N/R, B8 £38

D1758049

CONCR___
MASONRY
DESIGNER'S
HANDBOOK

by

J J ROBERTS BSc(Eng) PhD CEng MICE MIStructE MBIM
Research & Development Division, Cement and Concrete Association

A K TOVEY CEng MIStructE ACIArb
Advisory Division, Cement and Concrete Association

CRANSTON BSc PhD CEng MICE FIStructE FACI
·rch & Development Division, Cement and Concrete Association

BEEBY BSc PhD CEng MICE MIStructE
·ch & Development Division, Cement and Concrete Association

∿point Publication

VIEWPOINT PUBLICATIONS

Books published in the Viewpoint Publications series deal with all
practical aspects of concrete, concrete technology and allied subjects in
relation to civil and structural engineering, building and architecture.

First published 1983
13.024 (limp)
ISBN 0 86310 008 2
13.027 (hardback)
ISBN 086310 013 9

Viewpoint Publications are designed and published by
Eyre & Spottiswoode Publications Ltd
Swan House, 32 Swan Court, Leatherhead, Surrey KT22 8AH

Printed by Eyre & Spottiswoode Ltd, Thanet Press, Margate.

The Authors

The main authors of this Handbook are Dr John Roberts and Mr Alan Tovey, although important contributions were made by Dr Bill Cranston and Dr Andrew Beeby. All the authors are grateful to Mr Chris Harris for his Chapter on Statistics.

To anyone familiar with the industry it will be apparent that all of the authors are employed by the Cement & Concrete Association. With due modesty the authors would claim that many of the research developments in concrete masonry in the United Kingdom within the last two decades have occurred as a result of the Association's work.

Since 1935 the Association has provided an impartial service of technical advice and information to all users of Portland cement in the United Kingdom and has worked to promote standards of excellence in concrete design and construction. The scope and scale of the activities of the Association have grown in accordance with the growth in the use of concrete and other cement-based materials. The expertize of the Association's professional and technical staff has been crucial to the development of materials, design and construction philosophy and practice and is reflected in its major contributions to the British Standards and Codes of Practice. The reputation of the Cement & Concrete Association is recognized and respected throughout the world and the Research Station at Wexham Springs is internationally recognized as one of the leading establishments of its kind in the world.

Dr J J Roberts graduated from London University in 1969 and joined the Research and Development Division of the Cement & Concrete Association as a Research Engineer. Many of the projects on which he has subsequently been involved have considered various aspects of concrete masonry, including reinforced masonry, and he has published a number of papers on this topic. Currently he is Head of the Building Section of the Construction Research Department. In 1977 he was awarded the Henry Adams Bronze Medal of the Institution of Structural Engineers for a paper written jointly with Dr W B Cranston entitled *The Structural Behaviour of Concrete Masonry — Reinforced and Unreinforced*. He has been actively involved in several committees including CSB 33 dealing with the Structural Masonry Code and was closely involved with the drafting of BS 5628: Part 2.

Alan Tovey started his career with the Concrete Section of British Railways Western Region and later joined a major precast manufacturer where he was involved with both design and construction of a variety of precast concrete structures. He gained municipal engineering experience and practical design experience of loadbearing brickwork and blockwork with a London Borough Authority. He joined the Advisory Division of the Cement & Concrete Association in 1973, and is currently Principal Structural Engineer of the Building and Structural Engineering Department of the Advisory Division. He has been involved on many publications and British Standards, including the revision to CP 121.

Dr W B Cranston graduated from Glasgow University in 1955 and spent two years of national service in the Airfield Construction Branch of the Royal Air Force. The next four years were spent as an Assistant Lecturer, again at Glasgow University, where he carried out research work on metal columns. Since then he has been employed in the Research and Development Division of the Cement & Concrete Association where he was initially engaged on research into the behaviour of reinforced concrete framed structures. He was subsequently heavily involved in drafting parts of the limit state code for structural concrete, CP 110. His current responsibility as Head of the Design Research Department includes the supervision of a wide range of research on structural concrete and unreinforced masonry. As a member of CSB 33 he played a significant part in the drafting of BS 5628: Part 1 in limit state terms.

Dr A W Beeby graduated from London University in 1960. After working with John Laing & Sons for four years he joined the Cement & Concrete Association as a research engineer. During the past 19 years he has been involved in research on many aspects of the behaviour and design of concrete structures and he has published a number of papers. He was involved with the development of parts of CP 110 and was one of the authors of the Code handbook. Recently he has been deeply involved in work on the revision of the reinforced concrete sections of the Code. As Deputy Head of the Design Research Department, his duties include responsibility for work on the structural behaviour of unreinforced masonry.

Acknowledgements

The Publisher and Authors would like to acknowledge the kind permission of the British Standards Institution to reproduce the following Figures within this publication:

Figures 3.1, 3.2, 3.4 and 3.5 from BS 6073: Part 1: 1981
Figure 3.11 from BS 4551: 1980
Table 8.1 and Figures 8.6, 8.7, 8.8, 8.21, 10.7, 10.8, 10.11, 10.12 and 10.13 from BS 5628: Part 1: 1978
Figures 8.25, 8.26, 8.27, 8.29, 8.30, 13.1 and 13.2 from CP 121: Part 1: 1973
Figures 14.5 and 14.6 from CP 3: Ch.III: 1972
Figure 15.1 from BS 476: Part 8: 1972
Figure 19.8 which is adapted from a Figure in BS 6073: Part 1: 1981

The Authors would like to thank their friends and colleagues at the Cement and Concrete Association for their help and discussions, those who read and commented on the draft text and particularly Dr G Somerville, Director of Research and Technical Services, for his support and encouragement.

Thanks are also due to the patient families of the Authors for giving them the time to write this book.

Contents

Notations

A	horizontal cross sectional area	F_s	solid area divided by total area of slotted block
A_A	area of Part A } Figure 7.26		
A_B	area of Part B }	F_v	voided area divided by total area of slotted block
A_{ar}	actual area of roof lights		
A_{aw}	actual area of windows	f	a stress
A_c	area of compressive zone	f_o	characteristic anchorage bond strength between mortar or concrete infill and steel
A_e	area of the element		
A_f	area of opaque exposed floor (if any)	f_e	intrinsic unit strength (adjusted for aspect ratio)
A_m	cross sectional area of masonry		
A_r	area of opaque roof	f'_c	uniaxial compressive strength
A_{roof}	total area of roof including rooflights	f_d	design strength of a material
A_s	cross sectional area of primary reinforcing steel	f_f	characteristic compressive strength of masonry in bending
A_v	face area of void per block (mm²)	f_g	block strength based on gross area
A_{wall}	total area of wall including windows	f_{horiz}	applied horizontal stress
A_w	effective area of wall	f_k	characteristic compressive strength of masonry
A_{wo}	area of opaque wall		
a	deflection	f_{kb}	characteristic flexural strength (tension) of masonry when failure parallel to bed joint
a_r	reduced span (yield-line analysis)		
b	width of section	f_{kp}	characteristic flexural strength (tension) of masonry when failure perpendicular to bed joint
b_{eff}	effective breadth of opening (Figure 7.25)		
b_p	breadth of pier		
b_r	reduced span (yield-line analysis)	f_{kx}	characteristic flexural strength (tension) of masonry
C	internal compressive force		
C_f	coefficient of friction	f_m	block strength based on nett area
C_x	conductance of solid section	f_{self}	selfweight stress
C_y	conductance of voided section	f_{vert}	applied vertical stress
d	effective depth of tension reinforcement	f_v	characteristic shear strength of masonry
d_n	constant depending on sample size	f_w	applied vertical stress per unit area
E_i	modulus of elasticity of the part	f_y	characteristic tensile strength of reinforcing steel
e	eccentricity of load		
e_a	additional eccentricity due to deflection in walls	G	specified strength of blocks
		G_k	characteristic dead load
e_d	drying shrinkage	g_A	design vertical load per unit area
e_{lat}	eccentricity at mid-height resulting from lateral load	g_d	design vertical dead load per unit area
		H	overall height
e_m	the larger of e_x or e_t	h	clear distance between lateral supports (usually height)
e_{max}	numerically larger eccentricity		
e_{min}	numerically smaller eccentricity	h_{eff}	effective height of wall or column
e_t	total design eccentricity in the mid-height region of a wall	h_f	thickness of flange
		h_L	clear height of wall to point of application of lateral load
e_{temp}	temperature contraction		
e_u	ultimate tensile strain	h_p	panel height
e_x	eccentricity at top of a wall *or* eccentricity in x direction	h_w	window height
		I	second moment of area of total section
e_y	eccentricity in y direction	I_A	second moment of area of Part A

I_B	second moment of area of Part B
I_b	second moment of area of linking beam
I_i	second moment of area of the ith wall
i	individual specimen result from the sample
L	length or span
L_c	contact length
L_s	the reduction in length
l	span
l_g	distance between centroids of two parts of the wall
M	bending moment due to design load
M_d	design moment of resistance
M_u	ultimate moment of resistance
M_{uc}	ultimate moment of resistance when controlled by concrete
M_{us}	ultimate moment of resistance when controlled by reinforcement
M_w	total wind moment
M_{wi}	wind moment carried by the ith wall
M_y	moment in the y direction
m	design moment per unit length
N	design axial load on section under consideration
N_u	ultimate axial load
N_v	number of voids across thickness of slotted block
n	axial load per unit length of wall available to resist an arch thrust or sample size
n_y	vertical load per unit length of wall
P	force
P_m	ratio of average stress to maximum stress
P_w	wind force carried by wall
p	wind load
Q	heat flow rate through an element
Q_g	actual heat flow through glazing
$Q_{g\,max}$	maximum permissible heat flow through glazing
Q_k	characteristic imposed load
Q_{max}	maximum imposed load
$Q_{o\,actual}$	heat flow through opaque elements of structure
$Q_{o\,max}$	maximum permissible heat flow through opaque elements
q	a lateral load
q_{lat}	design lateral strength
R	thermal resistance of solid material or factor for degree of restraint
R_a	thermal resistance of ventilated air space
R_{ave}	total average thermal resistance of the construction
R_{ci}	average thermal resistance to centre line of cavity
R_e	equivalent thermal resistance of block
R_k	sum of known thermal resistances
R_{max}	maximum permissible percentage of rooflight glazing
R_{si}	inside surface resistance (thermal)
R_{su}	outside surface resistance (thermal)
R_v	thermal resistance of unventilated air space
R_x	thermal resistance of solid section
R_y	thermal resistance of voided section
r	radius of curvature
S	first moment of area of the section of wall to

	one side of the section considered about the neutral axis of the total section
s	standard deviation calculated from sample data
T_i	inside temperature
T_o	outside temperature
t	overall thickness of a wall or column
t_1	thickness of first leaf of a cavity wall
t_2	thickness of second leaf of a cavity wall
t_b	block thickness
t_{eff}	effective thickness of wall or column
t_f	thickness of the flange
t_p	thickness of the pier
t_v	thickness of void in slotted block
U	thermal transmittance value
U_{ar}	thermal transmittance value of rooflights
U_{aw}	thermal transmittance value of windows
U_f	thermal transmittance value of floor
U_r	thermal transmittance value of roof
U_w	thermal transmittance value of wall
V	shear force due to design loads
V_h	horizontal shear force acting on length of a wall
V_v	vertical shear stress on section considered
v	shear stress due to design loads
v_c	characteristic shear stress
v_h	design shear stress
W	applied load
W_k	characteristic wind load
W_{max}	maximum permissible percentage of glazing
W_u	ultimate capacity of the section
W_w	design wind load
w	range within a sample of size n
w_d	density of wall
X_i	each individual result in an example
X_n	average value of samples
x	a dimension
Y (or Y_n)	formulae simplification factors (for Chapter 8)
y	a dimension
Z	section modulus
z	lever arm
α	bending moment coefficient for laterally loaded panel
β	capacity reduction factor for walls allowing for effects of slenderness and eccentricity
γ_c	classification factor
γ_f	partial safety factor for load
γ_m	partial safety factor for material
γ_{mm}	partial safety factor for blockwork or partial safety factor for compressive strength of masonry
γ_{ms}	partial safety factor for strength of steel
γ_{mv}	partial safety factor for material in shear
δ	central deflection under lateral load or difference between average and actual result
θ	rotation of joint or an angle
κ	a constant or coefficient of variation
λ	thermal conductivity
μ	orthogonal ratio or true mean value
ρ	$\dfrac{A_s}{bd}$ or $\dfrac{A_s}{bt}$ as appropriate
σ	true standard deviation
ϕ	degree of fixity at support

1

Introduction

Concrete has a long history. It has been used since ancient times and was known to the Ancient Egyptians and even earlier civilizations. The oldest known concrete so far discovered dates back to 5600 BC and came to light during excavations on the banks of the River Danube at Lepenski Vir in Yugoslavia[1.1]. The modern, remarkable, developments with new structures, new techniques of handling concrete and even new kinds of concrete have all taken place within a comparatively short time and, in fact, 1974 was only the 150th anniversary of the patent for the manufacture of the first Porland cement.

The first all-concrete house was built in 1835 in Kent. The only part of this house which was not constructed in concrete was the suspended first floor as to build this successfully would have required reinforcement, the introduction of which was not pioneered until some years later. The first concrete blocks were made in the United Kingdom in about 1850 by Joseph Gibbs. The blocks were hollow with moulded faces which imitated the dressed stone of that period. The process, which provided a cheap alternative to dressed stone, was patented by Gibbs. It was not until about 1910, coinciding with the significant growth in the production of cement, that the concrete block industry became properly established. Major growth took place between 1918 and 1939 with the establishment of many small block manufacturers throughout the country. It was in 1918, with thousands of troops coming home from Europe, that the then Prime Minister, David Lloyd George, began his house building scheme of *homes fit for heroes*. These concrete block houses were built entirely of concrete and were the first in this country to be built in metric units. At this time the development of the industry was still based on a low price product, with the clinker from coal-fired power stations providing much of the aggregate used.

After the Second World War, as steel was in short supply, architects were obliged to make use of reinforced and prestressed concrete. The demand for concrete blocks also began to increase and both solid and hollow blocks became widely accepted for all purposes. The resumption of house building in the 1950s and 1960s and the rebuilding of cities demolished after the war brought emphasis to the important role to be played by concrete blocks — particularly in the use of lightweight blocks for the inner leaf of cavity walls. The low cost, lighter weight and ease of handling of these blocks ensured economy in terms of time and cost of construction. This in turn brought about the introduction of autoclaved aerated blocks which, at that time, were probably appreciated more for their operational advantages on site than for their thermal insulation properties. Concurrent with developments in the United Kingdom, many were also taking place in the United States of America, and it is here that the evolution of high quality facing concrete masonry, and machines associated with its production, can be discovered. Perhaps what was more important was the realization by American engineers of the potential for high rise concrete masonry. The seismic problems, associated with certain areas of the country, having also fostered the development of reinforced masonry.

Within the last two decades many developments have been incorporated in the uses of concrete masonry. A vast range of products are now available or can be made to order. The increased use of concrete blocks and bricks, at the expense of many other masonry materials, is such that concrete masonry can be claimed to be the major masonry material in the United Kingdom (Figure 1.1). The relative proportions of the types of block and brick used are illustrated in Figure 1.2. It is apparent that the growth in the market share of autoclaved aerated concrete blocks has taken place at the expense of some of the market held by lightweight aggregate blocks. The proportionate trend in the share of insulating blocks used does not appear to have been affected by changes in the thermal regulations. At present lightweight aggregate blocks account for about 40% of the market with dense and autoclaved aerated blocks accounting for about 30% each.

The renewed interest in all forms of masonry as a structural material has brought about the introduction of BS 5628[1.2], a Limit State Code, which enables the designer to take a more rational approach toward the use of concrete masonry. The purpose of this handbook is to cover the design of concrete masonry, including many aspects not covered by the various codes of practice, as well as to provide an insight into those other aspects of masonry performance to which the designer

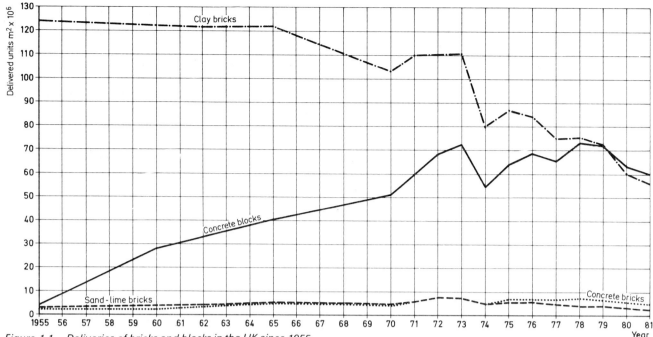

Figure 1.1   Deliveries of bricks and blocks in the UK since 1955

may need to give consideration.

Another factor which has encouraged the wider use of concrete masonry has been the scarcity of ideal building sites for dwellings and buildings in general. This has also widened the experience and expertise of the engineer involved in that the foundations and superstructure of even the most modest buildings have needed careful examination. The inherent need for further information on the engineering properties of masonry has thus been uncovered. The introduction of design requirements for lateral loading in the event of an accident has led to substantial amounts of work on the lateral load resistance of masonry, further widening the scope and ability of the engineer to effectively design with a basic understanding of the proposed masonry materials. There is no doubt that the attention recently paid to the need for conservation of energy has advanced the use of concrete masonry construction. Although Part F of the Building Regulations[1.3], when introduced in January 1975, was essentially a measure to reduce condensation, to achieve this an improvement in the resistance offered by buildings to the pas-

sage of heat through the various elements had to be effected. The use of thermal insulating blocks was therefore encouraged, and the introduction of Part FF of the Building Regulations in July 1979 gave further support to the use of blocks of this type. Familiarity with the larger size of concrete blocks compared with bricks has led to a realization of the economies possible with this material, while the best concrete brick and block facing materials are also favourably comparable to any other materials. Advances still continue to be made in the scope and imagination with which masonry can be employed and while there is still room for such innovation it has to be admitted that there is a bright outlook for such an old and well tried material.

Increasingly the tendency to try to codify every aspect of design brings with it the danger that the engineer will lose sight of the overall consideration and application of engineering principles. This potential problem is evident, for example, in the way in which domestic scale techniques of building have been extended to larger buildings without sufficient consideration being given to the fact that the larger scale will

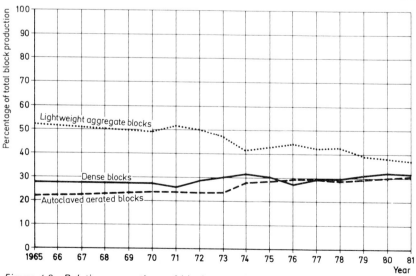

Figure 1.2   Relative proportions of block types delivered since 1965

have an effect on the overall stability of the building. It is hoped, therefore, that this handbook will provide a useful and practical guide to the engineer and other professionals. At the same time this handbook could not attempt to replace the training and experience of the qualified engineer. The authors have sought to classify and quantify their combined experiences in the use of concrete masonry, introducing the results of the extensive programme of research which has been undertaken by the Cement and Concrete Association. In addition extensive use has been made of the results of work carried out elsewhere in the United Kingdom and overseas, particularly in the United States, Australia and New Zealand.

The implementaton of the Building Regulations is an interesting aspect of the work of an engineer. Although he may show to the satisfaction of the Local Authority that his proposed building complies in every way with the relevant regulations, the structure, when complete, may substantially differ from that proposed. The Building Research Station at East Kilbride in Scotland has carried out a survey of public sector housing in Scotland for compliance with the thermal regulations, the results of which are illustrated in Figures 1.3 and 1.4. Quite apart from casting an interesting insight into the relative popularity of various construction methods, it is apparent that many buildings actually under construction, as recorded by BRE staff visiting the sites, did not comply with the Building Regulations. It is also interesting to speculate just how many other aspects of masonry performance, quite aside from thermal performance, are denigrated at the construction stage. It is comforting to note that except for the situation when there is vigorous engineering supervision on site, the global factor of safety for masonry at something approaching 4.5 has been retained in BS 5628. Although Part 1 of the Code does not deal with the use of reinforced and prestressed masonry, which will be covered in Part 2 of the Code, a chapter has been included in this handbook on reinforced masonry so that a rational limit state approach may be adopted as an interim design measure until such time as Part 2 eventually becomes available. An unfortunate aspect of the partitioning of the Code into two separate sections is that the various parts tend to be produced in isolation and consecutively.

It is currently considered necessary to pay much more attention to the overall integrity of buildings and their resistance to abnormal load. The explanation for this relates in part to the trend to codify methods of

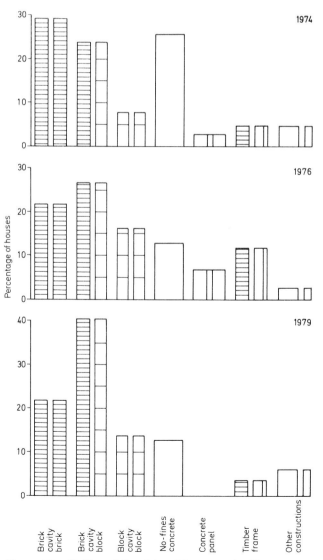

Figure 1.3   *Walling of Scottish public sector dwellings*
(adapted from BRE Current Paper 60/78 by kind permission of Building Research Establishment, together with private communication)

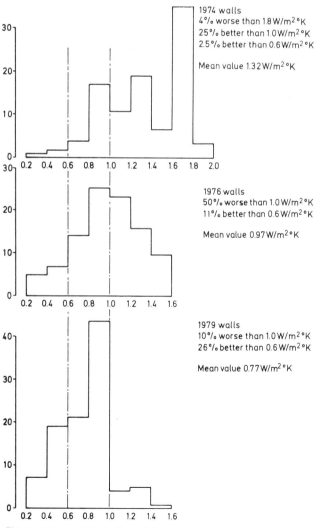

Figure 1.4   *U-values of walls in Scotland*
(adapted from BRE Current Paper 60/78 by kind permission of Building Research Establishment, together with private communication)

design into discrete packages thereby reducing the tendency to consider the behaviour of the building as a whole. Of course, this approach to overall stability was stimulated by the events at Ronan Point where a gas explosion blew a panel out of the side of a high rise block of flats resulting in the progressive collapse of the complete corner of the building, and subsequent attention being paid to the potential problems of progressive collapse. The fifth amendment to the Building Regulations proposed the following approach to reduce the risk of this form of collapse:

(1) The local resistance method whereby the structure is designed to have the required strength to resist abnormal loadings so that hazards will not cause any local failure.

(2) The alternative path method whereby the structure is examined to determine the effect of the removal of any single vertical or horizontal element within each storey, base or span, and ensure the ability of the remaining elements to redistribute and support the load.

The local resistance method is generally difficult to implement because of the cost implications of the approach, although there are a few masonry structures to which the method could be said to apply. The alternative path solution is the one which would seem most likely to commend itself to engineers. The philosophy of the alternative path approach is that any damage which occurs as a result of progressive collapse should be localized so that sufficient bridging is able to take place to ensure the integrity of the structure as a whole. Clearly there needs to be sufficient tying and localized redundancy within the building to confine the extent of the damage.

The background has, therefore, been set for the *Concrete Masonry Designer's Handbook*. The layout and arrangement of the subsequent chapters is classified in the contents list. A number of design examples have been provided as well as design charts. Feedback on the experience of designers in the use of these and of other contents of the handbook would be of interest to the authors, as would suggestions on further areas of development or improvements to the text.

References

1.1 STANLEY, C C. Highlights in the history of concrete. Cement and Concrete Association, Slough, 1979. Publication No 97.408.

1.2 BRITISH STANDARDS INSTITUTION. BS 5628: Part 1: 1978 *Code of Practice for the structural use of masonry*. Part 1: *Unreinforced masonry*. BSI, London. pp 40

1.3 The Building Regulations 1976. HMSO, London.

2

Principles of limit state design

2.1 Introduction

Building construction, in common with much else in this modern world, has become complex and sophisticated. Early types of construction provided minimal shelter from wind and rain whereas today's contrasting construction provides an internal environment where every aspect of climate and lighting can be under finger-tip control. With this progress has come the clearer definition and understanding of performance requirements. It is against this background that the ideas of limit state design have developed. It must be said at the outset that the introduction of limit state philosophy into Codes has caused considerable confusion and a general feeling that design has become even more complicated. In fact, limit state philosophy is nothing new, it is merely a method of formalizing what has always been done in design. Limit state philosophy is nothing more than a statement that, in design, all the possible ways in which a structure can become unfit for its desired use should be considered and, if necessary, designed against explicitly.

Limit state design was originally conceived for use in reinforced or prestressed concrete design and its operation can probably be seen most clearly by considering reinforced concrete. It is perfectly possible to design a beam or slab which is adequately strong but which, under service conditions, will deflect excessively. It is also possible to design a beam which will not deflect seriously under service loads but, nevertheless, will not be strong enough. Furthermore, it is possible to design members which are both sufficiently strong and sufficiently stiff but which will be disfigured by unsightly cracking. Design to satisfy one criterion (e.g. strength) thus does not guarantee that other aspects of performance will be satisfied. these other aspects have to be carefully considered.

CP 110[2.1], the first Limit State Code, sets down criteria which have to be met for each aspect of performance, and design procedures are given for satisfying these criteria. Equations are given for strength; span/effective depth ratios are given to ensure that deflections are not excessive and bar spacing rules and stress limitations are given to ensure that cracking is not excessive. It can thus be seen that limit state design is

not new, since most of these provisions have appeared in previous Codes, the only difference is a more formal statement of the design objectives.

2.2 Limit states appropriate to masonry

Clause 19 of BS 5628[2.2] states that "The design of loadbearing masonry members should be primarily to ensure an adequate margin of safety against the ultimate limit state being reached". This arises because the margin of safety specified is such that the loads in walls under service conditions are lower (in the order of one quarter or one fifth) than that which will cause collapse assuming the construction is built to specification. In tests on concrete block masonry walls to collapse severe deformation or cracking does not develop until loads of around 80% of ultimate are attained. In practice far more severe deformations can arise from shrinkage and temperature effects than will ever arise from loading. While shrinkage and expansion cracking due to temperature change can cause damage which affects the serviceability, they are not dealt with in limit state terms, but by simple detailing rules given in CP 121[2.3] which are referred to in *Chapter 16*.

It should be emphasized that although the Code does not specify any serviceability criteria such as acceptable crack widths or acceptable movements at expansion or contraction joints, the designer is not thereby excused from considering these matters. As an example, it may be necessary in tall structures to consider differential movement between the vertical walls which are carrying the vertical loads and those walls which function as partitions. These and other similar problems must be treated on their individual merits.

2.3 Partial safety factor format

The limit state method is normally associated in Codes with a partial safety factor format. This is a new departure but appears an eminently logical step forward. The idea is that instead of a global safety factor, different partial safety factors are associated with different types of loading and different materials. These factors are chosen to reflect the uncertainty with which the particular parameter can be assessed. Thus, dead load, which should be relatively accurately determinable, has a lower load factor associated with it than does a live load, which is less certain. Similarly, in reinforced concrete, concrete has a larger partial factor than steel since its quality is likely to be more variable. This approach gives results which accord with common sense; structures supporting dominantly their own self weight can be designed for lower overall safety factors than those carrying a large proportion of ill defined imposed loads; members where the strength depends mainly on concrete (e.g. columns) are built to higher safety factors than those where the strength depends dominantly on the reinforcement (e.g. lightly reinforced beams). In masonry, there is only one material — masonry. This limits the partial factors and makes life simpler. The factors are applied to the *characteristic strengths* of the material to give *design strengths*. Characteristic strengths are the specified strengths of materials (i.e., the characteristic strength of a 5 N/mm^2 block is 5 N/mm^2). Characteristic loads are those given in design regulations.

In the Code there are two types of partial safety factor:

γ_m — allows for variability of materials and workmanship

γ_m is applied to strengths

Thus, design strength is given by:

$$f_d = \frac{f_k}{\gamma_m}$$

for unreinforced masonry, γ_m varies from 3.5 to 2.5 depending on control (See BS 5628:Table 4).

γ_f — allows for variability in the loading. A design load $= \gamma_f \times$ characteristic load. Values for various combinations of load are given in BS 5628:Clause 22.

The factors for γ_f have been selected to be consistent with CP 110. This has the advantage that where reinforced concrete elements form part of the structure, loadings calculated for the design of those elements can be used directly in the masonry design. The γ_m factors have been derived by a process of calibration from the previous Code, CP 111:1970[2.4].

2.4 References

2.1   BRITISH STANDARDS INSTITUTION. CP 110: 1970 *The structural use of concrete.* BSI, London.

2.2   BRITISH STANDARDS INSTITUTION. BS 5628: Part 1: 1978 *Code of Practice for the structural use of masonry.* Part 1: *Unreinforced masonry.* BSI, London. pp 40

2.3   BRITISH STANDARDS INSTITUTION. CP 121: Part 1: 1973 *Code of Practice for walling.* Part 1: *Brick and block masonry.* BSI, London. pp 84

2.4   BRITISH STANDARDS INSTITUTION. CP 111: 1970 *Structural recommendations for loadbearing walls.* BSI, London.

3

Materials

3.1 Introduction

This chapter covers the general specification of concrete masonry units as given in BS 6073[3.1], together with their physical properties. More comprehensive information on thermal insulation, sound insulation, rain resistance and fire resistance is given in *Chapters 12 to 15*.

The specification of concrete masonry units is covered by BS 6073:1981[3.1]. This Standard replaces the two previous Standards, BS 2028, 1364:1968[3.2] *Precast concrete blocks* and BS 1180:1972[3.3] *Concrete bricks and fixing bricks*. As well as being simplified, the Standard has been separated into two parts — Part 1: *Specification for precast masonry units* and Part 2: *Methods of specifying precast masonry units* (see *Chapter 17*).

As there have been a number of modifications to the previous Standards, the current definitions as given in BS 6073 are repeated below:

Masonry unit
A block or brick.

Block
A masonry unit which, when used in its normal aspect, exceeds the length or width or height specified for bricks (see *Bricks* below), subject to the proviso that its work size does not exceed 650 mm in any dimension, and its height when used in its normal aspect does not exceed its length or six times its thickness.

Brick
A masonry unit not exceeding 337.5 mm in length, 225 mm in thickness, (thickness is termed *width* in BS 3921[3.15]) or 112.5 mm in height.

Types of block
The presence of transverse slots to facilitate cutting or the filling of holes or cavities with non-structural insulant shall not alter the definitions given below:

Solid block
A block which contains no formed holes or cavities other than those inherent in the material.
Note: An autoclaved aerated concrete block is a solid block under this definition.

Cellular block
A block which has one or more formed holes or cavities which do not wholly pass through the block.

Hollow block
A block which has one or more formed holes or cavities which pass through the block.

Types of brick

Solid brick
One in which small holes passing through, or nearly through, the brick do not exceed 25% of its volume, or in which frogs (depressions in the bed faces of a brick) do not exceed 20% of its volume. For the purposes of this definition small holes are defined as being less than 20 mm wide or less than 500 mm^2 in area. Up to three larger holes, not exceeding 3250 mm^2 each may be incorporated as aids to handling, within the total of 25%.

Perforated brick
One in which small holes (as defined above) passing through the brick exceed 25% of its volume. Up to three larger holes, not exceeding 3250 mm^2 each, may be incorporated as aids to handling.

Hollow brick
One in which holes passing through the brick exceed 25% of its volume and the holes are not small, as defined above.

Cellular brick
One in which the holes closed at one end exceed 20% of the volume of the brick.

Sizes

Co-ordinating size
The size of a co-ordinating space allocated to a masonry unit, including allowances for joints and tolerances.

Work size
The size of a masonry unit specified for its manufacture, to which its actual size should conform within specified permissible deviations.

Compressive strength
The average value of the crushing strengths of ten masonry units tested in accordance with Appendix B of BS 6073.

3.1.1 Strength

3.1.1.1 Concrete blocks

It should be noted that in BS 6073 only blocks equal to or greater than 75 mm are tested for compressive strength. Blocks less than 75 mm are only tested for transverse strength and are primarily intended for non-loadbearing partitions. BS 6073:Part 1 states that the average crushing strength of 75 mm or greater blocks shall be not less than 2.8 N/mm² and that the corresponding lowest crushing strength of any individual block in the test sample of ten, shall not be less than 80% of this minimum permissible average crushing strength.

A similar criteria applies to blocks of greater strength except that the strength specified shall apply in place of the 2.8 N/mm² minimum permissible average crushing strength quoted above. Concrete blocks are generally available with mean compressive strengths ranging from 2.8 to 20 N/mm², although blocks of greater strength can be produced. The average and corresponding lowest individual strengths for the strength ranges quoted in BS 5628[3,4] are given in Table 3.1. For blocks of thickness less than 75 mm the average transverse strength of the sample shall not be less than 0.65 N/mm².

3.1.1.2 Concrete bricks

In the case of concrete bricks, the average compressive strength shall not be less than 7.0 N/mm² and the corresponding coefficient for variation for the samples shall not exceed 20%. The physical requirements for the strength categories in BS 5628 are given in Table 3.2.

3.1.2 Dimensions and tolerances

3.1.2.1 Concrete blocks

The typical range of work size of concrete blocks is given in Table 3.3, although blocks of entirely non-standard dimensions or design may be produced. The maximum deviation on the sizes of units are as follows:

length + 3 mm and − 5 mm

height + 3 mm and − 5 mm

thickness + 2 mm and − 2 mm average

+ 4 mm and − 4 mm at any individual point.

In practice, since most blocks are produced in accurate steel moulds, it should be recognized that a consignment of blocks is likely to comprise of units all of a similar size, although within the tolerances specified. This can have an effect on joint width, especially for facing work.

Table 3.1 Compressive strength of blocks corresponding to BS 5628 strength categories

Block strength	Minimum compressive strength N/mm²	
	Average of ten blocks	Lowest individual block
2.8	2.8	2.24
3.5	3.5	2.8
5.0	5.0	4.0
7.0	7.0	5.6
10.0	10.0	8.0
15.0	15.0	12.0
20.0	21.0	16.8
35.0	35.0	28.0

Table 3.2 Physical requirements for concrete bricks

Physical property	Compressive strength category					
	7.0	10.0	15.0	20.0	30.0	40.0
Compressive strength (wet) Average of ten bricks not less than (N/mm²)	7.0	10.0	15.0	20.0	30.0	40.0
Coefficient of varients of compressive strength not to exceed (%)	20	20	20	20	20	20
Drying shrinkage not to exceed	0.06	0.04	0.04	0.04	0.04	0.04

Table 3.3 Work sizes of blocks

Length × height mm		Thickness mm														
		60	75	90	100	115	125	140	150	175	190	200	215	220	225	250
390 × 190		×	×	×	×	×		×	×		×	×				
440 × 140		×	×	×	×			×	×		×	×			×	
440 × 190		×	×	×	×			×	×		×		×	×		
440 × 215		×	×	×	×	×	×	×	×	×	×	×	×	×	×	×
440 × 290		×	×	×	×			×	×		×	×	×			
590 × 140			×	×	×			×	×		×	×	×			
590 × 190			×	×	×			×	×		×	×	×			
590 × 215			×	×	×		×	×	×	×		×	×		×	×

Notes:
1. To obtain the co-ordinating size of a masonry unit, add the nominal joint width, which is normally 10 mm, to the length and height of the unit given in the Table (The thickness remains unchanged).
2. Other work sizes are available and in use. No single manufacturer necessarily produces the complete range of work sizes shown.

3.1.2.2 Concrete bricks

Concrete brick sizes are typically manufactured to the work sizes shown in Table 3.4. The maximum dimensional deviation for bricks is as follows:

length + 4 mm and − 2 mm

height + 2 mm and − 2 mm

thickness + 2 mm and − 2 mm

3.1.3 Frost resistance

3.1.3.1 Concrete blocks

The concrete block is inherently durable and suitable for a variety of exposure conditions. The British Standard Code of Practice CP 121*[3.5] gives the following recommendations as to the minimum quality of blocks and mortar for durability (Table 3.5).

Table 3.4 Work sizes of bricks

Length × height		Thickness mm	
mm	mm	90	103
290	× 90	×	
215	× 65		×
190	× 90	×	
190	× 65	×	

Notes:
1. To obtain the co-ordinating size of a masonry unit, add the nominal joint width, which is normally 10 mm, to the length and height of the unit given in the Table (The thickness remains unchanged).
2. Other work sizes are available and in use No single manufacturer necessarily produces the complete range of work sizes shown.

The Code permits the use of blocks below ground level damp-proof course, as described in Table 3.5 providing that there is no likelihood of sulphate attack. If there is a possibility of such attack, additional precautions may be necessary.

Table 3.5 Minimum quality of concrete units and mortars for durability

Situation	Element of construction		Minimum quality of units[1]				Minimum quality of mortar[1]	
			Calcium silicate bricks (Class)	Concrete bricks (Category)	Concrete blocks (Type)		When there is no risk of frost during construction	When freezing may occur during construction
					Thickness mm	Density kg/m³		
a	Inner leaf of cavity walls and internal walls	Unplastered	2	7.0	Any	Any	(iv)	(iii) or plasticized[2] (iv)
		Plastered	1	7.0	Any	Any	(v)	(iii) or plasticized[2] (iv)
b	Backing to external solid walls	Unplastered	2	7.0	Any	Any	(iv)	(iii) or plasticized[2] (iv)
		Plastered	1	7.0	Any	Any	(iv)	(iii) or plasticized[2] (iv)
c	External walls including the outer leaf of cavity walls and facing to solid construction	Above damp-proof course near to ground level	2	15.0	⩾ 75	Any	(iv)	(iii)
		Below damp-proof course but more than 150 mm above finished ground level	2	15.0	⩾ 75	Any	(iii)	(iii)
		Within 150 mm of ground level or below ground	3	20.0	⩾ 75	⩾ 1500	(iii)[5]	(iii)[5]
d	External freestanding walls		3	15.0	⩾ 75	⩾ 1500	(iii)	(iii)
e	Parapets	Rendered	3	20.0	⩾ 75	Any	(iv)	(iii)
		Unrendered	3	20.0	⩾ 75	⩾ 1500	(iii)	(iii)
f	Sills and copings of bricks		4	30.0	—	—	(ii)	(ii)
g	Earth retaining walls[3,8]		4	30.0	⩾ 75	⩾ 1500	(ii)[5]	(ii)[5]

Notes:
(1) The designation of mortars is given in Table 3.11. Loading requirements or other factors may necessitate the use of a higher designation.
(2) Concrete bricks should not be used in contact with ground from which there is a danger of sulphate attack unless they are protected or have been made specifically for this purpose.
(3) Bricks of a lower strength category may be used if the supplier can provide direct evidence that they are suitable in the given location.
(4) Where sulphates are present in the ground water, the use of sulphate-resisting cement for the mortar may be necessary.
(5) An effective and continuous damp-proof course should be provided at the top of the wall as well as just above ground level.
(6) It is essential that rendering is on one side only.
(7) Walls should be backfilled with free draining material as recommended in the Civil Engineering Code of Practice No. 2:1951: *Earth retaining structures*.

*Currently being revised

9

3.1.3.2 Concrete bricks The frost resistance of a given combination of category of brick and mortar designation will be adequate if the requirements in Table 3.5, for a given use, are complied with.

3.1.4 Drying shrinkage and wetting expansion

3.1.4.1 Concrete blocks The average value of the drying shrinkage of the sample should not exceed 0.06% except for autoclaved aerated concrete blocks, for which the maximum permissible value shall be 0.09%.

3.1.4.2 Concrete bricks The maximum permitted drying shrinkage for concrete bricks is indicated in Table 3.2. It should be noted that if bricks are to be used under permanently damp conditions the drying shrinkage specification is of no significance.

3.1.5 Impact resistance

The most recent proposals on performance criteria for impact are those contained in the draft Code of Practice of external walls[3.6] in which an attempt has been made to provide a sensible framework for the evaluation of the performance of walls liable to suffer impact damage, although it is clear that there is a lack of information in some areas.

Two distinct criteria must be satisfied:

(1) Walling should be capable of withstanding hard and soft body impacts applied or transferred to either of its faces during normal use without sustaining damage and without deterioration of its performance. There should be no significant irreversible deformation, visually unacceptable indentation marks or irreparable damage resulting from such impact.

(2) The walling, if subjected to more severe accidental impact should not be penetrated or become dislodged from its supporting structure. Any fracture resulting from such impact should not produce debris which may be a hazard to occupants or to people outside the building.

The proposals cover the use of walling materials and therefore need to consider both the impact resistance required for the retention of performance, including appearance, and that needed for maintaining the safety of persons. The latter takes the form of larger soft body impacts for lateral stability and is applicable to very lightweight constructions. It is extremely unlikely that any masonry construction will fail to have adequate resistance in this situation.

In considering the performance levels required, the proposals recognise four levels of exposure:

(a) Walls in locations liable to vandalism and other rough use.

(b) Walls adjacent to pedestrian thoroughfare or playing fields where not in category (a).

(c) Walls adjacent to private open gardens.

(d) Walls sheltered from people (a wall adjacent to a small garden with no footpaths and enclosed by a fence is an example).

Table 3.6 Minimum test impact for retention of performance in location categories (b) and (c).

Type of impactor	Position in building	Location of wall	
		(b) Nm	(c) Nm
Hard body (a)	External at pedestrian level	15	7.5
	External not at pedestrian level	10	2
Soft body (b)	External at pedestrian level	120	60
	External not at pedestrian level	30	10

Recommendations for category (b) and (c) conditions are provided in Table 3.6. Two types of impactor are used in the tests:

(a) *Hard body* A steel ball, 50 mm in diameter and weighing 0.5 kg is either dropped vertically or swung as a pendulum (with a cord at least 3 m long), onto the weakest part of the test construction.

(b) *Soft body* A canvas or rubber bag of spherical shape and 200 mm diameter, filled with dry sand of 0.2 mm grading and weighing 2 kg is swung on a cord at least 3 m long against the weakest part of the specimen.

In practice testing with a soft body impactor is unlikely to damage a masonry construction. Tests on fairly soft unrendered aerated concrete blocks with the hard body impactor indicate that even at the highest energy levels specified in Table 3.6 blocks are unlikely to suffer visually unacceptable damage. The addition of a render coat further improves the performance of these blocks. The impact resistance of concrete bricks is very good and they are generally suitable for use in areas likely to be vandalized. Particular attention should, however, be paid to the impact resistance of tiling and other vertical cladding systems.

3.1.6 Density

BS 6073:Part 2 gives methods of measurement for both block density (gross density) i.e., oven dry mass ÷ gross volume, and also concrete density (nett density), i.e., oven dry mass ÷ concrete volume. The block density is used, for example, in determining loads on a structure and handling requirements. The concrete density can be used to assess the thermal conductivity of the material and hence the thermal resistance of the block.

3.1.7 Fire resistance

Concrete blocks and bricks have inherently good fire resistance. In the case of dwellings most concrete masonry constructions are capable of providing a degree of fire resistance far in excess of the notional required period of not less than half-an-hour. The fire resistance of different types of units depends upon the class of aggregate employed and the presence of hollows or slots. The notional fire resistance periods for masonry walls are given in *Chapter 15*. Being non-combustible, concrete masonry walling does not produce smoke or toxic gasses but consideration must be given to the performance of any added insulants or finishes.

3.1.8 Thermal insulation

There are number of ways of producing concrete blocks with good thermal insulation properties, such as aerated blocks, lightweight aggregate blocks, multi-slotted lightweight aggregate blocks and foam-filled blocks of lightweight or dense aggregate. It is simpler, therefore, to consider the thermal resistance required of the block. If a thermal transmittance (U value) of 1.0 W/m² °C is required when a typical brick-cavity-block wall is to be employed with dense plaster internally, then a block with resistance of 0.491 m² °C/W or larger will be needed.

While it is comparatively easy to calculate the resistance of a solid block given the material coefficient of thermal conductivity, special assumptions need to be made for multi-slotted blocks, and this is dealt with in further detail in *Chapter 12*.

Historically, it has been usual to relate the thermal conductivity of a given concrete to the density of the material — the Jacob curve. Whilst it appears that this relationship gives a reasonable prediction of thermal conductivity based on a knowledge of the material density, some types of units, e.g., blocks made with a foamslag aggregate, appear to differ considerably from the standard curve and have better thermal conductivity values than predicted by density.

In general terms, thermal insulating blocks will have a density less than 1400 kg/m³, except in the case of foam-filled dense blocks. The lowest density unit likely to be encountered is 475 kg/m³ for the lower density autoclaved aerated concrete blocks.

3.1.9 Acoustic performance

Concrete masonry walls in general, including those comprising two leaves of the lighter thermal insulating blocks, have sufficient mass to provide adequate levels of sound insulation, both between adjoining properties and between the property and an outside sound source. The use of blocks for internal partitions (provided joints are well filled with mortar) can also provide good levels of sound insulation between adjoining rooms where problems often arise with very lightweight partitions. Typical examples of walls able to satisfy the sound insulation requirements are shown in *Chapter 14*. These include usual 'deemed-to-satisfy' constructions, although some manufacturers are able to offer constructions which are lighter than those indicated while still complying with the regulations.

It is possible that the inner leaf of a cavity wall will be required to assist the separating wall in attaining the necessary level of sound insulation, in which case it is advisable to consult the manufacturer concerning the wide variety of blocks available.

Generally speaking, the sound insulation will be a consideration in selecting the density of the units employed, as the greater the mass built into the wall the greater its ability to resist sound waves. It is necessary to check on proprietary products, however, since even quite dense units may be sufficiently open textured to allow fairly direct transmission of sound. Conversely, the high proportion of closed cells in autoclaved aerated blocks appear to give these units a high resistance to sound transmission. Where a sound absorbent material is required, open textured units have the ability to provide a large reduction in reflected sound levels. Special blocks designed to absorb sound in set frequency ranges can be made available by a few manufacturers.

In practice, the in situ sound performance of a wall is very dependent on workmanship although a recent survey in Belgium has indicated that 50% of sound problems occurred as a result of faults in the conception of the building.

3.1.10 Water absorption

Unlike clay brickwork there are no test procedures or requirements for measurement of water absorption of concrete blocks or bricks so that this parameter is not referred to in determining any other aspect of performance.

3.1.11 Resistance to rain

There is no simple correlation between a standard unit test for permeability or porosity and the performance of 2 m square test panels tested in a rain rig in accordance with BS 4315[3.7]. Open textured facing blocks of very similar appearance and identical densities, but different manufacture, may perform very differently in terms of the amount of water passing through the block when tested in a rain penetration rig. Reference should be made to local experience when assessing a particular block for resistance to rain or a wall test could be commissioned, although the latter may prove fairly expensive and there are not many suitable rigs available in the UK.

Rendering or other forms of surface finish will generally provide a wall with very good resistance to rain penetration. In the case of very dense concrete blocks and bricks where large amounts of 'run-off' of water down the face of the wall may be expected to occur, the additional water will tend to be blown through points of weakness in the wall, such as poorly filled mortar joints.

The rain penetration resistance of various wall constructions is discussed in *Chapter 13*.

3.1.12 Bond to mortar

As the suction applied by concrete blocks is generally less than that applied by clay bricks it is not necessary to wet blocks before laying. If problems are encountered, for example with some aerated blocks, because of high suction (particularly in hot weather) then a proprietary water retaining admixture may be considered which might comprise of methyl cellulose, although others are available.

As a general recommendation the best compromise between performance and workability will be given by a 1:1:6 cement:lime:sand mortar, although a 1:2:9 cement:lime:sand mortar may be used for low strength lightweight aggregate blocks and for aerated blocks where there is no risk of freezing during construction. The alternative plasticized or masonry mortar may also be considered. If a strong mortar is employed particularly with lighter units, the shrinkage between the block and mortar may reduce the mortar bond strength. The mortar consistence will need to be adjusted by the block layer to suit both the weight and suction of the block in use. Dense concrete blocks, especially if hollow, exert more pressure on the mortar than lightweight blocks and a stiffer mortar may be required.

3.1.13 Ease of finishing

Most blocks are rendered without any problem, but the general rule applicable to the mortar used for rendering is that it should be weaker than the block to which it is applied. A 1:1:6 cement:lime:sand render is normally suitable for lightweight aggregate blocks while a 1:2:9 render is more suitable for aerated blocks. For dense blocks there is little point in using a render stronger than a 1:1:6 except in the case of special applications. The mix proportions of some proprietary render systems do differ and advice should be sought from the manufacturer. The texture and suction of blocks will also vary considerably and reference should be made to the specific recommendations applicable to the block in use.

Autoclaved aerated blocks are likely to have a fairly high suction compared to other types of blocks which may prove a problem, particularly in hot weather. Although it is common practice to wet these blocks on site before rendering, this is often done to excess and may give rise to cracking due to movement of the wall. It is recommended that either a pva:cement:sand bonding coat is applied before rendering, or a water retaining admixture, such as methyl cellulose, is added to the render mortar. Some manufacturers of aerated concrete blocks add a water repellent during the manufacture of the units to limit subsequent suction. A pva:cement:sand coat can be used to bond to very smooth dense blocks or bricks and other types of unit may also benefit if treated with a bonding coat before subsequent rendering. An extra key for the render may also be obtained by raking back the mortar joints.

Most blocks will provide a good base for paint but due consideration must be given to the manufacturer's recommendations. In particular, the alkali present in the block may attack some paints and this would require the use of an alkali resistant primer on the surface. Selection of an open textured block usually provides a very attractive finish when painted and allows the wall to 'breathe'. In general paint for use with blockwork should be vapour permeable.

3.1.14 Ease of providing fixings

There is a wide range of proprietary fixings available for use after construction of a wall. Some fixings are built-in during construction, but these are unlikely to vary in performance with different types of blocks unless the loads imposed are so high that local crushing failure occurs — an unlikely event in practice because most fixings are comparatively lightly loaded.

The ease with which small fixings may be provided will depend largely on the ease with which the block in question may be drilled. Some very dense open textured blocks may require the use of special drill heads and, as the dense aggregate may tend to deflect the drill, an undersized drill head may be required to avoid too large a hole. Aerated blocks are easily drilled but because of the friable nature of the material one of the proprietary fixings specifically for this type of block may be required. Cut nails may be used during construction for making fixings in autoclaved aerated concrete (see also *Section 3.10*).

3.1.15 Resistance to chemical attack

There is no simple means of assessing the resistance of a block to sulphate attack and reference should be made to the past experience of the manufacturer or specifier. Open textured units are likely to be more vulnerable to chemical attack than dense hydraulically pressed concrete units. Finishing specifications are available which will provide protection to blockwork against chemical attack, e.g., protection to silage retaining walls from attack by acid. However, in the case of the effect of particular chemicals on the durability of a given block, reference should be made to the manufacturer.

3.2 Standard tests for blocks

3.2.1 Strength

3.2.1.1 Concrete blocks The standard method of determining block strength is to test ten blocks capped with mortar. Strength tests to BS 6073 should be carried out on whole blocks. The old provision of BS 2028, 1364:1968 for testing sawn part blocks was unsatisfactory, particularly where the blocks which contained a void or other feature were used which resulted in an assymetric specimen on sawing.

Preparation of specimens
A smooth surface is required for a capping plate, for which machined steel plates or plate glass are employed, which is covered with a suitable release agent. The ten blocks must be immersed for at least 16 hours in water at a temperature between 10—25°C and allowed to drain for about 30 minutes under damp sacking or similar material before the capping procedure is carried out.

The mortar for capping each block should consist of one part by weight of rapid-hardening Portland cement to one part by weight of sand complying with the requirements of grading zones 2 or 3 of BS 882:1201[3.8].

From the sand, any material retained on a No. 7 fine mesh normal or special test sieve should have been rejected as specified in Part 1 of BS 410[3.9]. Water is added to produce a mortar having a consistence value of not less than 6 mm and not more than 9 mm when measured by the test for the determination of consistence by the dropping ball method specified on page 23. Prisms or cubes should be made from the mortar and tested for compressive strength in accordance with the procedures given in BS 1881[3.10]. Prisms should be cured using plain tap water and the compressive strength determined by a strength test carried out near the ends of the unbroken prisms. The results should be used to determine the age at which the mortar reaches an average compressive strength of at least 28 N/mm², which will normally be two to four days.

The mortar is placed as a uniform layer 5 mm thick on the capping plate. One bed face of the block is pressed into the mortar so that the vertical axis of the specimen is perpendicular to the plane of the plate. The verticality of the blocks is checked by using a level against each of the four vertical faces of the block, making allowance for any taper of the block sides. It is important to ensure that the mortar bed is at least 3 mm over the whole area and that any cavity in the bed face, which is normally filled when the blocks are laid in the wall, is completely filled with mortar. Surplus mortar is trimmed off flush with the sides of the block and the specimen is covered with cloth or polythene which is kept damp. The specimen should be left undisturbed for at least 16 hours before being carefully removed from the capping plate. If the bed is free from defects the second bed face should be capped using the same procedure. After checking, the complete specimens should be placed in water at a temperature of 20 ± 2°C until the mortar used for both test faces has attained the required minimum strength.

Determination of compressive strength

Each specimen is removed from the water and allowed to drain for about 30 minutes under damp sacking or similar material and is tested while still in a wet condition. The specimen is placed centrally in the machine (see details of testing machine below) and the load increased continually at a rate of 5 ± 0.5 N/mm² for blocks of specified strength less or equal to 7 N/mm², or 10 ± 1 N/mm² for blocks of specified strength greater than 7 N/mm². The rate of application of load should be maintained as far as possible right up to failure.

The maximum load in Newtons carried by each specimen during test is recorded. The maximum load divided by the gross area of the specimen in mm² is taken as the compressive strength of the block in N/mm² and is reported to the nearest 0.05 N/mm² for blocks with a specified strength less than 7 N/mm² and to the nearest 0.1 N/mm² for blocks with a specified strength greater than 7 N/mm². The mean of the compressive strength of ten blocks is taken as the average compressive strength of the sample and is reported to the same accuracy as the individual results.

The testing machine

A testing machine of sufficient capacity for the test and equipped with a means of providing the rate of loading specified and with a pacing device is used. The capacity of the machine shall be such that the expected ultimate load on a specimen is greater than one-fifth of the machine scale range. The machine shall comply, as regards accuracy, with the requirements of Grade A or B of BS 1610:1964[3.11].

The testing machine shall be equipped with two permanent ferrous bearing platens which shall normally be as large as the bedding faces of the specimen being tested. Where the permanent platens of the testing machine are not as large as the specimen to be tested, auxiliary bearing platens having dimensions not less than that of the specimen shall be used. These shall not be fixed to the permanent platens, but shall be brought to bear in intimate contact, care being taken to exclude dirt from the interfaces.

The upper machine platen shall be able to align freely with the specimen as contact is made but the platens shall be restrained by friction or other means from tilting with respect to each other during loading. The lower compression platen shall be a plain, non-tilting bearing block. The auxiliary platen that will bear on the upper surface of the specimen shall be attached loosely to the testing machine by flexible wire or chain, to prevent it falling if the specimen collapses suddenly under load.

The testing face of the main platen and both faces of each auxiliary platen shall be hardened and shall have:

(1) A flatness tolerance of 0.05 mm.

(2) A parallelism tolerance for one face of each platen with respect to the other face as datum of 0.10 mm.

(3) A surface texture not greater than 3.2 μm CLA, measured in accordance with BS 1134[3.12].

The testing faces, where case-hardened, shall have a diamond pyramid hardness number of at least 600. Where the platens are through-hardened, the steel shall have a minimum specification of EN 26Y. The permanent platens shall be solid and not less than 50 mm thick, unless blocks of specified compressive strength of 7 N/mm² or more are to be tested, in which case the platens shall be not less than 75 mm thick. Auxiliary platens shall be solid and have a thickness not less than two thirds the amount by which they overhang the permanent platens unless blocks of specified compressive strength of 7 N/mm² or more are to be tested, in which case the thickness shall not be less than the overhang. In no case, however, shall the auxiliary platen overhang the permanent platen by more than 75 mm.

Alternative rapid control test

An alternative to the use of mortar capping is the use of fibre board. The strength indicated in this test varies from that achieved using board capping (see page 14) and the simplified test procedure is generally only used by manufacturers as a rapid control test.

The procedure for preparing the blocks for test is simply to remove fins or small pieces of aggregate proud of the surface by means of a carborundum stone. The specimens are then immersed in water at a temperature between 10—25°C for at least 16 hours and are stored under damp sacking as described for the mortar capped test. Two new pieces of 12 mm insulation board, complying with BS 1142[3.13] and 10 mm larger than the bed faces of the specimens, are used as caps. The specimens are tested in the machine in a similar manner to the mortar capped specimens. In general, the source of manufacture of the capping board will not affect the indicated block strength.

Determination of transverse breaking load
This procedure is used for relatively thin non-loadbearing partition blocks. Five blocks are selected at random and immersed for at least 16 hours in water at a temperature of between 10—25°C. Each block is then covered with damp material and allowed to drain for 30—45 minutes before testing. The testing frame is shown in Figure 3.1. Each block is placed centrally on the support bearers with the bedding faces perpendicular to the plane of the bearers. Load is applied so that the extreme fibre stress increases at a rate of approximately 1.5 N/mm² per minute. Appropriate rates of loading are shown in Table 3.7. The maximum load carried by the block during the test is recorded to the nearest 25 N and the transverse strength determined from the expression $f = \frac{570P}{bt^2}$. The mean of the five determined strength loads is taken as the transverse breaking strength of the sample and is reported to the nearest 0.05 N/mm².

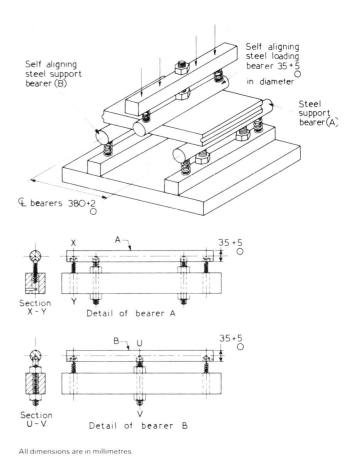

All dimensions are in millimetres.

Figure 3.1   Apparatus for transverse test

Table 3.7 Appropriate rates of loading

Height (work size) mm	Thickness (work size) mm	Approximate rate of loading N/mm.
190	60	1800
	75	2800
215	60	2000
	75	3200
290	60	2700
	75	4300

Table 3.8 Relationships between some of the test specimens

Test specimens compared	Ratio
Mortar cap, block dry / Mortar cap, block wet	1.15
Board cap, block dry / Board cap, block wet	1.14
Board cap prism / Mortar cap prism	0.90
Board cap, block wet / Mortar cap, block wet	0.80

Limitations of the standard test for block strength
The clauses in BS 6073 relating to the performance of the testing machine are insufficient to describe whether it will perform adequately in practice. Although the accuracy of load scale indication is specified, this does not ensure that the machine is of sufficient stiffness, that the ball seating moves to accommodate the specimen and subsequently locks under load and that the specimen fails correctly even if slightly misplaced. It is recommended that consideration be given to a more comprehensive machine performance specification, details of which have been published[3.1, 3.2].

The relationship between the strengths of blocks, wet and dry, and between mortar and board capped specimens have been investigated[3.14] and the results are summarized in Table 3.8. Although these relationships are obtained from tests on a wide range of blocks, it is possible that the ratio between particular conditions

might be slightly different for special materials or blocks. It must be remembered that because of the high variability of most concrete blocks a large number of specimens need to be tested to predict confidently the ratio between two forms of test.

One further point to note is the use of prism specimens which stems largely from testing small brick size units. Two block high specimens will not indicate significant differences in either mortar strength or joint thickness for most types of block as they affect the axial strength of a wall and their use is not, therefore, recommended[3.14].

3.2.1.2 Concrete bricks

The compressive strength of concrete bricks is found by testing a sample of ten units. The British Standard covering the testing of concrete bricks, BS 6073, includes a detailed sampling procedure to ensure that bricks selected are representative of the stack. The average overall dimensions of each brick, including the length and width of the frog if present, is measured to the nearest 1 mm and in the case of units with no frog or indentation, the area of the small bed face is calculated. For bricks containing a frog the gross area of the bed face in which the frog lies is calculated and the net area of application of the load is derived as the gross area minus the area of the frog. If the frog or indentation is so ill-defined that measurement is impracticable the bricks should be tested in accordance with Clause 43 of BS 3921[3.15] which applies to frogged bricks laid frog upwards. Where both bed faces contain frogs, the net area of the smaller bed face should be used and for bricks having holes or perforations the gross area of the smaller bed face is calculated.

Before testing the bricks must be immersed in water at a temperatrue of $20 \pm 5°C$ for approximately 16 hours. Each brick is taken from the water and placed on the platen of the testing machine with the bed faces perpendicular to the direction of application of load. The testing machine must meet the requirements for accuracy of Grade B of BS 1610[3.11] at the maximum load expected. To ensure uniform load the brick must be placed between plywood sheets of 2.4 to 4.8 mm thick, and the plywood must extend beyond the face of the bricks. Fresh plywood caps should be used for each brick. Load is applied at a rate of 200 ± 20 kN/minute for a frogged brick and 400 ± 40 kN/minute for a brick with no frog, until the brick has failed. The rate of loading may be doubled until half the anticipated maximum load has been applied. The compressive strength of each brick is taken as the maximum load divided by the area of the bed face. The strength of each brick is expressed in MN/m² to the nearest 0.5 MN/m² and the average of the ten bricks reported to the nearest 0.5 MN/m².

A procedure is included in BS 6073:1981 for calculating the coefficient of variation of compressive strength from the individual values.

3.2.2 Shrinkage

3.2.2.1 Concrete blocks

The test procedures for determining drying shrinkage given in the current Standard, also in BS 1881:Part 5[3.10], have been found to have certain drawbacks but have been included pending research by various organizations represented on the BSI Committee. If necessary an amendment will be issued. The following are the current test requirements.

Preparation of specimens

Four whole blocks are taken at random to determine drying shrinkage and wetting expansion and a specimen is sawn from each of the blocks. The length of each specimen must be not less than 150 mm and not more than 300 mm, the cross section of the specimen must have one dimension of 50 ± 3 mm and the second not less than 50 mm, and the centre area of the rectangle enclosing the cross section of the specimen must be solid. Reference points in the form of stainless steel balls 6.3 to 6.5 mm in diameter must be fixed to each end of the specimen such that they lie at the central axis. The balls may usually be fixed with neat rapid-hardening Portland cement and the specimens stored in moist air for at least one day to allow the cement to harden. The steel balls should ideally be located in holes, 2 mm deep, drilled in the ends of the specimen so that a hemispherical bearing is provided, but with some hard aggregates this may be difficult to achieve, in which case simple roughening of the ends of the blocks would have to suffice. The reference points should be cleaned and coated with lubricating grease, and the specimens stored in water at room temperature for a minimum of four days and a maximum of seven, the water being maintained at a temperature of $20 \pm 1°C$ for the final four hours. Each specimen is then measured to determine the distance over the steel balls to the nearest 1 mm and the length is taken as this distance minus 13 mm.

Procedure for testing

The specimens are removed from the water and the grease is immediately wiped from the steel balls. The length of each specimen is measured* on apparatus similar to that shown in Figure 3.2. The specimen is placed between the recessed seating of the frame and the recessed end of the gauge and is rotated, the minimum reading of numerator gauge being recorded. By reversing the specimen and repeating the reading, an average of two readings may be taken as the original wet measurement. The calibration of the apparatus is checked using a reference rod.

The specimens are dried in an oven, ensuring that there is free access of air to all surfaces (It is important not to place additional wet specimens in an oven containing partly dried specimens). The specimens are removed at the specified time and placed in a cooling cabinet.

Ideally measurements should be carried out in a controlled temperature of $20 \pm 2°C$ at a time when the specimen temperature in the cabinet does not change by more than 0.5°C in half an hour and is within 3°C of the measured room temperature. The length of each specimen is measured as soon as possible after removal from the cabinet, a correction of 0.001% being applied for each °C difference in temperature from 20°C and another correction made if the reading of length of the standard reference rod has changed. The cycle of drying, cooling, measuring and correcting is continued until the specified consistency and length are attained.

*Full details of this equipment are available in BS 6073. A detailed description of the oven is contained in BS 6073. Essentially the oven is designed to maintain a RH of 17% at a temperature of 55°C. Saturated air is provided by means of the apparatus shown in Figure 3.3 and two air changes per hour take place.

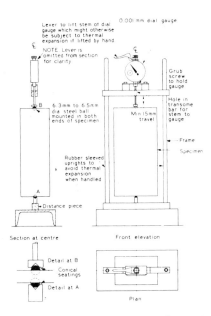

Figure 3.2 Typical measuring apparatus for drying shrinkage and wetting expansion

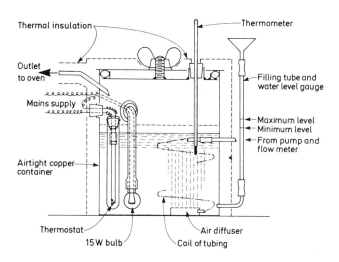

Figure 3.3 Air-conditioning equipment for supplying saturated air at controlled temperature to conditioning oven

Readings are taken at daily intervals each side of seven and fourteen day increments from the time the specimens are taken out of the water. The average of each pair is calculated as the seven and fourteen day values respectively. For at least two of the three specimens A, B and C the difference between the original wet measurement and the seven day value is not less than 90% of the difference between the fourteen day value and the original wet measurement and the third is not less than 85%, the dry measurement is regarded as the fourteen day value provided the test for consistency

is satisfied. If it is not satisfied, specimen D is substituted accordingly, and if the above requirement for completion of the dry measurement is then satisfied by the three specimens so obtained, take the fourteen day mean value as the dry measurement. If the criteria for completion of drying are not satisfied all the specimens are returned to the oven and readings taken at 20 and 22 days. Provided the test for consistency is satisfied the mean of the results from specimens A, B and C is regarded as the dry measurement. If the test for consistency is not satisfied substitute the result from specimen D and recalculate. Calculate the drying shrinkage for each specimen as the difference between the original wet measurement and the dry measurement expressed as a percentage of the length.

It is now necessary to measure the wetting expansion and the specimens must be immersed in water for four days, the water being maintained at 20° ± 1°C for the final few hours. The length of each specimen is then recorded and the wetting expansion is calculated as the difference between the dry measurement and the final wet measurement expressed as a percentage of the length.

Calculation of results

If the values for drying shrinkage or wetting expansion obtained with any one of the three specimens A, B and C differ from the average value for the same three specimens by more than 25% then the excessive shrinkage value of the individual specimen is discarded and the value obtained with specimen D substituted. The average value of drying shrinkage and wetting expansion is reported to the nearest 0.005%. If the value of D is also found to differ from the average for the second set of three specimens by more than 25% the result of the test is to be regarded as invalid.

Limitations of the test procedure

The regime of curing and testing at 55°C at a relative humidity of 17% is unrealistic in terms of being more severe than the worst conditions likely to be encountered by blockwork in practice. Furthermore, it is apparent that no limits are set to the age or initial curing applied to specimens, and drying shrinkage may change significantly because of further hydration of the cement or of atmospheric carbonation over a period of a few weeks. The rank applied to different types of blocks when tested to the above regime may differ from that observed in practice. This test procedure is, therefore, likely to be reviewed with the object of producing more practicable results.

3.2.2.2 Concrete bricks

Preparation of specimens

For the determination of drying shrinkage four whole bricks are taken at random. A depression not more than 2 mm deep is drilled or cut into the centre of each end of all four specimens although if the nature of the brick makes this difficult the surface should just be roughened. A 6.3 to 6.5 mm diameter stainless steel ball is cemented with neat rapid-hardening Portland cement into each depression, and is wiped dry and coated with lubricating grease to prevent corrosion.

The specimens marked A, B, C and D are stored in moist air for at least one day. They are then completely immersed in water at room temperature for a minimum of four days and a maximum of seven, the water is maintained at a temperature of 20 ± 1°C for the final four hours. Each specimen is measured to determine the distance over the steel balls to the nearest 1 mm and this distance minus 13 mm is taken as the length. The equipment and subsequent method of test is similar to that used for concrete blocks.

3.2.3 Determination of block density, concrete volume and net area of hollow blocks

3.2.3.1 Determination of density Measurement of volume of cavities:

(1) Place the blocks on a thin sheet of foam rubber or other resilient material with the open ends of the cavities uppermost.

(2) Close any cavities at the ends of the block by clamping flat sheets of 13 mm insulating board to the ends of the block without distortion. Ignore the effects of tongues or grooves.

(3) Fill a one litre glass measuring cylinder accurately with dry sand which has been graded between a 300 m BS test sieve and a 600 m BS test sieve, both sieves complying with BS 410[3.9].

(4) Fill the cavities with the sand by pouring from the cylinder, refilling if required, keeping the cylinder lip within 25 mm of the top of the cavity and pouring steadily and striking off level.

(5) Return to the cylinder any sand struck off and note, in ml, the total volume of sand used to the nearest 50 ml. Convert this volume to the equivalent volume in mm³ of the cavities to the nearest 250 mm³.

(6) Calculate the gross volume of the block to the nearest 250 mm³ by multiplying the average thickness by the specified length and height of the block (Ignore formed protrusions and indentations).

(7) Express the volume of cavities in each block as a percentage of the gross volume of the block.

(8) Record, to the nearest 5%, the greatest volume of cavity detected.

3.2.3.2 Determination of concrete volume

(1) Remove all random flashings with carborundum stone.

(2) Measure to the nearest 1 mm using callipers and rule the dimensions of formed indentations and protrusions on the external faces and ends of the block.

(3) Calculate the algebraic sum of the volume of all indentations and protrusions to the nearest 250 mm³ (Treat volume of indentation as negative and volume of protrusion as positive).

(4) Calculate the concrete volume, to the nearest 250 mm³, using the following equation:

Concrete volume = (gross volume of block)

        − (volume of cavities and voids)

        + (algebraic sum of volume of indentations and protrusions)

3.2.3.3 Determination of block density and concrete density

(1) Dry three blocks for at least 16 hours in a ventilated oven having the temperature controlled at 105 ± 5°C.

(2) Cool the blocks to ambient temperature and weigh.

(3) Repeat (1) and (2) until the mass lost in one cycle does not exceed 0.05 kg.

(4) Calculate the block density and the concrete density by using the following formulae:

Block density in kg/m³ = oven dry mass in kg ÷ gross volume in m³

Concrete density in kg/m² = oven dry mass in kg ÷ concrete volume in m³.

(5) Record the mean densities of the three blocks to the nearest 10 kg/m³.

3.2.3.4 Determination of net area of hollow blocks

(1) Obtain the mean height from six height measurements.

(2) Calculate the net area using the following equation:
Net area = concrete volume ÷ mean height.

NOTE: The net area of hollow blocks is required for assessing the characteristic compressive strength of walls of hollow concrete blocks, filled with in situ concrete (see Clause 23.1.7 of BS 5628:Part 1:1978).

3.2.4 Dimensions

To determine the dimensions of a batch of concrete blocks it is usual to take ten whole blocks from the consignment at random. Any fins may be removed with a carborundum stone before checking the dimensions at the points shown in Figure 3.4. There are four positions at which the length is checked, six positions for height and seven measurements of thickness. As a routine control of length and height GO/NOT GO gauges of the sort shown in Figure 3.5 may be used but callipers and a rule must be used for the thickness.

When checking compliance with dimensional tolerances it is necessary to calculate to the nearest 1 mm the average of the seven measurements of thickness of each block. If the dimensions are being employed to calculate the block density, the gross volume of the block is calculated to the nearest 50 000 mm³ from the average thickness and the specified length and height of the block. When the dimensions are being used to work out the area for compressive strength determinations, the average thickness at the top and bottom bed faces are calculated to the nearest 1 mm and the gross area is

(a) Four positions for checking length of whole blocks

(b) Six positions for checking height of whole blocks

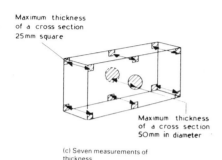

Maximum thickness of a cross section 25mm square

Maximum thickness of a cross section 50mm in diameter

(c) Seven measurements of thickness

Figure 3.4   Measuring points for block dimensions

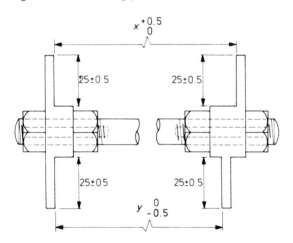

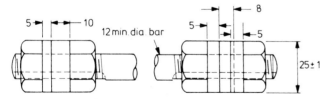

Figure 3.5   GO/NOT GO gauges for checking length and height of concrete blocks
Note 1: Keys are used for keeping fittings at both ends in the same plane
Note 2: Fittings may be made from the solid as shown or made up from separate pieces
Note 3: The two measuring dimensions are to be accurate to 0.5 mm

calculated to the nearest 500 mm² as the smaller of the two average thicknesses multiplied by the specified length of block.

3.2.5 Moisture content

There is no standard procedure for determining the moisture content of concrete masonry, but it is sug-

gested that a procedure similar to that indicated in BS 1881: Part 5:1970[3.10] *Methods of testing concrete* is adopted*.

The dry density may be determined by placing the weighed block or block sample, in a drying oven at a temperature of 105 ± 5°C. This may take up to three days for very dense concrete, after which the specimen should be removed from the oven and immediately transferred to a dessicator or dry airtight vessel. Once the temperature has fallen below 60°C it may be reweighed and the moisture content by weight then deduced. As with a concrete cube, the saturated weight may be determined by weighing the specimen under water and in air before drying in the oven.

3.2.6 Thermal insulation

In the United Kingdom the thermal insulation value of a concrete block is determined by measuring the thermal conductivity in accordance with BS 874:1973[3.16] *Methods for determining thermal insulating properties, with definitions of thermal insulating terms*†. This Standard allows a variety of procedures but aspects relating to building materials are considered here.

The basic specimens required for test are two 305 × 305 × 50 mm prisms from the block. If the face size of block is smaller than the above, sections must be sawn from the block, glued and the faces ground to an accurate thickness. A heating element is then placed between the prisms, with thermocouples on either side of each prism either on the surface or buried. The thermal conductivity of the material is calculated by applying a known input of electrical energy and measuring the surface temperatures. The apparatus can be a plain hot plate with surrounding layers of insulation to prevent edge lossses, or a guarded hot plate.

While materials as delivered can vary, the variation in results between laboratories testing the same type of block appears to be due to differences in the testing procedure. Among the observations made by Spooner[3.17] on the results of a 'round robin' thermal conductivity test were the following:

(1) A comparison of results taken from plain and guarded hot plate equipment recorded no difference for aerated concrete specimens but 7% difference for lightweight concrete.

(2) Good contact must be maintained between the thermocouples and the specimen surfaces and for thermal conductivities above 0.5 W/m K the thermocouples must be cemented into grooves in the surface of the specimens.

The British Calibration Service has set up a laboratory verification scheme which should obviate many of the discrepancies once it has become established.

---

*Several parts of BS 1881 have now been revised as BS 1881:1983.
†Currently being revised.

3.3 Quality control for blocks

3.3.1 Introduction

The Code of Practice, BS 5628, introduces the concept of quality control such that the value of γ_m should be commensurate with the degree of control exercized during the manufacture of the structural units, the site supervision and the quality of the mortar used during construction. Two levels of control are recognized for manufacture (See also *Chapter 19*):

Normal category   This category should be assumed when the requirements for compressive strength in the appropriate British Standard are met, but the requirements for the special category below are not.

Special category   This may be assumed where the manufacturer:

(1) agrees to supply consignments of structural units to a specified strength limit, referred to as the *acceptance limit* for compressive strength, such that the average compressive strength of a sample of structural units, taken from any consignment and tested in accordance with the appropriate British Standard specification has a probability of not more than 2½% being below the acceptance limit;

(2) operates a quality control scheme, the results of which can demonstrate to the satisfaction of the purchaser that the *acceptance limit* is consistently met in practice and the probability of failing to meet the limit is never greater than that stated above.

The British Standards Institution runs a quality control scheme whereby a registered certification trade mark (kitemark) and legend 'Approved to British Standard' may be marked on the blocks by manufacturers licensed under the scheme. The mark indicates that the units have been produced to comply with the requirements of the British Standard under a system of supervision, control and testing operated during manufacture and including periodical inspection at the manufacturers' works.

The lack of correlation between unit and wall strength for small units such as bricks has led to the concept of testing small assemblages or prisms of masonry. The use of prisms has also been applied to larger units such as concrete blocks, but there is little purpose in using more than single blocks, as unit tests correlate well with wall tests on blockwork panels, and prism tests in the case of blocks do not even reflect large changes in mortar strength, joint thickness or workmanship[3.14]. The use of these tests for site control of masonry construction is, therefore, not recommended, and block, mortar and workmanship quality is better controlled by means of separate tests. A detailed explanation of quality assurance procedures which might be operated by a manufacturer is provided in *Chapter 19*.

3.3.2 Performance of the testing machine

It is now widely accepted that such features as the stiffness of the testing machine frame, hydraulic system and the behaviour of the ball seat under load can all reduce the indicated strength of the specimen and thus affect the recorded strength of concrete cubes. These aspects are quite separate from the accuracy of load scale indication of the machine and whether it is Grade A or Grade B. Although the effect of poor machine performance on indicated block strengths has not been well researched, a limited number of tests carried out by The Cement and Concrete Association have indicated strengths 10% lower than those obtained on a good machine. For concrete cube machines, for which many more test results are available, differences of up to 30% have been recorded. It is important to ensure that testing is carried out in accordance with the correct British Standard for the particular product and on a machine performing satisfactorily. Many manufacturers of testing machines offered 'special' versions of standard concrete cube testing machines for block testing only—possibly the only concession to block testing being the provision of a larger platen. BS 6073 makes specific recommendations about platen thickness and such like, which should be followed. Purpose designed block testing machines are now available and providing these are regularly checked should provide good results. The Foote prooving device is one method of checking the performance of block testing machines, and is reported by Roberts[3.18] who has also published a testing machine specification[3.19] from which appropriate clauses can be extracted.

3.4 Mortar strength

Mortar fulfills a multi-purpose role in a masonry assemblage. In addition to providing a level bed so that the load is evenly spread over the bearing area of the units, the mortar bonds units together to help them resist lateral forces, allows the control of alignment and plumb, and prevents the ingress of rain through the joints.

3.4.1 Properties relevant to mortar selection

Mortar should be very workable and hence readily and economically used by the mason, it must offer adequate durability but should not be stronger than the units so that movements can be accommodated. Table 3.5 indicates the minimum quality of unit and mortar for a given exposure condition.

Traditionally, lime mortars were employed for masonry construction, typical proportions being 1:3 lime:sand. Although lime mortars offer excellent workability characteristics they rely on the loss of water and carbonation to slowly gain strength and this constraint on the rate of construction has lead to the widespread use of cement mortars. Portland cement mortar quickly gains strength allowing rapid construction. Lime is often added to the mix to improve workability producing the so called cement:lime:sand (compo) mortar. Masonry mortar consists of a mixture of Portland cement with a very fine mineral filler and an air-entraining agent. These mortars offer good working properties but should not be overmixed because an excessive amount of air could be entrained. Air-entrained or plasticized mortar is produced by using a plasticizer to replace the role of the lime with the cement:sand:mix, whereby the air bubbles increase the volume of the binder paste and fill the voids in the sand.

In Table 3.9 comparison is made of the properties of different types of mortar and their approximate equivalence. For most general purpose concrete masonry construction the lowest grade of mortar practicable should be employed. Thus for aerated concrete blocks a 1:2:9 cement:lime:sand mortar will be appropriate, providing:

(1) the sand grading is good;

(2) there is no risk of frost attack during setting;

(3) the surface finish to be applied as a decorative coat does not demand a stronger background.

For most general purpose concrete masonry construction a 1:1:6 cement:lime:sand mortar is suitable. High strength loadbearing masonry and reinforced masonry generally require a $1:\frac{1}{4}:3$ or $1:\frac{1}{2}:4\frac{1}{2}$ cement:lime:sand mortar. Table 3.10 indicates the lime:sand mixes required for specified cement:lime:sand mortars. Retarding agents can be added to delay the set and prolong the working life of the mortar, but cement mortars should otherwise be used within two hours of mixing. Table 3.10 also indicates the order of strength that may be aimed at for control purposes. In practice the strength achieved by a given mortar will depend on the quality and grading of the sand as well as the cement and water content. The bond strength of the mortar to the units is often far more important than the compressive strength which is not a prime requirement. Given a reasonable sand grading the bond strength achieved will depend on the workmanship of the masonry and the type and condition of the units at the time of laying, together with the subsequent curing regime. Sands for use with mortar should comply with BS 1198, 1199, 1200:1976[3.20].

Table 3.9 Lime:sand mixes required for specified cement:lime:sand mortars

Specified cement:lime:sand mortar	Lime:sand mix	Gauging of cement with lime:sand mix
Proportions by volume	Proportions by volume	Proportions by volume
$1:\frac{1}{2}:4-4\frac{1}{2}$	1:8-9	$1:4-4\frac{1}{2}$
1:1:5-6	1:5-6	1:5-6
1:2:8-9	$1:4-4\frac{1}{2}$	1:8-9
1:3:10-12	$1:3\frac{1}{2}-4$	1:10-12

Table 3.10 Requirements for mortar (adapted from BS 5628:Part 1:1978)

		Type of mortar						Mean compressive strength at 28 days (N/mm^2)	
	Mortar designation	Cement:lime:sand		Air-entraining mixes					
				Masonry cement:sand		Cement:sand with plasticizers			
		by volume	by weight (mass)	by volume	by weight (mass)	by volume	by weight (mass)	Preliminary laboratory tests	Site tests
Increasing strength and durability / Increasing ability to accommodate movements	(i)	$1:0-\frac{1}{4}:3$	$1:0-\frac{1}{8}:3\frac{1}{2}$	—	—	—	—	16.0	11.0
	(ii)	$1:\frac{1}{2}:4-4\frac{1}{2}$	$1:\frac{1}{4}:5$	$1:2\frac{1}{2}-3\frac{1}{2}$	$1:3\frac{1}{2}$	1:3-4	1:4	6.5	4.5
	(iii)	1:1:5-6	$1:\frac{1}{2}:6\frac{1}{2}$	1:4-5	$1:5\frac{1}{2}$	1:5-6	$1:6\frac{1}{2}$	3.6	2.5
	(iv)	1:2:8-9	1:1:10	$1:5\frac{1}{2}-6\frac{1}{2}$	$1:7\frac{1}{2}$	1:7-8	1:9	1.5	1.0
Direction of change in properties is shown by the arrows	Increasing resistance to frost attack during construction →								
	← Improvement in adhesion and consequent resistance to rain penetration								

Notes:

(1) Where mortar of a given compressive strength is required by the designer, the mix proportions should be determined from tests conforming to the recommendations of Appendix A of BS 5628:1978.

(2) The different types of mortar that comprise any one designation are approximately equivalent in strength and do not generally differ greatly in their other properties. Some general differences between types of mortar are indicated by the arrows at the bottom of the Table, but these differences can be reduced (see CP 121).

(3) 'Lime' refers to non-hydraulic or semi-hydraulic lime. The proportions are based on dry hydrated lime.

(4) **Proportions by volume.** The proportions of dry hydrated lime may be increased by up to 50% to improve workability. The range of sand contents is to allow for the effects of the differences in grading upon the properties of the mortar. Generally, the higher value is for sand that is well graded and the lower for coarse or uniformly fine sand. The designer should clearly indicate which proportions are required for the particular sand being used. Where no specific instructions are given, it will be assumed that the designer has satisfied himself that the sand will have no significant effect on the mortar and that it may be batched within the given range to achieve workability.

(5) **Proportions by weight (mass).** The proportions of dry hydrated lime may be increased by up to 25% to improve workability. The proportions for sand given are mean values for each mortar designation. The proportions by mass may alternatively be determined by the designer by measuring the actual bulk densities of the constituents of a volume-batched mix known to produce satisfactory results.

(6) An air-entrained admixture may, at the discretion of the designer, be added to a lime:sand mix to improve its early frost resistance.

3.4.2 Quality control for mortars

Specified quality control of mortars on site is generally confined to large jobs where loadbearing masonry is involved and construction is taking place under the special category indicated in BS 5628:Part 1[3.4]. It is prudent to specify effective sampling and test procedures for the mortar on any large site, particularly where, for reasons of strength or appearance, consistent batching and use is critical.

Cement for mortars should comply with the requirements of one of the following Standards: BS 12:1978[3.21] *Specification for ordinary and rapid-hardening Portland cement*; BS 146:Part 2:1973[3.22] *Portland blast furnace cement*; BS 4027:1980[3.23] *Specification for sulphate-resisting Portland cement* or BS 5224:1976[3.24] *Specification for masonry cement*.

Lime should be hydrated non-hydraulic (high calcium) or semi-hydraulic (calcium) conforming to BS 890:1972[3.25] *Building limes*. Sands for mortar should comply with the grading requirements of Table 2 of BS 1200[3.20] and with the general requirements of that Standard in respect of its limitations on deleterious substances.

Ragsdale and Birt[3.26] have conducted an extensive survey of the availability, usage and compliance with specification requirements of building sands. It is apparent that sands available in the UK for use in building mortars vary considerably in their properties and characteristics and that those which conform fully and consistently to the current British Standards are unobtainable from local sources in many parts of the country. As a result Ragsdale and Birt found that many sands which did not comply with the British Standards could satisfactorily be used and that the factors of prime importance were cleanliness and grading, rather than compliance with the appropriate British Standards gradings. Figures 3.6 and 3.7 reproduced from this survey indicate the specified grading limits for masonry mortar sands and for plastering sands respectively.

Pigments should comply with the requirements of BS 1014:1975[3.27] and generally should not exceed 10% by weight of the cement, except in the case of carbon black which should not exceed 3% by weight of the cement.

The mixing and use of mortars should be in accordance with the recommendations of CP 121:Part 1: 1973[3.5] and BS 5390:1976[3.28]. Ready mixed lime: sand for mortar should comply with the requirements of BS 4721:1971[3.29]. Wet ready mixed retarded cement:lime:sand mixes should only be used with the written permission of the designer.

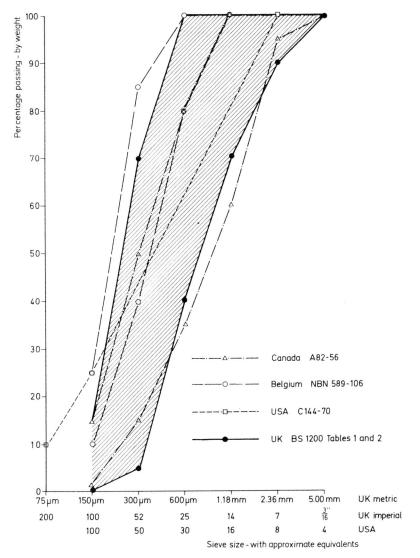

Figure 3.6   Specified grading limits for masonry mortar sands

Preliminary tests Six weeks prior to building the masonry, the strengths of the grades of mortar to be used should be determined in the laboratory with materials taken from the sources which are to supply the site. Six specimens should be produced of one of the following types: 75 mm cubes, 100 mm cubes or 100 mm × 25 mm × 25 mm prisms. The mortar should have a consistence corresponding to a 10 mm penetration of the dropping ball (without suction method) and should be cured hydraulically and tested in compression in accordance with the procedures given in BS 4551:1970[3.30]. The type of specimen to be used on the Site should be identical to that used for these preliminary tests.

Interpolation of test results The average compressive strengths for the various grades of mortar are shown in Table 3.10. If desired half of the specimens may be tested at seven days, the results of which will normally give an indication of the strength to be expected at 28 days. For the mortars in Table 3.10 the strengths at seven days will approximate to two thirds of the

strengths at 28 days provided that the mortars are based on Portland cement with no additive to retard or accelerate the rate of hardening. If the average of these seven day strengths equals or exceeds two thirds of the appropriate weight in the Table the requirements are likely to be satisfied, but if the average strength is less, the designer may choose to wait for 28 day strengths or to have the test repeated on a more suitable sand.

Site tests Six 100 mm × 25 mm × 25 mm prisms or four cubes should be prepared on Site for every 150 m² of wall of one grade of mortar, or for every storey of the building, whichever is the more frequent. Specimens should be stored and tested in accordance with BS 4551[3.30]. If required, half the site specimens may be tested at seven days. The average strength should exceed two thirds of the appropriate 28 day strength in Table 3.10. When the Site samples are tested at the age of 28 days, the results will be deemed to pass if the average strength of three 100 mm × 25 mm × 25 mm prisms or two cubes exceeds the appropriate Site values given in Table 3.10.

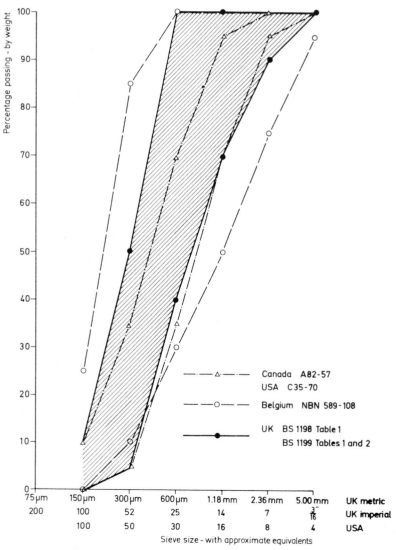

Figure 3.7 Specified grading limits for plastering sands

3.5 Standard tests for mortars

3.5.1 Consistence by dropping ball

Flow, stiffening time and strength properties of a mortar will all be affected by the consistence which may be determined by the dropping ball test. Since some other test procedures require a standard consistence of 10 ± 0.5 mm penetration of the dropping ball, preliminary tests in accordance with this Clause may have to be made for adjustment of the water content.

Suitable apparatus for carrying out the test, as shown in Figure 3.8, consists of a dropping mechanism for a methyl methacrylate ball. This release mechanism must be such that it does not impart any appreciable spin, friction or acceleration to the ball other than that due to gravity (Figure 3.9). The polished ball has a diameter of 25 ± 0.1 mm, weighs 9.8 ± 0.1 g and is dropped into the mortar contained in a brass mould of 100 mm internal diameter and 25 mm internal length. The apparatus includes a device for measuring the depth of penetration of the ball in mm to an accuracy of 0.1 mm, which also needs to be capable of measuring any fall in the surface level of the mortar for consistence retentivity. The brass mould is filled by pushing the mortar with the end of a palette knife in about ten stages. When the mortar is slightly above the rim the surface is levelled with the top of the mould using the palette knife, which is held at about 45° and moved once across the mould with a sawing motion to strike off excess material, and then at a slightly flatter angle to trowel the surface.

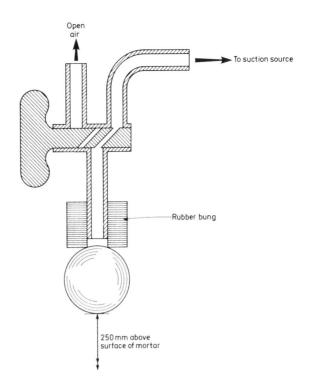

Figure 3.9   Diagrammatic representation of ball release

The methyl methacrylate ball is allowed to drop from a height of 250 mm and must land within 12 mm of the centre of the surface of the mortar. The penetration of the ball is measured and recorded to the nearest 0.1 mm. The test is repeated twice with two other samples of the mortar, after cleaning the apparatus, and the average of the three penetrations is recorded to the nearest 0.1 mm as the consistence.

3.5.2 Consistence retentivity and water retentivity

The retention of consistence and of water in mortars is of considerable practical importance, especially if the mortar is to be applied on materials of high suction. The consistence of any particular mortar will depend upon the water content and the content of entrained air. Thus, measuring the water retained under a standard test condition is not always adequate to describe the performance of some mortars, and the degree to which the mortar retains its consistence is the more useful measure for general use. In this test the properties of the mortar are measured before and after standard suction treatment. The final consistence value, expressed as a percentage of the original value, is termed the 'consistence retentivity'. The weight of water retained after suction, expressed as a percentage of the original water content, is termed the 'water retentivity'.

For this test, the mould used for the dropping ball test is filled and the average penetration is determined. The depresssion left by the ball is filled with mortar and struck off level. The surface of the mortar is then covered with two pieces of white cotton gauze (two circles, 110 mm in diameter or two squares of 110 mm wide) and eight circles of filter paper are placed on top.

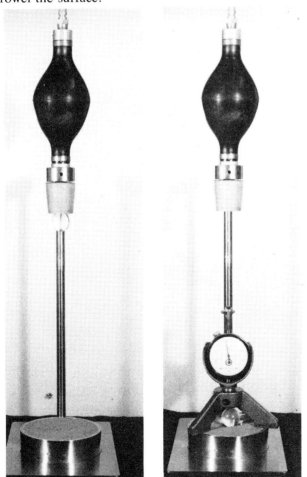

Figure 3.8   Dropping ball apparatus and a suitable device for measuring penetration

Extra thick white filter paper of weight 200 g/m² and 110 mm in diameter should be used on top of which a non-porous plate 110 mm in diameter should be placed loaded with a 2 Kg weight. After two minutes the weight, filter paper and cotton gauze are removed and the gauze discarded.

The fall in the level of the mortar is then measured and a single dropping ball test is carried out after suction. The apparent penetration of the ball is corrected by subtracting from it any measured fall in the level of the mortar so that the corrected penetration of the ball after suction, expressed as a percentage of the average penetration before suction, is the consistence retentivity. This procedure is repeated with a second sample of mortar, and the average of the two retentivity values to the nearest 5% is taken as the consistence retentivity of the mortar.

To measure the water retentivity the mould in a dry condition and light circles of filter paper are weighed. The mould is filled as for the dropping ball test and, with all mortar removed from the outside, the mould and its contents are weighed. The mortar is then subjected to suction as described earlier and the filter paper weighed to the nearest 0.05 g. The weight of water originally present in the mould is calculated from the weight of mortar in the mould and the moisture content of the mortar. The weight of water retained by the mortar after suction (i.e., the weight of water originally present in the mould minus the weight of water absorbed by the filter paper), expressed as a percentage of the weight of water originally present in the mould full of mortar, is the water retentivity. The procedure is repeated with a second sample of mortar and the average of the two retentivity values to the nearest 1% is taken as the water retentivity of the mortar.

3.5.3 Determination of the compressive strength of mortar

The standard cube for testing mortar is 100 mm but 75 mm moulds may also be used, or prisms 100 mm × 25 mm × 25 mm. The mould must be substantial in construction and comply with the requirements of BS 1881:Part 3:1970[3.10]*. Particular attention is paid to the dimensional tolerances of the mould.

A representative sample of the mortar should be taken and the test specimens made as soon as practicable. The mould should be filled in layers approximately 50 mm deep and each layer should be compacted by hand or by vibration. Once the top layer has been compacted the surface of the concrete should be finished level with the top of the trowel. Ideally vibration should be used to ensure compaction but a standard compacting bar may be used to complete compaction by hand.

Specimens made in the laboratory should be stored in a place free from vibration, in moist air of at least 90% relative humidity at a temperature of 20 ± 2°C for 16—24 hours. Either a moist curing room or damp matting covered by polythene should be used.

Demoulding can take place after 24 hours, and specimens should then be stored in a tank of clean water at a temperature of 20 ± 1°C until tested. Specimens made on site should be stored under damp matting covered with polythene at a temperature of 20 ± 5°C for 16—24 hours. After demoulding, usually 24 hours, the specimens should be stored in clean water contained in a tank maintained at a temperature of 20 ± 2°C until they are removed for testing. The specimens should be tested in a concrete cube testing machine of Grade A in terms of BS 1610[3.11] and the performance aspects of the machine should be verified by regular reference testing. Load should be applied to the specimens at a rate of 15 N/mm² per minute and the maximum load failure recorded.

It should be noted that BS 4551:1970[3.30] also contains a flexural test for mortar using the 100 mm × 25 mm × 25 mm prism but it is unlikely that the designer will require this information for the mortar in isolation.

3.5.4 Bond strength of mortar

A number of techniques have been developed for determining the bond strength of mortar to units but no direct methods are incorporated into a British Standard. The method of testing for the flexural strength of a masonry assemblage specified in BS 5628:Part 1[3.4], (Appendix A2) relies on testing panels 1.2 m to 1.8 m long by 2.4 m to 2.7 m high, where the bond of the mortar to the units plays an important part in the overall performance of such a panel.

A cross-brick couplet test was developed for incorporation in ASTM specifications[3.31] involving the use of a testing machine fitted with a special jig applying such tensile force that the unit eventually parts, thus giving a measure of the bond at the mortar. A diagram of the apparatus is shown in Figure 3.10.

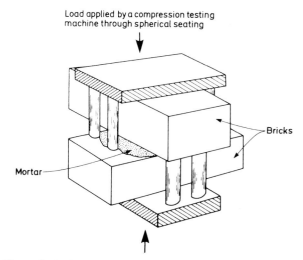

Figure 3.10 Crossed brick couplet test for mortar bond

3.5.5 Stiffening rate

This test involves an arbitrary procedure for determining the time taken after mixing for the resistance offered by the mortar to the penetration of a metal rod 30 mm³ in cross sectional area to reach 1.0, 1.5 or 2.0 N/mm². The higher value is suitable for higher cement

---

*Several parts of BS 1881 have now been revised as BS 1881:1983

24

content mortars when testing can be completed within the day, whereas the lower values are more appropriate for weaker mortars. This is a comparative test procedure which may, for example, be used to investigate the effect of an admixture. Alternatively a procedure may be used to compare the time to give an agreed resistance to penetration with that of a control mix.

The time of stiffening is taken from the time water or cement is added to the mix. Mortar should be prepared to a standard consistence of 10 ± 0.5 mm dropping ball penetration. A mould approximately 75 mm diameter and 50—100 mm high should be filled in ten layers and tapped on the bench four times after each increment. The top surface should be struck level and the whole operation completed within 15—20 minutes of commencement of stiffening time. The specimens should be stored in air at a temperature of 20 ± 2°C and a relative humidity greater than 90%. The resistance to penetration is measured after two hours, and then at hourly intervals until the value is greater than half the required resistance. Thereafter the resistance should be measured at half hourly intervals.

To carry out the measurement the mould is placed on a platform scale under the penetration rod, which is held in a drill stand independent of the platform. The level of the stand is used to lower the rod slowly into the mortar until the loose washer* just touches the surface at which point the reading of the scale in kg is noted. The resistance to penetration in N/mm² can then be calculated.

3.5.6 Air content of freshly mixed mortars

The air content of mortars can be determined by the density method or the pressure method. The density method probably gives more reproducible results, but requires a knowledge of the densities of the constituents and the mix proportions (including the water content) by weight. The pressure method does not require this information but involves the use of special equipment.

To determine the air content using the density method a thick walled brass measure is first weighed and then filled with mortar in ten increments, the measure being tapped against the bench four times after each increment. Filling is carried out in such a way that little excess has to be struck off with a palette knife, and the measure is wiped clean on the outside and weighed. It is then possible to calculate the density of mortar and, from a knowledge of the capacity of the measure, to determine the air content.

Using the pressure method the apparatus shown in Figure 3.11 must be employed. The bowl of the equipment is filled with mortar, filter paper wetted and placed on the surface of the mortar, and the head unit clamped into position. The glass tube is lowered through the gauge glass until the end is just above the filter paper. Water is poured slowly through this tube as the tube is slowly withdrawn until the water is up to the zero mark in the gauge glass. With the tube withdrawn, the assembly is tilted and rotated while being struck with a mallet to remove air bubbles. Water is again brought to the zero mark and the top opening capped. The required pressure, as determined during calibration, is then applied. The bowl is again tapped with the mallet and the pressure brought to calibration pressure. The air content may then be read. The pressure is reduced slightly and then returned to the calibration level, and the air content is read again. The cap is then removed and a check made to ensure that the water level returns to the zero mark. The value of air content is taken as the average of both readings.

3.5.7 Test for hardened mortars

3.5.7.1 Sampling of hardened mortars In a number of circumstances it may be considered necessary to carry out tests on hardened mortars. The following notes serve only to give guidance on the more important factors to be considered.

Sufficient samples of mortar should be taken from regularly spaced positions of those parts of the construction under consideration* to enable a representative picture of the mortar in the construction to be built up. A minimum of 100 g of material made up of not less than three equal increments will be required. In cases where only chemical analysis is required, and not sand grading, the sample may be obtained by drilling with a masonry drill as an alternative to cutting out work. Some care needs to be taken in evaluating the range of volume proportions determined by chemical analysis, and reference should be made to BS 4551:1970[3.30] for further details.

3.5.7.2 Analysis of hardened mortars Before any tests can be carried out it is necessary to separate the various layers of the construction and remove any contaminating materials, such as paint, gypsum plasters, spatter-dash, grime, brick and block. The main sample should be lightly crushed and, if necessary dried at 105 ± 5°C to remove all free moisture.

It is not within the scope of this book to detail all the test procedures for the chemical analysis of mortars and reference should be made to BS 4551:Part 1:1970. Sufficient information has, however, been included so that the reader is aware of the range of tests available.

Loss on ignition This test is only required when either it is suspected that organic ingredients are present in a substantial proportion, or where the composition is required on an anhydrous carbonate free basis for more accurate assessment of cement:lime:sand ratios with carbonate free sands. Lime in an old fully carbonated mortar, for example, will have a loss on ignition of 44 parts by weight for each 56 parts of calcium oxide, as against about 20 parts for each 56 parts of calcium oxide, in fresh, dry, hydrated lime.

---

*The brass rod is usually 65 mm long and 6.175 ± 0.025 mm in diameter. The end which penetrates the mortar has a reduced diameter of 5 mm for a length of 40 mm. A loosely fitting brass marker (washer) with an external diameter of 20 mm rests on the stop formed at the diameter change point.

---

*It is important to store the sample in an air-tight container.

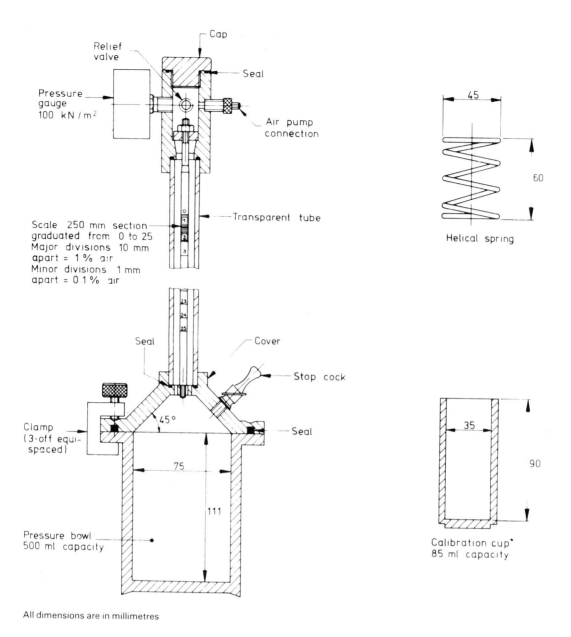

Relief valve

Cap

Seal

Pressure gauge 100 kN/m²

Air pump connection

Transparent tube

Scale 250 mm section graduated from 0 to 25
Major divisions 10 mm apart = 1% air
Minor divisions 1 mm apart = 0.1% air

45

60

Helical spring

Seal

Cover

Stop cock

45°

Seal

Clamp (3-off equi-spaced)

75

35

90

111

Pressure bowl 500 ml capacity

Calibration cup 85 ml capacity

All dimensions are in millimetres

Figure 3.11 Apparatus for measurement of air content (pressure method)

Sand content, sand grading, clay and silt content This test provides information on the suitability of the sand used in the mortar.

Soluble silica, mixed oxides, iron oxide, calcium oxide, magnesium oxide and chloride It is sometimes necessary for these tests to be carried out, particularly to differentiate between ordinary Portland cement and rapid-hardening Portland cement because both show a ratio of calcium oxide to soluble silica of approximately three. In the case of sulphate-resisting Portland cement the ratio of aluminium oxide to iron oxide will be 1.0 or less, but tests will also need to be carried out on a sample of the sand used because the amount of acid soluble aluminium and iron oxides may vary considerably. The use of extra rapid-hardening Portland cement will give a mortar which has a chloride content equivalent to approximately 2% of calcium chloride in the cement content, but chlorides may also be present in aggregates of marine origin and additives. White Portland cement is characterized by ratios of aluminium to iron oxide of the order of 20. High alumina cement will produce mortars (unless calcium carbonate has been added) with a ratio of calcium oxide to the aluminium oxide of approximately 1.0.

Mixes based on lime usually have calcium oxide to silica ratios much higher than 3. If a magnesium lime has been employed the magnesium oxide content of the mortar will usually be higher than 5% (i.e., higher than Portland cement, high calcium lime or hydraulic lime).

Sulphur trioxide content Where the sulphur trioxide content is higher than might be expected for the use of Portland cement (sulphur trioxide > 3%) and lime (sulphur trioxide > 1%) the following courses should be considered:

(1) the use of calcium sulphate plaster;

(2) attack of the mortar by sulphates from extraneous courses;

(3) the use of super sulphated cement.

26

Proportions by volume Most measurements will generally indicate the relative proportions of each constituent of a mortar by weight. To find out the relative proportions by volume the following relationship should be used:

$$\text{Amount of constituent by volume} = \frac{\%\ \text{of the constituent by weight}}{\text{bulk density of constituent}}$$

3.6 Wall ties

3.6.1 Durability

The purpose of a wall tie is to restrain together two leaves of masonry. The two common types of tie available are the metal strip tie with fish tails at both ends and a twist in the centre (the fish tail tie) and the wire type which is known as the butterfly because of its shape. Wall ties are made in a range of materials from hot dipped galvanized steel* (sometimes coated in bitumen) to stainless steel, copper, or copper alloy. Plastic wall ties are also available but are not accepted by some local authorities and are not generally recommended by the authors. In some areas all cavity wall ties are required to be of a non-ferrous metal to ensure long term durability and this is advocated as a sensible precaution for all large masonry constructions. The specification of ties is controlled by BS 1243[3.32].

3.6.2 Flexibility

Where the inner and outer leaves of the building are constructed from different materials, such as clay brick and concrete brick, differential movement has been known to lead to cracking when very stiff wall ties have been employed. Standard sizes of fish tail ties are 150 mm and 200 mm in length, 20 mm in width and thicknesses of 3.0 and 2.5 mm. Butterfly ties are of 12 SWG wire and 150, 200 and 300 mm in length. The latter will clearly impose less lateral restraint when differential thermal and moisture movements are expected to be a problem and should thus be employed in these situations†. In practice butterfly or double triangle ties are preferred for constructions using blockwork.

3.6.3 Location of ties

In the case of cavity walls, ties should be embedded in the mortar during construction so that at least 50 mm of the tie is embedded in the mortar of each leaf, and should be evenly spaced at a rate of not less than 2.5 per square metre. In non-loadbearing masonry they should normally be placed at intervals of no more than 900 mm horizontally and no more than 450 mm vertically. In loadbearing masonry the spacing should be in

accordance with Table 3.11. Additional ties must be provided around openings so that there is one tie for each 300 mm height of the opening.

When lateral loads on walls need to be calculated, reference should be made to Table 3.12 for guidance on working loads in ties.

Table 3.11 Spacing of ties

Minimum leaf thickness (one or both)	Cavity width	*Spacing of ties		Number of ties per square metre
		horizontally	vertically	
mm	mm	mm	mm	
75	50—75	450	450	4.9
90 or more	50—75	900	450	2.5
90 or more	75—100	750	450	3.0
90 or more	100—150	450	450	4.9

* This spacing may be varied provided that the number of ties per unit area is maintained.

3.7 Damp-proof courses

Materials for damp-proof courses should comply with the requirments of one of the following British Standards: BS 743: 1970[3.33], BS 988, 1076, 1097, 1451: 1973[3.34] or BS 1162, 1418, 1410: 1973[3.35]. Where there is no British Standard for a particular material, the manufacturer should provide evidence as to its suitability for the intended purpose and conditions of use.

A damp-proof course should be provided in a building to prevent the entry of water from an external source into the building or between parts of the structure and should be bedded in mortar and protected from damage during construction. Consideration must be given to the provision of a damp-proof course at the following points:

(1) where the floor is below ground level;

(2) 150 mm above ground level in external walls;

(3) under sills, jambs and over openings;

(4) in parapets;

(5) chimneys and other special details.

Stepped damp-proof courses at openings should extend beyond the end of the lintel by at least 100 mm. All horizontal damp-proof courses should protrude 10 mm from the external face of the wall and be turned downwards. Vertical damp-proof courses should be of adequate width and be fixed so as to separate the inner and outer leaves of the wall.

In loadbearing masonry, care must be taken to use a material which will not creep or otherwise spread under load for the damp-proof course. The type of damp-proof course provided can effect the restraint conditions to be assumed for design, for example, if engineering bricks are employed a wall might be assumed to be continuously supported in a situation where the use of a flexible damp-proof course would mean the assumption of simple support. On site rolls of flexible damp-proof course should be stored on a level surface protected from heat and other damage.

---

*It should be noted that the current methods of manufacture may result in butterfly ties which are likely to be less durable than the corresponding strip tie made from galvanized steel.

†It must be remembered that factors such as sound performance may be greatly influenced by the type of tie employed.

Table 3.12 Working loads in ties

Specification	Working loads in ties engaged in dovetail slots set in structural concrete	
	Tension	Shear
Dovetail slot types of ties	N	N
(1) Galvanized or stainless steel fishtail anchors 3 mm thick in 1.25 mm galvanized steel slots 150 mm long. Slots set in structural concrete	1000	1200
(2) Galvanized or stainless steel fishtail anchors 2 mm thick in 2 mm galvanized steel slots 150 mm long. Slots set in structural concrete	700	1100
(3) Copper fishtail anchors 3 mm thick in 1.25 mm copper slots 150 mm long. Slots set in structural concrete	850	1000

Specification	Working loads in ties embedded in mortar of different designations*			
	Tension			Shear
	(i)	(iii)	(iv)	(i), (ii) or (iii)
Cavity wall ties	N	N	N	N
(1) Wire butterfly				
(a) Zinc coated or stainless steel 3.25 mm diameter	650	650	500	550
(b) Copper 2.65 mm diameter	500	500	450	500
(2) Strip fishtail, 3 mm × 10 mm; zinc coated; copper, bronze or stainless steel	1400	1000	700	900

* Designations of mortar (i) to (iv) as in Table 3.11. Unless stress grading is carried out the above table of safe working loads may not be used when the percentage of colouring is in excess of the following:

(1) 10% by weight of the cement if pigments complying with the requirements of BS 1014 are used.
(2) 2% to 3% by weight of the cement if carbon black is used.

3.8 Reinforcement

Reinforcing steel should conform to the requirements of one of the following British Standards: BS 4449: 1978[3.36]; BS 4461: 1978[3.37]; BS 970: Part 4: 1970[3.38]; BS 1449: 1956[3.39]; BS 4482: 1969[3.40] or BS 4483: 1969[3.41]. Reinforcement may need to be galvanized according to the requirements of BS 729: 1971[3.42] or otherwise protected from corrosion. The characteristic tensile strengths of reinforcement are given in the appropriate British Standards and are quoted in Table 3.13. Bed joint reinforcement should be of the tram line type so that it does not deform under tensile load. The effective diameter should be between 3 and 5 mm.

Reference should be made to *Chapter 9* dealing with reinforced masonry for further information on detailing.

Table 3.13 Strength of reinforcement

Designation	Nominal size mm	Specified characteristic strength mm
Hot rolled steel grade 250 (BS 4449)	All sizes	250
Hot rolled steel grade 460/425 (BS 4449)	Up to and including 16	460
	Over 16	425
Cold worked steel grade 460/425 (BS 4461)	Up to and including 16	460
	Over 16	425
Hard drawn steel wire and fabric (BS 4482 and BS 4483)	Up to and including 12	485

3.9 Infill concrete and grout for reinforced masonry

Cement for use with infill concrete (grout) should comply with the requirements of one of the following British Standards: BS 12: 1978[3.21] *Specification for ordinary and rapid-hardening Portland cement*; BS 146: Part 2: 1973[3.22] *Portland blast furnace cement* or BS 4027: 1980[3.23] *Specification for sulphate-resisting Portland cement*. Masonry cement and high alumina cement should not be used. In some circumstances a small proportion of lime may be added to the mix and this should be non-hydraulic (high calcium) or semi-hydraulic (calcium) complying to BS 890:1972[3.25] *Building limes*. Sands and coarse aggregates should comply with BS 882:1201[3.8].

Concrete infill should be one of the following mixes:

Cement : lime (optional) : Sand : 10 mm aggregate

(1) 1   0—¼   3   —

(2) 1   0—¼   3   2

(Proportioned by volume of dry materials)

(3) A prescribed or designed mix of grade 25 or better in accordance with BS 5328 with a nominal maximum size of aggregate of 10 mm.

(4) A prescribed or designed mix of grade 25 or better in accordance with BS 5328 with a nominal maximum size of aggregate of 20 mm.

Mix (1) must be liquid and should be used for grouting internal joints not completely filled by mortar at the time of laying. Mixes (2), (3) and (4) should have a slump between 75 mm and 175 mm. Mixes (2) and (3) should be used for filling spaces with a minimum dimension of not less than 50 mm and mix (4) may be used for filling spaces with a minimum dimension of 100 mm.

Superplasticizers may be employed to produce high workability concrete of low water/cement ratio but should only be employed under supervision and on the authority of the engineer in charge. Expansive additives are also available to reduce the shrinkage of the infilling concrete within the masonry. This obviates the need for 'topping up' of cores and recompaction after the initial slump of the material.

The strength of the infilling concrete or grout should be checked by making 100 mm cubes in accordance with BS 1881[3.10], the details of which are essentially covered in *Section 3.5.3*. The characteristic strength should not fall below that specified or, alternatively, other forms of acceptance criteria must be proposed. The sampling rate should be set with respect to the method of mixing and the method of placing. Generally speaking a rate of sampling comparable to that for the mortar is appropriate.

3.10 Mechanical fixings for attaching components to masonry

The majority of fixings in masonry comprise of plugs placed in drilled holes to receive screws, bolts or nails, mechanical anchorages such as sockets or channels, or fired or precision fixed pins and nails. The performance requirement for the fixing can be summarized as:

(1) it must be strong enough to support the load (whether direct tension, shear or both);

(2) the fixing must be durable so that it will last the life of the building or at least the component, and will not deteriorate causing stains, etc;

(3) it must be economic.

It is beyond the scope of this book to consider in detail the various ways in which a fixing can be made, but the following general principles apply to most types of fixing.

In the case of drilled fixings it is necessary to ensure that the drilled hole is of the correct size for the plug and the side should be perpendicular to the surface of the wall. Certain forms of dense aggregate open textured block tend to deflect the tip of the drill, which can result in an oversized hole being produced. A variety of plugs may be inserted into the drilled hole, including fibre, metal and plastic and in the case of irregular holes a fibre plugging compound may be employed. Plugs are usually specified by British Screw Gauge, but there is an increasing tendency to produce fixings capable of taking a range of screw sizes, in which case it is important to note that the most efficient fixing in terms of strength performance will be obtained when the largest screw size is used.

The action of inserting the screw expands and distorts the plug to such an extent that a good mechanical bond is achieved between the screw, fixing and substrate. Fibre plugs and some metal type plugs will tend to be pushed too far into holes that have been over-drilled, whereas plastics and some forms of metal plug have a tip which prevents them disappearing into an oversize hole.

Special fixings may be used with aerated and other very light blocks, which usually incorporate some degree of expansion to provide mechanical bond. Cut nails can also be driven into the block to carry component loads.

Heavier fixing devices may be required for some purposes, and these may be of the single cone anchor form (Figure 3.12) which expand when the bolt is tightened, the retraction stud bolt type whereby a wedge expands on retraction of the stud, or the self drilling type where a plug is hammered into the anchor to cause expansion and the collar proud of the surface is snapped off. In addition to various other forms of expansion fixing there are a number of chemical fixings which rely on the breaking of a capsule of chemicals to initiate setting.

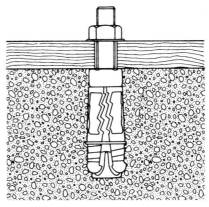

Figure 3.12 Single cone anchor

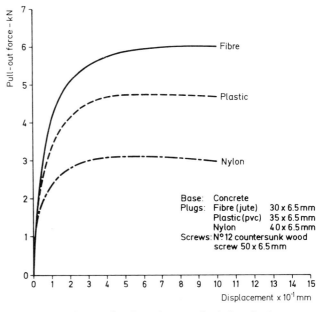

Figure 3.13 Graph of pull-out force and relative displacement

Most manufacturers will supply detailed information of the loadbearing performance of their products. For general information only, some pull out results are presented to indicate how a plug type fixing will perform under load. Figure 3.13 shows tests on the three types of plug shown in Figure 3.14. Note that an initial slip takes place leading to a bond type failure in most cases.

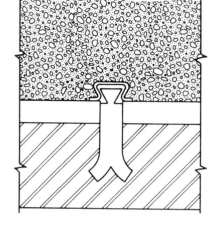

Figure 3.16 Masonry tied to a column by means of a metal tie held in a dovetail slot

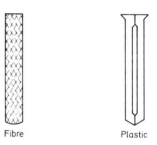

Fibre   Plastic   Nylon

Figure 3.14 Typical plugs

3.11 Mechanical fixing for tying structural elements

The most common form of mechanical fixing used in masonry is the wall tie, and the specifications and standards covering standard wall ties are discussed under that heading in *Section 3.6*. There are, in addition, a number of specialized ties, such as fishtail ties with lips or dowels (Figure 3.15) used to fix stone or precast concrete to masonry. Cramps may be used with some types of coping stone to locate adjacent stones.

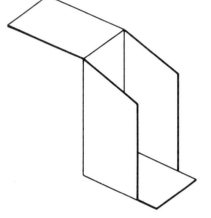

Figure 3.17 A joist hanger

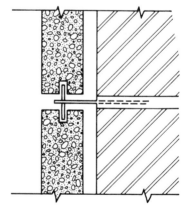

Figure 3.15 Dowelled tie holding precast concrete unit to masonry wall

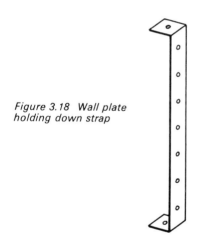

Figure 3.18 Wall plate holding down strap

Cast in slots or bolt connections are sometimes provided in concrete panels so that adjoining masonry can be tied in. The dovetail slot, as shown in Figure 3.16, overcomes one of the main problems of building masonry to the frame accurately, in that the ability of the tie to move up and down the slot provides some freedom. Specialist fixings are also available to tie brick slips to beams and such like.

Various forms of loadbearing devices, such as angle corbels, are available to restrain heavy structural members. Built-in devices such as joist hangers (Figure 3.17) or wall plates (Figure 3.18) holding down straps are very widely used. These devices should be designed and used in accordance with the manufacturers instructions, with due regard for the local stress concentration as detailed in *Chapter 10*.

3.12 Method of test for structural fixings

The method of test for structural fixings in concrete and masonry is covered in BS 5080:Part 1:1974[3.43]. The test procedure consists mainly of a means of applying a tensile force to a fixing installed in a solid base material. Figure 3.19 is a photograph of a test rig capable of carrying out such a test. The Standard gives information on the use of standard specimens as well as set procedures for the installation of the fixing. During the test, load is applied in discrete increments and measurements are taken of both the load and the movement of the fixing. A graph is then drawn of load against relative movement, similar to that shown in Figure 3.20. It may be necessary to test a number of samples of

Figure 3.19 *Equipment suitable for performing a tensile test on a fixing*

Figure 3.20 *Diagrammatic representation of equipment used to measure the creep of a fixing*

each type of fixing for a given substrate so that some idea of variation can be obtained. It is common practice to apply quite large safety factors, often a factor of 5, for pull-out loads.

It may well be that some fixings are required to operate with a high shear load rather than a direct pull-out load, while in other situations it may be necessary to provide a test rig which will enable both forms of loading to be applied simultaneously.

In the case of some chemical and plastic forms of fixing long term creep under load may need to be investigated.

3.13 References

3.1   BRITISH STANDARDS INSTITUTION. BS 6073: 1981 *Precast concrete masonry units.* Part 1: *Specification for precast masonry units* (pp 12) and Part 2: *Method for specifying precast masonry units* (pp 8). BSI, London.

3.2   BRITISH STANDARDS INSTITUTION. BS 2028, 1364: 1968 *Precast concrete blocks.* BSI, London. pp 44

3.3   BRITISH STANDARDS INSTITUTION. BS 1180: 1972 *Concrete bricks and fixing bricks.* BSI, London. pp 20

3.4   BRITISH STANDARDS INSTITUTION. BS 5628: Part 1: 1978 *Code of Practice for the structural use of masonry.* Part 1: *Unreinforced masonry.* BSI, London. pp 40

3.5   BRITISH STANDARDS INSTITUTION. CP 121: Part 1: 1973 *Code of Practice for walling.* Part 1: *Brick and block masonry.* BSI, London. pp 84

3.6   BRITISH STANDARDS INSTITUTION. Draft code of practice for vertical enclosures. BSI, London, June 1978.

3.7   BRITISH STANDARDS INSTITUTION. BS 4315: Part 2: 1970 *Methods of test for resistance to air and water penetration.* Part 2: *Permeable walling constructions (water penetration).* BSI, London. pp 16

3.8   BRITISH STANDARDS INSTITUTION. BS 882: 1201 *Aggregates from natural sources for concrete (including granolithic).* BSI, London.

3.9   BRITISH STANDARDS INSTITUTION. BS 410: 1976 *Specification for test sieves.* BSI, London. pp 16

3.10 BRITISH STANDARDS INSTITUTION. BS 1881: Part 3: 1970 *Methods of testing concrete.* BSI, London.

3.11 BRITISH STANDARDS INSTITUTION. BS 1610: 1964 *Methods for the load verification of testing machines.* BSI, London. pp 24

3.12 BRITISH STANDARDS INSTITUTION. BS 1134: Part 1: 1972 *Method for the assessment of surface texture.* Part 1: *Method and instrumentation.* BSI, London. pp 20

3.13 BRITISH STANDARDS INSTITUTION. BS 1142: Part 3: 1972 *Fibre building boards.* Part 3: *Insulating board (softboard).* BSI, London. pp 12

3.14 ROBERTS, J J. The effect of different test procedures upon the indicated strength of concrete blocks in compression. *Magazine of Concrete Research, Vol 25,* No 83, June 1973. pp 87—98

3.15 BRITISH STANDARDS INSTITUTION. BS 3921 *Clay bricks and blocks.* BSI, London. pp 32

3.16 BRITISH STANDARDS INSTITUTION. BS 874: 1973 *Methods for determining thermal insulating properties, with definitions of thermal insulating terms.* BSI, London. pp 40

3.17 SPOONER, D C. Results of a round robin thermal conductivity test organized on behalf of the British Standards Institution. *Magazine of Concrete Research, Vol 32,* No 111, June 1980. pp 117—122

3.18 ROBERTS, J J. The performance of concrete block testing machines as assessed by the Foote proving device. Cement and Concrete Association, London, January 1973. Publication No 42.478. pp 5

3.19 ROBERTS, J J. Specification for a machine for testing concrete blocks in compression. Cement and Concrete Association, London, October 1974. Publication No 42.499. pp 12

3.20 BRITISH STANDARDS INSTITUTION. BS 1198, 1199, 1200: 1976 *Building sands from natural sources.* BSI, London. pp 8

3.21 BRITISH STANDARDS INSTITUTION. BS 12: 1978 *Specification for ordinary and rapid hardening Portland cement*. BSI, London. pp 4

3.22 BRITISH STANDARDS INSTITUTION. BS 146: Part 2: 1973 *Portland blast furnace cement*. Part 2: *Metric units*. BSI, London. pp 8

3.23 BRITISH STANDARDS INSTITUTION. BS 4027: 1980 *Specification for sulphate resisting Portland cement*. BSI, London. pp 4

3.24 BRITISH STANDARDS INSTITUTION. BS 5224: 1976 *Specification for masonry cement*. BSI, London. pp 8

3.25 BRITISH STANDARDS INSTITUTION. BS 890: 1972 *Building limes*. BSI, London. pp 32

3.26 RAGSDALE, L A, AND BIRT, J C. Building sands: availability, usage and compliance with specification requirements. *CIRIA Report 59*. London, June 1976. pp 30

3.27 BRITISH STANDARDS INSTITUTION. BS 1014: 1975 *Pigments for Portland cement and Portland cement products*. BSI, London. pp 12

3.28 BRITISH STANDARDS INSTITUTION. BS 5390: 1976 *Code of Practice for stone masonry*. BSI, London. pp 40

3.29 BRITISH STANDARDS INSTITUTION. BS 4721: 1971 *Ready-mixed lime: sand for mortar*. BSI, London. pp 20

3.30 BRITISH STANDARDS INSTITUTION. BS 4551: 1970 *Methods of testing mortars and specification for mortar testing sand*. BSI, London. pp 80

3.31 AMERICAN SOCIETY FOR TESTING AND MATERIALS. ASTM: E149-66 *Tentative method of test for the bond strength of mortar to masonry units*. Philadelphia, 1966. pp 10

3.32 BRITISH STANDARDS INSTITUTION. BS 1243: 1978 *Specification for metal ties for cavity wall construction*. BSI, London. pp 4

3.33 BRITISH STANDARDS INSTITUTION. BS 743: 1970 *Materials for damp-proof courses*. Metric units. BSI, London. pp 24

3.34 BRITISH STANDARDS INSTITUTION. BS 988, 1076, 1097, 1451: 1973 *Mastic asphalt for building (limestone aggregate)*. BSI, London. pp 12

3.35 BRITISH STANDARDS INSTITUTION. BS 1162, 1418, 1410: 1973 *Mastic asphalt for building (natural rock asphalt aggregate)*. BSI, London. pp 12

3.36 BRITISH STANDARDS INSTITUTION. BS 4449: 1978 *Specification for hot rolled steel bars for the reinforcement of concrete*. BSI, London. pp 12

3.37 BRITISH STANDARDS INSTITUTION. BS 4461: 1978 *Specification for cold worked steel bars for the reinforcement of concrete*. BSI, London. pp 8

3.38 BRITISH STANDARDS INSTITUTION. BS 970: Part 4: 1970 *Wrought steels in the form of blooms, billets, bars and forgings*. Part 4: *Stainless, heat resisting and valve steels*. BSI, London. pp 76

3.39 BRITISH STANDARDS INSTITUTION. BS 1449: 1956 *Steel plate, sheet and strip*. BSI, London. pp 12

3.40 BRITISH STANDARDS INSTITUTION. BS 4482: 1969 *Hard drawn mild steel wire for the reinforcement of concrete*. BSI, London. pp 12

3.41 BRITISH STANDARDS INSTITUTION. BS 4483: 1969 *Steel fabric for the reinforcement of concrete*. BSI, London. pp 12

3.42 BRITISH STANDARDS INSTITUTION. BS 729: 1971 *Hot dip galvanized coatings on iron and steel articles*. BSI, London. pp 16

3.43 BRITISH STANDARDS INSTITUTION. BS 5080: Part 1: 1974 *Methods of test for structural fixing in concrete and masonry*. Part 1: *Tensile loading*. BSI, London. pp 12

4

Types of block and brick

4.1 Introduction

When categorizing the types of block and brick available, a number of factors need to be considered, the influences of which are discussed under the following headings:

(1) methods of manufacture

(2) appearance

(3) performance

(4) ease of use

The possible compromises which may need to be made with respect, for example, to producing a facing block with good thermal insulation properties, are covered to some extent in each section, but it should be recognized that the above categories must widely overlap.

It is not within the scope of this book to go into details of materials used for manufacturing concrete blocks. The reader should, however, be aware that in addition to various dense aggregates, materials such as pulverized fuel ash, pumice, clinker, foamed slag, expanded clay, expanded shale and sawdust are employed.

4.2 Methods of manufacture

4.2.1 Concrete blocks

Concrete blocks in the United Kingdom are generally manufactured by the following processes:

(1) a foaming process in the case of autoclaved aerated concrete

(2) a mobile machine called an egglayer

(3) a static machine

4.2.1.1 Autoclaved aerated blocks Aerated concrete blocks are manufactured under controlled factory conditions. The constituent materials are usually cement and sand, although in many cases pulverized fuel ash is used as a replacement for some or all of the sand. The raw materials are mixed with a foaming agent

and discharged into large steel moulds. These moulds are usually wheeled through the various stages of manufacture on a track or rails. The 'cake' in the mould rises due to the action of the foaming agent until it is completely filled with the aerated material, and is then cut by wires to give the desired unit size before being placed in an autoclave — a high pressure steam curing chamber — where curing takes place at pressures up to 15 atmosphere.

This method of production is only used for making very lightweight blocks, typically between 475-750 kg/m³, which are primarily produced for their good thermal insulation properties. Two particular advantages in this are:

(1) it is comparatively easy to alter the position of the wires and produce non-standard block sizes given a substantial order.

(2) the dimensional use of autoclaves stabilizes the blocks at a comparatively early stage and enables them to be used direct from the factory.*

Although autoclaved aerated blocks are sometimes used fair-faced and painted, it is not possible to produce a facing block using this process. To overcome this problem some manufacturers bond their blocks to a 10—25 mm facing to produce a faced aerated block. Whilst such a process is expensive it does enable very high quality faces to be used. This technique of manufacture of facing units also necessitates the provision of a number of special units to maintain the appearance of the corners, etc.

It should also be noted that it is only possible to manufacture solid blocks in aerated concrete and that it is not possible to produce blocks stronger than 6 N/mm² without greatly increasing the density.

4.2.1.2 The egglayer This appropriately named machine may be used to produce a very wide range of dense and lightweight blocks. Essentially the plant comprises a central batching and mixing facility, tipping

---

*Note, however, that the building of hot blocks into a wall is not necessarily desirable.

bucket truck, the egglayer machine and a large flat concrete apron. The mix is discharged from the mixer into the bucket of the truck and transferred to the hopper of the egglayer. The egglayer moves in small steps along the concrete apron and at each step stamps out blocks directly onto the surface of the concrete. The blocks are produced by drawing some of the mix contained in the hopper into a steel mould where it is vibrated and compacted. The design and control of the mix has to be such that the blocks are free standing directly from the mould without subsequent slumping. The blocks are then left to air cure although in the summer they may be wetted down or covered.

The obvious limitations to this method of production are:

(1) the large area of concrete apron required means that in bad weather most manufacturers can only afford to cover a small part of the apron;

(2) the apron needs to be well laid and regularly maintained to ensure good dimensional accuracy;

(3) the open air curing means that the blocks are subject to the vagaries of the weather, although in practice manufacturers adjust the design of the mix to compensate for the prevailing weather conditions;

(4) although there are some exceptions most egglayers are not suitable for producing good quality facing units or very high strength blocks.

In spite of these limitations the egglayer produces very economic dense and lightweight blocks. Recent developments for greater production include the double drop machine, which produces two layers of blocks, and the production of blocks on end, rather than laid, on the bed face.

To produce blocks of different sizes or configurations, it is necessary to change the mould in both the egglayer and the static machine discussed in the next section. Whilst manufacturers do have a range of moulds available they are very expensive, and custom made sizes, faces and configurations are only likely to be economic for large orders. Because of the wear that will occur on moulds, block tolerances from a given mould will inevitably change from minus to plus over a large manufacturing cycle. As is also the case with the static machine, the vertical casting method makes the height of the block the most difficult dimension to control.

4.2.1.3 The static machine The static machine is the most consistent method of producing good quality dense and lightweight blocks. A central automatically controlled batching plant is used to feed the mixing plant which directly links with the block machine or machines. Blocks are stamped out by a combination of vibration and compaction onto steel or wooden pallets. The effect of the vibration and compaction effort on the mix is usually much greater than can be applied by an egglayer so that it is possible to produce very dense, high strength blocks using this technique. Once the

blocks have been produced on the pallet they move along a conveyor system and are stored on a large metal frame which, when full, is carried by a transfer car to a curing chamber. In the majority of cases low pressure steam curing is employed, but in some cases burner curing or autoclaving is used. When curing has been completed the frames are removed from the curing chambers by the transfer cars, the blocks are automatically cubed ready for despatch and the pallets returned into the system.

Low pressure curing gives the blocks high early strength. In the case of autoclaved blocks, however, the crystalline structure of the cementitious products is changed and offers a number of advantages:

(1) shrinkage is reduced;

(2) greater uniformity of colour is possible — blocks which are autoclaved tend, in general, to be lighter in colour;

(3) autoclaving can utilize the pozzolanic properties of some of the mix constituents.

Autoclaving is, however, an expensive process both in terms of capital plant costs and in energy costs.

The type of mould box required can vary between machine manufacturers but the observations made in the previous section regarding costs and use are equally applicable to this method of manufacture.

Both egglayers and static machines may be used to produce solid, cellular or hollow blocks with densities from 800—2100 kg/m³ and strengths of 2.8—35 N/mm² although the higher densities and strengths are more likely to be produced by static machines.

4.2.2 Concrete bricks

Concrete bricks may be produced on the static machine as previously described or by hydraulic pressing. This technique involves the use of very dry mixes which are pressed into shape by high loads on a continuous production basis. Using this method it is possible to produce high strength, durable units. Most of the types of blocks described in the following sections can also be made available as concrete bricks.

4.3 Appearance

4.3.1 Plain facing blocks

It will already be clear that not only the method of manufacture, but also the type of aggregate, will greatly affect the appearance of a block. In dense facing blocks, local aggregates will invariably be used (indeed the availability of local materials would have played a large part in the siting of the plant), for example, a limestone aggregate might be used. The manufacturer generally has the option of changing the grading of the aggregate, which may be continuous or gap graded, employing different fine aggregates, employing an admixture, varying the degree of compaction and employing a pigment. In addition, the surface of the finished block may be grit or sand blasted to further change the appearance. By using a combination of the possible variables a large manufacturer will have available a range of open textured facing blocks which could be made in a range of strengths and sizes solid, cellular or hollow. Examples of typical dense aggregate facing blocks of the type described are shown in Figure 4.1. Because of the high cost of the natural material, plain facing blocks can be produced specifically to replace local stone as a building material.

In addition to dense aggregates, lightweight aggregates may be used to produce plain facing blocks. Units made from graded wood particles are also available but the very lightweight blocks are not generally produced as homogeneous facing units.

4.3.2 Split face blocks

Split face blocks are made by splitting a dense block (often a hydraulically pressed block) so that the aggregate is split and exposed. The appearance of this type of block will clearly depend upon the aggregate employed and its size. The heavy emphasis of the aggregate tends to make this type of block suitable in areas where stone is a traditional building material. The technique can be used to produce very attractive concrete bricks as shown in Figure 4.1.

Figure 4.1   Split faced concrete bricks which can be either flat or frogged

4.3.3 Tooled face blocks

The faces of dense blocks may be tooled to expose the aggregate but, unlike split face units, this operation is often carried out so that the face of the unit has a more rounded appearance. Blocks and bricks produced using this technique tend to be relatively expensive but are widely employed in certain areas of the country.

4.3.4 Profiled blocks

A profiled face can be obtained during casting by sim-

ply adapting the mould box although it may be necessary to change the mix design when making this type of block. The portion of the profiled face proud of the main face of the block should not be counted when working out the thickness of the unit for design purposes.

4.3.5 Slump blocks

The slump or 'Adobe' block is produced by using a comparatively wet fine aggregate mix so that after demoulding the face slumps or bulges in a fairly random manner. Although not widely produced or used in the United Kingdom this type of block is popular in some parts of the world. The random and variable nature of the unit places less emphasis on the quality of the blocklaying.

4.3.6 Exposed aggregate blocks

Some manufacturers can offer blocks with exposed aggregate faces. This is achieved by bonding a prepared face to an aerated or lightweight block or by casting the face wet on the back-up block. Traditional methods of washing to expose the aggregate are still used, as is abrasive blasting. The aggregates used in production of this type of unit need to be selected with great care.

4.3.7 Scored face blocks

With this type of block alterations are made to the mould producing 'dummy' mortar joints on the faces so that when the blocks are laid with an appropriate colour of mortar the wall appears to be built from smaller units.

4.3.8 Screen wall blocks

These blocks are not generally used for designed load-bearing purposes but are included for completeness. They are made from dense concrete and are produced in a number of designs of perforation so that attractive screen walls can be produced.

4.3.9 Coloured units

To achieve a coloured finish on the unit pigments may be incorporated at the mixing stage or the colour may be imparted by the careful selection and bleaching of natural aggregates. Some forms of pigment can, however, be prone to fading which could lead to problems, particularly where a building is subject to differential weathering. There may also be problems with batch to batch variations of fresh blocks, so that it is wise to intermix different batches of facing blocks and bricks to ensure random rather than localized variations.

4.4. Performance

This section deals with performance as it affects the type of block available in general terms only. More detailed information on particular properties is given elsewhere in the book.

Good thermal insulation has been of greatest significance in promoting the use of lightweight concrete blocks, but other properties have also been exploited for specific markets.

4.4.1 Thermal insulating blocks

Thermal insulating blocks typically have resistances between 0.445 and 0.625 m² °C/W. This category includes all aerated autoclaved blocks, some solid lightweight aggregate blocks, slotted lightweight aggregate blocks and foam or similarly filled dense aggregate blocks. The latter may prove to have a higher thermal resistance than that quoted above but more measured values are required to substantiate calculated values. A range of thermal insulating blocks is shown in Figure 4.2.

Figure 4.2   Thermal insulating blocks

4.4.2 Separating wall blocks

Some manufacturers offer special dense blocks specifically for producing solid separating walls meeting the statutory requirements described in *Chapter 16*. Proprietary lifting devices are also available for use in carrying and laying.

4.5 Ease of use

4.5.1 Hollow blocks

These have been defined in *Chapter 3* and an example is shown in Figure 4.3. Hollow blocks are generally made of dense aggregates and are particularly useful in

the following circumstances:

(1) for producing single leaf walls 150—225 mm thick for which dense solid blocks might be too heavy to lay rapidly;

(2) for producing reinforced masonry by incorporating reinforcing steel in the core and filling with in situ concrete;

(3) where it is required to incorporate services within the thickness of the wall.

4.5.2 Cellular blocks

These blocks are made with dense and lightweight aggregates so that the face is similar to a corresponding solid block. The main advantage is that this type of block is lighter than the corresponding solid block and the voids can present a convenient hand hold. One end of the voids should be effectively sealed to prevent mortar droppings falling into the voids when that end is used to support the bed joint mortar. An example is shown in Figure 4.3.

Some manufacturers include blocks designed for easy cutting as a standard proportion of each delivery. These incorporate special slots which enable the unit to be split into a half or part block with the aid of a bolster.

4.5.3 Specials

Special shaped units are produced to make maintenance of bonding patterns easier particularly in facing work or as cavity closers. Other blocks such as lintel or beam blocks are designed to provide permanent formwork to in situ lintels and beam courses cut within the wall. Examples of some specials are shown in Figures 4.4, 4.5, 4.6 and 4.7. The high cost of moulds and the need to interrupt manufacturing runs to produce a small number of units tend to make production of special blocks expensive.

Figure 4.3   Solid, cellular and hollow blocks

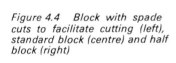

Figure 4.4   Block with spade cuts to facilitate cutting (left), standard block (centre) and half block (right)

Figure 4.5   Cavity closure and Quoin blocks

5.2.2 Other bonding patterns

There are a number of potential bonding patterns, some of which differ little from the running bond pattern in terms of wall performance. Perhaps the smallest variation from the conventional running bond is the use of quarter bond and running with half block units. It is important to remember that a change in the bonding pattern may well result in the necessity for additional specials, and a masonry saw on site will be particularly useful. There are, of course, big differences in the use of brick size units, for which there are many traditional intricate bonding patterns, and concrete blocks, where the size and 'scale' effect tends to limit the number of options available. Accepting this, and the penalty of cost and laying rate which may prove apparent when an unusual bonding is employed, it is necessary to consider the structural implications of changes. Perhaps the most extreme example occurs with the use of stack bonded walls, where there is no interlock between the units. Even if such a wall is essentially non-loadbearing it will almost certainly prove necessary to incorporate bed joint reinforcement in order to prevent cracking due to movement.

5.3 Single leaf wall

The definition of a single leaf wall contained in BS 5628 is "a wall of bricks or blocks laid to overlap in one or more directions and set solidly in mortar". For many years the single leaf or 'solid' wall comprised of a 9 in. brick wall, i.e. made from 4½ in. thick bricks. When, in the period between the World Wars, the cavity wall came to be more widely used in an effort to reduce the incidence of rain penetration, the use of the solid wall declined so much that in England and Wales it was rarely used, although it enjoys some use in Scotland where it is still encompassed by the Scottish Building Regulations[5.4] and in many other parts of the world where it has continued to be widely used such as the USA and Europe. Climatic differences as well as indigenous building resources greatly influence methods of construction. In Germany, for example, cavity walling would be considered uneconomic in the South of the country whereas in the North, with natural clay resources and a wetter climate, cavity walls are more common.

The main factors which have to be considered with a single leaf wall are as follows:

(1) prevention of rain penetration — to this end the wall will have to be well constructed and the provision of a protective coating, such as rendering, may be necessary;

(2) timber joists may need to be specially treated if they are to be built into the wall — otherwise joist hangers may be used with due allowance for the eccentricity of the load on the wall;

(3) to meet current and proposed thermal regulations, the use of added insultants may need to be considered.

One system developed in Scotland is the 'posted' solid wall, as shown in Figure 5.2, which employs a single leaf of 150—250 mm of insulating block, usually rendered externally. A completely separate inner lining of plasterboard, 50 mm or more away from the inner face of the masonry, is supported by means of a series of timber posts spanning from roof to floor. Traditionally such posts would be supported on sleeper walls but more recently solid floors have been employed with one and two storey dwellings. External insulation systems also provide a useful means of protecting the outside of single leaf constructions because such systems are generally very effective in preventing rain penetration and enable simple construction details to be employed without the risk of cold bridging. An example is shown in Figure 5.3.

There is no doubt that single leaf walling is very competitive in terms of overall construction costs compared to other constructions, and given the changes occurring in thermal insulation requirements the use of solid walling may receive a substantial boost. A new development in the use of solid blockwork is the use of glass reinforced cement render to bond together dry-stacked blocks.

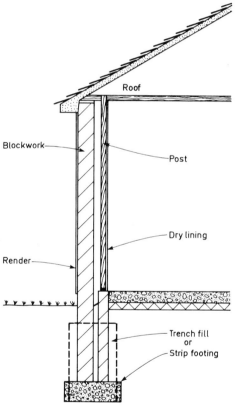

Figure 5.2   Single leaf posted construction

5.4. Cavity walls

The original concept of providing a cavity wall is basically quite sound. Even using permeable walling materials, separated by a gap of perhaps 50 mm, the ingress of water through a well built wall should be eliminated. Although water might pass through the outer leaf of the wall this would subsequently run down the back face of the outer leaf and be discharged from

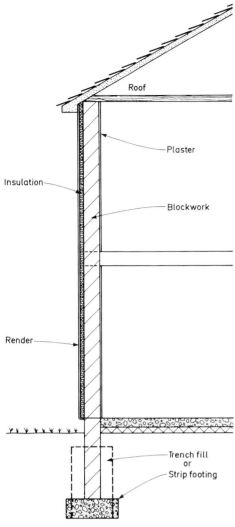

Figure 5.3   Single leaf – externally insulated

A factor which has had a profound influence upon construction of cavity walls has been the necessity for better thermal insulation as a health measure, to prevent undue condensation or as an energy saving measure. This has lead to the use of lower density blocks in the inner leaf to increase the thermal insulation as shown in Figure 5.4 and as a direct result, blocks with a density as low as 475 kg/m³ may be employed. These blocks may be used in such a way that other aspects of

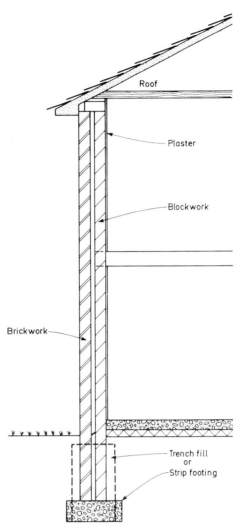

Figure 5.4   Brick – cavity – block

the bottom of the cavity — providing no bridge was encountered which enabled the water to pass to the inner leaf of the construction.

Since the introduction of the cavity wall the incidence of rain penetration has indeed been reduced and problems can now be traced to:

(1) the desire to use walling materials which are more permeable than those traditionally used;

(2) poor workmanship;

(3) poor understanding of design — especially the difficulty in executing such features as stepped cavity trays, etc.

The growth in the use of cavity walls has also resulted in structural design changes. The bearing of timber joists on the inner leaf is a sensible precaution in overcoming the risk of moisture reaching the wood, and this has lead to the situation where the inner leaf is usually loadbearing and the outer leaf is not. To stop the non-loadbearing leaf from 'waving in the wind' it has been considered essential to tie the two leaves together, although the long term efficiency of this must be doubted when the durability of the ties is considered. The tying of the two leaves has also given rise to the consideration of composite action between the two leaves from a design viewpoint.

performance, such as sound resistance, are not necessarily impaired, but they are usually of low strengths between 2.8 to 5 N/mm². The shape factor, however, is more favourable for blocks than for brick shaped units and using cross-wall construction, it is possible to produce two storey constructions with precast concrete floors using blocks only 4.35 N/mm² in strength, as shown in Figure 5.5. To overcome the more stringent thermal resistances required of walls since January 1975 for Part F, and June 1979 for Part FF of the Building Regulations[5.5] there has been a tendency to construct cavity walls with two leaves of lightweight block, as shown in Figure 5.6, and to build with a thicker inner leaf.

Although the width of the cavity between two leaves is generally considered as 50 mm, this figure is in no way sacrasanct. For a large blockwork building using two 100 mm leaves it might be very useful to incorporate a 100 mm cavity so that the whole design is based on the 300 mm module. Increasingly encroachments are being made into the cavity space to incorporate added insulation and this is discussed more fully in *Chapter 12*.

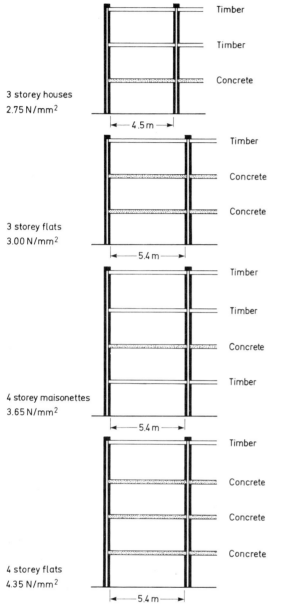

3 storey houses
2.75 N/mm²
← 4.5 m →
Timber
Timber
Concrete

3 storey flats
3.00 N/mm²
← 5.4 m →
Timber
Concrete
Concrete

4 storey maisonettes
3.65 N/mm²
← 5.4 m →
Timber
Timber
Concrete
Timber

4 storey flats
4.35 N/mm²
← 5.4 m →
Timber
Concrete
Concrete
Concrete

Figure 5.5   Structural performance: calculated required concrete block strengths for various loadbearing wall constructions up to four storeys

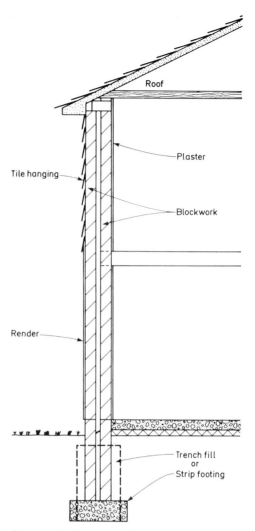

Roof
Plaster
Tile hanging
Blockwork
Render
Trench fill
or
Strip footing

Figure 5.6   Block – cavity – block

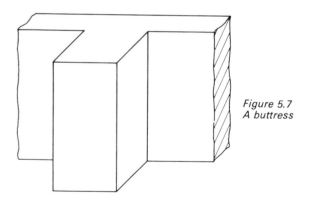

Figure 5.7
A buttress

5.5 Buttress

A buttress is a portion of wall thicker than the main run of wall of which it is an integral part, as shown in Figure 5.7, usually projecting on one side of the wall only, but in some cases projecting on both sides. Generally, a buttress is provided either to provide local support under a structural member or reduce the eccentricity of loading at that point, or to provide lateral stability for the wall. In addition to providing a stiffer bending element buttresses also provide end fixity for walls spanning between them. Occasionally buttresses are provided solely as architectural features. They may be constructed by toothing masonry into the bonding pattern of the main wall or by building the buttress separately and using substantial metal ties to ensure composite action.

5.6 Infill panels

Where masonry panels are used in framed buildings as non-loadbearing panels, the main aspects of design are that the panel should have adequate resistance to lateral load and service loads, it should be effectively tied to the frame and should not cause distress as a result of long term movements.

The use of loadbearing material to provide panels within a frame of a different material, although consi-

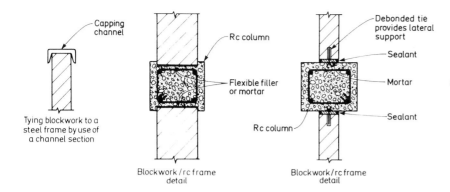

Figure 5.8 Typical panel/frame details

Labels in figure: Capping channel; Rc column; Flexible filler or mortar; Debonded tie provides lateral support; Sealant; Mortar; Sealant; Rc column; Tying blockwork to a steel frame by use of a channel section; Blockwork/rc frame detail; Blockwork/rc frame detail

dered structurally inefficient, for some types of building may still be economically viable.

There are a number of techniques for tying in panels to the frame, and a few examples of steel and concrete frames are shown in Figure 5.8. It must be remembered that concrete masonry walls tend to undergo shrinkage and a wall/frame detail is often a good place to introduce a movement joint, as discussed in *Chapter 16*.

5.7 Gravity retaining walls

Gravity retaining walls rely upon the weight of masonry built into the wall and are, therefore, if of any great height, massive in construction and costly to build. For retaining walls over 4—5 m high it will generally be cheaper to use reinforced concrete, but for walls up to 3—4 m high reinforced masonry may be a more economic solution.

Design of gravity retaining walls is usually carried out using the 'classic' theory with no tension being assumed in the masonry, and as such no further consideration is given to this aspect in this book. It should be remembered, however, that only blocks suitable for use below ground should be built into a retaining wall. Where the ground is subject to high levels of sulphates, reference should be made to the manufacturer as to the suitability of the blocks for use in the prevailing conditions. The durability of the blocks may be enhanced by tanking or otherwise providing a protective coating which will reduce the effect of aggressive conditions.

5.8 Separating (or party) walls

Separating walls between dwellings are primarily designed to reduce sound transmission and the spread of fire, although they may also serve as loadbearing walls. Sound reduction is satisfied by traditionally solid walls but lighter building materials, when built into a cavity wall with a 50 mm or 75 mm cavity and plastered, may also prove to be perfectly satisfactory in service. This is covered in detail in *Chapter 14*.

5.9 Fair faced walls

Building a fair faced wall with concrete blocks or bricks requires attention to detail over and above that required for normal walls. Careful planning is necessary at the design stage in terms of module, layout of openings, sizing of components, etc., to obviate unnecessary cutting of blocks and breaking of the bonding pattern. The appearance of masonry openings may be maintained by using reinforced masonry lintels, or certain forms of pressed steel lintels.

The use of special blocks at corners and reveals will probably be necessary and any cutting on site should be carried out with a mechanical saw. An important point to be considered is that it is very much more difficult to build a wall fair faced on both sides than fair faced on just one side.

The mortar joint is an important feature of all facing work and must be given due attention. As the mortar joints need to be regular in appearance and properly finished, the block will need to be dimensionally accurate, more so for ordinary blocks (this is as important with bricks) and the arrisses clean and sharp. The colour of the mortar should be selected to enhance the appearance of the units, and to avoid colour variations due to batching or re-tamping, a central batching facility should be considered or, alternatively, pre-bagged materials employed.

There are a number of tools for finishing joints and various types of joint profile that may be employed. Generally, a lightly tooled or flush finish is to be preferred, both from the point of view of preventing water ingress and of helping to ensure the long term durability of the materials used. It should also be remembered that a deeply recessed joint may affect the loadbearing performance of the wall.

When cavity trays are incorporated into the wall weep holes should be provided to allow water to drain away, and consideration should be given to the effect of water weeping out of such holes on the appearance of the building. Clearly, all materials to be used need to be carefully handled and stored on site. Further guidance is available in the publication *Concrete Masonry for the Designer*[5.6]. Figures 5.9, 5.10 and 5.11 show examples of the use of fair faced blockwork.

5.10 Rendered masonry walls

Rendering a wall greatly increases the resistance of the wall to rain penetration and reduces the rate of air infiltration as well as providing an attractive finish. There are, however, a number of guidelines which should be followed.

Figure 5.9   Fair-faced blocks used for flats

Figure 5.10   Fair-faced blocks used externally

In general, render should be weaker than the block or brick to which it is to be applied. Thus, a 1:1:6 cement:lime:sand render would be suitable for light-weight aggregate blocks and most bricks, while a 1:2:9 cement:lime:sand render is more suitable for some types of aerated blocks. For two or three coat work it is recommended that each successive coat should be weaker or thinner than the coat preceding it. Newly applied rendering, including stipple and spatter dash coats, should be kept damp for the first three days. The second coat should be delayed until the previous coat has had time to harden. Specifications generally require

Figure 5.11   Fair-faced blocks used
internally

44

Figure 5.12 Rendered housing

a delay period of seven days between coats and this should enable most types of cement:lime:sand render to harden sufficiently, even under cold conditions. A shorter period, depending upon prevailing conditions, may be suitable for weaker 1:2:9/1:1:6 renders. In some cases the masonry and subsequent rendering coats may need to be dampened to reduce suction but free water should never be left on the surface. Some blocks may form a very high suction background, particularly in hot weather, and an admixture such as a methylcellulose may be useful to reduce the loss of water from the mix. Renderings should not be applied to frost bound walls or during frosty conditions.

Most types of lightweight blocks provide sufficient key so that raked joints may not be required. Rough struck joints will usually be adequate, but in view of the variety of blocks available the manufacturer should be consulted at an early stage regarding specification of render and the preparation of the background.

Render is available in a range of types, colours and textures, some examples of which are discussed in the publication *External Rendering*[5.7]. An example of rendered housing is illustrated in Figure 5.12.

5.11 Diaphragm or cellular walls

Two parallel leaves of masonry joined by masonry cross ribs so that I or box sections are formed are referred to as diaphragm walls, as shown in Figure 5.13, which are

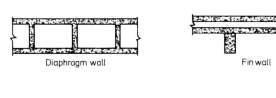

Diaphragm wall   Fin wall

Reinforced hollow block masonry   Reinforced cavity construction

Figure 5.13 Selection of wall types

very useful and economic for single storey buildings 4—5 m high such as sports halls and warehouses. Cellular walls are usually designed to span vertically as propped cantilevers with the wall either considered to be cracked or uncracked, as discussed in *Chapter 7*.

This type of construction can incorporate McAlloy bars within the cavity so that a moderate prestress may be applied to the masonry, and can prove very economic if adequate provision is made to protect the prestressing bar.

5.12 Fin walls

A fin wall is similar in appearance to a buttressed wall and consists essentially of a cavity wall stiffened with fins to act as a series of T sections as shown in Figure 5.13. As with the diaphragm wall, it is particularly applicable to 4—5 m single storey structures such as sports halls.

5.13 Reinforced masonry

The simplest and most economic form of reinforced masonry construction is the use of hollow blocks, the cores of which are filled after construction with reinforcing steel and in situ concrete. This method of construction is described fully in *Chapter 9*. The incorporation of reinforcement does not greatly alter the axial load carrying capability of the wall but significantly alters the lateral load performance. It can be useful to reinforce locally at door joints, lintels, etc.

In addition to hollow blocks it is possible to reinforce walls using special bonding patterns or filled cavity construction. Special bonding patterns tend to be expensive to execute, but filled reinforced cavity construction can be viable under certain circumstances. A comparison of the two techniques is shown in Figure 5.13.

Reinforced masonry is particularly useful as a tech-

Figure 5.14 High rise reinforced blockwork in the USA

nique for tying buildings together, for assisting performance of tall walls subjected to lateral loading and for retaining walls. An example of a high rise block in the USA is shown in Figure 5.14.

5.14 Veneered and faced walls

A veneered wall comprises of a facing unit attached to a backing (usually loadbearing) unit, but not bonded to such an extent that common action occurs under loads. There are a number of fixing and anchorage devices designed to facilitate this technique, but it is not widely used in the United Kingdom. Unlike a veneered wall, the facing of a faced wall is attached to the backing and bonded so that common action results under load.

5.15 Collar jointed walls

This wall comprises two parallel single leaf walls not further than 25 mm apart with the space between them filled with mortar and the walls tied together so that common action occurs under load. Construction of this type is useful for building an essentially 'solid' wall with brick size units.

5.16 References

5.1 BRITISH STANDARDS INSTITUTION. BS 5628: Part 1: 1978 *Code of Practice for the structural use of masonry*. Part 1: *Unreinforced masonry*. BSI, London. pp 40

5.2 READ, J B, AND CLEMENTS, S W. The strength of concrete block walls. Phase II: Under uniaxial loading. Cement and Concrete Association, London, 1972. Publication No 42.473. pp 17

5.3 HEDSTRÖM, R O. Load tests on patterned concrete masonry walls. *Journal of the American Concrete Institute, Vol 32,* No 10, April 1961. pp 1265—1286

5.4 The Building Standards (Scotland Consolidation) Regulations 1971. HMSO, London.

5.5 The Building Regulations 1976. HMSO, London.

5.6 TOVEY, A. K. *Concrete masonry for the designer* (Publication No. 48.049) and *Concrete masonry for the contractor* (Publication No. 48.050). Cement and Concrete Association, Slough. 1981

5.7 MONKS, W L, AND WARD, F. External rendering. Cement and Concrete Association, London, 1980. Publication No 47.102. pp 32

6

Stability, robustness and overall layout

BS 5628, in common with CP 110, contains provisions relating to stability and robustness, which arise from the *Report of the inquiry into the collapse of flats at Ronan Point.*[6.1]. There are four recommendations applicable to all masonry buildings and some special recommendations for structures of five storeys and over.

The four main recommendations are:

(1) a layout should be chosen for the structure to ensure 'a robust and stable design';

(2) the structure must be capable of resisting a horizontal force equal to 1.5% of the total characteristic dead load above the level being considered;

(3) adequate connections should be made between walls and floors and between walls and roofs;

(4) in regard to accidental forces, there should be 'a reasonable probability' that the structure 'will not collapse catastrophically under the effect of misuse or accident'. The Code goes on to say that "no structure can be expected to be resistant to the excessive loads or forces that could arise due to an extreme cause, but it should not be damaged to an extent disproportionate to the original cause".

The special recommendations for buildings of five storeys and over effectively spell out ways in which condition (4) above, can be satisfied for such buildings. The recommendations give three options which can be followed to limit accidental damage. The first of these (*Section 6.5.1*) requires that each structural element be capable *either* of resisting a design load of 34 kN/m² applied from any direction *or* of being removed without leading to collapse of a *significant portion of the structure*. The second and third options involve the introduction of ties into the structure. As well as the aforementioned recommendations which apply to the completed structure, the Code also emphasises the need to consider stability during construction, both of individual walls and of the structure as a whole.

The following Sections contain remarks with regard to each of the recommendations in turn.

6.1 Layout

Low and medium rise masonry structures are almost always inherently stable, firstly because walls are naturally strong in resisting lateral forces applied in their plane and secondly because it is usual for such a building to contain walls arranged in different directions. To ensure stability it is necessary to provide sufficient walls to resist lateral and torsional movements. Figure 6.1 illustrates layouts of walls which would ensure stability. It should be noted that wind loads normally applied to the face of a building have to be transmitted via the floors to the walls providing lateral resistance.

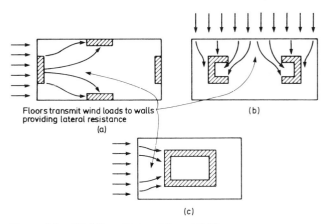

Figure 6.1   Wall layouts providing stability

Figure 6.2 shows arrangements of walls which are not symmetrical thus giving rise to torsional moments. The possibility of a torsional deformation under a gust loading applied to part of the structure should not be forgotten. Figure 6.3 shows a building stable against uniform lateral pressure but not against an eccentric gust.

In most instances the layout of a masonry building will be far more complex than is shown in Figures 6.1 to 6.3, with many more loadbearing walls continuous from foundation to roof. There will also be internal partitions which, despite being of weaker blocks and perforated by door openings, will still contribute to lateral load resistance and stability. An accurate analysis of response to lateral load is not normally possible, so that

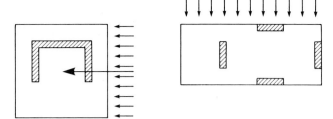

Figure 6.2   Wall layouts introducing torsional response

simplifying assumptions, ignoring the action of particular walls or parts of walls, are justified and will be on the safe side.

Where shear walls intersect, as shown in Figure 6.1 (b) and (c), it is necessary to limit the length of wall which can be assumed to act as a flange. This is analogous to the limitations on flange width applied to T and L beams of reinforced and prestressed concrete. American practice[6.2, 6.3] limits the width taken into account in the case of T and I sections to be one-sixth of the total wall height above the level being considered but with the outstand on either side not exceeding six times the thickness of the intersected walls. In the case of L, Z and   sections, the outstand is limited to one-sixteenth of the total wall height above the level being considered or to six times the thickness of the intersected wall, whichever is the less. Figure 6.4 shows how the provisions apply to T and L walls. For detailed analysis of such walls, refer to *Chapter 5*.

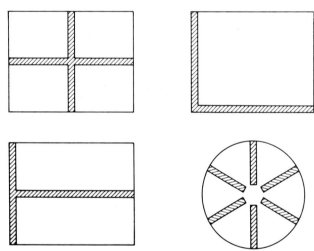

Figure 6.3   Layouts unable to resist torsion

Temperature and shrinkage movements also require consideration when deciding on a layout for walls. A layout such as that illustrated in Figure 6.1(b) will be susceptible to this problem. As has already been said, walls are naturally strong in resisting lateral forces and will be equally strong in resisting lateral movements. Shear walls acting in the same plane should, if possible, not be located further apart in that plane than 10 m. If this recommendation is exceeded it is possible that severe cracking will develop in one or other of the shear walls or in the connecting floor or roof.

The provision of movement joints also requires special care (see *Chapter 16*). Figure 6.5(a) illustrates a layout actually used on a single storey building which

collapsed catastrophically when wall *A* was sucked out by wind. Walls *B* and *C*, being left supported at one end only, then fell over with the roof, taking wall *D* with them. A less convenient but stable alternative is shown (Figure 6.5(b)). Another alternative would have been to have provided ties at roof level between walls *A* and *D*.

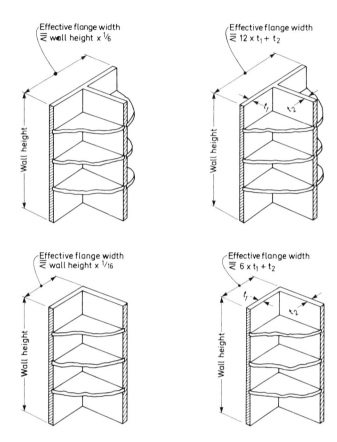

Figure 6.4   Intersecting walls

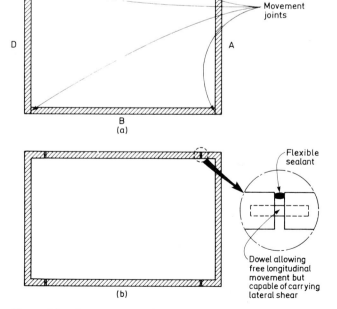

Figure 6.5   Arrangement of movement joints giving: (a) an unstable structure (b) a stable structure

6.2 1.5% horizontal load

In Clause 20.1 it is stated that the horizontal load should be uniformly distributed. This is to avoid stress concentrations which would arise in analysis if it was considered acting at, say, the centre of gravity of the part of the building above the level being considered. It should be considered as uniformly distributed in both horizontal and vertical directions in the case of a building of rectangular plan form. In the case of a non-rectangular plan form it is suggested that the forces be calculated on convenient rectangles of the plan area. Examples are shown in Figure 6.6. It will be seen that unless separate rectangles are considered, an altogether excessive load requirement could arise on projecting wings of a building. In the case of a long building considered end-on, it will be permissible to consider the load as arising at various points distributed along the length of the building, otherwise very high local stresses may arise.

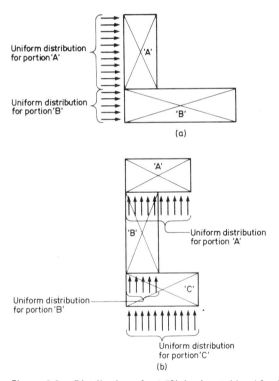

Figure 6.6   Distribution of a 1.5% horizontal load for buildings of non-rectangular plan form

It can be noted that the design for a lateral load equal to a percentage of the load of the building is a simple way of designing for the effect of earthquakes. In parts of the world prone to earthquakes, percentages much higher than 1.5 are used in design. However, the 1.5% may certainly be considered as adequate to deal with the very minor earthquakes which occur in the UK.

6.3 Roof and floor connections

In Clause 20.1 it is recommended that roof and floor connections should be as in Appendix C and as appropriate. The fixings in Appendix C are designed to provide simple resistance to lateral movement to ensure that there is no possibility of a wall buckling above a height of two storeys (see *Chapter 16*). It should be noted that more onerous tie requirements are specified for structures of five or more storeys.

6.4 Misuse or accident

A proper layout and the provision of an ability to withstand a 1.5% horizontal force will provide a considerable safeguard against excessive damage following an accidental load in a normal building. Consideration should, however, be given to the excessive risks which might arise from any particular type of occupancy and to structures exposed to vehicle impact. With regard to gas explosions, studies[6.4] have shown that these accidents occur quite frequently in dwellings, although the pressures reached in the Ronan Point collapse are attained in only a handful of cases in any given year. Therefore, there can be no question of individual dwelling units being designed to resist the effects of an explosion of the severity of that at Ronan Point. The general question of what level of damage is acceptable from a given cause is a matter of judgement. Special consideration will be appropriate for buildings such as concert halls or sports centres which may contain a large number of people.

6.5 Special recommendations — buildings of five storeys and over

At present, buildings of five storeys and over are not very common in the UK. There is, however, no reason why, for some particular occupancies at least, such structures should not become as popular as they already are in certain areas of America. As structures over five storeys are likely to cover a fairly large plan area, there will usually be many loadbearing walls inserted in various directions. Such structures are naturally robust, but even so, particular requirements are specified in the Code. These arise essentially from Building Regulation D17. The detailed provisions are given in Section 5 of BS 5628 and, as previously mentioned, comprise of three options, each of which is discussed below.

6.5.1 Option 1

In this option it is necessary to consider each individual loadbearing element in turn and either *demonstrate that it can withstand a force of 34 kN/m² applied in any direction* or *prove that no significant portion of the structure will collapse if it is removed.*

The figure of 34 kN/m² is close to the pressure which occurred in the Ronan Point collapse which, as previously mentioned, is only likely to be reached or exceeded in a handful of incidents in a given year[6.4].

It may initially appear unreasonable to consider only one element at a time since an explosion inside a building will produce pressure on both slabs and walls. In practice, however, once the weakest element begins to fail, the burning gas in a gas explosion will begin to vent

49

so that the load will begin to drop off. In the case of high explosives, the pressure is dependent on the distance from the centre of the explosion so that, except in extreme cases, the only severe effect will be to the elements nearest to the centre of the explosion.

The option to resist 34 kN/m² is probably only practicable for walls. Most slabs in structures will have a dead weight of only around 6 kN/m² and so will fail by being uplifted unless a lot of top steel is provided. Short span slabs may be able to withstand 34 kN/m² in a downward direction.

In the case of walls it is possible for 34 kN/m² to be resisted, provided the wall carries a substantial vertical load and is of reasonable thickness, and is also restrained between concrete floors. The formula for arch action given in Clause 36.8 can then be applied, which is based on the assumption of arching as illustrated in Figure 6.7.

Taking moments about C:

$$n\,(t - \delta) + q \cdot \frac{h}{2} \cdot \frac{h}{4} = q \cdot \frac{h}{2} \cdot \frac{h}{2}$$

$$n\,(t - \delta) = \frac{qh^2}{8}$$

Ignoring δ as being small gives:

$$nt = \frac{qh^2}{8}$$

$$\text{or} \quad q = \frac{8tn}{h^2}$$

Finally γ_m is introduced to give the equation:

$$q = \frac{8 \times t \times n}{h^2\,\gamma_m}$$

as in Clause 36.8 of BS 5628.

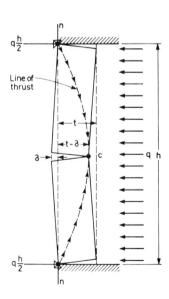

Figure 6.7 Arching failure under pre-compression load, n

It will be seen that the compressive load actually increases the capacity of arching so that the design value of n, the axial load/unit length of wall, is derived from an imposed load of $0.35\,Q_k$ and a dead load of $0.9\,G_k$. For the purpose of accidental loading γ_m is taken as 1.05. This is much lower than that used for ordinary

compression in accidental loading ($0.5 \times 3.5 = 1.75$). This is because the load arising from $0.35\,Q_k$ and $0.9\,G_k$ is much lower than that for which the wall is designed. The actual depth of the stress block carrying the axial load at the arch hinges is usually a small fraction of the wall thickness. A shortfall in arch capacity is more likely to arise in these cases due to the wall being out-of-plumb. In practice it will be found that for walls 150—200 mm thick the compressive load will be insufficient unless the wall supports three or more storeys of construction. Thus it is concluded at this point that under *Option 1* it is necessary to consider the removal firstly of floors and roofs and secondly of walls in upper storeys.

It should be noted that for checking after removal, reduced γ_f and enhanced γ_m factors are used. The γ_f factors for dead, imposed and wind loads are given in Clause 22(d), while the γ_m factors are to be taken as half of those specified for normal design (Clause 27.3). It may be noted that the 0.35 factor for imposed load is the result of a two-thirds reduction from 1.05 in accordance with Building Regulation D17. These reduced safety factors take account of the reduced probability of excessive imposed loads or understrength coinciding with the occurrence of very severe (and therefore unlikely) accident.

The definition of loadbearing elements which may be removed is given in Table 11 of BS 5628. For internal walls, any length between vertical lateral supports should be considered removable subject to an upper limit of $2.25\,h$, where h is the height of the wall. For external walls the full length between lateral supports should be taken. For slabs the whole area should be considered removable unless there are partitions or other construction underneath which can form temporary supports for the reduced design load ($0.35\,Q_k + 1.05\,G_k$) on the remaining slab. Table 11 of BS 5628 does not deal specifically with one way slabs, but it would seem reasonable to assume that an upper limit of $2.25\,l$, where l is the span, could be applied for internal slabs in cases where there are no substantial partitions to provide temporary supports.

It is necessary to consider the portion of the structure liable to collapse after removal and judge whether it is a 'significant portion'. Building Regulation D17 provides some assistance here in that it allows removal of a portion of any one structural member provided that:

"(a) structural failure consequent on that removal would not occur within any storey other than the storey of which the portion forms part, the storey next above (if any) and the storey next below (if any); and

(b) any structural failure would be localized within each such storey".

Regulation D17 goes on to state that in regard to (b) the regulation may be "deemed to be satisfied if the area within which structural failure might occur would not exceed 70 m² or 15% of the area of the storey (measured in the horizontal plane), whichever is the less".

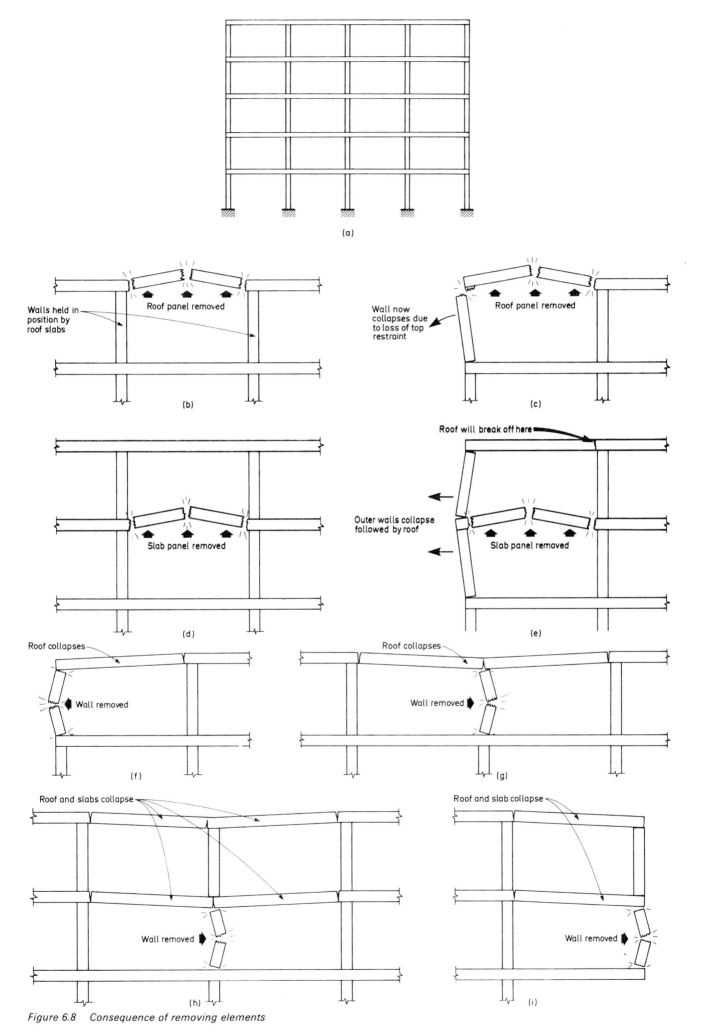

Figure 6.8   Consequence of removing elements

51

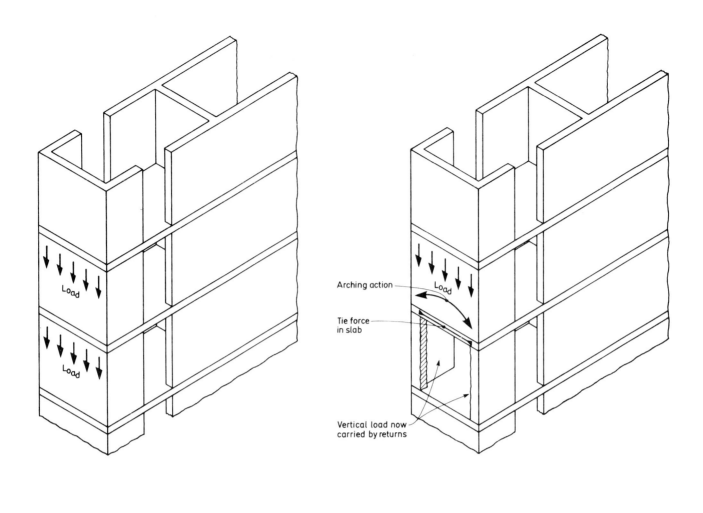

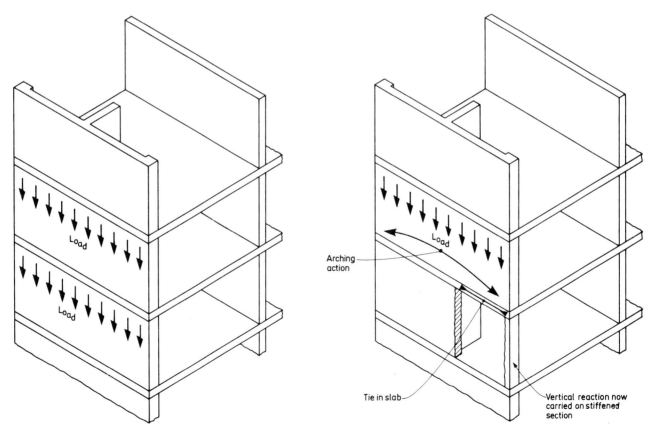

Figure 6.9   Ensuring stability following removal of an element

The matter is clearly one for the exercise of engineering judgement. It may be helpful to consider the particular case of a cross wall type of construction as in Figure 6.8. Various cases of removal and conse-

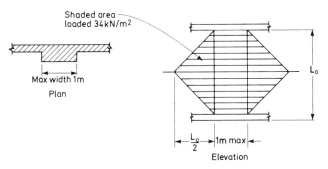

Figure 6.10 Wall braced by stiffened section

quential collapse are indicated for removal of elements in the top two storeys, all of which, in the authors' view, are acceptable as being damage which is not *disproportionate to the original cause*. Interior slab removal lower down the structure is also acceptable since it will not cause any further collapse (Figure 6.8(d)). However, exterior slab removal and wall removal in lower storeys will not be acceptable. Potential solutions in respect of removal of the external slab or wall are sketched in Figure 6.9 where the external or flank wall is provided with returns or with stiffened sections which are designed to withstand 34 kN/m². It should be noted that the latter solution involves designing the stiffened sections to carry a proportion of load transmitted from the adjoining panel (Figure 6.10). This solution can also be adopted where necessary for internal walls below the top most storeys. More sophisticated solutions than those suggested in Figure 6.9 can obviously be conceived, for instance allowing cantilevering out of portions which can lose support, but it may be preferable to use the procedures given under *Options 2* and *3* (*Sections 6.5.2* and *6.5.3*) below rather than rely on extensive calculations which will, of necessity, involve many assumptions.

6.5.2 Option 2

In this option horizontal ties are provided at all floor levels in accordance with rules specified in the Code and the vertical elements are proved to be removable, one at a time, without collapse of a significant portion of the structure.

For detailed operation of this option, reference should be made to the comments under *Option 3* for the provision of horizontal ties and those under *Option 1* for ways of dealing with vertical elements, i.e., walls.

6.5.3 Option 3

In this option both horizontal ties and vertical ties are provided at specified positions around, across and down the building.

It is worth commenting at the outset that the provision of ties in masonry buildings is not new. Many older

buildings, where the masonry has deformed or where settlement has occurred, have been fitted with ties, passing to iron anchor plates which can be seen on the outer walls, so that the principle of providing ties is well established.

The primary objective may be seen as providing integrity to the structure as a whole, but there is a secondary objective in that the ties will limit the possible spread of damage. Ties in a portion of wall above a removed storey allow it to act as a tied arch. Horizontal ties acting in a catenary manner may also permit slabs to continue to carry load in a severely deformed state, thus avoiding collapse on to floors below and subsequent further damage. Where vertical ties are provided at intervals in walls, they essentially give locally protected elements; in this instance there is a close parallel in effect between *Option 3* and *Option 1*.

The provision of peripheral and internal ties is a simple matter where in situ reinforced concrete floors are used, in which instance CP 110 specifies a minimum percentage of steel which must be provided in both directions throughout. There may be some difficulties in dealing with floors made up of precast elements, but the detailed provisions of CP 110 should be consulted here. Manufacturers of precast floor units are aware of the problems and can advise designers on solutions appropriate to their own products.

The provision of column and wall ties can be achieved in two ways. Firstly by friction or shear arising from direct bearing of floor slabs on the wall, or secondly by arranging ties along the lines of Figures 15—17 of Appendix C to BS 5628.

The requirements for vertical ties are clearly specified in Table 14 of BS 5628. In masonry incorporating hollow units it is probably simplest to provide ties at spacings of 1 m or so. In other cases it will be necessary to provide special masonry units every so often which provide a suitable vertical void into which ties and surrounding concrete can be placed; in this instance it would be preferable to use a larger spacing. While it is not specifically mentioned in Table 12 under *Option 3*, a statement in Clause 37.4 implies that vertical ties need not be extended to the foundation but only to a level where the wall can be proved capable of resisting 34 kN/m². This would appear sensible since the precompression load from five or six storeys will produce a wall robust enough to resist removal in nearly all cases.

6.6 References

6.1 Report of the inquiry into the collapse of flats at Ronan Point, Canning Town. HMSO, London, 1968.

6.2 Building Code requirements for concrete masonry structures. *ACI Journal Proceedings, Vol 7*, No 8, August 1978. pp 384—403

6.3 Commentary on Building Code requirements for concrete masonry structures. *ACI Journal Proceedings, Vol 7*, No 9, September 1978. pp 460—498

6.4 TAYLOR, N, AND ALEXANDER, S J. Strutural damage in buildings caused by gaseous explosions and other accidental loadings. *BRE Current Paper CP 45/74*, Building Research Establishment.

7

Walls under vertical load

7.1 Background

7.1.1 Mortar strength and block strength

In the previous chapters, the properties of blocks and mortars have been discussed and are classified by their characteristic strengths. A plain wall is a composite structure made of these two materials and, under compressive loading, its strength would be expected to be influenced by the strengths of both materials. What sort of interaction between block and mortar strength might be expected? Two extreme possibilities can be put forward: (a) Between horizontal joints, all loads will effectively be carried by the blocks while at the horizontal joints, all the load is carried by the mortar so that the wall strength might be expected to correspond to the strength of the weaker material; (b) The function of the mortar joint is simply to produce a good uniform bearing between the blocks and provided the mortar is not so fluid that it could squeeze out like toothpaste, its strength is irrelevant and the wall strength will correspond to the strength of the blocks. In fact, the second of these possibilities is the closest to the truth though the properties of the mortar may have some influence on the strength. Walls tend to be weaker than the average strength of the blocks for a number of reasons which will now be considered.

7.1.1.1 Behaviour of a thin mortar layer between stronger blocks
Assuming for the moment that both mortar and block are elastic, one influence of the mortar on the block can easily be determined. The elastic modulus of the mortar is commonly substantially less than that of the block and, as a consequence, the vertical strains under axial load are greater. This in turn implies a greater transverse dilation due to Poissons ratio. Since the stronger block will not tend to dilate so much, it will restrain the mortar which will be put into horizontal compression, thus putting the mortar into a state of triaxial compression. Very roughly, concrete or mortar in triaxial compression will be able to withstand a vertical stress, f_{vert}, given by

$$f_{\text{vert}} = f'_c + 4f_{\text{horiz}}$$

where f'_c = the uniaxial compressive strength
f_{horiz} = the applied horizontal stress

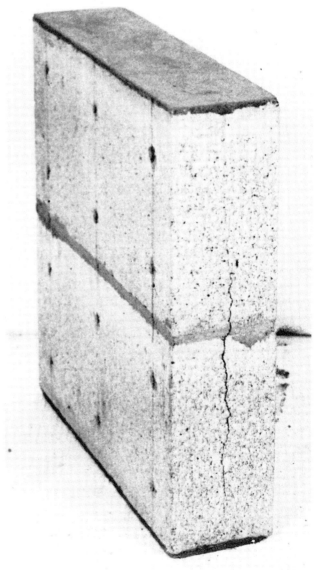

Figure 7.1   Mode of failure of couplet

The restraint from the blocks ensures that f_{horiz} can attain whatever value is required to sustain the applied vertical load and hence the mortar joint cannot fail

would be assumed if the deflection were ignored. In the limit, this extra eccentricity can cause more deflection, resulting in more eccentricity and an instability failure can result. The normal situation, however, is simply that the increased eccentricity causes the centre section to fail at a lower load than would otherwise be the case.

To estimate the reduction in capacity of the wall, it is necessary to obtain an estimate of the deflections, for which it is necessary to know the moment-curvature relationship for a blockwork wall. Moment-rotation relationships have been reported by Cranston[7.2] for small units made up of two blocks plus a single mortar joint. Figure 7.7 shows typical results for different levels of axial load. It will be seen that as the eccentricity increases, the stiffness decreases. For the lower loads the behaviour could almost be considered to be elastic-plastic. The basic reasons for this type of behaviour are quite easy to discern if the behaviour of the joint is considered (see Figure 7.8(a) and (b)). For low eccentricities of load (Figure 7.8(a)) the joint is completely in compression and the rotation of the joint will be given by:

$$\theta = \frac{N\,e\,t_i}{E_j\,I} \quad \dots \dots \dots \dots \dots (1)$$

The tensile stress that can develop between the block and the mortar is very low and cracks will develop in the joints almost as soon as any part of the joint goes into tension. Also, the mortar on the compressive face will start to spall at quite an early stage. This leaves the load to be carried on a relatively small and decreasing area of mortar. The stress and deformations in this piece of mortar become very large as eccentricity increases. As a consequence of the lower strength and stiffness of the mortar relative to the block and of the small area of mortar actually supporting the loads, a large proportion of the total rotation takes place in the joints. This is illustrated in Figure 7.9 which shows the proportion of the rotation occurring in the joint as a function of the total rotation for various situations. As the eccentricities· increase or the axial load

lowers, the behaviour of the joint begins to dominate the overall behaviour.

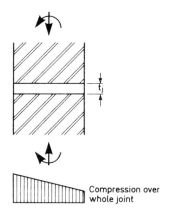

(a) Low eccentricity

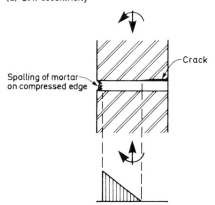

(b) Higher eccentricity

Figure 7.8   Behaviour of joint under eccentric load: (a) low eccentricity (b) high eccentricity

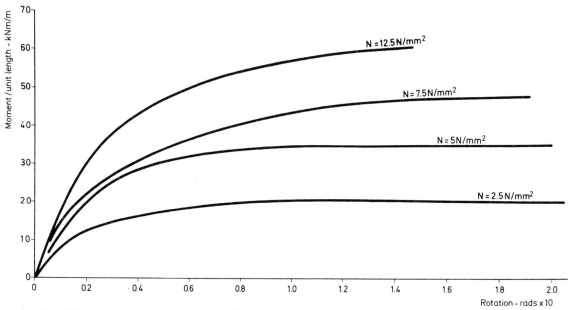

Figure 7.7   Moment rotation characteristics of blockwork

There are two modes of failure of the critical section of a wall:

(1) for relatively higher vertical loads, failure will occur in the block when the eccentricity reaches the value given by the relation below:

$$e = \frac{1}{2} \left(t - \frac{N}{bf_c} \right)$$

(this can be obtained from equation (1) above);

(2) for walls with relatively light vertical loads the mortar in the joint crushes. This crushing starts at the compression face and as the deformations increase, the crushing works its way into the joint until there is insufficient sound mortar to sustain the load at the required eccentricity.

From the above it will be seen that the behaviour of very slender walls, which will inevitably be lightly loaded at failure, will be dominated by the behaviour of the mortar and the properties of the block will be largely irrelevant. This is opposite to the situation for heavily loaded short walls where the strength depends upon the properties of the block and properties of the mortar are largely irrelevant.

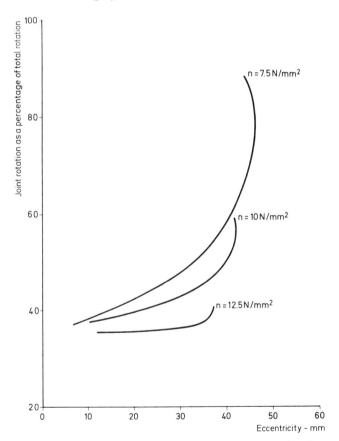

Figure 7.9 *Proportion of total rotation accommodated in joints for various levels of axial load*

7.1.5 Development of theoretical equations for slender walls

Information on the basic moment-curvature behaviour of blockwork can be obtained by numerical methods, and can be used to predict the strengths of vertically loaded slender walls. However, for design purposes such an approach is impracticable and, in any case, insufficient data on basic behaviour exists. As a conse-

quence, some alternative approach is required and it has been found that the approach used for reinforced concrete slender columns in CP 110 can be adapted for use on masonry walls.

In very simple terms, the derivation for a reinforced concrete member is as follows. Consider a pinned ended strut of height h. At failure, the strain in the concrete on the compression face at mid-height will be 0.0035. Assuming a balanced section, the strain in the steel at yield will be, say, about 0.002. The curvature of the critical section will thus be given by:

$$\frac{1}{r} = \frac{0.0035 + 0.002}{d} \quad \dots \dots \dots \dots \dots (2)$$

The central deflection will be given by the relation

$$a = \kappa h^2 \frac{1}{r} \quad \dots \dots \dots \dots \dots \dots (3)$$

where κ is a constant which depends upon the shape of the curvature diagram. If the axial load on the column is N_u then this deflection under ultimate conditions will increase the central moment on the column by an amount equal to $N_u a$. The column is then designed for the initial applied moment plus this additional moment. Equation (3) above can be rearranged as follows by substituting for $\frac{1}{r}$ from (2).

$$\frac{a}{d} = \kappa' \frac{h^2}{d^2}$$

From this it can be seen that all columns with the same slenderness ratio are predicted to have the same ultimate deflection expressed as a fraction of the effective depth. Figure 7.10 shows a series of load-central deflection curves for 140 mm masonry walls with various eccentricities of load. It will be seen that despite the great variation in ultimate load obtained and the differences in form of some of the curves, all the walls are at, or close to, their maximum load at the same deflection of about 10 mm. Thus, the same form of equation as that used for reinforced concrete can be expected to work reasonably well for masonry. Such an equation would have the form:

$$\frac{e_a}{t} = \kappa \left(\frac{h_{ef}}{t} \right)^2 \quad \dots \dots \dots \dots \dots (4)$$

where:

e_a = additional eccentricity
h_{ef} = effective height

This is the equation used in Appendix C of the Code. A value of $\frac{1}{2400}$ is used for κ and an arbitrary adjustment has been made so that there will be zero additional moment for an eccentricity of $0.05t$. This additional eccentricity has to be added to the eccentricity of the vertical loading. To achieve this, it is necessary to know the distribution of the initial and additional eccentricities up the height of the wall. For convenience, Appendix B makes the assumptions shown in Figure 7.11.

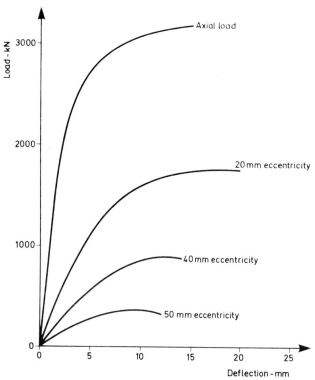

Figure 7.10 Load-deflection curves for a series of 13 course high walls

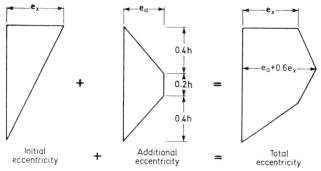

Figure 7.11 Assumed variations of eccentricity over the height of a wall

7.2 Walls under vertical load — design

7.2.1 General

The basic information required for the design of a wall to resist a vertical load (eccentric or axial) is as follows:

(1) the loading appropriate to the ultimate limit state which consists of the characteristic loads (dead, imposed, wind) and appropriate partial safety factors;

(2) a characteristic compressive strength for the particular type of masonry being adopted and an appropriate partial safety factor for reducing the characteristic strength to a design value;

(3) to assess the effects of slenderness and eccentricity of load, it is necessary to estimate the effective height and effective thickness of the wall;

(4) an assement is needed of the effective eccentricity of the loading at the top of the wall.

Each of these aspects of design will be considered in turn and, where appropriate, the provisions of the Code described and explained.

7.2.2 Design loads and partial safety factors

Characteristic loads are obtained from CP 3 Chapter V. These are multiplied by partial safety factors which take account of:

(1) possible unusual increases in load beyond the characteristic values;

(2) possible inaccuracies in assessment of load effects or unforeseen stress redistributions within the structure;

(3) variations in dimensional accuracy.

These statements are given in Clause 19.

Since the characteristic load is ideally a load with a 5% chance of being exceeded during the life of a structure, it is clear that design should be carried out for a load somewhat greater than this as a 1 in 20 chance of collapse due to overload would be unacceptable. The size of this increase can be expected to depend upon the inherent variability of the type of loading considered, hence a larger factor will be expected for live loads than for dead.

In (2) above, load effects are the moments, stress axial forces, and such like, at particular points in the structure resulting from the loading; they are the results of structural analysis. This part of the safety factor is thus to allow for inaccuracies in analysis. An effect of constructional inaccuracies is also to produce errors in the assessed load effects and in the ISO Standard setting out the limit state format errors in analysis and errors due to tolerances are combined together into a partial factor, γ_{f3}. This is also employed in the Bridge Code, BS 5400. In the most rigorous formulations this factor is applied to the load effects and not, as in BS 5628, to the loads.

A further function of the partial factors on the loads is to take account of the relative probability of various combinations of loading occurring. This function is not explicitly mentioned in Clause 19 but is nevertheless implicit in the values given for the factors in Clause 22. It is clearly less likely that maximum dead, live and wind loads will all occur simultaneously than that maximum dead and wind loads or dead and live loads will occur simultaneously. Thus for combination (3), dead, imposed and wind load, the partial factors are all lower than those adopted for combinations (1) and (2). This is not new; in CP 111, a 25% overstress was permitted for this combination of loads, which produced the same result but by a different means.

Two factors may be given for the dead loading because in some cases, the capacity of a wall may actually be increased by the addition of load, an example of which would be a wall subjected to a substantial wind load. The vertical load on such a wall provides a degree of prestress and increases the capacity of the wall to withstand the wind. In this case, the wall's ability to withstand the wind should be checked under the lower value of dead load $(0.9\ G_k)$.

7.2.3 Characteristic compressive strength of masonry

Appendix A2 specifies a test procedure for determining the characteristic strength of masonry, from which it will be seen that the characteristic strength of a particular type of masonry is that strength obtained for a panel of the masonry 1.2 to 1.8 m wide and from 2.4 to 2.7 m in height. The load should be axial and the top and bottom of the panel are restrained against rotation. In the absence of a value obtained from such a test, the Code gives charts and tables which may be used to estimate a value appropriate to the particular units and mortar employed. Interpolation is required between these tables for particular sizes of block and so, to simplify this procedure, Table 7.1 gives values of the design ultimate strength of masonry for common types and thickness of block.

Occasionally it may be convenient to build a wall of hollow blocks and then fill the cavity with concrete. The assessment of an appropriate characteristic strength in this case is dealt with in Clause 23.1.7. This states that, provided the infill concrete is at least as strong as that in the blocks, the blocks may be treated as solid and an appropriate characteristic strength obtained using Code Tables (b) and (d). For this purpose, the characteristic strength of the concrete in the block is assessed using the net cross sectional area of the block rather than the gross area of the block as is normally used when assessing block strength.

Another problem which sometimes arises is the assessment of a suitable characteristic strength for a wall constructed of blocks laid flat. This is an area where there is little evidence from actual wall tests and so the following can only be considered as an interim proposal until such time as reliable test data become available. The relationship between unit strength and wall strength will depend upon how the unit strength was obtained:

(1) if the block was tested in the testing machine on its side then the characteristic masonry strength should be obtained by interpolation between Tables 2(b) and 2(d) on the basis of the aspect ratio *as laid*. It may be necessary to extrapolate below Table 2(b) to obtain a value;

(2) if the block was tested vertically in the normal way then it is suggested that the characteristic masonry strength is obtained by interpolating between Tables 2(b) and 2(d) on the basis of the aspect ratio *as tested*. The result obtained should then be reduced slightly (say by 20%) to allow for the fact that the quality of the mortar joints is likely to have more effect of the strengths for blocks laid flat.

Walls have occasionally been built in stack bond. This in fact, lies outside the scope of BS 5628 since CP 121, to which BS 5628 refers, requires that the horizontal distance between joints in successive courses should not be less than a quarter of the unit length. Nevertheless, there may be reasons why the use of stack bond is desired and test work has been carried out in America and the National Masonry Association of America have developed recommendations for its use[7.4]. In principle, this report suggests the following:

(1) the vertical loadbearing capacity may be considered to be the same as for normal masonry except that concentrated loads should be considered to be carried only by the tier of masonry on which the load acts;

(2) the flexural strength across the horizontal joints can be considered to be the same as in normal masonry;

(3) the flexural strength across the vertical joints should be considered to be zero. To compensate for this, horizontal reinforcement should be provided.

The report gives recommendations as to amounts and arrangements of steel but it would seem reasonable to ensure sufficient steel in the joints to provide the same vertical flexural strength as given in Table 7.3 for the particular block used.

Hollow blocks are sometimes laid with mortar on the two outer strips of the blocks only. This is referred to as shell bedding. Clause 23.3 states that, where this is done, the appropriate value of f_k is obtained in the usual way from Tables (a) and (b) of the Code but that the design strength is then reduced by the ratio of the bedded area to the *gross* area of the block. This is incorrect; the design strength should be reduced by the ratio of the bedded area to the *net* area of the block.

7.2.4 Design strength

The design strength of masonry is obtained from the characteristic strength by dividing it by a material partial safety factor, γ_m. This factor makes allowance for variations in quality of the materials and differences between the strength of masonry constructed under site conditions and those built under laboratory conditions. Bearing this in mind, it is to be expected that a higher degree of quality control in the manufacture of the units will permit the use of a lower partial safety factor and similarly for construction control. A proportion of this safety factor must allow for the approximate nature of the tables given in the Code for determining characteristic masonry strength as a function of unit and mortar strength. Consequently, one would expect some reduction if the characteristic strength were determined directly. Hence the 10% reduction permitted when the Appendix A2 test has been used. If the special category of unit control and construction control are employed and if the characteristic strength has been obtained by test, a 36% increase in design strength can be obtained.

7.2.5 Effective height of wall

The concept of effective height appears to have been adopted almost universally for the treatment of instability effects in design. In an earlier section consideration was given to the failure by buckling of a pinned ended column as sketched in Figure 7.12(a). Analysis of a fixed ended column gives points of zero moment at the quarter points. The centre half of the column is thus behaving exactly as the pinned ended column and will fail at the same load as a pinned ended column of height $l/2$. A cantilever may be considered as half of a

Table 7.1 Design ultimate strength of masonry (kN/m)

Mortar designation	Compressive strength of unit (N/mm²)							Block type
	2.8	3.5	5.0	7.0	10.5	14.0	21.0	
(a)	Block height = 215		Block thickness = 100		Partial safety factor = 3.5			
(I)	80	100	143	194	261	325	438	solid
	80	100	143	163	176	190	222	hollow
(II)	80	100	143	183	246	290	377	solid
	80	100	143	157	164	172	191	hollow
(III)	80	100	143	183	239	275	342	solid
	80	100	143	154	158	162	174	hollow
(IV)	80	100	126	160	205	241	305	solid
	80	100	126	137	141	145	155	hollow
(b)	Block height = 215		Block thickness = 140		Partial safety factor = 3.5			
(I)	93	116	167	227	304	379	512	solid
	93	116	167	197	225	253	309	hollow
(II)	93	116	167	214	288	339	440	solid
	93	116	167	189	211	228	266	hollow
(III)	93	116	167	214	280	322	399	solid
	93	116	167	187	203	215	242	hollow
(IV)	93	116	147	187	240	282	256	solid
	93	116	147	165	179	191	216	hollow
(c)	Block height = 215		Block thickness = 190		Partial safety factor = 3.5			
(I)	105	129	187	255	342	425	574	solid
	105	129	187	232	281	329	418	hollow
(II)	105	129	187	240	323	380	494	solid
	105	129	187	221	263	295	360	hollow
(III)	105	129	187	240	314	361	448	solid
	105	129	187	219	255	279	327	hollow
(IV)	105	129	165	210	269	316	400	solid
	105	129	165	193	222	246	292	hollow
(d)	Block height = 215		Block thickness = 215		Partial safety factor = 3.5			
(I)	111	136	197	269	360	449	606	solid
	111	136	197	249	308	366	473	hollow
(II)	111	136	197	253	340	401	521	solid
	111	136	197	237	290	329	407	hollow
(III)	111	136	197	253	331	381	472	solid
	111	136	197	235	281	311	369	hollow
(IV)	111	136	174	221	284	333	422	solid
	111	136	174	207	244	274	330	hollow

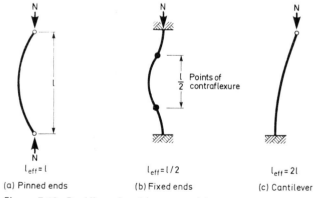

Figure 7.12 Buckling of various struts: (a) pinned ends (b) fixed ends (c) cantilever

pinned ended strut; its strength will thus be the same as a pinned ended strut of length $2l$. Obviously, a convenient way of dealing with these in design is to treat them all as pinned ended struts but with effective lengths chosen to given the correct failure load for the particular end conditions. The 'effective' lengths are thus:

Pinned ended strut	l
fixed ended strut	$l/2$

cantilever strut $\qquad 2l$

Actual structural situations differ from these ideal structures; the tops and bottoms of columns are not totally rigidly restrained and their effective lengths will exceed $l/2$. A common assumption is to take 0.75 times the actual height.

A failure of slender masonry walls is not strictly by buckling in the classical sense; nevertheless, the concept of effective height remains useful. Clause 28.3.1.1 defines the effective height as either

(1) ¾ of the clear distance between lateral supports where some rotation restraint exists; or

(2) the clear distance between lateral supports where the restraint is only to lateral movement and not to rotation.

The question remains as to what constitutes a lateral support.

Consider the buckling of an external wall (see Figure 7.13). If the tie to the intermediate floor were to break, the buckling mode would become as shown in Figure 7.13(b).

The effective height is doubled and the capacity of

Table 7.1 ....continued .....

Mortar designation	Compressive strength of unit (N/mm²)							Block type
	2.8	3.5	5.0	7.0	10.5	14.0	21.0	
(e)	Block height = 190		Block thickness = 90		Partial safety factor = 3.5			
(I)	72	90	129	175	235	292	394	solid
	72	90	129	147	159	171	200	hollow
(II)	72	90	129	165	222	261	339	solid
	72	90	129	141	148	155	172	hollow
(III)	72	90	129	165	215	248	308	solid
	72	90	129	139	142	146	156	hollow
(IV)	72	90	113	144	185	217	275	solid
	72	90	113	123	127	130	140	hollow
(f)	Block height = 190		Block thickness = 100		Partial safety factor = 3.5			
(I)	77	96	138	187	251	313	422	solid
	77	96	138	158	173	188	222	hollow
(II)	77	96	138	176	237	280	364	solid
	77	96	138	152	161	170	191	hollow
(III)	77	96	138	176	231	266	330	solid
	77	96	138	150	155	160	173	hollow
(IV)	77	96	121	154	198	233	294	solid
	77	96	121	133	138	143	155	hollow
(g)	Block height = 190		Block thickness = 140		Partial safety factor = 3.5			
(I)	86	107	154	210	281	350	473	solid
	86	107	154	186	217	248	309	hollow
(II)	86	107	154	197	266	313	407	solid
	86	107	154	178	203	224	266	hollow
(III)	86	107	154	197	258	297	369	solid
	86	107	154	176	196	211	241	hollow
(IV)	86	107	136	173	221	260	329	solid
	86	107	136	155	172	187	216	hollow
(h)	Block height = 190		Block thickness = 190		Partial safety factor = 3.5			
(I)	98	120	174	237	318	396	535	solid
	98	120	174	220	273	324	418	hollow
(II)	98	120	174	223	301	355	461	solid
	98	120	174	209	256	290	360	hollow
(III)	98	120	174	223	292	336	417	solid
	98	120	174	208	248	275	326	hollow
(IV)	98	120	154	195	251	295	373	solid
	98	120	154	183	216	242	291	hollow

the wall is reduced catastrophically, and a tie of sufficient strength must be provided to ensure that this cannot happen. Clause 28.2.1 states that a lateral support must be able to carry a horizontal force of 2.5% of the design vertical load on the wall in addition to any horizontal forces induced by the design loads (e.g., wind suction). This force would develop if the upper and lower walls were both 1.25% out of plumb (i.e. 40 mm in 3 m height), which should cope with the worst that is likely to arise in practice. Details of what will constitute a simple lateral support (giving no rotation restraint) and an enhanced lateral support which can be assumed to provide some restraint to rotation are given in Clauses 28.2.2.1 and 28.2.2.2 respectively.

In assessing the effective height of short lengths of wall where the length is less than or equal to four times the thickness, the rules in Clauses 28.3.1.2 or 28.3.1.3 for columns should be used rather than the provisions of 28.3.1.1. In the case of cavity walls, the thickness should be taken as the thickness of the loaded leaf.

7.2.6 Effective thickness

In the same way that it is convenient to reduce all buckling problems to equivalent pinned ended struts by using effective heights, it is convenient to reduce problems to consideration of solid rectangular sections by introducing an effective thickness. For solid walls or piers, the effective thickness equals the actual thickness. Clause 28.4 gives values of effective thickness for walls stiffened by piers and cavity walls.

The precise derivation of these factors is unclear but the basic principles can be illustrated without difficulty. The buckling strength of a wall depends upon its stiffness and a convenient measure of stiffness is the moment of inertia of a section. Consider a wall stiffened with piers spaced at a centre to centre distance of six times the pier width (top line of Table 5 in the Code) as shown in Figure 7.14. If $t_p = 2t$, the moment of inertia of the section is given as $0.03 \times 6l_p \times 8t^3$. The moment of inertia of an equivalent rectangular section is given by $\dfrac{6\,l_p\,t^3_{ef}}{12}$. Equating these gives $t_{ef} = 1.42\,t$ which is (to one decimal place) the same as given in Table 5. If the same operation is carried out for $\dfrac{t_p}{t} = 3$, then $\dfrac{t_{ef}}{t} = 2$; again as given in Table 5. However, if these calculations are carried out for the case where the pier spacing is 10 or 20 times the pier width, then

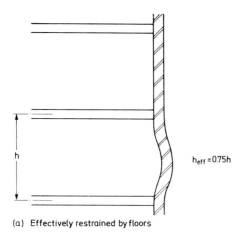

(a) Effectively restrained by floors

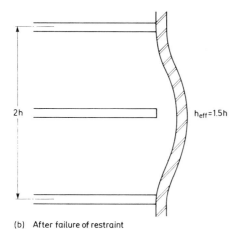

(b) After failure of restraint

Figure 7.13 Buckling of external wall: (a) effectively restrained by floors (b) after failure of restraint

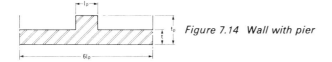

Figure 7.14 Wall with pier

larger values than those given in Table 5 will be obtained. This indicates that while a pier can fully stiffen a length of wall equal to six times its width, it is not fully effective when the spacing is larger. By the time the pier spacing reaches 20, large areas of wall between the piers must be considered to be unstiffened.

The effective thickness of a cavity wall can only be obtained empirically as it will depend upon the effectiveness of the ties in inducing some composite action between the two leaves.

7.2.7 The strength of short walls under eccentric loads

Under axial loading, the design strength of a wall which is sufficiently short for there to be a negligible deflection under ultimate loads is simply the characteristic strength of the wall divided by the appropriate partial safety factor. Once the load is applied eccentrically, however, the load capacity is reduced. Appendix B of BS 5628 indicates that the reduced capacity may be calculated on the assumption that, at ultimate load a plastic distribution of stress will act over the whole compression zone. The assumptions are illustrated in Figure 7.15.

64

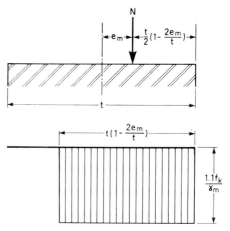

Figure 7.15 Stress block under ultimate conditions

In Figure 7.15 e_p = the eccentricity of the load

n_γ = the vertical load per unit length of wall

t = the thickness of the wall

f_k = the characteristic strength of the masonry

γ_m = the partial safety factor

It will be seen that the vertical load must act at the centre of the compression block and hence the neutral axis depth is given by:

$$x = t\left(1 - \frac{2e_m}{t}\right) \quad\cdots\cdots\cdots\cdots\cdots(5)$$

By equilibrium of forces:

$$n_\gamma = \frac{1.1f_k}{\gamma_m}x = \frac{1.1f_k t\left(1 - \frac{2e_m}{t}\right)}{\gamma_m}\cdots\cdots\cdots(6)$$

For very small eccentricities this equation will give a value of n_γ greater than the axial capacity. This is clearly not permissible and so an upper limit on the value of the load of $\frac{f_k t}{\gamma_m}$ must be applied.

If this is substituted into equation (5) we get, for the limiting case:

$$\frac{f_k t}{\gamma_m} = \frac{1.1f_k t\left(1 - \frac{2e_m}{t}\right)}{\gamma_m}\cdots\cdots\cdots(7)$$

This gives a limiting value of $\frac{e_m}{t} = 0.045$ (the Code rounds this to 0.05). Below this value of eccentricity, the capacity of the section is unaffected by the eccentric loading. Above this eccentricity, the capacity will be reduced to that given by equation (5). Writing $n_\gamma = \beta n_\gamma$ axial, it will be seen that: $\beta = 1.1\left(1 - \frac{2e_m}{t}\right)$

This gives the following values for β as a function of $\dfrac{e_m}{t}$

Table 7.2   Values of β as a function of e_m/t

Ratio $\dfrac{\text{eccentricity}}{\text{wall thickness}}$	Capacity reduction factor
0.05	1.00
0.10	0.88
0.15	0.77
0.20	0.66
0.25	0.55
0.30	0.44
0.35	0.33
0.40	0.22
0.45	0.11
0.50	0.00

When the wall is sufficiently slender for the deflection at its centre to have a significant influence on the central eccentricity, there will be a further reduction in load capacity. The derivation of equations for estimating the increase in eccentricity due to deflection of the wall was given in *Section 7.1.5*. Appendix B gives the relationship:

$$e_a = t \left[\frac{1}{2400} \left(\frac{h_{ef}}{t_{ef}} \right)^2 - 0.015 \right] \quad \ldots\ldots\ldots(8)$$

and, as discussed in *Section 7.1.5*, the eccentricity in the middle region of the wall is assumed to be:

$$e_t = e_a + 0.6e_x \quad \ldots\ldots\ldots\ldots\ldots(9)$$

where e_x is the eccentricity at the top of the wall. Clearly, if e_a is small, e_t can be smaller than e_x. If this is the case, then, obviously e_x governs. The design eccentricity e_m, is thus the greater of e_t and e_x. The capacity of the wall has to be estimated for this eccentricity.

If a value of $\dfrac{h_{ef}}{t}$ of 6 is used, it will be seen that e_a will be calculated to be zero. Thus, slenderness effects are assumed in the Code to be zero for slenderness ratios of 6 or less.

Equations (7), (8) and (9) may be used to derive the capacity reduction factors in Table 7 of the Code. A typical example will show how this is achieved. Assume a slenderness ratio of 12. Substituting this into (8) gives an additional eccentricity in the central region of $0.045t$. If the eccentricity at the top is $0.1t$, then (9) gives the total eccentricity in the central region as $0.105t$. This is greater than the eccentricity at the top and hence $\dfrac{e_m}{t} = 0.105$. For this eccentricity, equation (7) gives a value of β of 0.869. If the eccentricity at the top is $0.3t$, then the central eccentricity will be found to be $0.225t$. Since this is less than the eccentricity at the top, $\dfrac{e_m}{t}$ becomes the top value of 0.3. For this, equation (7) gives a β value of 0.44. These values can be seen to be the same as are given in Table 7 of the Code for the particular eccentricities and slenderness ratios chosen.

From the design point of view then, calculation of the strength of a vertically loaded wall can be achieved using the formula

$$\text{Vertical load resistance} = \frac{\beta b t f_k}{\gamma_m}$$

Columns are tackled in exactly the same way as walls except that it may be necessary to consider the effects of bending about both axes. Where the eccentricities are small about either or both axes (less than $\frac{1}{20}$ of the section size) the strength can be checked by assuming a value of β from Table 7 of the Code on the basis of the larger ratio of eccentricity to section dimension in that direction and the slenderness ratio appropriate to the minor axis. Where both eccentricities exceed $\frac{1}{20}$ of the section dimension, the Code states that a capacity reduction factor must be calculated using the assumption made in Appendix B. The exact procedure envisaged by the Code in this latter situation is not set out but the following would appear satisfactory:

(1) for the eccentricity about each axis in turn calculate the additional eccentricity using equation (8), assess the design eccentricity as either the initial eccentricity at the top or that derived from equation (9), whichever is the greater;

(2) by trial and error, define a neutral axis position so that the centroid of the compression zone coincides with the centroid of the applied load. The vertical load capacity of the section is then given by:

$$N_u = \frac{1.1 A_c f_k}{\gamma_m}$$

where N_u = ultimate axial load
A_c = area of compression zone

(see Figure 7.16).

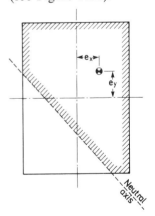

Figure 7.16 Biaxial bending of a column section

Provided the section is rectangular, this problem can be solved by the use of the design chart in Figure 7.17. To use the chart, calculate the ratio of the eccentricity to the section dimension in the minor axis and major axis bending directions. Using these two values, obtain a capacity reduction factor β from Figure 7.17. The vertical load capacity is then given by:

$$N_u = \beta \frac{b t f_k}{\gamma_m}$$

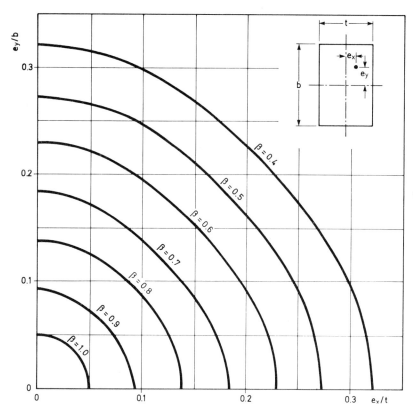

Figure 7.17 Design chart for biaxial bending of masonry piers

7.2.8 Assessment of eccentricity

Practice in the assessment of eccentricity is summarized in Building Research Establishment Digest No 246. The introductory paragraph of the section of this digest dealing with eccentricity is worth quoting in full:

"The assessment of eccentricity of vertical loading at a particular junction in a brickwork or blockwork wall is made complex by the many possible combinations of wall and floor systems. The structural behaviour of the junction will be affected by the magnitude of the loads, the rigidity of the interconnected members and the geometry of the junction. It is seldom possible to determine the eccentricity of load at a junction by calculation alone, and the designer's experience must be his guide."

The advice given may be summarised as follows:

(1) bearing on external walls

In general eccentricity $= \dfrac{t}{2} + \dfrac{x}{3}$

where a concrete floor of short span spans the full width of the wall or the load is applied by a centered wall plate, it may be more reasonable to regard the load as axial.

(2) bearing on internal walls

(a) span on either side not differing by more than 50%

eccentricity $= 0$

(b) spans differing by more than 50%

Imagine the floor split along the centreline of the wall and treat each side as for an external wall (see Figure 7.18(b)). Treat each side as for (1) above to obtain eccentricities for N_1 and N_2. Combine these to obtain overall eccentricity.

(3) joints supported on hangers

Load assumed to act 25 mm outside face of wall.

In all cases, the Code makes the assumption that the eccentricities apply at the top of the wall and that the eccentricity at the bottom is zero. If this is clearly unreasonable then the Code approach should be modified appropriately.

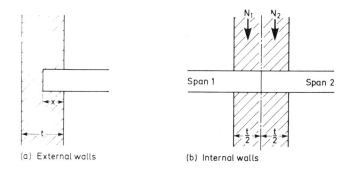

(a) External walls   (b) Internal walls

Figure 7.18 Assessment of eccentricities: (a) external walls (b) internal walls

7.2.9 Cavity walls with both leaves loaded

If, at the level where the load is applied, both leaves are spanned by some form of spreader which carries the applied load, each leaf may be designed to carry an axial load of magnitude such that, acting together, they equilibrate the applied load. This is illustrated in Figure 7.19.

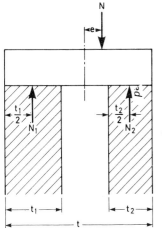

Figure 7.19 Cavity wall with both leaves loaded

From this Figure,

$$N_e = N_2 \left(\frac{t}{2} - \frac{t_1}{2} \right) - N_1 \frac{t}{2} - \frac{t_1}{2}$$

$$N = N_1 + N_2$$

These equations may be solved for N_1 and N_2

Failure will occur as soon as one or other leaf reaches its capacity. This will commonly be the inner leaf of an external wall.

A modification to this procedure is required as soon as the line of action of the load passes outside the centroid of one of the leaves. When this occurs, the load is clearly carried by only the one leaf at an appropriate eccentricity.

7.2.10 Diaphragm walls

This is a relatively new form of construction where the two leaves of a double leaf wall are effectively connected by diaphragms which permit the whole wall to act as a cellular section. This is distinct from the normal cavity wall where the connection, via wall ties, does not provide sufficient connection to allow the two leaves to act compositely in resisting load.

Clearly, the fundamental requirement for a double leaf wall to behave as a diaphragm or cellular wall is that diaphragms should be provided at sufficiently close spacings and should be adequately bonded into the two leaves. Provided this is done, stresses in the wall may be estimated on the basis of the properties of the whole section. If the spacing of the diaphragms is too large, areas of wall between the diaphragms will become ineffective (this is similar to the effective flange widths which have to be used in reinforced concrete design). Provided the spacing of the diaphragms is not greater than twelve times the width of the thinner leaf, it can be assumed that the whole wall is effective. If wider spacings become essential, then a reasonable approach would seem to be to assume that any part of the wall at a distance further than six times the leaf thickness from the centre line of the nearest diaphragm is incapable of resisting load.

The vertical shear stress at the junction between the diaphragms and the leaves of the wall may be calculated using the standard elastic formulae. Thus, the vertical shear stress is given by:

$$v_v = \frac{V_h S}{It} \quad \dots \dots \dots \dots \dots (10)$$

where v_v = vertical shear stress on section considered

V_h = the horizontal shear force acting on the length of wall equal to the spacing of the diaphragms

I = second moment of area of total section

t = thickness of section on which shear is being checked

S = first moment of area of the section of wall to one side of the section considered about the neutral axis of the total section.

(see Figure 7.20 for clarification).

Thus, for the section sketched in Figure 7.20, the stress across the junction between the diaphragm and the leaf is given by:

$$v = \frac{V_h b t_1 (h - t_1)}{2 I t_d}$$

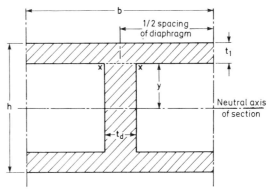

Figure 7.20 Diaphragm wall

If the diaphragm is thick compared with the thickness of the leaves, the vertical shear should be checked in the leaf rather than at the joint (see Figure 7.21). Obviously, this is only likely to be critical where the diaphragm is more than twice the thickness of the leaves.

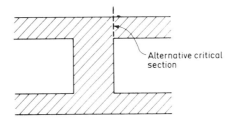

Figure 7.21 Alternative critical section for shear

It is suggested that the vertical shear force in the walls should be limited to $\frac{0.7}{\gamma_m}$ N/mm². This is twice the value given in Clause 25 for shear across a bed joint with mortar classes (i), (ii) or (iii) and, in the absence of better information, seems a reasonable value.

Assuming that the diaphragms are not bonded into the leaves, the vertical shear across the joint between them should be carried by the provision of ties.

One of two approaches may now be used to design the wall to resist vertical and horizontal loads. Firstly, it can be designed entirely elastically so that the tensile stress does not exceed half the design flexural stress and the compressive stress does not exceed 0.8 of the design compressive stress $\left(0.8 \frac{f_k}{\gamma_m}\right)$. Thus:

$$\frac{N_{u\,max}}{A_c} - \frac{N_{u\,max}ey_1}{I} \leq 0.8 \frac{f_k}{\gamma_m} \quad \ldots\ldots\ldots(11)$$

$$\frac{N_{u\,min}}{A_c} - \frac{N_{u\,min}ey_2}{I} \geq \tfrac{1}{2}f_t \quad \ldots\ldots\ldots(12)$$

where y = distance from the neutral axis to the face of the wall

A_c = cross-sectional area of wall

If walls are designed in this way, it may be assumed that deflections under the design loads are negligible and thus there will be no slenderness effects.

Secondly, they can be designed as cracked sections and thus unable to carry tensile stresses. In this case, the vertical load may be assumed to be resisted by a stress block as shown in Appendix B of BS 5628. Slenderness effects have to be allowed for and a capacity reduction factor can be estimated using equation (1) from Appendix B and equation (2) modified to:

$$e_t = 0.6 e_{xt} + e_a + e_{lat}$$

where e_{lat} is the eccentricity at mid height resulting from the lateral loading. Equation (3) will require re-definition as follows (see Figure 7.22).

(i) by moments about section centroid:

$$\left(b - t_d\right)\left(y_1 - \frac{t_1}{2}\right)t_1 + xt_d\left(y_1 - \frac{x}{2}\right)$$
$$+ [\tfrac{1}{2}(t_2 - h + x)(b - t_d)(2y_2 - t_2 - h + x)]$$
$$= e[(b - t_d)t_1 + t_d x + [(t - h + x)(b - t_d)]]$$
$$\leftarrow \quad \text{Area of compressive zone, } A_c \quad \rightarrow$$

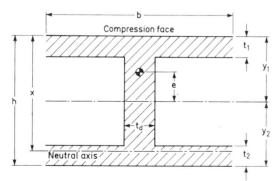

Figure 7.22 Definitions used in ultimate load equations

Solve equation (1) for x. If $x < y_2 - t_2$ (i.e. x is not within leaf) delete terms in square brackets and solve

again for x. If $x < t_1$ (i.e. compression zone is entirely in one leaf) design as single wall of thickness t. Having found x, the area of the compression zone A_c is found and the vertical load capacity is given as:

$$n_\gamma = \frac{1.1 A_c f_k}{\gamma_m}$$

Using Equation (1) in Appendix B, the effective thickness of the wall may be taken as the overall wall thickness.

7.2.11 Non-standard eccentricities of load

As stated earlier, the assumption has been made in the derivation of the capacity reduction factors that the eccentricity used in design is present at the top of the wall reducing to zero at the bottom. In practice, the eccentricity at the bottom of the wall will commonly be in the opposite direction to that at the top. As far as consideration of slenderness effects are concerned, it is the eccentricity in the central region of the wall which is required and thus to assume opposite eccentricities at top and bottom will lead to a smaller central eccentricity and a larger load capacity. Since the precise behaviour of the bottom of walls is difficult to define, it would be inadvisable to assume that the eccentricities changed sign unless the wall was constructed in such a way as to make this inevitable. If, however, the nature of the structure was such that the eccentricity at the top and bottom were in the same direction, then it would be advisable to make allowances for this since the capacity of the wall will be reduced. The required modification to the design procedure is to change equation (2) in Appendix B from:

$$e_t = 0.6 e_x + e_a$$

to:

$$e_t = e_a + e_{min} + 0.6 (e_{max} - e_{min})$$

where e_{max} is the numerically larger eccentricity

e_{min} is the numerically smaller eccentricity

e_{max} and e_{min} have the same sign if they are in the same direction

Suitable values of β may now be calculated using equations (1) (3) and (4) from Appendix B together with the modified equation (2).

7.2.12 Walls with eccentricities in their own plane (shear walls)

The overall stability of masonry structures subjected to wind loads will commonly be provided by walls or

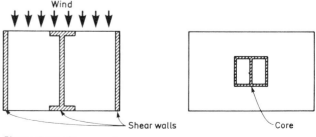

Figure 7.23 Shear walls or cores

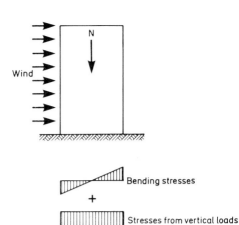

Figure 7.24 Stresses in a shear wall

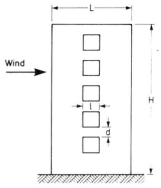

(a) Pierced wall

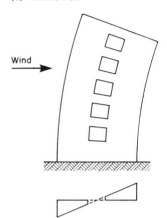

(b) Conditions in an unpierced wall

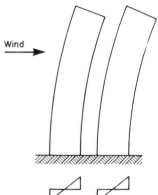

Figure 7.25 Pierced shear
walls : (a) pierced wall
(b) conditions in an
unpierced wall (c) conditions
of wall if openings produce
a complete break

(c) Conditions in wall if openings produce
a complete break

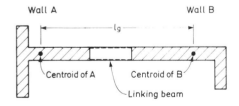

Figure 7.26 Pierced shear wall – definitions

groups of walls acting as 'shear walls' or 'cores' (see Figures 7.23 and 7.24).

In principle these act as cantilevers in resisting the horizontal forces shown in Figure 7.25.

In most cases stress can be checked on this basis.

$$\text{Stress at base of wall} = \frac{N_y}{A} \pm \frac{M_w}{I} \, y$$

where N_y = vertical load

A = cross sectional area of wall

M_w = total wind moment

I = moment of inertia of wall section

y = distance form cetroid to point considered

This approach will work for single walls or groups of connected walls. Where wind loads are resisted by a series of separate walls, the total wind forces will be carried by the various walls in proportion to their relative stiffness. Thus the wind moment carried by a particular wall is given by:

$$M_{wi} = M_w \frac{I_i}{\Sigma I}$$

M_{wi} = wind moment carried by $i\,th$ wall

M_w = total wind moment

I_i = moment of inertia or $i\,th$ wall

ΣI = sum of moments of inertia of all walls assumed to be resisting wind moments

Possible difficulties can arise where a wall is pierced by a series of openings so that it may not be clear whether it can be considered as a single unit or whether it should be considered as separate walls. Consider the wall illustrated in Figure 7.26. Clearly, the actual conditions will lie between those illustrated in Figure 7.25 (b) and (c). If the openings are relatively small, assumption (b) will be closest while, if they are larger (a) will be more appropriate. For walls with a single line of openings, Pierce and Matthews[7.5] give a simplified

design approach which should be applicable to masonry structures. The wind moments are considered in two parts

$\beta_1 M_w$ is carried by the two parts of the wall acting independently (as in Figure 7.25(c))

$(1-\beta_1)M_w$ is assumed to be carried by the wall acting as fully connected wall (see Figure 7.25(b))

The stress can then be found by summing the stress obtained from the two calculations. β_1 is given by the following relationship

69

$$\beta_1 = \frac{2}{\alpha H} \left(\frac{\alpha H - 1}{\alpha H} \right)$$

where

$$\alpha = \sqrt{\frac{12 I_b}{h b_{eff}^3} \left(\frac{l_g}{I_A + I_B} + \frac{1}{A_A} + \frac{1}{A_B} \right)}$$

H = overall height

I_b = moment of inertia of linking beam

h = storey height

b_{eff} = effective breadth of opening = $l + d$ in Figure 7.25(a)

l_g = distance between centroids of the two parts of the wall (designated as A and B)

I_A, I_B respectively the moments of inertia of parts A and B

A_A, A_B respectively the areas of parts A and B

If $\alpha H > 16$ then the wall should be considered fully coupled (i.e. $\beta_1 = 0$).

If $\alpha H < 4$ the two halves should be considered to act independently.

Calculation of β for $\alpha H = 4$ does not give $\beta_1 = 1$ which this would suggest, but Pierce and Matthews say at this end of the range the result is so sensitive to minor changes in the parameters that it is advisable to take $\beta_1 = 1$ for $\alpha H < 4$.

The calculation outlined above is tedious and a further simplification has been made. Figure 7.27 gives values of β_1, as a function the parameters $\frac{d}{h} \times \frac{l}{L}$ and $\frac{h}{L}$.

This Figure is an approximation to the approach given above but is probably adequate for most design purposes.

The maximum and minimum vertical stress can now be assessed as:

$$f = \frac{P}{A_A + A_B} \pm \frac{\beta_1 M y_1}{I_A \text{ or } I_B} \pm \frac{(1 - \beta_1) M y_2}{I'}$$

I' is the moment of inertia of A and B acting together

Having found the maximum stress, this can be compared with the design stress, making due allowance for the capacity reduction factors in Table 9. In assessing the eccentricity for use with Table 9, the forces resulting from the wind can be assumed to be acting axially. Appropriate assumptions should be made about the eccentricities of loads applied by floors supported by the wall.

The problem which remains is the stress condition which may arise in the connecting beams in pierced shear walls. Pearce and Matthews give the following formula for the maximum shear force carried by a connecting beam:

$$Q_{max} = \beta_2 P_w \frac{h}{\mu l_g} \dots \dots \dots \dots (13)$$

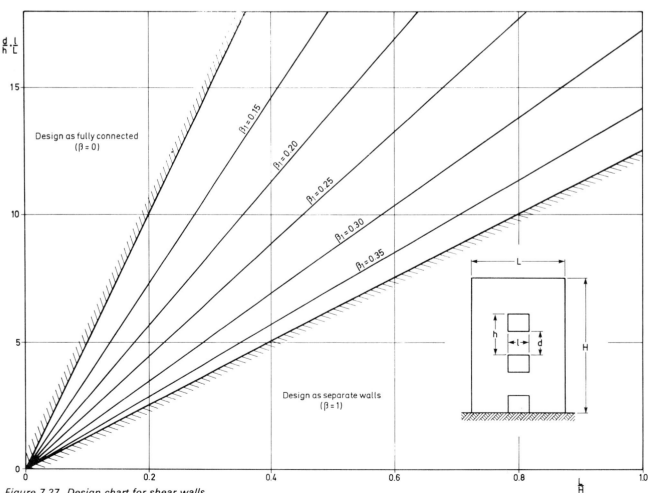

Figure 7.27 Design chart for shear walls

70

where

$$\mu = 1 + \frac{(I_A + I_B)(A_A + A_B)}{A_A A_B l_g^2}$$

P_w = wind force carried by wall
and β_2 is obtained from Table 7.3.

Table 7.3 Values of coefficient β_2 as a function of β_1

β_1	β_2
.1	.79
.15	.71
.2	.54
.25	.58
.3	.51
.35	.44
.4	.40

In most cases it will be sufficiently accurate to take μ as equal to 1.15.

The shear stress in the connecting beam should not exceed $\dfrac{0.2 \sqrt{f_k}}{\gamma_m}$

7.3 Examples

7.3.1 Combined vertical and lateral load

BS 5628:Clause 36.8 gives two possible approaches to check the lateral load capacity of a wall carrying significant vertical loads. The most direct method is to use the equation given in the clauses:

$$q_{lat} = \frac{8 \, n_\gamma t}{h^2 \gamma_m}$$

where q_{lat} = lateral load per unit area
$\quad n_\gamma$ = vertical load per unit length of wall
$\quad t$ = wall thickness
$\quad h$ = clear height of wall

This equation is based on arch action and the derivation can be seen to be approximately as follows:

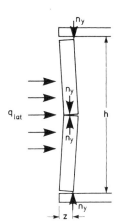

taking moments about the centre of the wall,

$$\frac{q_{lat} h^2}{8} = n_\gamma z$$

z is the distance between the lines of action of the vertical load at the centre and at the ends.

Assuming z to be roughly equal to t and introducing a safety factor gives:

$$q_{lat} = \frac{8 \, n_\gamma t}{h^2 \gamma_m}$$

The second approach is by consideration of the effective eccentricity due to the lateral load and any other eccentricity, using Clause 32 and Appendix B. No indication of how this should be attempted is given so there may be ways other than the approach suggested below.

There are three sources of eccentricity and the distribution of eccentricity up the height of the wall needs to be assessed for each.

(i) *Vertical loads*
The eccentricity at the top of the wall is assessed in the normal way and is assumed to reduce linearly from this value to zero at the foot of the wall,
i.e.

(ii) *Additional moments due to slenderness effects*
e_a can be calculated from equation 1 in Appendix B. The distribution of this eccentricity up the wall is open to interpretation. Appendix B states that the value may be taken as zero at top and bottom and e_a over the middle fifth of the height. However, this is derived from consideration of vertical load only. Consideration of buckling behaviour suggests that it would be more realistic to assume zero at points of contraflexure, giving the distribution sketched below:

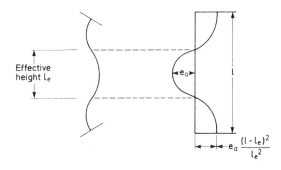

(iii) *Eccentricty due to lateral load*
The problem here is to assess the distribution of moment over the height of the wall. Provided there is some reasonable degree of axial load acting it seems unreasonable to assume the wall to be pinned top and bottom; the ends will have some moment capacity. A reasonable assumption for most cases would seem to be to assume the distribution as follows:

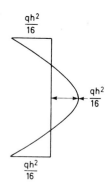

The eccentricity can be found by dividing these moments by the axial load, i.e.,

$$e_q = \frac{qh^2}{16n}$$

The total eccentricities can now be obtained by addition. The additional eccentricity due to slenderness effects is applied in the direction which will produce the worst effect.

The wall strength can now be checked by applying equation 3 in Appendix B to the section with the greatest eccentricity.

7.3.2 Combined vertical and horizontal load

For convenience this example is based on the same structure as that in *Problem 2* on vertical load. Also, so that the vertical loads previously assessed can be used, the example will consider the wall between ground and first floor, though in practice this might not necessarily be the most severe case and other floors would also have to be checked.

PROBLEM

Check that 10.5 N/mm² blocks are satisfactory for the wall between ground floor and first floor if the characteristic wind load is 0.55 kN/m² over the whole height of the building.

SOLUTION

To check that 10.5 N/mm² blocks are satisfactory for the wall between gound and first floor is the characteristic wind load is 0.55 kN/m² over the whole height of the building, the structure and loading are the same as used in *Problem 2* on vertical loads (*Section 7.3.3*).

Clause 36.8 gives two methods of carrying out the design:

(a) by using the formula provided in Clause 36.8, or
(b) by consideration of effective eccentricities and the principles of Clause 32 and Appendix B.

Both methods will be used in this example.

METHOD (A)

$$q_{lat} = \frac{8 \times t \times n_y}{h^2 \gamma_m}$$

using kN and m units

t = 140 mm = 0.14 m

h = 2.9 m

γ_m = 3.5

72

The design vertical load for this load case, $(0.9\,G_k + 1.4\,W_k) = 0.9 \times 76.4 = 68.8$ kN/m

$$\therefore q_{lat} = \frac{8 \times 0.14 \times 68.8}{2.9^2 \times 3.5} = 2.62 \text{ kN/m}^2$$

the required capacity = $1.4 \times 0.55 = 0.77$ kN/m²

$\therefore$ design is OK.

METHOD (B)

As before, the design vertical load is 68.8 kN/m.

The connection with the slabs above and below will provide some moment restraint, therefore assume the distribution of lateral moment is as sketched below:

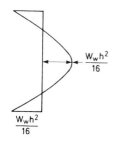

$$\frac{W_w h^2}{16} = \frac{1.4 \times 0.55 \times 2.9^2}{16} = 0.40 \text{ kN/m}$$

This moment corresponds to an eccentricity of:

$$\frac{0.4 \times 10^6}{68.8 \times 10^2} \text{mm} = 5.88 \text{ mm}$$

The eccentricity of the load at the top of the wall can be assessed as follows:

(i) load from second, third floors and roof, axial

(ii) load from first floor at eccentricity of $\frac{t}{6}$

by moments centre of wall,

$$\frac{0.9 \times 12 \times 140}{6} = 0.9 \times 57.15 \times e_t$$

$\therefore e_t = 4.9$ mm

(57.15 load of roof + two floors + three heights of wall)

The eccentricity of the vertical load at the base of the wall can be taken at zero.

Additional moments

$$\frac{l_e}{t} = 14.18$$

hence, from equation 1 in Appendix B, the additional eccentricity developing due to slenderness effect is:

$$e_a = 140 \left[\frac{1}{2400} (14.18)^2 - 0.015 \right]$$

$$= 9.63 \text{ mm}$$

The Code does not define how the eccentricity varies up a wall in bending with some fixity but a reasonable assumption is as follows:

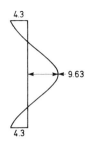

The total eccentricity can now be obtained by adding the additional eccentricities to the initial eccentricity and the eccentricity due to lateral load:

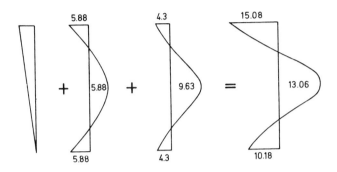

Hence maximum eccentricity = 15.08
Vertical load capacity

$\dfrac{f_k}{\gamma_m}$ for 10.5 N/mm² block = 1.84 N/mm²

$$= 1.1 \left(1 - \dfrac{2 \times 15.08}{140} \right) 140 \times 1.84$$

$$= 222 \text{ kN/m}$$

This exceeds 68.8 kN/m ∴ wall is OK.
By inspection, load case (c) will be OK.

7.3.3 Vertical load

PROBLEM 1
Find the characteristic strength of masonry built from 5 N/mm² solid blocks 190 mm high by 140 mm thick using 1:1:6 mortar. What design load will an axially loaded short wall (i.e., no slenderness effects) made from this masonry carry per metre at the ultimate limit state?

PROBLEM 2
The sketch below illustrates part of a four storey building of loadbearing masonry. The floors and roof spanning onto the inner leaf of the wall shown have a span of 6 m. Carry out calculations for the load case of vertical loads only (load case (a) in Clause 22 of BS 5628) for the wall between ground and first floor. What strength of block will be needed?

Loadings

      Roof   Dead load = 3.8 kN/m²

               Live load = 0.75 kN/m²

      Floors Dead load = 4.0 kN/m²

               Live load = 3.5 kN/m²

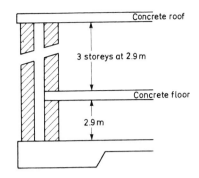

Weight of inner skin of masonry assume 2.5 kN/m²

Assume 90 mm thick outer skin

          140 mm thick inner skin

          50 mm cavity

PROBLEM 3
A precast floor unit is supported on a 140 mm wide block wall as sketched below. The wall is constructed of 140 mm thick modular blocks of 5 N/mm² strength. The wall is 2.9 m high and the beams on the wall at 0.75 m centres. If the design ultimate end reaction from the beams is 20.18 kN, check that the local bearing stresses are satisfactory.

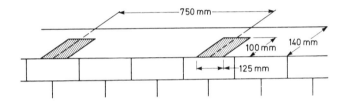

PROBLEM 4
The 12 m high structure sketched below is subjected to a wind load of 0.5 kN/m² over the whole height. Assuming that the walls are built of 190 mm thick solid blocks and that the characteristic dead and live loads at the base of the wall are as given below, check that a 10.5 N/mm² block will be satisfactory.

Loads in kN/m	Wall A	Wall B	Wall C
Dead	76.4	152.0	76.4
Imposed	33.8	67.5	33.8

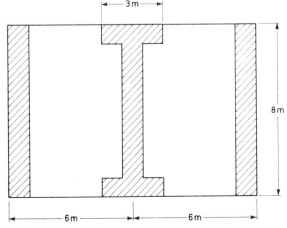

SOLUTION 1

Find the characteristic strength of masonry made of 5 N/mm² solid blocks 190 mm high by 140 mm thick using 1:1:6 mortar. What design load will a low wall made from this masonry carry per metre?

To find the characteristic strength, f_k, it is necessary to interpolate between Tables 2(b) and 2(d) in BS 5628. A 1:1:6 mortar is a Type (iii) mortar as defined in Table 7.1.

The height to thickness ratio of the block is

$$\frac{190}{140} = 1.36.$$

Table 2(b) is for blocks with $\frac{h}{t} = 0.6$

Table 2(d) is for blocks with $\frac{h}{t} \geq 2.0$

The characteristic strengths are given for those $\frac{h}{t}$ ratios as:

$$\frac{h}{t} = 0.6, \qquad f_k = 2.5$$

$$\frac{h}{t} \geq 2.0, \qquad f_k = 5.0$$

Hence, by linear interpolation, f_k for $\frac{h}{t} = 1.36$ can be found to be:

$$2.5 + \frac{(1.36 - 0.6)}{(2 - 0.6)} (5 - 2.5) = 3.86 \text{ N/mm}^2$$

Assuming normal control on site and in the manufacture of the blocks, the partial safety factor should be 3.5 (From Table 4). The design ultimate strength is thus:

$$\frac{3.86}{3.5} = 1.10 \text{ N/mm}^2$$

The load capacity of a metre of wall is thus:

$$\frac{1.10 \times 1000 \times 140}{1000} \text{ kN} = 154 \text{ kN/m}.$$

A similar calculation can be done for the common sizes of block and the standard specified compressive strengths. This has been done in Table 7.4. In all following examples, the figures from Table 7.4 will be used as the basic data. It will be seen that this Table gives a value of 154 kN/m for a 140 mm thick 5 N/mm² modular block.

Table 7.4 BS 5628 Design strengths of blockwork (kN/m) 1:1:6 mortar
$$\gamma_m = 3.5$$

Type	Thickness	Characteristic block strength N/mm²				
		3	5	10.5	21	28
Metric blocks 215 mm high	100	86	143	239	342	414
	140	100	167	280	399	483
	215	118	197	331	472	572
Modular blocks 190 mm high	90	77	129	215	308	372
	140	92	154	258	369	446
	190	104	174	292	417	505

(i.e., this is the strength of an axially loaded wall where there are no effects due to slenderness)

74

SOLUTION 2

Design wall for bottom floor of the four storey building sketched below. The roof and floors span 6 m onto the wall.

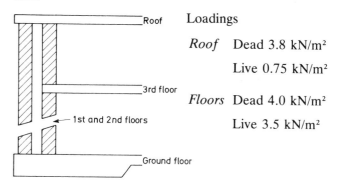

Loadings

Roof   Dead 3.8 kN/m²

Live 0.75 kN/m²

Floors   Dead 4.0 kN/m²

Live 3.5 kN/m²

Weight of inner skin of masonry —assume 2.5 kN/m²

Assume   90 mm thick outer skin

140 mm thick inner skin

50 mm cavity

Assess loading to ground floor level

	Dead
Roof	½ × 6 × 3.8 = 11.4
Three floors	3 × ½ × 6 × 4.0 = 36.0
Four storey heights of wall	4 × 2.9 × 2.5 = 29.0
Total kN/m	76.4

	Live
Roof	½ × 6 × 0.75 = 2.25
Three floors	3 × ½ × 6 × 3.5 = 31.50
Four storey heights of wall	0
Total kN/m	33.75

Design ultimate load
= 1.4 × dead load + 1.6 imposed load
= 1.4 × 76.4 + 1.6 × 33.75
= 161 kN/m

Eccentricity of load
Building Research Station Digest No. 246 gives guidance on the assessment of eccentricity. For an end wall with a concrete floor supported over the whole thickness of the leaf, *BRS Digest 61* suggests that if the ratio of span to wall thickness is less than 30, the eccentricity of the load from the floor may be taken as zero but where the ratio of span to wall thickness exceeds 30, a value of $\frac{1}{6}$ of the wall thickness will be more appropriate. In this case, $\frac{l}{t} = \frac{6000}{140} = 43$, hence $\frac{t}{6}$ is used. The load from the first floor is therefore taken at this eccentricity while the loads from the floors above are assumed to be axial.

Ultimate load from first floor

$$= 1.4 \times 12 + 1.6 \times 10.5 = 33.6$$

hence eccentricity of total load

$$= \frac{33.6 \times 1/6}{161} = 0.035$$

This is less than 0.05 which is the minimum design value.

Slenderness ratio
Effective thickness of cavity wall = ⅔ (90 + 140)
$$= 153.33$$
effective height = 0.75 × 2900 = 2175

$$\frac{l_e}{t} = 14.18$$

Design equation

$$N = \beta \frac{f_k}{\gamma_m} bt$$

$$\text{or} \quad \frac{N}{\beta} = \frac{f_k}{\gamma_m} bt$$

Table 7.4 gives values of $\frac{f_k}{\gamma_m} bt$ per metre of wall, hence we calculate $\frac{N}{\beta}$ and then look for a suitable block in Table 7.4.

From Table 7 of BS 5628

$$\beta = 0.89$$

hence $\quad \dfrac{N}{\beta} = \dfrac{161}{0.89} = 181 \text{ kN/m}$

As will be seen from Table 7.4 this is too much for a 5 N/mm² modular block (capacity 154 kN/m) and one would have to use a 10.5 N/mm² block (capacity 258 kN/m).

SOLUTION 3
Concentrated load under bearing*.
A precast floor unit is supported on a 140 mm wide block wall as sketched below. The wall is constructed from 5 N/mm² modular blocks. The wall is 2.9 m high. The beams are at 0.75 m centres.

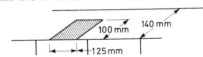

The end reactions from the beams are:
    Dead 5.5 kN
    Live 7.8 kN
The design ultimate reaction is thus:

$$5.5 \times 1.4 + 7.8 \times 1.6 = 20.18 \text{ kN}$$

The bearing stress is thus:

$$\frac{20.18 \times 1000}{125 \times 100} = 1.61 \text{ N/mm}^2$$

Inspection of Figure 4 in BS 5628 indicates that the bearing is Type 2. The local design stress is therefore $1.5 \frac{f_k}{\gamma_m}$. From Example 1, $\frac{f_k}{\gamma_m}$ for a 140 mm thick

*See *Chapter 10

modular block of 5 N/mm² is 1.10 N/mm². The permissible bearing stress is thus 1.65 N/mm². The stress immediately below the bearing is thus OK.

A check should also be done to ensure that the stress at 0.4 times the wall height below the bearing is less than $\beta \frac{f_k}{\gamma_m}$ assuming a 45° spread of load. 0.4 × 2.9 m = 1.07 m. However, since the beams are at 0.75 m intervals, the stresses will be uniform at a level of 0.75 m below the joint. A check on the whole wall for 1.6 L + 1.4 D will have ensured that this stress is OK, no further check is therefore needed.

SOLUTION 4
Simple shear wall

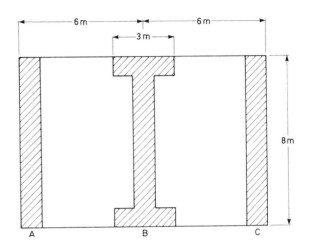

Structure is 12 m high, walls are of 140 mm thick solid blocks. Loading from floors and roof as in *Example 2*. The wind load may be assumed to be 0.5 kN/m² over the whole height.

Wind load on N face = 12 × 12 × 0.5 = 75 kN
Wind load on E face =   8 × 12 × 0.5 = 48 kN

These forces at 6 m from the ground.

Loads at base of walls (kN/m)

	A	B	C
Dead	76.4	152	76.4
Imposed	33.8	67.5	33.8

Consider wind from E or W. The only wall which will provide significant resistance is wall B.

Calculate second moment of area of B about N—S axis

$$= \frac{8 \times 0.19^3}{12} + \frac{2 \times 0.19 \times 3^3}{12} \text{ m}^4$$

$$= 0.0046 + 0.86 = 0.86 \text{ m}^4$$

Consider load case (b):

$$0.9 \, G_k + \text{greater of } 1.4 \, W_k \text{ or } 0.015 \, G_k$$

$$1.4 \, W_k = 1.4 \times 48 = 67.2 \text{ kN}$$

$$0.015 \, G_k = 8 \times (152 + 2 \times 76.4) \times 0.015$$

$$= 36.48 \text{ kN}$$

Design horizontal load = 67.2
Design vertical load = 0.9 × 152 × 8 = 1094

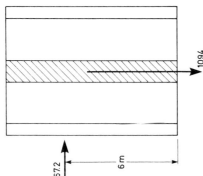

Length of wall = (8 + 3 + 3) = 14 m

∴ load on wall per metre = $\dfrac{1094}{14}$ = 78 kN/m

Stress at outer edges

$$= \frac{M_y}{I} + \frac{N_u}{A}$$

$$= \frac{3}{2} \frac{67.2 \times 6}{186} + \frac{78}{0.19}$$

$$= 703 + 411$$

$$= 114 \text{ kN/m}^2 = 1.1 \text{ N/mm}^2$$

$$= 212 \text{ kN/m}^2 \text{ of wall}$$

Slenderness ratio of wall = $\dfrac{2900 \times 0.15}{190}$ = 11.45

Eccentricity of load from floor onto returns can be assumed to be zero.

Hence β = 0.94

Hence required design capacity in kN/m

$$= \frac{212}{0.94} = 225 \text{ kN/m}$$

Table 7.4 shows that this can be achieved using a 10.5 N/mm² block.

Load case (c) should also be considered

Horizontal load = 1.2 × 48 − 57.6 kN

Vertical load = 1.2 × (152 + 67.5) × 8 = 2107.2 kN

similar to before:

$$\frac{N_u}{A} + \frac{M_y}{I} = \frac{2107}{14 \times 0.19} + \frac{57.6 \times 6 \times 3}{0.86 \times 2} \text{ kN/m}^2$$

$$= 792 + 603$$

$$= 1395 \text{ kN/m}^2$$

$$= 265 \text{ kN/m of wall}$$

As before, β = 0.94

∴ Design resistance = 282 kN/m

This is more critical than load case (b) but still within the capacity of a 10.5 N/mm² block which will take 292 kN/m (see Table 7.4).

Now consider wind from the other direction. This will be much less critical and is being done purely to illustrate the principal of splitting the wind forces be-

76

tween the three walls.

Calculate moments of intertia of walls about E—W axis

Walls A and C

$$I = \frac{0.19 \times 8^3}{12} = 8.11$$

Wall B

$$I = \frac{0.19 \times 8^3}{12} + 2 \times 0.19 \times 3 \times 4^2$$

$$= 26.35$$

Wind force is shared between walls in proportion to their stiffness. For load case (c) the design force is 57.6 kN

Wall A takes $\dfrac{57.6 \times 8.11}{2 \times 8.11 + 26.35}$ = 11 kN

Wall C will also take 11 kN
Wall B will take 35.6 kN

The capacity of the walls is checked as for bending in the other phase.

7.3.4 Strength of biaxially bent pier

PROBLEM AND SOLUTION 5

This is not a problem which is likely to arise very often in practice. Should such a problem arise, however, this example illustrates how it may be tackled within the intentions of the Code.

Check whether the pier having the cross section drawn below can withstand a vertical design load of 130 kN at an eccentricity in one direction of 125 mm and of 90 mm in the direction at right angles. The pier is hollow and is constructed of 5 N/mm² blocks in 1:1:6 mortar for which the value of $\dfrac{f_k}{\gamma_m}$ is 1.1 N/mm².

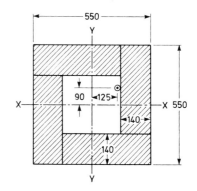

This problem can be solved by trial and error by guessing a neutral axis position and then estimating the position of the centroid of the area of the cross section in compression. When a neutral axis position has been found such that the centroid of the compressed area coincides with the centroid of the load, the axial load capacity can be calculated from the equation:

$$N = 1.1 \frac{f_k}{\gamma_m} A_c$$

where A_c = area of masonry in compression

If $N > 130$ kN, the section is satisfactory. The problem is probably best solved by drawing out the section to scale. Only two tries will be set out in detail here.

Try 1

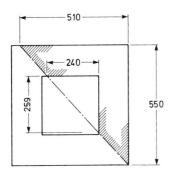

Area of compression zone $= \dfrac{510 \times 550}{2} - \dfrac{240 \times 259}{2}$

$$= 140\ 250 - 31\ 080$$

$$= 109\ 170 \text{ mm}^2$$

moments about Y—Y

$$140\ 250 \times \left(\frac{550}{2} - \frac{510}{3} \right)$$

$$- 31\ 080 \left(\frac{270}{2} - \frac{240}{3} \right) = 109\ 170\ \bar{x}$$

hence $\bar{x} = 119$

moments about X—X

$$140\ 250 \times \left(\frac{550}{2} - \frac{550}{3} \right)$$

$$- 31\ 080 \left(\frac{270}{2} - \frac{259}{3} \right) = 109\ 170\ \bar{y}$$

hence $\bar{y} = 104$ mm

$\bar{x} = 125$, $\bar{y} = 90$ is required.

It is necessary to increase $\bar{x}$ very slightly and decrease $\bar{y}$ by about 14%. Moving the neutral axis to the right without rotation will increase $\bar{x}$, clockwise rotation of the neutral axis line will decrease $\bar{y}$.

Try 2

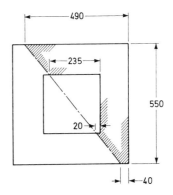

Area of compression zone

$$= 550 \times 40 + \frac{450 \times 550}{2} - 270 \times 20 - \frac{215 \times 270}{2}$$

$$= 22\ 000 + 123\ 750 - 5400 - 29\ 029$$

$$= 111\ 325 \text{ mm}^2$$

Moments about Y—Y

$$22\ 000 \times \left(\frac{550}{2} - \frac{40}{13} \right)$$

$$+ 123\ 750 \left(\frac{550}{2} - 40 - \frac{450}{3} \right)$$

$$- 5400 \left(\frac{270}{2} - \frac{20}{2} \right)$$

$$- 29\ 029 \left(\frac{270}{2} - \frac{215}{3} \right) = 111\ 325\ \bar{x}$$

Hence $\bar{x} = 122.3$

Moments about X—X

$$123\ 750 \left(\frac{550}{2} - \frac{550}{3} \right)$$

$$- 29\ 029 \left(\frac{270}{2} - \frac{270}{3} \right) = 111\ 325\ \bar{y}$$

Hence $\bar{y} = 90.16$

This is close enough to 125 and 90.

Vertical load capacity with this eccentricity

$$= \frac{1.1 \times 1.1 \times 111\ 325}{10\ 000} \text{ kN}$$

$$= 134.7 \text{ kN}$$

This is greater than 130 therefore design is satisfactory.

7.4 References

7.1 READ, J B, AND CLEMENTS, S W. The strength of concrete block walls. Phase III: Effects of workmanship, mortar strength and bond pattern. Cement and Concrete Association, London, 1977. Publication No 42.518. pp 10

7.2 CRANSTON, W B, AND ROBERTS, J J. The structural behaviour of concrete masonry — reinforced and unreinforced. *The Structural Engineer, Vol 54,* No 11, November 1976. pp 423—436

7.3 INTERNATIONAL STANDARDS ORGANIZATION. General principles for the verification of safety of structures. *ISO 2394,* February 1973.

7.4 NATIONAL CONCRETE MASONRY ASSOCIATION OF AMERICA, VIRGINIA. Technical Report No 37, 1952.

7.5 PEARCE, D J, AND MATTHEWS, D D. An appraisal of the design of shear walls in box frame structures. Property Services Agency, London, 1972.

8

Lateral loading on plain masonry

8.1 Background

Chapter 7 deals with the design of walls subject to vertical loads and walls subject to both vertical and lateral loads. There are, however, many walls, for instance those used for cladding steel or concrete portal framed buildings, subjected to predominantly lateral loads with the vertical load being very small or limited to self weight. Thus it is often necessary to check the adequacy of a non-vertical loadbearing wall to resist wind pressure. This need for some specific design information for laterally loaded walls was brought sharply into focus when the deemed-to-satisfy *Schedule 7* of the *1972 Building Regulations*[8.1] introduced restrictions limiting its application to residential buildings of not more than three storeys and certain small single storey structures in areas where the design wind speed does not exceed 44 m/sec. Previously *Schedule 7* covered a wider range of structures.

The application of CP 111[8.2] to the design of walls to resist wind pressures has caused difficulties to engineers over the years despite the introduction of an amendment in 1970 specifying permissible tensile stresses in the bed and perpend joints, because the scope of the Code remained unamended and can be interpreted as applying only to walls with significant vertical load. There was also a somewhat ambiguous statement that in general no reliance should be placed on the tensile strength of masonry in calculations but that the engineer could, at his discretion, design for tensile stresses. To complicate matters further the designer, having already taken responsibility to allow for tensile stresses, had very little published information to enable him to evaluate the bending moments in the panel. In practice, however, many designs were carried out using the permissible tensile values given in CP 111. Bending moments being either arbitrarily assessed or determined by using, for example, the bending moment coefficients available for two way spanning reinforced concrete slabs. It must be said that few failures of such designs have occurred, and those which have, have been due to inadequate edge fixing of the panels or because no structural calculations were carried out at all. To partially remedy the situation some simple rules for assessing the size of a wall subject to wind pressures were introduced in 1975 as an amendment to CP 121[8.3]. These rules are currently being amended to include panels with openings and will be given in the next edition of this Code. This is a useful approach but is limited in application. It became clear when drafting BS 5628[8.4] that the engineer still required more comprehensive design methods properly supported by research evidence.

Some work was carried out by Isaacs[8.5] as early as 1948. Several other papers on the strength of walls in lateral loading and the effect of the bond between the mortar and the masonry have been written, the most notable ones being referred to in the following sections. However, there was still insufficient data available in the early 1970s to put forward a positive design procedure. As a result, considerable research was undertaken in the UK from around 1973 with the result that for the first time a definite design procedure has been given in BS 5628[8.4], the current limit state version of CP 111[8.2]. The majority of the research[8.6, 8.7] was conducted by the British Ceramic Research Association for clay brickwork and by the Concrete Block Association for concrete blockwork. In addition, some special sponsored work on flexural strength, supervized by the Building Research Establishment has been carried out at the British Ceramic Research

Association at the request of the Property Services Agency on both brick and concrete block masonry. This work was extended to deal with calcium silicate bricks and concrete bricks.

So far reference has only been made to the stability of walls as determined by the flexural strength of the masonry. As well as this method BS 5628 permits an approach based on arching. Most of the information in this Chapter is devoted to the flexural strength method although some guidance is given on the arching method.

8.1.1 Method 1—Flexural strength approach

Determining the lateral load capacity of a wall panel based on attainment of ultimate tensile stresses in the bed joint and perpend joints.

The problem of determining the lateral load capacity of a masonry wall revolves around two basic points: (a) the flexural strength of the masonry and (b) the distribution of bending moments induced in the panel.

8.1.1.1 Characteristic flexural strengths The research work referred to above demonstrates that items which have the major influence on the flexural strength of masonry are: (i) the composition and strength of the mortar, (ii) the initial flow of the mortar and (iii) the curing conditions. Of these items it is reasonable to expect the safety factors and permitted stresses to accommodate (ii) and (iii). With regard to item (i), this is covered by allowing different stresses for different strength mortars. The variation in the air content of the various mortar mixes within any particular designation, i.e. cement:sand:lime, cement:sand with plasticizer and masonry cement:sand, is not considered to make an appreciable difference to the adhesion according to BS 5628, although subsequent evidence indicates this may have some effect.

In addition, the flexural strength of concrete block masonry was found to be broadly related to the compressive strength of the units. With clay bricks it was found in contrast that the water absorption of the unit was a major parameter. Thus in Table 8.1 (taken from BS 5628) the characteristic flexural strength of clay bricks relates to water absorption and that of concrete blocks to compressive strength. The strength and water absorption of calcium silicate and concrete bricks are fairly constant and therefore only one stress is given.

Table 8.1 Characteristic flexural strength of masonry (f_{kx})

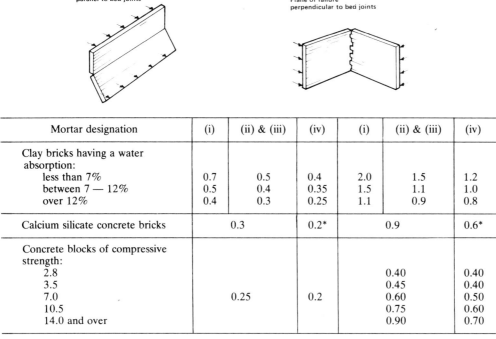

Mortar designation	(i)	(ii) & (iii)	(iv)	(i)	(ii) & (iii)	(iv)
Clay bricks having a water absorption:						
less than 7%	0.7	0.5	0.4	2.0	1.5	1.2
between 7 — 12%	0.5	0.4	0.35	1.5	1.1	1.0
over 12%	0.4	0.3	0.25	1.1	0.9	0.8
Calcium silicate concrete bricks		0.3	0.2*		0.9	0.6*
Concrete blocks of compressive strength:						
2.8					0.40	0.40
3.5					0.45	0.40
7.0		0.25	0.2		0.60	0.50
10.5					0.75	0.60
14.0 and over					0.90	0.70

*Applicable to calcium silicate bricks; values for concrete bricks to be established.

8.1.1.2 Behaviour of wall panels The research work on flexural strength was mainly carried out on prisms of masonry or on small wallettes subject to bending either across the bed joints or across the perpend joints. Quite a number of tests[8.6, 8.7] on actual wall

80

panels have also been carried out, covering clay, calcium silicate and concrete units. The failure loads were found to be different depending upon the flexural strength of the materials, but the actual mode of failure was broadly similar for panels of similar size and having the same support conditions. Patterns of cracking observed on the inside faces for typical walls are shown in Figure 8.1. The failure patterns are reasonably similar to what would be expected from reinforced concrete slabs analysed in accordance with yield line theory. Yield line theory was, of course, developed for use with reinforced concrete in which it is assumed that the element has sufficient ductility to enable several lines to develop with constant moment until there are sufficient to cause failure. It is clear that a masonry wall cannot truly behave in the same manner since it is a brittle material and is thus not capable of holding its moment across a line after a crack has formed. Despite this, however, yield line theory has been found to be a reasonable method for predicting the capacity of walls. The coefficients given in Table 9 of the Code and the tables to this Chapter (*Section 8.4*) were derived by yield line theory. For many designs it will be a simple matter of using the coefficients given but there will be occasions where it may be desirable to refer directly to the basic yield line equation as, for example, in the case of a wall of irregular shape or one with openings.

There are a number of text books and publications on the subject of yield line analysis but the most commonly available are those by Johansen[8.9, 8.15] Jones[8.10], Jones and Wood[8.11] and the publication by Comité Européan du Béton[8.12]. The derivation of yield line formula is outside the scope of this handbook as indeed would a comprehensive review of formula for various panel shapes be.

Reference should, therefore, be made to the above documents when detailed information is required, but for convenience, formula relating to the three standard panel shapes as given in the Code are given below. Further information with regard to panels of irregular shape and with openings is given in *Sections 8.2.6* and *8.2.7*. An alternative ultimate load analysis using a fracture line approach has also been proposed by Sinha[8.13, 8.14].

A comprehensive thesis dealing with laterally loaded masonry walls both unreinforced and reinforced with bed joint reinforcement has recently been prepared by Cajdert[8.16] of Sweden. The thesis covers work carried out in Sweden and other countries including the UK.

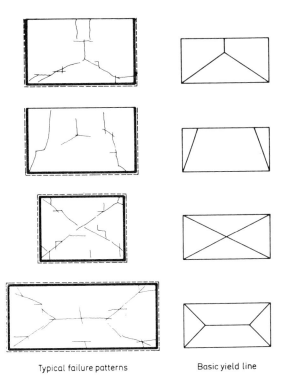

Typical failure patterns   Basic yield line

Figure 8.1 Patterns of cracking observed on the inside faces for typical walls

PANEL WITH FREE TOP EDGE

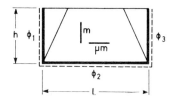

$$\alpha = \dfrac{\left(\dfrac{h}{L}\right)^2}{6\mu}\left(\dfrac{1}{[(3 + \phi_2) \div Y^2] - 1}\right)$$

where $Y = \sqrt{\left(\left[\dfrac{\sqrt{1 + \phi_1} + \sqrt{1 + \phi_3}}{\sqrt{\left[\dfrac{\mu}{\left(\dfrac{h}{L}\right)^2}(3 + \phi_2)\right]}}\right]^2 + 3\right) - \left(\dfrac{\sqrt{1 + \phi_1} + \sqrt{1 + \phi_3}}{\sqrt{\left[\dfrac{\mu}{\left(\dfrac{h}{L}\right)^2}(3 + \phi_2)\right]}}\right)}$

Failure pattern (ii)

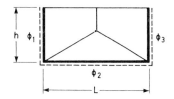

$$\alpha = \dfrac{1}{6Y_{13}{}^2}\left[\sqrt{\left(3 + \dfrac{\mu Y_2{}^2}{\left(\dfrac{h}{L}\right)^2 Y_{13}{}^2}\right)} - \dfrac{\sqrt{\mu}\, Y_2}{\left(\dfrac{h}{L}\right)Y_{13}}\right]^2$$

where $Y_2 = \sqrt{1 + \phi_2}$ $Y_{13} = \sqrt{1 + \phi_1} + \sqrt{1 + \phi_3}$

The perpend moment of resistance required so that a uniform lateral load, W_k, can be carried is given by:

$$m = \alpha\, W_k\, \lambda_f\, L^2$$

where α = bending moment coefficient greater of above equations

W_k = characteristic wind load

λ_f = partial safety factor for load

In both yield line equations

μ = orthogonal ratio

$= \dfrac{\text{moment of resistance on bed joint}}{\text{moment of resistance perpendicular to bed joint}}$

ϕ = degree of fixity at support

$= \dfrac{\text{moment of resistance at support}}{\text{moment of resistance of span}}$

i.e. 0 for pinned (simple) support

    1 for fixed support

Failure pattern (i)

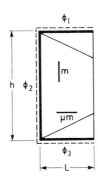

$$\alpha = \frac{1}{6}\left(\frac{1}{[3 + \phi_2) \div Y^2] - 1}\right)$$

where $Y = \sqrt{\left(\left[\frac{\sqrt{1 + \phi_1} + \sqrt{1 + \phi_3}}{\sqrt{\left[\frac{\left(\frac{h}{L}\right)^2}{\mu}(3 + \phi_2)\right]}}\right]^2 + 3\right) - \left(\frac{\sqrt{1 + \phi_1} + \sqrt{1 + \phi_3}}{\sqrt{\left[\frac{\left(\frac{h}{L}\right)^2}{\mu}(3 + \phi_2)\right]}}\right)}$

Failure pattern (ii)

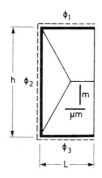

$$\alpha = \frac{\left(\frac{h}{L}\right)^2}{6\mu Y_{13}{}^2}\left[\sqrt{\left(3 + \frac{\left(\frac{h}{L}\right)^2 Y_2{}^2}{\mu Y_{13}{}^2}\right)} - \frac{\sqrt{\frac{1}{\mu}}\left(\frac{h}{L}\right)Y_2}{Y_{13}}\right]^2$$

where $Y_2 = \sqrt{1 + \phi_2}$ $Y_{13} = \sqrt{1 + \phi_1} + \sqrt{1 + \phi_3}$

again $m = \alpha W_k \lambda_f L^2$

W_k, λ_f, μ and ϕ as before

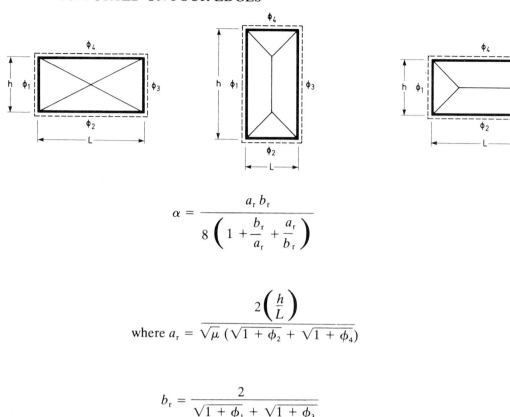

$$\alpha = \frac{a_r b_r}{8\left(1 + \dfrac{b_r}{a_r} + \dfrac{a_r}{b_r}\right)}$$

$$\text{where } a_r = \frac{2\left(\dfrac{h}{L}\right)}{\sqrt{\mu}\left(\sqrt{1 + \phi_2} + \sqrt{1 + \phi_4}\right)}$$

$$b_r = \frac{2}{\sqrt{1 + \phi_1} + \sqrt{1 + \phi_3}}$$

$$m = \alpha W_k \lambda_f L^2$$

W_k, λ_f, μ and ϕ as before

8.1.2 Method 2—Arching approach

The alternative method given in BS 5628 for the design of walls subjected to lateral loads is, as mentioned previously, based on the assumption that an arch thrust can be developed in the plane of a wall which is built solidly between rigid supports. The concept of this design approach may be illustrated by considering the member shown in Figure 8.2 which illustrates a horizontally spanning wall being subjected to a lateral load q_{lat}, the central deflection under this load being δ.

From Figure 8.1, and by reference to Figure 8.3 which shows the compressive blocks at supports and mid span, the internal compressive force n is equal to the permitted compressive stress multiplied by the depth of the compressive block. Thus $n = fx$

This force is being applied internally over a level arm a. The internal moment of resistance

$$\begin{aligned} M_i &= na \\ &= f_x\left(t - \frac{x}{2} - \frac{x}{2} - \delta\right) \\ &= f_x(t - x - \delta) \end{aligned}$$

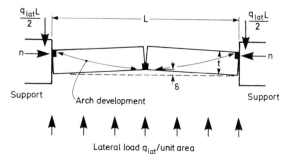

Figure 8.2

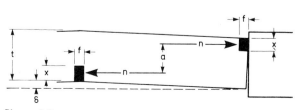

Figure 8.3

The applied moment over the span L gives:

$$M = \frac{q_{lat}L^2}{8}$$

Since for equilibrium the internal and external moments must balance, then:

$$\frac{q_{lat}L^2}{8} = fx\,(t - x - \delta)$$

$$\text{i.e. } q_{lat} = 8fx\frac{(t - x - \delta)}{L^2}$$

Now from BS 5628 the characteristic strength of masonry under these conditions may be taken as $1.5\,f_k$, and the depth of the compressive block is assumed to be $0.1\,t$. The ultimate design load q_{lat} predicted using the simplified and conservative approach with a partial safety factor for masonry of γ_m is determined as follows:

$$q_{lat} = \frac{8 \times 1.5\,f_k \times 0.1\,t\,(t - 0.1\,t - \delta)}{\gamma_m L^2}$$

$$= \frac{f_k}{\gamma_m}\frac{1.2\,t\,(0.9\,t - \delta)}{L^2}$$

When deflection, δ, equals 0 then the ultimate design load tends towards

$$q_{lat} = \frac{f_k}{\gamma_m}\left(\frac{t}{L}\right)^2 1.08$$

In BS 5628, Clause 36.4, we find for simplicity that in a panel of $L/t < 25$ the deflection can be ignored and that the design load may be found from the equation:

$$q_{lat} = \frac{f_k}{\gamma_m}\left(\frac{t}{L}\right)^2$$

It is reasonable to consider that the 1.08 figure was rounded down to 1.0 since some small deflections even at $L/t < 25$ may occur. An alternative and perhaps better way is to simply state that the equation given in Clause 36.4 of BS 5628:Part 1 will be conservative providing $\delta \leq 0.067\,t$ since putting this value into the above equation results in $q_{lat} = f_k/\gamma_m\,(t/L)^2$

The statement made in the opening paragraph of this section with regard to rigid supports and the subsequent illustration given in Figure 8.3 seem to suggest that the arch approach can only be made when a panel spans between two columns. This is not necessarily the case since the Code also makes reference to walls built continuously past the support. In this instance the arch approach can be applied to a section of wall providing that the wall which continues past the support has sufficient strength to resist the internal arch force n. Obviously even the column or member providing the support, as in the case of a wall as shown in Figure 8.2, must also be capable of resisting the arch thrust. The support itself must also be able to resist the applied lateral load with negligible deflection.

The formula for q_{lat} given in BS 5628 and reproduced above may be used provided that the length/thickness is not greater than 25 and provided that there is no appreciable reduction in the length of the wall due to moisture and thermal movements. The Code gives no guidance on determination of the deflection in the wall or allowance for the effects of movement. These aspects have been considered and the following approach is suggested. Shortening will arise due to:

(a) the axial load or thrust in the arch

(b) shrinkage movements

(c) thermal movements

The deflection of the supports must of course also be small. To put the matter into perspective, it is of interest to look at the effects of shortening. Consider Figures 8.4 and 8.5 which show a wall in which shortening of L_s has taken place. It is required to assess the deflection, δ. Assuming that θ is small (an assumption that is checked later), then

$$t \sin \theta = t\,\theta$$

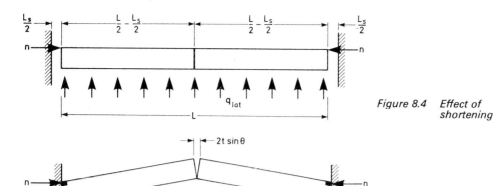

Figure 8.4 Effect of shortening

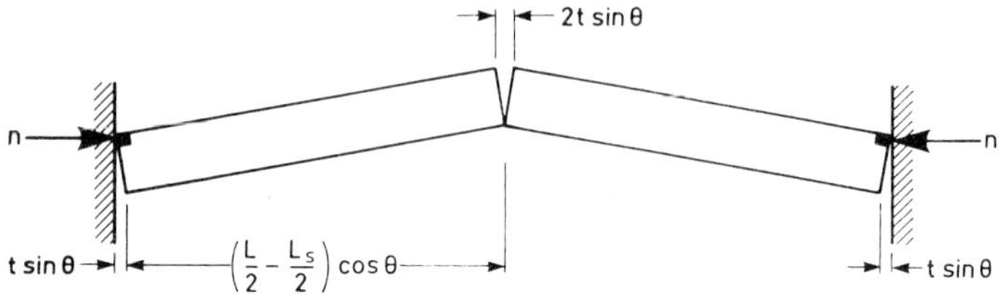

Figure 8.5 Effect of shortening

$$\frac{L}{2} - \frac{L_s}{2} \cos \theta = \frac{L}{2} - \frac{L_s}{2} = \frac{L}{2}$$

It follows then that

$$L_s = 4\, t\, \theta = \frac{4\, t\, \delta}{\dfrac{L}{2}} = \frac{8\, t\, \delta}{L}$$

and hence

$$\delta = \frac{L_s\, L}{8\, t}$$

It can also be useful to be able to calculate the actual arch thrust per unit depth of wall. The application of statics gives

$$n = \frac{q_{\text{lat}}\, L^2}{8\, (0.9\, t - \delta)}$$

Two practical examples will now be considered.

EXAMPLE 1

Consider a wall with a span of 4.75 m and a thickness of 190 mm (i.e., span/depth 25). The effects of shortening due to a shrinkage strain of 400×10^{-6} and a shortening under axial load of 100×10^{-6}, are to be assessed.

$$L_s = 4.75 \times 5 \times 10^{-6} \times 10^{-3} = 2.4 \text{ mm}$$

$$\therefore \delta = \frac{2.4 \times 4.75 \times 10^{-3}}{8 \times 190} = 7.5 \text{ mm} = 0.039\, t$$

The strain used in the example is tending towards the maximum which would normally be expected in practice and yet δ is considerably less than $0.067\, t$ and therefore indicates why the effect of deflection in members with a span/depth ratio not greater than 25 may be neglected.

Now $\theta = \dfrac{7.5}{2375} = 0.00316$ rad.

and $\cos \theta = 0.999995$

This is equivalent to a further shortening strain of 5×10^{-6} which is negligible in comparison to the basic 500×10^{-6} originally considered. Thus the capacity of the arch may be determined from formula

$$q_{\text{lat}} = \frac{f_k}{\gamma_m} \frac{1.2\, t\, (0.9\, t - \delta)}{L^2}$$

For a unit with a characteristic strength of 3.5 N/mm² and adopting $\gamma_m = 3.5$, this gives:

$$q_{\text{lat}} = \frac{3.5 \times 1.2 \times 0.19\, (0.9 \times 0.19 - 0.0075) \times 10^{-6}}{3.5 \times 4.75^2}$$

$$= 1.65 \text{ kN/m}^2$$

If the effect of the deflection had not been determined, the q_{lat} from Clause 36.4 would have been:

$$q_{lat} = \frac{3.5 \times 10^{-6}}{3.5} \left(\frac{0.19}{4.75}\right)^2 = 1.6 \text{ kN/m}^2$$

EXAMPLE 2

Consider a wall which spans 5.00 m and is 100 mm thick and resisting an ultimate load q_{lat} of 0.6 kN/m². Estimate the deflection arising from an axial shortening due to thrust and shrinkage of 400×10^{-6}. Check the design assuming $f_k = 6.4$ N/mm².

$$L_s = 400 \times 5.0 \times 10^{-6} = 2 \text{ mm}$$

$$\delta = \frac{L_s L}{8\, t} = \frac{2 \times 5000}{800} = 12.5 \text{ mm}$$

$$\theta = \frac{12.5}{2500} = 0.05 \text{ radians}$$

$$\therefore \text{Cos } \theta = 0.9999875$$

This is equivalent to a further shortening strain of 12.5×10^{-6}, which is negligible. Thus the capacity of q_{lat}

$$= \frac{7 \times 1.2 \times 100\,(90 - 12.5) \times 10^3}{3.5 \times 5000^2}$$

$$= 0.74 \text{ kN/m}^2 > 0.6 \text{ kN/m}^2$$

therefore wall will be acceptable..

The actual thrust developed at ultimate

$$= \frac{q_{lat}\, L^2}{8\,(0.9\, t - \delta)}$$

$$= \frac{0.6 \times 5^2 \times 10^3}{8\,(90 - 12.5)}$$

$$= 24.2 \text{ kN/m depth of wall.}$$

To check that the support is acceptable it is simply a matter of determining the deflection of the support member carrying the thrust, in this case 24.2 kN/m, and adding this additional δ into the q_{lat} formula. If q_{lat} is still greater than the applied lateral load then the supports are adequate. If not, the support must be stiffer.

8.2 Design to BS 5628:Part 1

The general design procedure of BS 5628 is interactive in that the following approach is required:

(1) make initial assumption of support conditions;

(2) make assumptions as to strength of unit required;

(3) determine orthogonal ratio μ and hence bending moment coefficient α;

(4) determine flexural strength required;

(5) check flexural strength of chosen masonry;

(6) if too low return to either (1) or (2) and modify.

In addition, a similar approach is required to check for shear, slenderness and ties to supports. These various factors are examined in greater detail as follows.

8.2.1 Support conditions

The support conditions have to be assessed first. The Code covers most of the common uses (Figure 8.6). A free edge is easily identified but some judgement is necessary in deciding between simply supported or fixed. In the examples given in the Code reference is made to "fixity at the discretion of the engineer". The engineer appears to have two alternatives, to consider the support as either pinned or fixed. It would be simple to

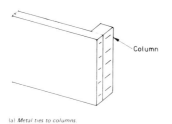

(a) Metal ties to columns.

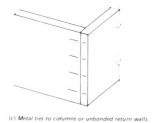

(c) Metal ties to columns or unbonded return walls.

(b) Bonded return walls.

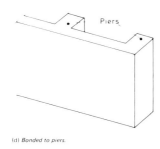

(d) Bonded to piers.

Figure 8.6   (a) metal ties to column – normally simple support but possible degree of fixity with rigid supports and stiff well anchored ties
(b) bonded return walls – degree of fixity at the discretion of the designer, the shorter the return the less the fixity – very short returns could reach free edge condition
(c) metal ties to return walls – normally simple support but possible degree of fixity with stiff wall anchored ties
(d) bonded to piers – intermediate pier, degree of fixity at discretion of engineer. End pier, simple support or free edge where pier insufficient to carry reaction

suggest that if in doubt the worst condition should be assumed. Unfortunately, this wording tends to be rather restrictive and it would appear better to suggest that the worst *practical* condition should be assumed. This would then allow an engineer and a checking authority to take a more reasonable line to a particular problem. For example, if in a certain design it is clear that the support is not a pinned condition, but there is doubt about the support being fully fixed then it would seem reasonable to allow for partial fixity. Obviously, if serious doubts do exist then the worst condition, pinned, must be assumed. If doubts exist about a pinned condition then it would certainly be better to consider that as a free edge. The text to the illustration (Figure 8.6) in the handbook showing support conditions has deliberately been reworded to bring the readers attention to the fact that only partial fixity may exist.

8.2.1.1 Accommodation for movement   It is appropriate while considering the vertical support condition to draw the readers attention to the question of accommodation of movements within the wall. Provision for movement may necessitate the inclusion of movement joints within the wall which may alter the initial assessment of the support conditions. This matter will also need to be reconsidered when the actual panel size is being determined to ensure that the designed length is not greater than the acceptable length between movement joints otherwise cracking may result.

8.2.1.2 Effect of tied piers   It is usual with concrete blockwork to use tied piers rather than fully bonded piers. This, however, will make little difference to the support condition since end piers are generally only taken as simple supports. Intermediate piers are often taken as fixed supports but since it is the continuing wall rather than the pier which provides the fixity it again makes little difference.

8.2.2 Design of solid single leaf walls

Having considered and assessed the support conditions the next stage is to determine the bending moments which occur in the panel as a result of the applied lateral load and hence calculate the required thickness or characteristic flexural strength.

The general design procedure may be split into four basic forms: (a) free standing walls, (b) vertically spanning walls, (c) horizontally spanning walls, and (d) walls which span in two directions — these include both three-sided and four-sided supported walls.

8.2.2.1 Free standing walls   From Clause 36.5.2 it may be seen that the design moment of resistance of a free standing wall subject to horizontal forces is given by:

$$m = W_k \, \gamma_f \, \frac{h^2}{2} + Q_k \, \gamma_f \, h_L$$

88

where

m = design moment per unit length

W_k = characteristic lateral load

γ_f = partial safety factor for loads

h = clear height of wall or pier above restraint

Q_k = characteristic imposed load

h_L = vertical distance between the point of application of the horizontal load, Q_k, and the lateral restraint.

In the case of wind load only: $\qquad m = W_k\, \gamma_f\, \dfrac{h^2}{2}$

8.2.2.2 Vertically spanning walls In accordance with Clause 36.4.2 it will be found that the design bending moment per unit length of a wall spanning vertically may be written as:

$$m = \alpha\, W_k\, \gamma_f\, h^2$$

where:

m = design moment per unit length

W_k = characteristic lateral load

γ_f = partial safety factor for loads

h = height between horizontal supports

α = bending moment coefficient

For walls which have simple supports at both top and bottom we find that the bending moment coefficient is taken as for any other member which has a uniformly distributed load over a simple span, i.e.

$$\alpha = 0.125$$

thus $m = 0.125\, W_k\, \gamma_f\, h^2$

or $\dfrac{W_k\, \gamma_f\, h^2}{8}$ as given in the Code.

The general approach has been explained in this way rather than giving the Code formula directly since the general formula $m = \alpha\, W_k\, \gamma_f\, X^2$ can be used to apply to all walls.

Vertically spanning walls will often have simple supports top and bottom as may be the case in single storey structures. However, the Code does indicate that allowance may be made, even in walls which span vertically, for any fixity which occurs at the supports. In this type of member the bending moment may be determined from the following formula:

$$m = \frac{W_k\, \gamma_f\, h^2}{2} \left[\frac{1}{\sqrt{1 \times \phi_1} + \sqrt{1 \times \phi_2}} \right]^2$$

where m = design bending moment per unit length

ϕ_1 and ϕ_2 = degree of fixity at each support

W_k = characteristic wind load

γ_f = partial safety factor for loads

h = distance between supports

Some attention, however, needs to be given to the values of fixity taken at the supports since the presence of horizontal damp-proof courses may limit the amount of flexural strength which can be developed. This is particularly important with walls spanning vertically only since total reliance is made on the flexural strength of the bed joints.

Obviously where the self weight stresses and any stress due to light vertical loads at the support under consideration is greater than the characteristic strength of the bed joint divided by the partial safety factor for materials, i.e. $g_d \geq f_b/\gamma_m$ then full fixity may be assumed. Where the stress is less than f_b/γ_m then the fixity will be at least $g_d/(f_b/\gamma_m)$.

It may be argued that this approach does not allow for any direct flexural strength given by the bed joint. However, this may be justified since some redistribution of bending moments over that found by normal elastic analysis of moments in beams has already been used to produce the yield line moments. If direct flexural strengths are allowed for, it may be more appropriate to determine the moments by normal elastic analysis with no allowance for redistribution. Where appreciable vertical loads are in existence then it will be advisable to design as indicated in *Chapter 7*.

Where piers are incorporated in a vertical spanning wall the load carried by the pier should be assessed from normal structural principles — for example, in a wall with piers the walls may be considered as spanning horizontally between the pier and the piers designed as spanning vertically carrying the load exerted on it by the span of the wall, the section modulus of the pier being assessed as recommended in Clause 36.4.3 of BS 5628. When the piers are closely spaced (flange width equal to distance between piers) then the wall will tend to act as a stiffened plate and thus the full section modulus may be adopted in assessing the moment of resistance of the wall.

8.2.2.3 Horizontally spanning walls There is no section in the Code dealing directly with the design of walls assumed to span horizontally. However, in the text to Table 9 it is indicated that a panel having h/l greater than 1.75 will tend to span horizontally, thus it may be taken that it is acceptable to design a panel on the assumption of only spanning horizontally. When the aspect ratio is less than 1.75 it will be more economical to design as a two way span.

By reference to Clause 36.4.2 and to the general design approach adopted earlier, the design bending moment per unit *height* for a wall spanning horizontally may be taken as:

$$M = \alpha\, W_k\, \gamma_f\, L^2$$

in which W_k and γ_f are as before,

L = length between vertical supports and α is again the bending moment coefficient for which a span between simple supports may be taken as $\alpha = 0.125$.
Thus

$$m = 0.125\, W_k\, \gamma_f\, L^2$$

$$\frac{W_k\, \gamma_f\, L^2}{8}$$

It is again logical that account may be taken for any fixity that occurs at the supports but since there is no direct reference made to partially fixed edges as there is with vertically spanning walls it may be assumed that full fixity can be taken in cases where this is justified. Therefore, the bending moment coefficient for a panel with fully fixed supports can be expected to reach 0.063, giving:

$$m = 0.063\, W_k\, \gamma_f\, L^2$$

$$\frac{W_k\, \gamma_f\, L^2}{16}$$

8.2.2.4 Walls spanning in two directions This type of wall includes panels with one free edge such as the U shape and C shape panels as they are referred to as well as panels which are supported on all four sides.

The general expression for the required design bending moment per unit *height* of these types of panels is given in Clause 36.4.2 as:

$$m = \alpha W_k\, \gamma_f L^2$$

The symbols α, W_k and γ_f are as previously defined, but it is important to note that L = horizontal distance between vertical supports or the distance between the vertical support and the free edge in the case of C shaped panels.

The coefficients given in Table 9 of BS 5628 and in the tables given in *Section 8.4* of this handbook for C shaped panels (panels J, K, L, p.22, Table 9) are given for use with the horizontal length L. Thus in the text given in the first edition of the Code, Clause 36.4.2, 'L' is misleading in stating that L is the length between supports.

With this type of panel α depends on:

(a) support conditions — free, pinned, fixed;

90

(b) aspect ratio $\dfrac{h}{L}$

(c) orthogonal ratio μ.

Support conditions
To establish the bending moment coefficient, α, account must first be taken of the support conditions as explained in detail in *Section 8.2.1.*

Aspect ratio
Another factor which influences the bending moments in a panel is its aspect ratio, which is simply the ratio of the height between supports divided by the length of the panel either between supports or between a vertical support and the free edge h/l. Where the aspect ratio is between 0.3 and 1.75 the panel will tend to span in two directions. When h/l is less than 0.3 the Code indicates that the wall will tend to cantilever towards the free edge. When h/l is greater than 1.75 the wall will tend to span one way across the shortest dimension.

Orthogonal ratio
The orthogonal ratio is defined as being the ratio of the flexural strength of the masonry when failure is parallel to the bed joints to that when failure is perpendicular to the bed joints. The charcteristic flexural strength of masonry is given in Table 3 of the Code and is given the general symbol f_{kx}. For convenience, however, and to avoid confusion as to which strength is used under which conditions, the following terms will be used in the following text and examples:

f_{kb} = characteristic flexural strength when failure is parallel to the bed joints (see Figure 8.7)

f_{kp} = characteristic flexural strength when failure is perpendicular to the bed joints (see Figure 8.8)

thus for general cases the orthogonal ratio, $\mu = \dfrac{f_{kb}}{f_{kp}}$

Clause 36.4.2 indicates that the orthogonal ratio may be calculated allowing for any vertical load that acts so as to increase the flexural strength along the bed joint. Generally, it is the self weight of the wall which is to be considered, but to take accurate account of the effect of self weight is difficult since the effective stress on the bed joints, and thus the orthogonal ratio, varies within the height of the wall. An acceptable simplification is to determine the self weight stress at mid-height of the panel and to use this with the characteristic flexural strength, f_{kb}, to determine a constant orthogonal ratio.

As the flexural strength in Table 3 of BS 5628 is given in characteristic terms and the self weight stresses in ultimate design terms, the former may be modified by the partial safety factor for material before adding to g_d. Thus the modification to allow for self weight gives:

$$\mu = \dfrac{\dfrac{f_{kb}}{\gamma_m} + f_{self}}{\dfrac{f_{kp}}{\gamma_m}}$$

where f_{self} = design self weight stress at mid-height
γ_m = partial safety factor for materials
which can be simplified to give the Code formula: $\mu = \dfrac{f_{kb} + f_{self} \cdot \gamma_m}{f_{kp}}$

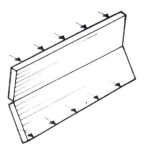

Figure 8.7 Plane of failure parallel to bed joints

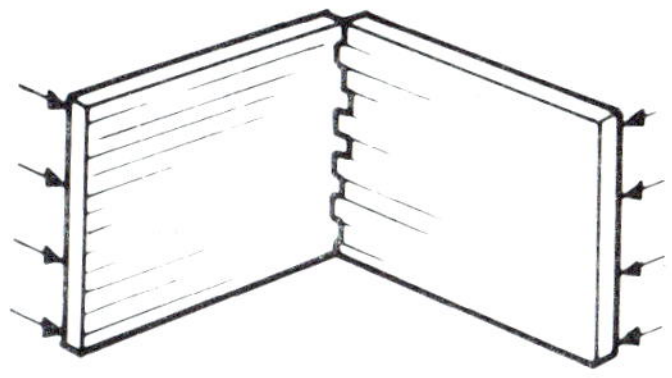

Figure 8.8 Plane of failure perpendicular to bed joints

Adopting the suggestion of using the self weight stress at mid-height of the panel and allowing for a partial safety factor for load of 0.9 gives, for single storey panel:

$$f_{self} = 0.5\,h\,W_d\,9.81 \times 10^{-6} \times 0.9$$
$$= 4.4 \times 10^{-6}\,h\,W_d$$

where h = panel height
W_d = density of wall

8.2.2.5 Moment of resistance of panel Having determined required m, a check has to be made that the masonry can be of that strength.

The ultimate moment of resistance of panels subject to bending, when assuming elastic distribution, is given in Clause 36.4.3 of the Code as:

$$M_u = \frac{f_{kx}}{\gamma_m} Z$$

for panels spanning vertically this is more conveniently written as:

$$M_u = \frac{f_{kb}}{\gamma_m} Z \text{ or } M_u = \left(\frac{f_{kb}}{\gamma_m} + f_{self} \right) Z$$

where self weight and small vertical loads act on the wall.

For panels spanning either horizontally or in two directions this is again more conveniently written as:

$$M_u = \frac{f_{kp}}{\gamma_m} Z$$

where γ_m = partial safety factor for materials
Z = section modulus

With panels spanning in two directions it is only necessary to determine M_u in the direction parallel to the perpend joint. This is because the coefficients given in Table 9 of BS 5628 have been derived to give moments in this direction. Moments and hence stresses along the bed joints do not need to be determined since these are automatically allowed for by using the orthogonal ratio in the formula used to determine coefficients.

For a plain wall spanning vertically $Z = \frac{bt^2}{6}$

In assessing the section modulus of a wall containing piers (Figure 8.9), the outstanding length of flange from the face of the pier should be taken as (a) $4 \times$ thickness of wall forming the flange when the flange is unrestrained, or (b) $6 \times$ thickness of wall forming the flange when the flange is continuous, but in no case more than half* the distance between the piers. Obviously the appropriate section modulus must be determined depending on which face is in tension. Allowance for the section modulus of a wall with piers only applies when assessing the bending stresses in a vertically spanning element.

Where the wall is spanning horizontally or in two directions, the section modulus should be taken in a vertical plane between any piers, i.e.

$$Z = \frac{ht^2}{6}$$

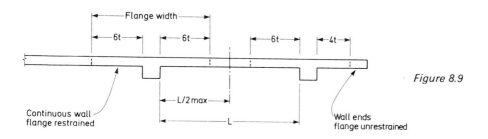

Figure 8.9

---

*The Code states the distance between piers but this is really related to the total flange width and not to the outstand.

8.2.2.6 Shear strength of panel The characteristic shear strength of masonry, f_v, is given in Clause 25 of the Code* as:

$0.35 + 0.6\, g_A \leqslant f_v < 1.75$ N/mm² except for mortars of designation iv where the maximum shear strength must not be greater than 1.4 N/mm². g_A = design vertical load per unit area.

The design for shear stress, v_h, along the bed joints must be controlled so that:

$$v_h \leqslant \frac{f_v}{\gamma_{mv}}$$

where γ_{mv} = partial safety factor for material strength in shear

= 2.5 for general use.

Taking the design shear stress, v_h, being equal to the design wind force, $\gamma_f W_k$, acting on the wall times the effective area of wall A_w on which it is assumed to act divided by the cross sectional area resisting the shear force A

That is:
$$v_h = \frac{\gamma_f\, W_k\, A_w}{A}$$

thus
$$\frac{f_v\, A}{\gamma_{mv}} \geqslant \gamma_f\, W_k\, A_w$$

If yield line analysis were adopted it would be possible to determine the total reactions on each panel support. However, as has been explained, this method of analysis is not strictly applicable to a brittle material and although it can assist in determining the moments in a wall it does not seem appropriate to go to the necessary lengths to determine reactions. It will generally be acceptable to consider the edge reactions to be due to an area bounded by a line drawn at 45° to form the supported corners and for such to be uniformly distributed along the supports (Figure 8.10).

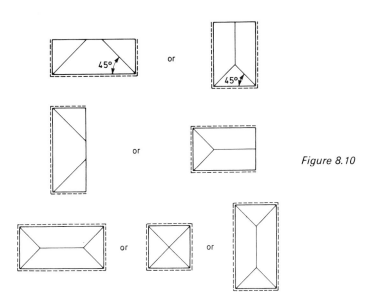

or

Figure 8.10

8.2.2.7 Slenderness limits The control on slenderness limits or limiting dimensions is given by Clause 36 which states that the dimensions of a laterally loaded panel should be limited as follows:

(1) panel supported on three edges
   (a) two or more sides continuous: height × length equal to $1500\, t_{ef}^2$ or less

   (b) all other cases: height × length equal to $1350\, t_{ef}^2$ or less

---

*No information is given on the effects of a flexible damp-proof course. The actual shear stress developed at such positions will depend on the type of damp-proof course present and it is hoped that the manufacturers of such materials will be in a position to provide relevant data. Tests which have been carried out suggest that most damp-proof course mortar joints should attain a characteristic shear strength of at least 0.09 N/mm². Alternatively, a shear strength equal to the self weight/stress times a coefficient of friction of say 0.4 could be adopted. The stress so derived would need to be multiplied by γ_{mv} to give a characteristic value. In addition, no information is given on the shear strength perpendicular to the bed joints. The authors would suggest a value of twice that given in Clause 25, although of course no allowance can be made for any design vertical load.

(2) panel supported on four edges

(a) three or more sides continuous: height × length equal to 2250 t_{ef}^2 or less

(b) all other cases: height × length equal to 2025 t_{ef}^2 or less

(3) panel simply supported at top and bottom
height equal to 40 t_{ef} or less

(4) free standing wall
height equal to 12 t_{ef} or less

In cases (1) and (2) no dimension should exceed 50 times the effective thickness, t_{ef}.

No direct reference is made to panels which are assumed to span horizontally but it may be deduced from (1)(a) and (b) that where the distance to the free edge is less than 30 t_{ef} the horizontal span for both simple and fixed supports should not exceed 50 t_{ef}. Where the distance to the free edge exceeds 30 t_{ef} the horizontal span should be limited to 45 t_{ef} for single supports and 50 t_{ef} for fixed supports. In the case of panels spanning vertically with partial fixity at the supports the limit of 40 t_{ef} should still be assumed to be applied. The effect of these controls may readily be seen by reference to Figure 8.11. The symbol t_{ef} = effective thickness as given in Figure 8.12.

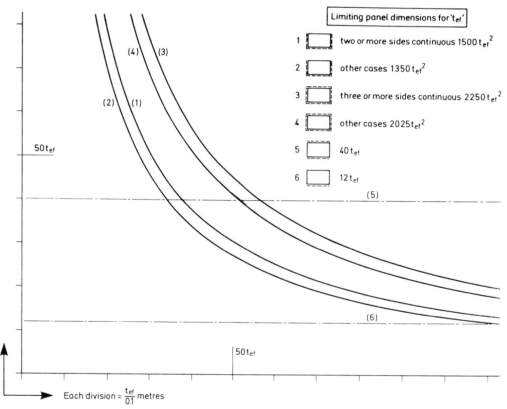

Figure 8.11

8.2.2.8 Summary of design requirements The detailed information contained in the last section may be summarized into an overall design procedure as follows:

Noting that h = panel height

L = panel length

w_k = characteristic wind load

and γ_f = partial safety factor for loads

Walls spanning vertically

$$m = \alpha \, \gamma_f \, W_k \, h^2$$

where α = 0.125 simple supports (for fixed supports — see *Section 8.2.2.2*)

$$M_u = \frac{f_{kb}}{\gamma_m} Z \text{ or } \left(\frac{f_{kb}}{\gamma_m} + f_{self} \right) Z$$

94

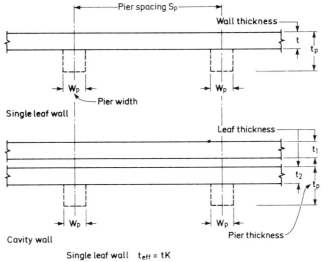

Single leaf wall $t_{eff} = tK$

Cavity wall $t_{eff} = \frac{2}{3}(t_1 + Kt_2)$ or t_1 or Kt_2
whichever is the greater

$\frac{S_p}{W_p}$	Values of K		
	$\frac{t_p}{t}$ or $\frac{t_p}{t_2}$		
	1 or NO piers	2	3
6	1.0	1.4	2.0
10	1.0	1.2	1.4
20 or NO piers	1.0	1.0	1.0

Figure 8.12

Walls spanning horizontally

$$m = \alpha \, \gamma_f \, W_k \, L^2$$

where $\alpha = 0.125$ simple support (0.063 fixed support — see *Section 8.2.2.3*)

$$M_u = \frac{f_{kp}}{\gamma_m} \, Z$$

Walls spanning two directions

$$m = \alpha \, \gamma_f \, W_k \, L^2$$

where α depends on (i) support conditions, (ii) orthogonal ratio (μ), (iii) aspect ratio $\frac{h}{l}$

This may be found from Table 9 (BS 5628), the tables in *Section 8.4*, or in appropriate cases by yield line analysis *(8.1.1.2)*.

$$M_u = \frac{f_{kp}}{\gamma_m} \, Z$$

Then for all panels:

(1) the thickness is so determined so that $M_u \geqslant m$ and since

$$m = \alpha \, \gamma_f \, W_k \, L^2 \text{ and } M_u = \frac{f_{kp} \, b \, t^2}{6\gamma_m}$$

thickness required: $t = \sqrt{\dfrac{6 \, \gamma_m \, \alpha \, \gamma_f \, W_k \, L^2}{f_{kp} \, b}}$

Note: for vertically spanning walls L is replaced by h and f_{kp} by f_{kb}. Values of t for a range of panels and loading are given in the span/thickness tables in *Section 8.5*.
(2) the shear stress should be limited so that

$$v_h \leqslant \frac{f_v}{\gamma_{mv}}$$

$$\leqslant \frac{f_v}{2.5}$$

95

(3) the panel dimensions must be checked against the limiting dimension requirements of Clause 36.3.

8.2.3 Design of double leaf (cavity) walls

Section 8.2.2. dealt with the basic design of laterally loaded walls as applicable to single leaf walls in general. With cavity walls the same basic procedure is adopted but the contribution of two leaves must be considered. Before the introduction of BS 5628 many engineers would have assessed the strength of a cavity wall to flexural loads by proportioning the applied loads to the two leaves in accordance with their stiffness. This approach was perhaps reasonable, although in practice the difference in the stiffness of the two leaves was not particularly marked since either the leaves were of similar thickness, or, where a difference in thickness did exist, the thicker leaf invariably had a lower modulus of elasticity. There is also a tendency for outer leaves to be more continuous than inner leaves. Table 9 of BS 5628:Part 1 is derived from yield-line analysis which relates to strength rather than stiffness.

These are some possible explanations to why the Code allows the design moment of resistance of a cavity wall to be taken as the sum of the design moments of resistance of the two leaves, except when the wall ties are not capable of transmitting the full force, in which case the contribution of the appropriate leaf should be limited accordingly (Figure 8.13). It would be unlikely for an engineer to actually design in the latter case and no doubt it would only be used in instances where a check is to be made on an already completed wall.

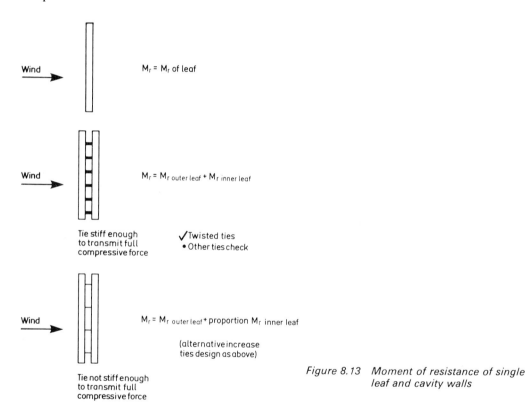

Wind

$M_r = M_r$ of leaf

Wind

$M_r = M_r$ outer leaf $+ M_r$ inner leaf

Tie stiff enough
to transmit full
compressive force

✓Twisted ties
• Other ties check

Wind

$M_r = M_r$ outer leaf $+$ proportion M_r inner leaf

(alternative increase
ties design as above)

Tie not stiff enough
to transmit full
compressive force

Figure 8.13 Moment of resistance of single leaf and cavity walls

With regard to the ties, the Code indicates that vertical twist type ties will always provide sufficient strength when placed at normal centres (Clause 29.1.4 of the Code), but butterfly or double triangle ties should be checked. In addition, recent tests indicate the possibility of some composite action with the stiffer ties. An important point here is for engineers not to take the simple way out and specify vertical twist ties at all times, since the greater stiffness of these ties may cause problems of cracking due to the differential movement between the two leaves, particularly if the leaves are built of different materials such as fired clay bricks and concrete blocks. It will, therefore, often be desirable to retain the more flexible type of ties and carry out a simple check on the compression in the ties (see Chapter 3 with regard to durability of ties). In fact, from Clause 36.2 it is given that the characteristic strength of a double triangle or wire butterfly tie, in a cavity not wider than 75 mm, may be taken as 1.25 kN. Since, by reference to Clause 29.1.4, ties must be provided at not less than 2.5/m^2 it may readily be deduced, taking the partial safety factor for ties $\gamma_m = 3.0$ as given by Clause 27.5, that this type of tie will be quite acceptable where the design wind load acting on the outer leaf does not exceed: $2.5 \times 1.25/3 = 1.04$ kN/m² and hence where the design wind pressure exceeds this figure ties will be required at not less than:

$$\frac{3.0 \; W_k \; \gamma_f}{1.25}$$

i.e. $2.4 \; W_k \; \gamma_f$ ties per m².

The slenderness limits applicable to cavity walls are the same as for single leaf walls except the effective thickness as explained in the previous section is modified as for any loadbearing cavity wall.

8.2.4 Design with small vertical precompression

Where a panel carries a small vertical load in addition to its self weight, the characteristic flexural strength may be modified in a similar manner to that explained in *Section 8.2.2.4* for accommodation of the self weight. Thus in designing a wall that spans vertically or in two directions the characteristic flexural strength may be modified to $f_{kb}/\gamma_m + f_{self}$, where f_{self} includes both self weight and dead load, and used to determine a modified orthogonal ratio or the strength of a vertically spanning member. As the vertical load gradually increases the panel will behave as a loadbearing element subject to lateral pressure and no longer controlled by flexural stresses. No precise value can be given but it is likely that it would be preferable to design as a loadbearing wall when the applied vertical design stress exceeds 0.1 N/mm².

8.2.5 Design with substantial vertical load

The design of this type of wall would be carried out by effectively modifying the applied vertical load and the appropriate capacity reduction factors as explained in *Chapter 7*.

8.2.6 Design of irregular shaped panels

Generally, most masonry walls will be rectangular. However, on occasions it is necessary to evaluate a trapezoidal shaped wall such as the gable wall to a mono pitched structure or the familiar gable wall to a conventionally pitched structure. With the first of these walls, as shown in Figure 8.14, the panel may be designed assuming an aspect ratio based on the mean height of the wall, i.e. $(h_1 + h_2) \; 0.5/L$ with three or four sided support being taken as appropriate. In the case of a vertical free edge, two cases arise as shown in Figure 8.15 and discussed below.

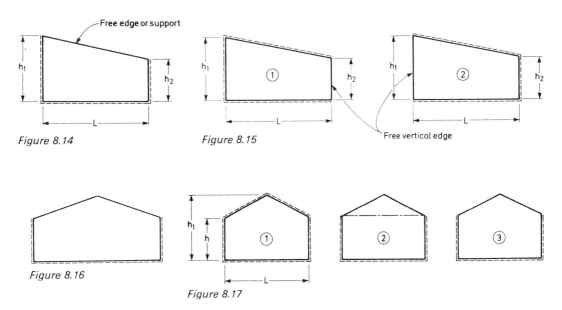

Figure 8.14   Figure 8.15

Figure 8.16   Figure 8.17

Since the vertical free edge will tend to dominate the moments induced in the panels, it will be conservative in case (1) to design to an assumed aspect ratio based on the mean height of the wall, i.e. $(h_1 + h_2) \; 0.5/L$.

Case (2) suggests a more critical situation than the first and thus a different aspect ratio seems justified. It would appear unnecessary to design for the full height of the unsupported edge and thus a reasonable compromise would be to design for an aspect ratio between the height in case (1) and the height, h, which gives $0.75 (h_1 + h_2)/L$. This height may also be reasonable to apply to the case where both vertical edges are free.

With the conventional shaped gable, as shown in Figure 8.16, three distinct support conditions may occur which will influence the way in which design should be tackled, as shown in Figure 8.17.

In case (1) the panel may be designed on an assumed rectangular panel supported on four sides with an aspect ratio equal to $0.5 (h_1 + h)/L$. The degree of fixity being determined as usual, the top support generally being assumed as a simple support. In case (2) the panel supported in this fashion will need two designs. Firstly, to design the main body of the wall as being supported on four sides with an aspect ratio equal to h/L, appropriate allowance being made for any fixity that occurs along the supports. Secondly, to design the triangular section as a cantilever from the top support. In the particular case of support to the sloping portion as well as a top horizontal support, the general design of the main section will suffice, unless the pitch is very steep, in which case it would seem appropriate to design the triangular section as a panel spanning between two opposite edges having a height of $(h_1 - h)/2$ or alternatively, yield line theory could be used.

The type of panel in case (3) should be tackled directly by yield line theory, but the following simple approach may be used to give an indication of the thickness required. The suggestion is to tackle the wall in two parts, the top triangular section being designed as a cantilever. Since, due to the triangular section, some concentration of stress will occur towards the centre of the wall and as the horizontal support to the cantilever is the underlying masonry and thus undefined, it is suggested that this section could reasonably be designed as a rectangular section of height equal to two thirds of the height from eaves to apex, i.e. $2 (h_1 - h)/3$ which would give an effective bending moment coefficient of 0.22 instead of 0.17 for a full triangular section. This approach would also seem appropriate for the cantilever section of case (2). The main wall section may then be designed as a panel supported on three sides with a line load acting on the free edge, the line load being taken as the reaction from the cantilever section. In effect this will give a result similar to that of a panel with a full length window of height equal to twice cantilever span, i.e. $h_w = 4(h_1 - h)/3$ (see Section 8.2.7), again allowance being made for any fixity to the supports.

Cases (2) and (3) are not particularly desirable situations and every effort should be made to provide support to the wall along the sloping portion of the roof. However, in certain situations, as with a large studio roof window, support may not be possible, in which case the approach given here may be used.

8.2.7 Design of panels with openings and line loads

The influence of openings on a laterally loaded masonry wall is very difficult to determine in specific terms since very few, if any, results are available on this type of wall. Appendix D of the Code gives some guidance and introduces the concept of using yield line analysis to determine the bending moments. It has already been stated that the current analytical methods are not particularly applicable for use with a brittle material with discrete planes of weakness, such as masonry and it is important, therefore, to emphasize the final determination of thickness which will require some engineering judgement rather than relying solely on single mathematical answers. It is not possible at present to give a definitive mathematical solution to panels with openings or additional line loads. The information given in this section should, however, provide the designer with sufficient guidance to provide a more confident answer.

It is convenient to start with the reference to the frame surround to the opening made in Appendix D of the Code. Most frames will possess a reasonable amount of strength such that they may either have sufficient strength to replace that lost by the area of the opening (particularly when the opening is small) or the strength of the frame will tend to transfer the loading from the opening towards the corners of the frame. This latter point could in many cases have the effect of a reduction of the bending moment in the panel from that which would otherwise be obtained by consideration of the opening to apply a full uniformly distributed load along the unsupported edge.

There are several analytical methods which could be used to give an indication of the effect of openings in masonry walls but yield line analysis appears the most adaptable, is well documented and has, therefore, been adopted as the basic mathematical approach

used in the following part of this section. The most useful reference for this type of problem is that written by Johansen[8.9].

8.2.7.1 Line loads on panels

8.2.7.1 Line loads on panels Before dealing with the actual case of openings within the panel, such as windows and doors, it will be useful to consider the situation where a load is applied along the entire length of an unsupported edge as shown in Figure 8.18, since it should be noted that the bending moment coefficients as given in Table 9 of BS 5628 for U and C shaped panels (panels A, B, C, D, J, K and H — Table 9) do not allow for any load on the unsupported edge. The solution to this problem will generally be either, (a) to simply consider the load on the free edge to be carried by a given band of wall adjacent to the opening, or (b) to determine a new yield line analysis with a line load included. The first approach needs little explanation and is simply a matter of assuming a width of wall over which the loading is considered to be distributed. Many widths have been suggested, some as low as 300 mm. However, by consideration of the distribution of line loads on slabs as given by Johansen[8.9] (Section 1.4) and the normal distribution of edge loads as given in CP 110, it would be reasonable to consider the additional load from the opening to be carried by a band of masonry $0.25\,L$ wide, the bending moments being taken as suggested in *Section 8.1* for walls spanning vertically or horizontally as appropriate. The second approach is more complex in that it is necessary for a yield line analysis to be carried out. For certain panel shapes it is possible to use standard formulae such as that given by Johansen. The panel supported on three sides with a uniformly distributed load and line load on the free edge is usefully given in Section 1.2 of Johansen. In fact, by using the approach given by Johansen, a simple modification to the coefficients given in the Code can be proposed as follows.

Johansen indicates that a slab with a uniformly distributed load and a line load may be converted to the case of a slab with a uniformly distributed load only by use of certain transformations. The transformations given by Johansen basically modify the aspect ratio of the slab and effectively increase the uniformly distributed load applied. The equations given by Johansen (Section 1.2) are in terms of a variable line load in two directions and a variable uniformly distributed load. In the case of the wall shown in Figure 8.18, it is only necessary to consider the line load along the free edge and, since the line load will thus be a product of the applied uniformly distributed load, the equations may be simplified in terms of only one variable load, i.e. the wind load.

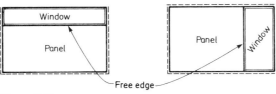

Figure 8.18

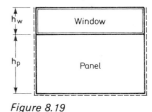

Figure 8.19

Taking the example in Figure 8.19 and defining the window height as h_w and the panel heights as h_p, the transformations or modifications to the panel dimensions are controlled by an expression

$$\sqrt{\frac{1 + 3\beta}{1 + 2\beta}} \text{ for height and}$$

$$\sqrt{\frac{1 + 2\beta}{1 + 3\beta}} \text{ for length, which in effect increases the aspect ratio } \frac{h}{L} \text{ by}$$

$$\frac{1 + 3\beta}{1 + 2\beta} \text{ where } \beta = \frac{\text{total line load}}{\text{total uniformly distributed load}}.$$

The total line load for the panel is shown as $h_w/2 \times L \times p$ (p = wind load).

The total uniformly distributed load is $h_p \times L \times p$. Hence $\beta = 0.5\, h_w/h_p$.

The transformation or modification to the applied distributed load is controlled by $1 + 2\beta$ where β is as indicated previously.

The modifications to the aspect ratio and applied uniformly distributed load, i.e. that which is required to convert a panel with uniformly distributed and line load to a panel with uniformly distributed load only, may be tabulated in terms of the ratio of the window height to the panel height as shown in Table 8.2.

Table 8.2

$\dfrac{h_w}{h_p}$	Modification to load $(1 + 2\beta)$	Modification to aspect ratio $\dfrac{(1 + 3\beta)}{(1 + 2\beta)}$
0.5	1.5	1.17
0.4	1.4	1.14
0.3	1.3	1.12
0.2	1.2	1.08
0.1	1.1	1.04

By inspection of the bending moment coefficients given in Table 9 of the Code it will be found that the modification of the aspect ratio by the small factor given in Table 8.2 has no significant effect. The transformation also allows for modification to the fixity of the base but by considering the worst case when the fixity = 0 (i.e., simple support), this term can conveniently be neglected, thus leaving only the modification to load and aspect ratio to be considered. However, by ignoring the modification to the aspect ratio, which is reasonable on the grounds that its effect is small and that the argument of the stiffness of the frame can be used to counter this, it can be suggested that the effect of a panel with a line load can be catered for by simply increasing the applied uniformly distributed load by the factor $1 + 2\beta$. This can be rewritten as $[1 + h_w/h_p]$. Thus for panels with line loads it can be suggested that the design moment is given by $m = \alpha W_k\, \gamma_f\, [1 + h_w/h_p]\, L^2$ for U shaped panels or $m = \alpha W_k\, \gamma_f\, [1 + L_w/L_p]\, L^2$ for C shaped panels where α is taken from Table 9 of the Code. An alternative and perhaps better way is to suggest that the coefficient α should be multiplied by $[1 + h_w/h_p]$ or $[1 + L_w/L_p]$, as appropriate.

In effect this approach suggests that the bending moment coefficient should be increased by a factor equal to the window height divided by the panel height, i.e., if the window is 10% of the height of the panel, increase the coefficient by 10%. The transformation for the alternative yield line pattern can be tackled in a similar way. This tends to give lower modification factors than for the previous case and therefore indicates that the simple modification still applies. Due to the simplification made and because the coefficients given in Table 9 of the Code may be from a different basic formula to that given by Johansen, the simple modification may not be technically correct but gives good agreement with a full rigorous analysis. When it is remembered that yield line analysis is only an approximate solution to masonry walls, the simple suggestion for dealing with a panel with a line load appears quite reasonable.

A rigorous analysis of the panel shown in Figure 8.20 gives a bending moment coefficient in the region of 0.09. The basic coefficient from Table 9 for $h/L = 2.4/3.6 = 0.68$ and orthogonal ratio $\mu = 0.35$ gives $\alpha = 0.074$.

Now height of window = 0.6 m and height of panel 2.4 m, therefore $h_w/h_p = 0.6/2.4 = 0.25$. Therefore increase coefficient by 25%, i.e. $0.074 \times 1.25 = 0.093$. This gives good agreement with the rigorous analysis.

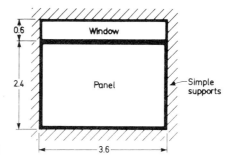

Figure 8.20

8.2.7.2 Panels with openings It is mentioned in the Code that small openings, due in part to the strength of the surrounds, will have little effect on the strength of the wall. The Code gives no guidance as to what a small opening is. An opening of only 5% each way of the panel is small but the effect of the opening will depend on exactly how the openings are distributed within the panel. A small slit completely up one edge will have a negligible area but will convert a panel from four edge support to three edge support. When openings become larger one basic suggestion made in the Code is to divide the panel into sub panels and then to design each part in accordance with the rules given in

100

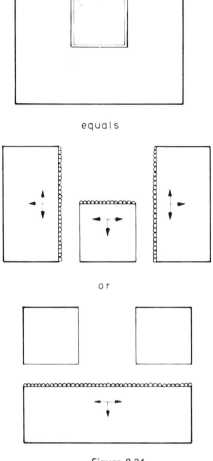

equals

or

Figure 8.21

Section 3.6 of the Code. This example given in the Code is illustrated in Figure 8.21. Unfortunately, it is difficult to see how this can be done since the panels as shown have line loads on the free edge which, as explained in previous sections, are not calculated for in the Code. However, by using methods suggested in the previous section this can now be done.

The alternative suggestion made in the Code, Appendix D, is to design the panel using a recognized method of obtaining bending moments in flat planes, e.g. finite element or yield line. Since the use of yield line was made in the previous section dealing with line loads on the free edge, it will be continued within this section.

Section 1.15 of Johansen will be found to be invaluable for openings within panels since several commonly occurring situations have been dealt with. In the previous section a simplification for dealing with the problem was made using Johansen's work as a basis. In the case of panels with openings, however, Johansen himself gives a simple method for dealing with the problem, suggesting in Section 1.24 that slabs with small holes may be dealt with by simply reducing the fixity of the supports to an amount equal to the length of the opening divided by the length of the side. The approach used by Johansen can be made selective by determining the basic yield line pattern and modifying for any openings which interfere with a yield line. However, adoption of the basic transformation approach and modification of the fixity of all supported edges in proportion to the total length of openings adjacent to each side, can provide the designer with a method for assessing the strength of panels with openings. The question of 'what is small' must be considered and indeed some limitation as to the disposition of the openings must be made. Since this method is not an attempt to replace a rigorous analysis but purely the provision of a simple indication or rule of thumb which may be used to assess the required panel thickness, a limit of openings up to 25% of the panel area is suggested since this conveniently reduces the fixity by 50%, i.e., it reduces a panel with fully fixed edges to half way between this and a simple support condition. In addition the maximum length of any opening should not exceed half the panel dimension. Where the dimensions or area of openings are in excess of these limits the tendency will be to reduce the panel to a different form, for example, a four sided support may well reduce to a panel with three supports and a three sided support may reduce to a two sided support or a dangerous condition where the panel is supported on two adjacent edges. Where a panel has initially simple supports the transformation will reduce the fixity to effectively a negative condition.

The determination of the bending moment or coefficient may be made using the formula given in *Section 8.1.1.2*. For convenience the coefficients given in the Code are repeated. The simplifications for dealing with panels with openings can be demonstrated by considering the panel shown in Figure 8.22.

Taking the orthogonal ratio of the basic panel to be 0.5 and the aspect ratio of $h/L = 3/6 = 0.5$ the bending moment coefficient for a wall with fixed supports from Table 9.1 of the Code is given as 0.014. The corresponding coefficient for a simple support condition from Table 9A is 0.028. Reducing the fixity of the support gives a partial fixity of 0.75 which, by linear interpolation, suggests a bending moment coefficient for the panel shown in Figure 8.22 of $0.014 + 0.014 \times 0.25$, i.e., 0.0175, say 0.018.

Where the opening is such that the modifications give a different change in fixity to adjacent sides it will be necessary to determine a new bending moment coefficient by use of the formula given in *Section 8.1.1.2* with modified fixity to the supports, or a rigorous analysis of the type given by Johansen. In the case of a panel with a line load and openings this may be tackled by first adjusting for modified fixity to take care of the openings and then modifying the coefficients so obtained by the method suggested in the previous section.

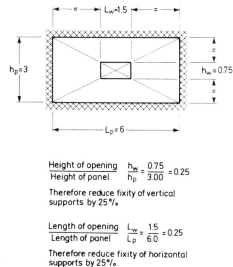

Height of opening $\dfrac{h_w}{h_p} = \dfrac{0.75}{3.00} = 0.25$
Height of panel

Therefore reduce fixity of vertical supports by 25%

Length of opening $\dfrac{L_w}{L_p} = \dfrac{1.5}{6.0} = 0.25$
Length of panel

Therefore reduce fixity of horizontal supports by 25%

Figure 8.22

8.2.7.3 Final assessment It has already been mentioned several times that any method of analysis, either rigorous analysis or the simplification given, should not automatically be taken to give an absolute answer. It is essential to give the matter some thought before reaching a final design solution. One way to tackle the general subject of laterally loaded panels with either line load and/or openings would perhaps be to assess initially what thickness or strength of unit would be required without openings, then to carry out either a rigorous design or the simple design approach given in this Section to assess the thickness or strength required for the panel with openings. In some situations it may be necessary to consider what thickness would be required if the panel were idealized into separate elements as suggested by the Code. Having done this and with consideration to the fixity of the frame to the opening, the engineer should be able to confidently select the units for the wall. In many cases the engineer will also be able to draw on previous experience.

8.2.8 Influence of hollow blocks

In Table 3 of BS 5628 no particular reference is made to the flexural strength of hollow blocks. Since no restriction is made in the Code with regard to the use of hollow or cellular blocks in a laterally loaded wall it can be taken that solid, hollow and cellular blocks should be treated in the same way. There is insufficient information to clarify this point in terms of the Code and it is therefore necessary to consider this matter in a little more detail.

As mentioned in *Section 8.1* the test results give some correlation for concrete blocks between the unit strength and the flexural strength. This aspect is not uncommon as there is also a good relationship between the tensile and cube strength of normal concrete. Since the unit strength of blocks is assessed on the gross area (see *Chapter 3*) it follows that the concrete strength or nett compressive strength of a hollow block will be higher than its quoted unit strength. If the relationship between the compressive strength and the flexural strength is correct it may be found that the flexural strength of a hollow block will be greater than for the solid block, when bending occurs perpendicular to the bed joints. Hence for hollow blocks it could be argued that the characteristic flexural strength of hollow blocks could be obtained from Table 3 of BS 5628 by using the nett strength of the unit instead of the normally quoted gross strength. This will give an increase in the flexural strength of some 35% for the typical hollow block.

The presence of voids, although possibly increasing the flexural strength, will reduce the section modulus of the wall. If a vertical section through a wall containing hollow blocks is considered to be depicted by the section shown in Figure 8.23, with a mean void width of 0.6 t, the section modulus is given as $(1 - 0.6^2) bt^2/6 = 0.64 bt^2/6$, i.e., some 36% less than a solid block. The conclusion drawn from this is that the reduction in the section modulus is counteracted by the possible increase in flexural strength of the unit and that a hollow block could be treated as if it were solid when bending occurs perpendicular to the bed joints.

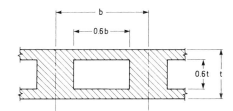

Figure 8.24

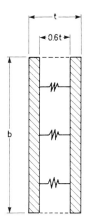

Figure 8.23

A slightly different approach is necessary when considering failure parallel to the bed joint since the flexural strength in this direction is controlled by the adhesion between the mortar and the unit rather than by the tensile or flexural strength of the concrete within the unit. It will be noted from Table 3 (BS 5628) that only one value of the characteristic flexural strength along the bed joint is given, i.e., 0.25 N/mm² (0.20 N/mm² in the case of mortar designation iv) for all block strengths. Although some increase in the flexural strength with respect to unit strength was indicated from research the amount was relatively small and was ignored. Again this work was conducted on solid units but should be reasonable for hollow blocks since the stresses quoted are basically quite low (with $\gamma_m = 3.5$, $\gamma_f = 1.2$, the bed joint stresses are effectively slightly less than those given in CP 111).

A horizontal section through a wall built with hollow blocks may be represented by Figure 8.24 which gives the section modulus as $(1 - 0.6 \times 0.6^2) bt^2/6$ i.e., $0.784 bt^2/6$.

Rather than determining the section modulus of the particular block being used, the maximum reduced section modulus, as given above, could be adopted which would effectively mean the same as treating the block as solid with flexural strengths from Table 3 of BS 5628 reduced by 0.8. However, as hollow blocks are likely to be better bedded than solid blocks, and as there is some test evidence to indicate that bed joint stresses tend to increase with the unit strength, it may be justifiable to ignore the reduction in the section modulus and just treat hollow blocks as solid with flexural strengths directly from Table 3. This procedure for dealing with hollow blocks in flexure is given pending the results of future research.

8.2.9 Influence of damp-proof courses

The introduction of a damp-proof course in a wall subject to flexure may alter the degree of fixity that occurs at the base. Clause 36.4.2 indicates that the bending moment coefficient, α, at a damp-proof course may be taken as for an edge over which their full continuity exists when there is sufficient vertical load on the damp-proof course to ensure that its flexural strength is not exceeded. The degree of fixity may thus be written as:

$$\left[\frac{\text{design vertical load per unit area}}{\dfrac{f_{kx}}{\gamma_m}} \right]$$

or using the approach used in *Section 8.2.2.4*, as $\left(\dfrac{f_{self}}{\dfrac{f_{kb}}{\gamma_m}} \right)$

the result of this equation gives the degree of fixity that is present, when ≥ 1 the base is fully fixed.

Where a damp-proof course occurs in a free standing wall the wall should generally be designed as a mass retaining wall. Should the damp-proof course be of the brick type sometimes used, the flexural strength of Table 3 may be used although consideration should be given to the effect of differential movement.

8.3 Design examples to BS 5628:Part 1

In the following examples it should be noted that the values for γ_m and γ_f are arbitrary values and in practice these values will need to be adjusted to suit the actual category of manufacturing and construction control being used. Also, in instances where the panel *is* providing stability to the structure, then γ_f of 1.4 will be required.

8.3.1 Laterally loaded masonry walls: Basic design example

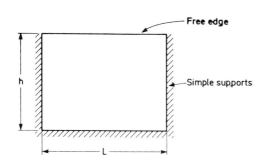

Determine the required thickness of a single leaf wall supported as shown above using the following criteria:

Characteristic wind load	$= 0.45 \text{ kN/m}^2$
Height of wall to free edge	$= 5 \text{ m}$
Length of wall between restraints	$= 5 \text{ m}$
Concrete blocks (solid) strength	$= 3.5 \text{ N/mm}^2$
Normal category construction control Special category manufacturing control	$= \gamma_m = 3.1$
Panel *not* providing stability to structure	$= \gamma_f = 1.2$

8.3.1.1 Flexural design The design bending moment per unit height of the wall is given by the following expression (Clause 36.4.2):

$$m = \alpha \, W_k \, \gamma_f \, L^2$$

The bending moment coefficient depends on: (i) orthogonal ratio, (ii) aspect ratio, h/L, (iii) support conditions.

(i) Concrete blocks strength 3.5 N/mm², therefore from Table 3, BS 5628 (Table 8.0):

$$\mu = \frac{0.25}{0.45} = 0.56$$

(ii) Aspect ratio

$$\frac{h}{L} = \frac{5}{5} = 1.0$$

(iii) Support conditions — simple

From BS 5628, Table 9A (Table 8.4.1), for $\frac{h}{L} = 1.0$

$\alpha = 0.080$ with $\mu = 0.6$

$\alpha = 0.083$ with $\mu = 0.5$

therefore by linear interpolation $\alpha = 0.0812$ when $\mu = 0.56$. Since $W_k = 0.45$ kN/mm² $\gamma_f = 1.2$ $L = 5$, then applied design moment per unit height $m = 0.0812 \times 0.45 \times 1.2 \times 5^2$ = *1.096 kN m/m*. The design moment of resistance (Clause 36.4.3) is given as:

$$M_d = \frac{f_{kx}}{\gamma_m} Z = \frac{f_{kp}}{\gamma_m} Z$$

where $f_{kp} = 0.45$ N/mm² and Z = section modulus.

Since $M_d \geq m$ and $M_d = \frac{f_{kp}}{\gamma_m} Z$ and as $Z = \frac{bt^2}{6}$

then

$$t \geq \sqrt{\frac{m \, \gamma_m 6}{f_{kp} \, b}}$$

$$\sqrt{\frac{1.096 \times 3.1 \times 6 \times 10^6}{0.45 \times 1000}}$$

$t \geq 213$ mm (see Table 8.1).

8.3.1.2 Slenderness limits Panel simply supported on more than one side, therefore, from Clause 36.3, $h \times L \leq 1350 \, t_{ef}^2$

Since wall is single leaf $t_{ef} = t$

therefore:

$$t \geq \sqrt{\frac{h \times L}{1350}} \geq \sqrt{\frac{5 \times 5 \times 10^6}{1350}} \geq 136 \text{ mm}$$

In addition no dimension shall exceed $50 \, t_{ef}$. Since h and L both = 5 m, then $t \geq \frac{5 \times 10^3}{50} \leq 100$ mm.

8.3.1.3 Design for shear Consider the wind load to be distributed to the supports as shown below:

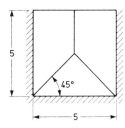

Then total load to support = $\gamma_f \times W_k \times$ loaded area

Thus the total shear along base = $\dfrac{1.2 \times 0.45 \times (5 \times 2.5)}{2}$ = 3.375 kN

Assuming that this load is uniformly distributed along base, the design shear force per metre run = $\dfrac{3.375}{5}$ = 0.675 kN.

The design shear stress (v_h) is therefore $\dfrac{0.675 \times 10^3}{215 \times 1000} = 0.003$ N/mm².

The characteristic shear strength (f_v) from Clause 25 = $0.35 + 0.6\,g_A$.
Since the self weight is to be ignored, characteristic strength, f_v, = 0.35 N/mm². A lower value may be required with the presence of a damp-proof course (see *Section 8.2.2.6*).

The design shear stress (v_h) must be limited so that $v_h \leqslant \dfrac{f_v}{\gamma_{mv}}$

In this case $v_h = 0.003$ N/mm² and $\dfrac{f_v}{\gamma_{mv}} = \dfrac{0.35}{2.5} = 0.14$ N/mm².

Therefore shear resistance is adequate along base

Total shear to each vertical support = $1.2 \times 0.45 \times 2.5\,(2.5 + 5)/2 = 5.06$ kN. Again, considering load to be uniformly distributed along support, then design shear force per metre run = 5.06/5 = 1.02 kN.

Using 2 mm thick anchors into dovetail slots in column, characteristic strength of each tie = 4.5 kN (Table 8, BS 5828 — see Table 8.1). Placing ties at 900 mm centres and taking the partial safety factor for material as 3.5. The design load resistance per metre run of wall = $4.5/3.5 \times 1000/900 = 1.43$ kN. This is greater than the design shear force and therefore adequate.

8.3.2 Example 1

PROBLEM
A single leaf wall to a warehouse, as shown below, has to be designed to withstand a characteristic wind load of 0.6 kN/m². Architectural requirements stipulate a maximum wall thickness of 140 mm. The panel does not provide stability to the structure. Both construction and manufacturing control are to be normal category.

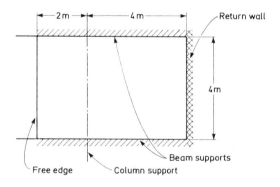

SOLUTION

Design for flexure

(1) *Right hand portion of panel 4 m long by 4 m high.* This panel is simply supported top and bottom. Consider return wall and support at column to give fixed vertical edges, i.e.

Using 7 N/mm² solid block.
From BS 5628 Table 3 characteristic bed joint strength = 0.25 N/mm² and in perpend direction = 0.60 N/mm², thus $\mu = 0.25/0.60 = 0.42$ ignoring self weight.

Aspect ratio of panel $\dfrac{h}{L} = \dfrac{4}{4} = 1.0$

Using support condition as above, bending moment coefficient from BS 5628 Table 9G (Table 8.4.13) = 0.037.

Now, $W_k = 0.60$ kN/m² $\quad \gamma_f = 1.2 \quad L = 4$ m

therefore, applied design moment per unit height

$$m = 0.037 \times 0.60 \times 1.2 \times 4^2$$
$$= 0.426 \text{ kN m/m}$$

The design moment of resistance $M_d = \dfrac{f_{kp}}{\gamma_m} Z$

thus required thickness

$$t \geqslant \sqrt{\frac{m \, \gamma_m \, 6}{f_{kp} \, b}}$$

$$t \geqslant \sqrt{\frac{0.426 \times 3.5 \times 6 \times 10^6}{0.60 \times 1000}} \geqslant 122 \text{ mm}$$

Slenderness limits Panel has less than three sides continuous, therefore Clause 36.3 (b)(2) controls. $h \times L \leqslant 2025 \, t_{ef}^2$

$t_{ef} = t$ since single leaf wall. Therefore

$$t \geqslant \sqrt{\frac{4 \times 4 \times 10^6}{2025}} \geqslant 89 \text{ mm}$$

Check 50 t_{ef} requirement

$$t \geqslant \frac{4 \times 10^3}{50} = 80 \text{ mm}$$

Loading condition controls therefore panel must be not less than 122 mm

(2) Left hand portion of panel 2 m long by 4 m high. This portion of the panel is simply supported top and bottom. One vertical edge is free, the other is to be considered as fixed, i.e.

Again, using 7 N/mm² solid block.

Thus, as before, $\mu = 0.42$ (ignoring self weight).

Aspect ratio of panel $\dfrac{h}{L} = \dfrac{4}{2} = 2.0$

Although this is outside the extent of Table 9 (BS 5628) it does not mean that the panel cannot be designed. However, it is necessary to consider the panel behaviour more closely since there may be a tendency for the panel to span in one direction or for an alternative yield line pattern to develop. Note 2 to Table 9 (BS 5628) relates to a panel with a free top edge. In the case of a panel with a free vertical edge it is reasonable to consider the panel cantilevering from the vertical support at a ratio h/L of $1/0.3$, i.e., around 3.0.

In addition the bending moment coefficient for a horizontal cantilever span would be of the order of $0.5 \, \gamma_f \, W_k \, L^2$, i.e., a coefficient of 0.5. The coefficient in Table 9, Figure K, for $\mu = 0.42$ and $h/L = 1.75$ is in the order of 0.16. It is therefore clear that the panel under consideration with a h/L of 2.0 is still spanning significantly in two directions. In addition, since the panel is only slightly outside Table 9 the yield line pattern will remain basically the same and thus the bending moment coefficient may be determined by use of the formula given in *Section 8.1.1.2*.

For the panel given

$$\phi_1 = \phi_3 = 0 \qquad \phi_2 = 1.0 \qquad \mu = 0.42 \qquad h = 4 \qquad L = 2 \qquad \frac{h}{L} = \frac{4}{2} = 2.0$$

107

For failure pattern (i):

$$\alpha = \frac{1}{6}\left(\frac{1}{[(3 + \phi_2) \div Y^2] - 1}\right)$$

where $Y = \sqrt{\left(\left[\frac{\sqrt{1 + \phi_1} + \sqrt{1 + \phi_3}}{\sqrt{\left[\left(\frac{h}{L}\right)^2 (3 + \phi_2)\right]}{\mu}}\right]^2 + 3\right) - \left(\frac{\sqrt{1 + \phi_1} + \sqrt{1 + \phi_3}}{\left[\left(\frac{h}{L}\right)^2 (3 + \phi_2)\right]{\mu}}\right)}$

thus $Y = \left(\left[\frac{\sqrt{1} + \sqrt{1}}{\sqrt{\frac{2^2}{0.42}} (4)}\right]^2 + 3\right) - \left(\frac{\sqrt{1} + \sqrt{1}}{\sqrt{\frac{2^2}{0.42}} 4}\right)$

$= 1.44$

Then $\alpha = \dfrac{1}{6} \dfrac{1}{\dfrac{4}{1.44^2} - 1}$

$= 0.178$

For failure pattern (ii)

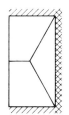

$$\alpha = \frac{\left(\frac{h}{L}\right)^2}{6\mu Y_{13}{}^2}\left[\sqrt{\left(3 + \frac{\left(\frac{h}{L}\right)^2 Y_2{}^2}{\mu Y_{13}{}^2}\right)} - \frac{\sqrt{\frac{1}{\mu}\left(\frac{h}{L}\right)} Y_2}{Y_{13}}\right]^2$$

where $Y_{13} = \sqrt{1 + \phi_1} + \sqrt{1 + \phi_3}$ and $Y_2 = \sqrt{1 + \phi_2}$

thus $Y_{13} = \sqrt{1} + \sqrt{1} = 2 \qquad Y_2 = \sqrt{2} \qquad \dfrac{h}{L} = \dfrac{4}{2} = 2$

hence $\alpha = \dfrac{2^2}{6 \times 0.42 \times 2^2}\left[\sqrt{\left(3 + \dfrac{2^2 (\sqrt{2})^2}{0.42 \times 2^2}\right)} - \dfrac{\sqrt{\frac{1}{0.42}} (2)\sqrt{2}}{2}\right]^2$

$= 0.145$

$\therefore$ Critical coefficient $= 0.178$

$W_k = 0.60 \qquad \gamma_f = 1.2 \qquad L = 2$ therefore $m = 0.178 \times 0.60 \times 1.2 \times 2^2$
$= 0.513$ kN m/m

hence $t \geq \sqrt{\dfrac{0.513 \times 3.5 \times 6 \times 10^6}{0.60 \times 1000}}$

≥ 134 mm

Slenderness limits   The panel has two simply supported edges, therefore, Clause 36.3 (1)(b) is applied. $h \times L \leq 1350 \, t_{ef}^2$

$$\therefore t \geq \sqrt{\frac{4 \times 2 \times 10^6}{1350}} \geq 77 \text{ mm}$$

$$50\ t_{\text{ef}}\ \text{requirement requires}\ \frac{4 \times 10^3}{50} = 80\ \text{mm}$$

Again loading condition controls panel size
The overall panel requires to be not less than 122 mm for the right hand portion and not less than 134 mm for the left hand portion. In this instance since both panels need to be approximately the same, the assumption that the central column support is fixed is confirmed. Had the panel sizes been significantly different then some readjustment would be required to allow for only partial fixity to the column support to the right hand panel. *Therefore, select 7 N/mm² block of thickness 140 mm.*

Shear
The wind load to be assumed to be distributed to the supports as shown.

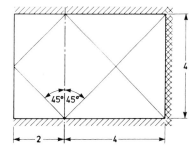

$$\text{Total shear load to base (also top support)} = 1.2 \times 0.6\ \left(\frac{4 \times 2}{2} + \frac{2 \times 2}{2} \right)$$

$$= 4.32\ \text{kN}$$

Assuming a uniform distribution the design shear force per metre run

$$= \frac{4.32}{6} = 0.72\ \text{kN}.$$

The design shear stress, $\quad v_{\text{h}} = \dfrac{0.72 \times 10^3}{140 \times 1000} = 0.005\ \text{N/mm}^2$

Since self weight is to be ignored, design shear strength

$$= \frac{f_{\text{v}}}{\gamma_{\text{mv}}} = \frac{0.35}{2.5} = 0.14\ \text{N/mm}^2.$$

Therefore, shear resistance is adequate.

Central column support
The central column support must be designed to withstand a total applied design load = 1.2 × 0.6 × 2 (4 × 2)/2 = 5.76 kN or 5.76/4 = 1.44 kN/metre. This should be capable of taking the load without undue deflection, say span/500. Top support to be designed to resist design load 0.72 kN/metre. Connections also required to transmit forces to support.

8.3.3 Example 2

PROBLEM
This example illustrates how allowance may be made for the self weight of the wall. A wall as used in the basic design example is to be used but allowance made for the density of the wall at 1200 kg/m³. Determine the characteristic pressure that may be carried.

Height of wall to free edge	= 5 m
Length of wall between restraints	= 5 m
Concrete blocks (solid) strength	= 3.5 N/mm²
Normal category construction control ⎱ ∴ $\gamma_{\text{m}} = 3.1$	
Special category manufacturing control ⎰	
Panel *not* providing stability to structure ∴ $\gamma_{\text{f}} = 1.2$	
Density of wall	= 1200 kg/m³

SOLUTION

Design for flexure

$$m = \alpha \, W_k \, \gamma_f \, L^2$$

Determination of bending moment coefficient

(1) Modified orthogonal ratio $\quad \mu = \dfrac{\dfrac{f_{kb}}{\gamma_m} + f_{self}}{\dfrac{f_{kp}}{\gamma_m}}$

where f_{self} is the self weight stress at mid height of the panel. Other symbols are as indicated previously.

$$f_{self} = 0.5 \, h \, \rho \, 9.81 \times 10^{-6} \, \gamma_f$$

$\quad\quad \gamma_f$ for maximum criteria is 0.9

$\quad\quad \rho$ is density of wall 1200 kg/m^3

$\therefore f_{self} = 0.5 \times 5 \times 1200 \times 9.81 \times 10^{-6} \times 0.9 = 0.0265$

now $f_{kb} = 0.25 \, f_{kp} = 0.45 \, \gamma_m = 3.1$

$$\therefore \mu = \frac{\dfrac{0.25}{3.1} + 0.0265}{\dfrac{0.45}{3.1}} = 0.74$$

(2) Aspect ratio $h/L = 5/5 = 1.0$

(3) Support conditions — edge supports are again simple supports. Both supports have an effective restraint equivalent to that exerted by the self weight of the wall. Since full wall height acts at base self weight, stress $= 0.265 \times 2 = 0.053$ N/mm^2.

Therefore, effective fixity at base $= \dfrac{0.053}{\dfrac{0.25}{3.1}} = 0.66$, i.e., effectively between a simple and fixed support.

There is no table that deals directly with partial supports and therefore the coefficient must be determined directly from a yield line formula, i.e., as given in *Section 8.1.1.2* or alternatively, an approximate solution may be obtained by linear interpolation from the standard bending moment coefficient tables.

In this particular case, the condition for fixed base with simple side supports is not contained in the Code and therefore Tables 8.4.1 and 8.4.2 may need to be used.

From $\mu = 0.74$ $h/L = 1.0$ $\alpha = 0.076$ for simple base

From $\mu = 0.74$ $h/L = 1.0$ $\alpha = 0.063$ for fixed base

Hence, for partial fixity $\phi_2 = 0.66$ $\alpha = 0.067$
Analysis by formula given in *Section 8.1.1.2* gives $\alpha = 0.0667$
Since design moment $m = \alpha \, W_k \, \gamma_f \, L^2$

$$= 0.067 \, W_k \, 1.2 \times 5^2$$

$$= 2.01 \, W_k$$

Design moment of resistance $\quad M = \dfrac{f_{kp}}{\gamma_m} Z$

now $t = 215$ mm and $Z = bt^2/6$

Therefore:
$$W_k \leqslant \frac{f_{kp} \, b \, t^2}{2.01 \times \gamma_m \times 6}$$

$$\leqslant \frac{0.45 \times 1000 \times 215^2}{2.01 \times 3.1 \times 6 \times 10^6}$$

$$\leqslant 0.55 \text{ kN/m}^2$$

110

Therefore, by allowing for the self weight of the wall (density 1200 kg/m³) an additional 0.1 N/m wind may be carried on the wall as shown in the basic example.

Shear
By comparison with *Example 1* shear is adequate at base. Shear to vertical supports is increased to 1.02 × 0.55/0.45 = 1.25 kN/metre. This is less than that provided by the ties (1.43 kN/metre), therefore, adequate.

8.3.4 Example 3

PROBLEM
In this example a continuous window opening along the upper edge of a wall panel is to be designed. The loading on the window applies an effective line load on the free edge.

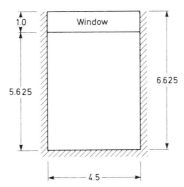

The wall is to be built with concrete bricks. γ_m to be taken as 3.5 and γ_f as 1.2. The characteristic wind pressure has been determined as 0.7 kN/m².

SOLUTION

Design for flexure
Adopting the approach given in *Section 8.2.7*, then for the basic bending moment coefficient:

(1) orthogonal ratio $\mu = 0.3/0.9 = 0.33$ − consider as 0.35 since some self weight will exist

(2) aspect ratio $h/L = 5.625/4.5 = 1.25$

(3) support conditions — consider as simple.

Then BS 5628, Table 9A (Table 8.4.1) for $h/L = 1.25$ $\alpha = 0.095$
Height of window $h_w = 1.0$ m and height of panel $h_p = 5.625$ m
therefore $h_w/h_p = 1.0/5.625 = 0.23$
Modification factor for line load $= 1 + 0.23 = 1.23$
hence modified bending coefficient $0.095 \times 1.23 = 0.117$
Now $W_k = 0.7$ kN/m² $\gamma_f = 1.2$ $L = 4.5$ m
Then applied design moment per unit height $m = 0.117 \times 0.7 \times 1.2 \times 4.5^2$

$$= 1.99 \text{ kN m/m}$$

Design moment of resistance $\qquad M_d = \dfrac{f_{kp}}{\gamma_m} Z$

therefore required thickness $t \geqslant \sqrt{\dfrac{1.99 \times 3.5 \times 6 \times 10^6}{0.9 \times 1000}} \geqslant 215.5$ mm

Since some strength will be obtained from window surround and as self weight has already been effectively neglected, use *215 mm thick wall.*

The example may be continued by considering what thickness would be required for the basic wall panel without the window and what thickness would be required had the panel been taken for the full 6.625 m height.

For the basic wall panel 5.625 × 4.5 m, bending moment coefficient α as determined previously is 0.095 which gives a required thickness of $215.5 \times 0.095/0.117 = 194$ mm.

Had the panel been 6.625×4.5 m then the aspect ratio is $6.625/4.5 = 1.47$ and BS 5628, Table 9A (Table 8.4.1) for h/L say 1.5 $\alpha = 0.100$. Hence thickness required $= 215.5 \times 0.100/0.117 = 199$ mm. This latter value is useful in comparing to the original case with window opening since both panels are subject to a similar total wind load but in the case of the panel with openings the total length of yield line is less and hence a slightly greater panel thickness, as determined as 215 mm, seems justified.

The loading from the window could be considered to be simply carried by a strip of brickwork running parallel to the opening. Had this method been adopted then an additional loading, as illustrated below, could be assumed to be carried by the top 1.125 m of wall (i.e., $0.25\ L$ as given in *Section 8.2.7*).

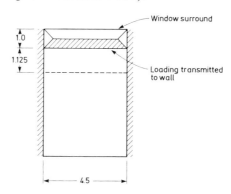

Equivalent uniformly distributed loading transferred to strip

$$= \frac{0.7 \times 0.5 \times (3.5 + 4.5)}{1.125 \times 4.5 \times 2} = 0.28 \text{ kN/m}^2$$

Total uniformly distributed loading on strip therefore $= 0.7 + 0.28 = 0.98$ kN/m². Designing strip as simply supported span $m = 0.125 \times 0.98 \times 1.2 \times 4.5^2 = 2.98$ kN/metre, giving t required $= 264$ mm.

If moment were arbitrary, assessed as $\dfrac{W_k\, \gamma_m\, L^2}{10}$ then t required reduces to 236 mm.

Considering this, and that there will be some stiffness within the window frame, then a wall thickness as originally derived of 215 mm would appear adequate.

8.3.5 *Example 4*

PROBLEM

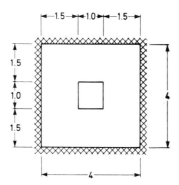

A single leaf panel 4 m long by 4 m high with a centrally placed window 1 m × 1 m has to be designed to resist a characteristic wind pressure of 0.6 kN/m². All edges are considered to be fixed.

$$\gamma_m = 3.5 \qquad \gamma_f = 1.2 \qquad 7 \text{ N/mm}^2 \text{ blocks.}$$

SOLUTION

Using the method indicated in *Section 8.1.1.2* fixity to edges is reduced by $\frac{1}{4} = 0.25$, i.e. $\phi = 0.75$. Now by use of the formula given in *Section 8.1.1.2* the bending moment coefficient may be determined as $= 0.035$. An approximate solution may, however, be obtained by interpolating between E and I of Table 9 (BS 5628) — see Tables 8.4.7 and 8.4.15.

112

Now $$\mu = \frac{0.25}{0.60} = 0.42 \quad \frac{h}{L} = \frac{4}{4} = 1.0$$

For the pinned edged condition panel E ($\phi = 0$) then $\alpha = 0.061$ (Table 8.4.7)
For fixed edged condition panel I ($\phi = 1$) then $\alpha = 0.030$ (Table 8.4.15)
For linear interpolation for all edges with fixity $\phi = 0.75$ $\alpha = 0.038$.
To continue with the simple interpolated figure $m = 0.038 \times 0.60 \times 1.2 \times 4^2$
$$= 0.438 \text{ kN/m per metre}$$

thus t required
$$= \sqrt{\frac{0.438 \times 3.5 \times 6 \times 10^6}{0.60 \times 1000}}$$
$$= 124 \text{ mm.}$$

Had the panel had simply supported edges top and bottom then the following would arise.

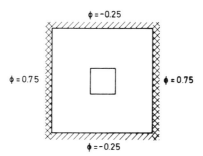

This could not be interpolated from Tables in BS 5628 and the formula would have been necessary. In this case the bending moment coefficient may be derived as:
$$\alpha = 0.045$$
$$m = 124 \times \sqrt{\frac{0.045}{0.035}} = 140.6 \text{ mm}$$

Since some strength will be obtained from window surround a 140 mm would be adequate.

Referring back to *Example 2*, it is indicated that an opening of 1 m × 1 m could also have been incorporated in the wall since the basic design thickness of 122 mm had to be increased to 140 mm to cater for the left hand panel.

8.3.6 Example 5

PROBLEM

A cavity wall of span 4.5 m by 3.375 m high has to be designed to withstand a wind pressure of 0.6 kN/m². The outside leaf is brickwork running past supporting columns. The inner leaf is blockwork abutting the columns with a soft control joint.

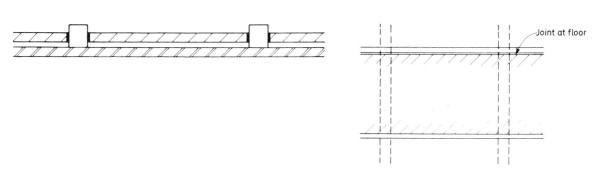

SOLUTION

Outer leaf

Consider brick f_{kb} = 0.3 and f_{kp} = 0.9. Wall density 1700 kg/m³. Orthogonal ratio = 0.3/0.9 = 0.33.

Consider as simply supported at base but allow for self weight of wall. Self weight stress at mid-height = 0.5 × 3.375 × 1700 × 9.81 × 10⁻⁶ × 0.9 = 0.025. Modified orthogonal ratio

$$\mu = \frac{\dfrac{0.3}{3.1} + 0.025}{\dfrac{0.9}{3.1}} = 0.42 \text{ consider as } 0.4$$

Therefore bending moment coefficient α from Table 9C, BS 5628 (Table 8.4.5) for aspect ratio 3.375/4.5 = 0.75 α = 0.044

Consider thickness as 100 mm. Thus design moment capacity of wall

$$M_d = \frac{f_{kx}}{\gamma_m} Z = \frac{f_{kp} b\, t^2}{\gamma_m 6} = \frac{0.9 \times 1000 \times 100^2}{3.1 \times 6 \times 10^6} = 0.484 \text{ kN/m per metre.}$$

The applied design moment $m = \alpha W_k \gamma_f L^2$ and since this may be allowed to equal the design moment capacity of the wall then

$$W_k = \frac{M_d}{\alpha \gamma_f L^2} = \frac{0.484}{0.044 \times 1.2 \times 4.5^2} = 0.45 \text{ kN/m}^2$$

The total characteristic wind pressure to be applied is 0.6 kN/m². Therefore, the excess force to be carried by the inner leaf is 0.6 − 0.45 = 0.15 kN/m².

Try 3.5 N/mm² blocks, 100 mm thick. Aspect ratio as before = 0.75. Orthogonal ratio = 0.25/0.45 = 0.55. Consider self weight as 1000 kg/m³. Then self weight stress at mid-height = 0.025 × 1000/1700 = 0.015 N/mm².

Modified orthogonal ratio $\mu = \dfrac{\dfrac{0.25}{3.1} + 0.015}{\dfrac{0.45}{3.1}} = 0.65$

Now, considering simple support to all edges, from BS 5628, Table 9A (Table 8.4.1) α = 0.0675. Thickness is 100 mm, therefore

$$M_d = \frac{0.45 \times 1000 \times 100^2}{3.1 \times 6 \times 10}$$
$$= 0.242 \text{ kN/metre}$$

Therefore, characteristic wind force that can be carried

$$W_k = \frac{0.242}{0.0675 \times 1.2 \times 4.5^2} = 0.15 \text{ kN/m}^2.$$

Total capacity of cavity wall is therefore acceptable.

It should be noted that the wall panel could be shown to carry a greater wind force since some degree of fixity could be allowed at the base of both walls. In addition, if mortar jointing were used between the inner block wall and the columns, then some degree of fixity could effectively be taken at the support due to the anchoring action of the wall.

In the example the total wind load was determined on the assumption that both leaves attain their ultimate stress simultaneously as inferred by the first paragraph to Clause 36.4.5. If, however, the wind load were shared between the two leaves in proportion to

114

their design moments of resistance, as given by the last clause, then the stress in the leaves would be as follows:

M_d brick = 0.484 M_d block = 0.242, thus W_k to be shared in ratio

$$\frac{0.484}{0.726} \times 0.6 = 0.4 \text{ kN/m}^2 \text{ to brick and } \frac{0.242}{0.726} \times 0.6 = 0.2 \text{ kN/m}^2 \text{ to block.}$$

This in turn gives

$$f_{kp} \text{ in bricks} = \frac{0.4 \times 1.2 \times 0.044 \times 4.5^2 \times 3.1 \times 6 \times 10^6}{1000 \times 100^2} = 0.8 \text{ kN/mm}^2$$

$$f_{kp} \text{ in blocks} = \frac{0.8 \times 0.2 \times 0.0675}{0.4 \times 0.044} = 0.61 \text{ kN/mm}^2$$

This tends to suggest an overstress in the blockwork. However, as we are working in ultimate terms and since the wind pressure will actually be distributed as suction and positive pressure on both leaves, then it would appear reasonable to accept the first method for design purposes. In this instance the additional allowance for self weight fixity could be shown to prove the wall adequate.

8.4 Bending moment coefficient tables

For the purpose of the following tables:
μ = orthogonal ratio
H = panel height
L = panel length
ϕ = degree of fixity 0.0 pinned/simple support
1.0 fixed support

Table 8.4.1

μ	H/L						
	0.30	0.50	0.75	1.00	1.25	1.50	1.75
1.20	0.029	0.042	0.055	0.067	0.076	0.082	0.087
1.10	0.030	0.044	0.057	0.069	0.077	0.084	0.089
1.00	0.031	0.045	0.059	0.071	0.079	0.085	0.090
0.90	0.032	0.047	0.061	0.073	0.081	0.087	0.092
0.80	0.034	0.049	0.064	0.075	0.083	0.089	0.093
0.70	0.035	0.051	0.066	0.077	0.085	0.091	0.095
0.60	0.038	0.053	0.069	0.080	0.088	0.093	0.097
0.50	0.040	0.056	0.073	0.083	0.090	0.095	0.099
0.40	0.043	0.061	0.077	0.087	0.093	0.098	0.101
0.30	0.048	0.067	0.082	0.091	0.097	0.101	0.104

$\phi 1 = 0.0$ $\phi 3 = 0.0$ $\phi 2 = 0.0$

Table 8.4.2

μ	H/L						
	0.30	0.50	0.75	1.00	1.25	1.50	1.75
1.20	0.015	0.028	0.041	0.053	0.062	0.069	0.075
1.10	0.016	0.029	0.043	0.054	0.064	0.071	0.077
1.00	0.017	0.031	0.045	0.056	0.066	0.073	0.079
0.90	0.018	0.032	0.047	0.059	0.068	0.075	0.081
0.80	0.020	0.034	0.049	0.061	0.070	0.077	0.083
0.70	0.021	0.037	0.052	0.064	0.073	0.080	0.085
0.60	0.023	0.039	0.055	0.067	0.076	0.082	0.087
0.50	0.026	0.043	0.059	0.071	0.079	0.085	0.090
0.40	0.029	0.047	0.064	0.075	0.083	0.089	0.093
0.30	0.034	0.053	0.069	0.080	0.088	0.093	0.097

$\phi 1 = 0.0$ $\phi 3 = 0.0$ $\phi 2 = 1.0$

Table 8.4.3

$\phi 1 = 0.0$ (diagram) $\phi 3 = 1.0$

$\phi 2 = 0.0$

μ				H/L			
	0.30	0.50	0.75	1.00	1.25	1.50	1.75
1.20	0.023	0.033	0.043	0.051	0.057	0.061	0.064
1.10	0.024	0.034	0.044	0.052	0.058	0.061	0.064
1.00	0.024	0.035	0.046	0.053	0.059	0.062	0.065
0.90	0.025	0.036	0.047	0.055	0.060	0.063	0.066
0.80	0.027	0.037	0.049	0.056	0.061	0.065	0.067
0.70	0.028	0.039	0.051	0.058	0.062	0.066	0.068
0.60	0.030	0.042	0.053	0.059	0.064	0.067	0.069
0.50	0.031	0.044	0.055	0.061	0.066	0.069	0.071
0.40	0.034	0.047	0.057	0.063	0.067	0.070	0.072
0.30	0.037	0.051	0.061	0.066	0.070	0.072	0.074

Table 8.4.4

$\phi 1 = 0.0$ (diagram) $\phi 3 = 1.0$

$\phi 2 = 1.0$

μ				H/L			
	0.30	0.50	0.75	1.00	1.25	1.50	1.75
1.20	0.013	0.023	0.033	0.042	0.048	0.053	0.056
1.10	0.014	0.024	0.034	0.043	0.049	0.054	0.057
1.00	0.015	0.025	0.036	0.044	0.050	0.055	0.058
0.90	0.016	0.027	0.037	0.046	0.052	0.056	0.060
0.80	0.017	0.028	0.039	0.047	0.053	0.057	0.061
0.70	0.018	0.030	0.041	0.049	0.055	0.059	0.062
0.60	0.020	0.032	0.043	0.051	0.057	0.061	0.064
0.50	0.022	0.034	0.046	0.053	0.059	0.062	0.065
0.40	0.024	0.037	0.049	0.056	0.061	0.065	0.067
0.30	0.028	0.042	0.053	0.059	0.064	0.067	0.069

Table 8.4.5

$\phi 1 = 1.0$ (diagram) $\phi 3 = 1.0$

$\phi 2 = 0.0$

μ				H/L			
	0.30	0.50	0.75	1.00	1.25	1.50	1.75
1.20	0.019	0.027	0.035	0.040	0.044	0.046	0.048
1.10	0.019	0.027	0.036	0.041	0.044	0.047	0.049
1.00	0.020	0.028	0.037	0.042	0.045	0.048	0.050
0.90	0.021	0.029	0.038	0.043	0.046	0.048	0.050
0.80	0.022	0.031	0.039	0.043	0.047	0.049	0.051
0.70	0.023	0.032	0.040	0.044	0.048	0.050	0.051
0.60	0.024	0.034	0.041	0.046	0.049	0.051	0.052
0.50	0.025	0.035	0.043	0.047	0.050	0.052	0.053
0.40	0.027	0.038	0.044	0.048	0.051	0.053	0.054
0.30	0.030	0.040	0.046	0.050	0.052	0.054	0.055

Table 8.4.6

$\phi 1 = 1.0$ (diagram) $\phi 3 = 1.0$

$\phi 2 = 1.0$

μ				H/L			
	0.30	0.50	0.75	1.00	1.25	1.50	1.75
1.20	0.012	0.020	0.028	0.034	0.038	0.041	0.044
1.10	0.012	0.020	0.028	0.034	0.039	0.042	0.044
1.00	0.013	0.021	0.029	0.035	0.040	0.043	0.045
0.90	0.014	0.022	0.031	0.036	0.040	0.043	0.046
0.80	0.015	0.023	0.032	0.038	0.041	0.044	0.047
0.70	0.016	0.025	0.033	0.039	0.043	0.045	0.047
0.60	0.017	0.026	0.035	0.040	0.044	0.046	0.048
0.50	0.018	0.028	0.037	0.042	0.045	0.048	0.050
0.40	0.020	0.031	0.039	0.043	0.047	0.049	0.051
0.30	0.023	0.034	0.041	0.046	0.049	0.051	0.052

Table 8.4.7

$\phi4 = 0.0$

$\phi1 = 0.0$ $\phi0 = 0.0$

$\phi2 = 0.0$

μ	H/L						
	0.30	0.50	0.75	1.00	1.25	1.50	1.75
1.20	0.007	0.016	0.027	0.038	0.047	0.055	0.062
1.10	0.007	0.017	0.029	0.040	0.049	0.057	0.064
1.00	0.008	0.018	0.030	0.042	0.051	0.059	0.066
0.90	0.009	0.019	0.032	0.044	0.054	0.062	0.068
0.80	0.010	0.021	0.035	0.046	0.056	0.064	0.071
0.70	0.011	0.023	0.037	0.049	0.059	0.067	0.073
0.60	0.012	0.025	0.040	0.053	0.062	0.070	0.076
0.50	0.014	0.028	0.044	0.057	0.066	0.074	0.080
0.40	0.017	0.032	0.049	0.062	0.071	0.078	0.084
0.30	0.020	0.038	0.055	0.068	0.077	0.083	0.089

Table 8.4.8

$\phi4 = 1.0$

$\phi1 = 0.0$ $\phi3 = 0.0$

$\phi2 = 0.0$

μ	H/L						
	0.30	0.50	0.75	1.00	1.25	1.50	1.75
1.20	0.005	0.012	0.021	0.031	0.039	0.047	0.054
1.10	0.005	0.013	0.023	0.032	0.041	0.049	0.056
1.00	0.006	0.014	0.024	0.034	0.043	0.051	0.058
0.90	0.006	0.015	0.026	0.036	0.045	0.053	0.060
0.80	0.007	0.016	0.028	0.039	0.048	0.056	0.063
0.70	0.008	0.018	0.030	0.041	0.051	0.059	0.065
0.60	0.009	0.020	0.033	0.044	0.054	0.062	0.069
0.50	0.010	0.022	0.036	0.048	0.058	0.066	0.072
0.40	0.012	0.026	0.041	0.053	0.063	0.071	0.077
0.30	0.016	0.031	0.047	0.060	0.069	0.076	0.082

Table 8.4.9

$\phi4 = 1.0$

$\phi1 = 0.0$ $\phi3 = 0.0$

$\phi2 = 1.0$

μ	H/L						
	0.30	0.50	0.75	1.00	1.25	1.50	1.75
1.20	0.004	0.009	0.017	0.025	0.033	0.040	0.047
1.10	0.004	0.010	0.018	0.027	0.035	0.042	0.049
1.00	0.004	0.011	0.019	0.028	0.037	0.044	0.051
0.90	0.005	0.011	0.021	0.030	0.039	0.046	0.053
0.80	0.005	0.013	0.023	0.032	0.041	0.049	0.056
0.70	0.006	0.014	0.025	0.035	0.044	0.052	0.059
0.60	0.007	0.016	0.027	0.038	0.047	0.055	0.062
0.50	0.008	0.018	0.030	0.042	0.051	0.059	0.066
0.40	0.010	0.021	0.035	0.046	0.056	0.064	0.071
0.30	0.012	0.025	0.040	0.053	0.062	0.070	0.076

Table 8.4.10

$\phi4 = 0.0$

$\phi1 = 0.0$ $\phi3 = 1.0$

$\phi2 = 0.0$

μ	H/L						
	0.30	0.50	0.75	1.00	1.25	1.50	1.75
1.20	0.007	0.014	0.023	0.031	0.038	0.044	0.048
1.10	0.007	0.015	0.025	0.033	0.039	0.045	0.049
1.00	0.008	0.016	0.026	0.034	0.041	0.046	0.051
0.90	0.008	0.017	0.027	0.036	0.042	0.048	0.052
0.80	0.009	0.018	0.029	0.037	0.044	0.049	0.054
0.70	0.010	0.020	0.031	0.039	0.046	0.051	0.055
0.60	0.011	0.022	0.033	0.042	0.048	0.053	0.057
0.50	0.013	0.024	0.036	0.044	0.051	0.056	0.059
0.40	0.015	0.027	0.039	0.048	0.054	0.058	0.062
0.30	0.018	0.031	0.044	0.052	0.057	0.062	0.065

Table 8.4.11

$\phi 1 = 0.0$ $\phi 4 = 0.0$ $\phi 3 = 1.0$ $\phi 2 = 1.0$

```
* * * * * * * * *
*               *
*               *
*               *
*               *
*               *
*               *
* * * * * * * * *
```

μ	0.30	0.50	0.75	H/L 1.00	1.25	1.50	1.75
1.20	0.005	0.011	0.019	0.026	0.032	0.038	0.043
1.10	0.005	0.011	0.020	0.027	0.034	0.039	0.044
1.00	0.006	0.012	0.021	0.029	0.035	0.041	0.045
0.90	0.006	0.013	0.022	0.030	0.037	0.042	0.047
0.80	0.007	0.014	0.024	0.032	0.039	0.044	0.048
0.70	0.007	0.016	0.026	0.034	0.041	0.046	0.050
0.60	0.008	0.017	0.028	0.036	0.043	0.048	0.052
0.50	0.010	0.019	0.030	0.039	0.045	0.051	0.055
0.40	0.011	0.022	0.034	0.042	0.049	0.054	0.057
0.30	0.014	0.026	0.038	0.046	0.053	0.057	0.061

Table 8.4.12

$\phi 1 = 1.0$ $\phi 4 = 1.0$ $\phi 3 = 0.0$ $\phi 2 = 1.0$

```
* * * * * * * * *
*               *
*               *
*               *
*               *
*               *
*               *
* * * * * * * * *
```

μ	0.30	0.50	0.75	H/L 1.00	1.25	1.50	1.75
1.20	0.004	0.008	0.015	0.022	0.028	0.033	0.038
1.10	0.004	0.009	0.016	0.023	0.029	0.034	0.039
1.00	0.004	0.010	0.017	0.024	0.030	0.036	0.041
0.90	0.005	0.011	0.018	0.026	0.032	0.037	0.042
0.80	0.005	0.011	0.020	0.027	0.034	0.039	0.044
0.70	0.006	0.013	0.021	0.029	0.036	0.041	0.046
0.60	0.007	0.014	0.023	0.031	0.038	0.044	0.048
0.50	0.008	0.016	0.026	0.034	0.041	0.046	0.051
0.40	0.009	0.018	0.029	0.037	0.044	0.049	0.054
0.30	0.011	0.022	0.033	0.042	0.048	0.053	0.057

Table 8.4.13

$\phi 1 = 1.0$ $\phi 4 = 0.0$ $\phi 3 = 1.0$ $\phi 2 = 0.0$

```
* * * * * * * * *
*               *
*               *
*               *
*               *
*               *
*               *
* * * * * * * * *
```

μ	0.30	0.50	0.75	H/L 1.00	1.25	1.50	1.75
1.20	0.006	0.013	0.020	0.026	0.031	0.035	0.038
1.10	0.007	0.013	0.021	0.027	0.032	0.036	0.039
1.00	0.007	0.014	0.022	0.028	0.033	0.037	0.040
0.90	0.008	0.015	0.023	0.029	0.034	0.038	0.041
0.80	0.008	0.016	0.024	0.031	0.035	0.039	0.042
0.70	0.009	0.017	0.026	0.032	0.037	0.040	0.043
0.60	0.010	0.019	0.028	0.034	0.038	0.042	0.044
0.50	0.011	0.021	0.030	0.036	0.040	0.043	0.046
0.40	0.013	0.023	0.032	0.038	0.042	0.045	0.047
0.30	0.016	0.026	0.035	0.041	0.044	0.047	0.049

Table 8.4.14

$\phi 1 = 1.0$ $\phi 4 = 0.0$ $\phi 3 = 1.0$ $\phi 2 = 1.0$

```
* * * * * * * * *
*               *
*               *
*               *
*               *
*               *
*               *
* * * * * * * * *
```

μ	0.30	0.50	0.75	H/L 1.00	1.25	1.50	1.75
1.20	0.005	0.010	0.016	0.022	0.027	0.031	0.034
1.10	0.005	0.010	0.017	0.023	0.028	0.032	0.035
1.00	0.005	0.011	0.018	0.024	0.029	0.033	0.036
0.90	0.006	0.012	0.019	0.025	0.030	0.034	0.037
0.80	0.006	0.013	0.020	0.027	0.032	0.035	0.038
0.70	0.007	0.014	0.022	0.028	0.033	0.037	0.040
0.60	0.008	0.015	0.024	0.030	0.035	0.038	0.041
0.50	0.009	0.017	0.025	0.032	0.036	0.040	0.043
0.40	0.010	0.019	0.028	0.034	0.039	0.042	0.045
0.30	0.013	0.022	0.031	0.037	0.041	0.044	0.047

Table 8.4.15

$\phi1 = 1.0$ $\phi3 = 1.0$ $\phi4 = 1.0$ $\phi2 = 1.0$

μ	\multicolumn{7}{c}{H/L}
	0.30	0.50	0.75	1.00	1.25	1.50	1.75
1.20	0.003	0.008	0.014	0.019	0.024	0.028	0.031
1.10	0.004	0.008	0.014	0.020	0.025	0.029	0.032
1.00	0.004	0.009	0.015	0.021	0.026	0.030	0.033
0.90	0.004	0.010	0.016	0.022	0.027	0.031	0.034
0.80	0.005	0.010	0.017	0.023	0.028	0.032	0.035
0.70	0.005	0.011	0.019	0.025	0.030	0.033	0.037
0.60	0.006	0.013	0.020	0.026	0.031	0.035	0.038
0.50	0.007	0.014	0.022	0.028	0.033	0.037	0.040
0.40	0.008	0.016	0.024	0.031	0.035	0.039	0.042
0.30	0.010	0.019	0.028	0.034	0.038	0.042	0.044

Table 8.4.16

$\phi1 = 0.0$ $\phi2 = 0.0$ $\phi3 = 0.0$

μ	\multicolumn{7}{c}{H/L}
	0.30	0.50	0.75	1.00	1.25	1.50	1.75
1.20	0.008	0.020	0.040	0.062	0.085	0.108	0.133
1.10	0.009	0.022	0.042	0.066	0.090	0.114	0.141
1.00	0.009	0.023	0.046	0.071	0.096	0.122	0.151
0.90	0.010	0.026	0.050	0.076	0.103	0.131	0.162
0.80	0.012	0.028	0.054	0.083	0.111	0.142	0.175
0.70	0.013	0.032	0.060	0.091	0.121	0.156	0.191
0.60	0.015	0.036	0.067	0.100	0.135	0.173	0.211
0.50	0.018	0.042	0.077	0.113	0.153	0.195	0.237
0.40	0.021	0.050	0.090	0.131	0.177	0.225	0.272
0.30	0.027	0.062	0.108	0.160	0.214	0.269	0.325

Table 8.4.17

$\phi1 = 0.0$ $\phi2 = 0.0$ $\phi3 = 1.0$

μ	\multicolumn{7}{c}{H/L}
	0.30	0.50	0.75	1.00	1.25	1.50	1.75
1.20	0.006	0.014	0.029	0.046	0.065	0.084	0.104
1.10	0.006	0.016	0.031	0.050	0.069	0.090	0.110
1.00	0.007	0.017	0.034	0.053	0.074	0.096	0.116
0.90	0.007	0.019	0.037	0.058	0.080	0.102	0.125
0.80	0.008	0.021	0.040	0.063	0.087	0.110	0.136
0.70	0.009	0.023	0.045	0.070	0.095	0.120	0.149
0.60	0.011	0.026	0.051	0.078	0.105	0.134	0.165
0.50	0.013	0.031	0.058	0.088	0.118	0.152	0.186
0.40	0.015	0.037	0.069	0.102	0.138	0.176	0.215
0.30	0.020	0.046	0.084	0.123	0.167	0.212	0.258

Table 8.4.18

$\phi1 = 1.0$ $\phi2 = 0.0$ $\phi3 = 1.0$

μ	\multicolumn{7}{c}{H/L}
	0.30	0.50	0.75	1.00	1.25	1.50	1.75
1.20	0.004	0.011	0.022	0.036	0.051	0.067	0.084
1.10	0.005	0.012	0.024	0.039	0.055	0.072	0.089
1.00	0.005	0.013	0.026	0.042	0.059	0.077	0.095
0.90	0.005	0.014	0.028	0.045	0.064	0.083	0.102
0.80	0.006	0.016	0.031	0.050	0.070	0.090	0.110
0.70	0.007	0.017	0.035	0.055	0.076	0.098	0.119
0.60	0.008	0.020	0.040	0.062	0.085	0.108	0.133
0.50	0.009	0.023	0.046	0.071	0.096	0.122	0.151
0.40	0.012	0.028	0.054	0.083	0.111	0.142	0.175
0.30	0.015	0.036	0.067	0.100	0.135	0.173	0.211

Table 8.4.19

μ	0.30	0.50	0.75	H/L 1.00	1.25	1.50	1.75
1.20	0.008	0.018	0.034	0.050	0.066	0.082	0.098
1.10	0.008	0.019	0.036	0.053	0.070	0.086	0.102
1.00	0.009	0.021	0.038	0.056	0.074	0.091	0.108
0.90	0.010	0.023	0.041	0.060	0.079	0.097	0.113
0.80	0.011	0.025	0.045	0.065	0.084	0.103	0.120
0.70	0.012	0.028	0.049	0.070	0.091	0.110	0.128
0.60	0.014	0.031	0.054	0.077	0.099	0.119	0.138
0.50	0.016	0.035	0.061	0.085	0.109	0.130	0.149
0.40	0.019	0.041	0.069	0.097	0.121	0.144	0.164
0.30	0.024	0.050	0.082	0.112	0.139	0.162	0.183

$\phi 1 = 0.0$

$\phi 2 = 1.0$

```
* * * * * * * *
*
*
*
*
* * * * * * * *
```

$\phi 3 = 0.0$

Table 8.4.20

μ	0.30	0.50	0.75	H/L 1.00	1.25	1.50	1.75
1.20	0.005	0.013	0.025	0.039	0.053	0.066	0.079
1.10	0.006	0.014	0.027	0.041	0.056	0.069	0.083
1.00	0.006	0.015	0.029	0.044	0.059	0.073	0.088
0.90	0.007	0.017	0.032	0.047	0.063	0.078	0.093
0.80	0.008	0.018	0.034	0.051	0.067	0.084	0.099
0.70	0.009	0.021	0.038	0.056	0.073	0.090	0.106
0.60	0.010	0.023	0.042	0.061	0.080	0.098	0.115
0.50	0.012	0.027	0.048	0.068	0.089	0.108	0.126
0.40	0.014	0.032	0.055	0.078	0.100	0.121	0.139
0.30	0.018	0.039	0.066	0.092	0.116	0.138	0.158

$\phi 1 = 0.0$

$\phi 2 = 1.0$

```
* * * * * * * *
*
*
*
*
* * * * * * * *
```

$\phi 3 = 1.0$

Table 8.4.21

μ	0.30	0.50	0.75	H/L 1.00	1.25	1.50	1.75
1.20	0.004	0.010	0.020	0.031	0.043	0.054	0.065
1.10	0.004	0.011	0.021	0.033	0.045	0.057	0.069
1.00	0.005	0.012	0.023	0.035	0.048	0.061	0.073
0.90	0.005	0.013	0.025	0.038	0.052	0.065	0.078
0.80	0.006	0.014	0.027	0.041	0.056	0.069	0.083
0.70	0.007	0.016	0.030	0.045	0.060	0.075	0.090
0.60	0.008	0.018	0.034	0.050	0.066	0.082	0.098
0.50	0.009	0.021	0.038	0.056	0.074	0.091	0.108
0.40	0.011	0.025	0.045	0.065	0.084	0.103	0.120
0.30	0.014	0.031	0.054	0.077	0.099	0.119	0.138

$\phi 1 = 1.0$

$\phi 2 = 1.0$

```
* * * * * * * *
*
*
*
*
* * * * * * * *
```

$\phi 3 = 1.0$

8.5 Span/thickness design tables

For the purpose of the following tables:

Density = kg/m³
Wind = N/m²
ϕ = degree of fixity
  0.00 pinned
  1.00 fixed
f_b, f_p = N/mm²
Limit as per Clause 36.3
Notes: When not given, the panels tend to span in one direction
  *Controlled by slenderness limits.

Tables 8.5.1. to 8.5.16 inclusive — three sides horizontal

```
*              *
*              *
*              *
*              *
*              *
*              *
*              *
*              *
* * * * * * * * *
```

Table 8.5.1

Density 600 f_b 0.25		Wind 550 f_p 0.45		γ_m 3.5	ϕ1 0.00	ϕ2 0.00 γ_f 1.2		ϕ3 0.00 Limit 1350
Height				Length				
	1	2	3	4	5	6	7	8
1	50	80	105					
2		98	131	158	182	204		
3		105	145	179	207	233	257	278
4			153	191	225	254	279	304
5			158	200	237	269	298	324
6				205	245	281	313	342
7				210	251	289	324	356
8					256	296	332	366

Table 8.5.2

Density 600 f_b 0.25	Wind 550	f_p 0.45		γ_m 3.5	ϕ1 1.00	ϕ2 1.00 γ_f 1.2		ϕ3 1.00 Limit 1500
Height				Length				
	1	2	3	4	5	6	7	8
1	35	57	72					
2		70	94	112	128	141		
3		75	104	128	149	166	182	196
4			109	137	162	183	202	218
5			113	143	170	195	216	236
6				147	177	203	227	249
7				150	181	209	235	259
8					184	214	241	266

Table 8.5.3

Density 600		Wind 650			φ1 0.00		φ2 0.00		φ3 0.00
f_b 0.25		f_p 0.45			γ_m 3.5		γ_f 1.2		Limit 1350

Height	Length							
	1	2	3	4	5	6	7	8
1	54	87	114					
2		106	142	172	198	222		
3		114	158	194	225	253	279	303
4			166	208	244	276	303	331
5			172	217	257	293	325	353
6				223	266	305	340	372
7				228	273	314	352	386
8					278	322	361	398

Table 8.5.4

Density 600		Wind 650			φ1 1.00		φ2 1.00		φ3 1.00
f_b 0.25		f_p 0.45			γ_m 3.5		γ_f 1.2		Limit 1500

Height	Length							
	1	2	3	4	5	6	7	8
1	38	62	78					
2		76	102	122	139	153		
3		81	113	139	162	180	198	213
4			119	149	176	199	219	237
5			123	156	185	212	235	256
6				160	192	221	247	271
7				164	197	227	255	281
8					201	233	262	290

Table 8.5.5

Density 600		Wind 750			φ1 0.00		φ2 0.00		φ3 0.00
f_b 0.25		f_p 0.45			γ_m 3.5		γ_f 1.2		Limit 1350

Height	Length							
	1	2	3	4	5	6	7	8
1	58	94	122					
2		114	153	184	213	238		
3		123	170	209	241	272	300	325
4			179	224	262	296	326	356
5			185	233	276	315	349	379
6				240	286	328	365	399
7				245	293	338	378	415
8					299	345	388	428

Table 8.5.6

Density 600		Wind 750			φ1 1.00		φ2 1.00		φ3 1.00
f_b 0.25		f_p 0.45			γ_m 3.5		γ_f 1.2		Limit 1500

Height	Length							
	1	2	3	4	5	6	7	8
1	41	66	84					
2		81	109	131	149	165		
3		87	121	150	174	194	212	229
4			128	160	189	214	236	255
5			132	167	199	227	253	275
6				172	206	237	265	291
7				176	211	244	274	302
8					215	250	282	311

Table 8.5.7

Density 600 f_b 0.25	Wind 900 f_p 0.45		γ_m 3.5	$\phi1$ 0.00		$\phi2$ 0.00 γ_f 1.2		$\phi3$ 0.00 Limit 1350
Height				Length				
	1	2	3	4	5	6	7	8
1	63	103	134					
2		125	168	202	233	261		
3		134	186	229	264	297	328	356
4			196	245	287	324	357	389
5			202	255	303	345	382	415
6				263	313	359	400	437
7				268	321	370	414	455
8					328	378	425	460

Table 8.5.8

Density 600 f_b 0.25	Wind 900 f_p 0.45		γ_m 3.5	$\phi1$ 1.00		$\phi2$ 1.00 γ_f 1.2		$\phi3$ 1.00 Limit 1500
Height				Length				
	1	2	3	4	5	6	7	8
1	45	73	92					
2		89	120	144	164	181		
3		96	133	164	190	212	232	250
4			140	176	207	234	258	279
5			145	183	218	249	277	302
6				189	226	260	290	318
7				192	232	268	301	331
8					236	274	309	341

Table 8.5.9

Density 600 f_b 0.25	Wind 550 f_p 0.60		γ_m 3.5	$\phi1$ 0.00		$\phi2$ 0.00 γ_f 1.2		$\phi3$ 0.00 Limit 1350
Height				Length				
	1	2	3	4	5	6	7	8
1	44	73	96					
2		88	119	144	166	187		
.3		93	130	162	188	211	234	255
4			136	172	203	231	255	277
5			140	178	212	243	271	297
6				182	219	252	283	311
7				186	224	259	292	322
8					227	264	298	330

Table 8.5.10

Density 600 f_b 0.25	Wind 550 f_p 0.60		γ_m 3.5	$\phi1$ 1.00		$\phi2$ 1.00 γ_f 1.2		$\phi3$ 1.00 Limit 1500
Height				Length				
	1	2	3	4	5	6	7	8
1	31	52	66					
2		62	85	103	118	131		
3		66	93	116	135	152	167	181
4			97	123	146	166	184	201
5			100*	127	153	175	196	215
6				131	157	182	205	225
7				140*	161	187	211	233
8					163	190	216	239

Table 8.5.11

Density 600								
f_b 0.25	Wind 650 f_p 0.60		γ_m 3.5	ϕ1 0.00	γ_f 1.2	ϕ2 0.00		ϕ3 0.00 Limit 1350

Height	Length							
	1	2	3	4	5	6	7	8
1	48	80	104					
2		95	129	156	181	203		
3		101	141	176	205	230	254	277
4			148	187	221	251	277	301
5			152	193	231	265	295	322
6				198	238	274	308	338
7				202	243	282	317	350
8					247	287	324	359

Table 8.5.12

Density 600								
f_b 0.25	Wind 650 f_p 0.60		γ_m 3.5	ϕ1 1.00	γ_f 1.2	ϕ2 1.00		ϕ3 1.00 Limit 1500

Height	Length							
	1	2	3	4	5	6	7	8
1	34	57	72					
2		68	92	112	128	142		
3		72	101	126	147	166	181	196
4			106	134	159	181	200	218
5			109	139	166	191	213	234
6				142	171	198	222	245
7				145	175	203	229	254
8					178	207	234	260

Table 8.5.13

Density 600								
f_b 0.25	Wind 750 f_p 0.60		γ_m 3.5	ϕ1 0.00	γ_f 1.2	ϕ2 0.00		ϕ3 0.00 Limit 1350

Height	Length							
	1	2	3	4	5	6	7	8
1	52	85	112					
2		102	139	168	194	218		
3		109	152	189	220	247	273	298
4			159	200	237	269	298	324
5			163	208	248	284	317	346
6				213	256	295	330	363
7				217	261	302	340	375
8					266	308	348	385

Table 8.5.14

Density 600								
f_b 0.25	Wind 750 f_p 0.60		γ_m 3.5	ϕ1 1.00	γ_f 1.2	ϕ2 1.00		ϕ3 1.00 Limit 1500

Height	Length							
	1	2	3	4	5	6	7	8
1	37	61	78					
2		73	99	120	137	153		
3		77	108	135	158	178	195	211
4			113	144	170	194	215	234
5			117	149	178	205	229	251
6				153	184	212	239	263
7				155	188	218	246	272
8					191	222	252	279

Table 8.5.15

Density 600		Wind 900		$\phi 1$ 0.00		$\phi 2$ 0.00		$\phi 3$ 0.00
f_b 0.25		f_p 0.60		γ_m 3.5		γ_f 1.2		Limit 1350

Height	\multicolumn{8}{c}{Length}
	1	2	3	4	5	6	7	8
1	57	94	122					
2		112	152	184	213	239		
3		119	166	207	241	271	299	326
4			174	219	260	295	326	355
5			179	228	272	311	347	379
6				233	280	323	362	398
7				237	286	331	373	411
8					291	338	381	422

Table 8.5.16

Density 600		Wind 900		$\phi 1$ 1.00		$\phi 2$ 1.00		$\phi 3$ 1.00
f_b 0.25		f_p 0.60		γ_m 3.5		γ_f 1.2		Limit 1500

Height	\multicolumn{8}{c}{Length}
	1	2	3	4	5	6	7	8
1	40	67	85					
2		80	108	132	150	167		
3		85	119	148	173	195	213	231
4			124	157	187	213	236	257
5			128	163	195	224	251	275
6				167	201	233	262	288
7				170	206	239	270	298
8					209	244	276	306

Tables 8.5.17 to 8.5.32 inclusive — four sides

```
* * * * * * * * *
*               *
*               *
*               *
*               *
*               *
*               *
*               *
* * * * * * * * *
```

Table 8.5.17

Density 600		Wind 550		$\phi 1$ 0.00	$\phi 2$ 0.00	$\phi 3$ 0.00	$\phi 4$ 0.00
f_b 0.25		f_p 0.45		γ_m 3.5		γ_f 1.2	Limit 2025

Height	\multicolumn{8}{c}{Length}
	1	2	3	4	5	6	7	8
1	40	56	63					
2		79	98	109	117	123		
3		91	117	136	150	160	168	175
4			130	154	173	188	200	209
5			138	167	190	209	224	237
6				177	203	225	244	259
7				184	214	238	259	277
8					222	249	272	292

Table 8.5.18

Density 600 f_b 0.25		f_p 0.45		γ_m 3.5		$\phi1$ 1.00 $\phi2$ 1.00 γ_f 1.2	$\phi3$ 1.00	$\phi4$ 1.00 Limit 2250

Height	Length							
	1	2	3	4	5	6	7	8
1	29	40*	60*					
2		57	70	80*	100*	120*		
3		65	84	98	108	120*	140*	160*
4			93	111	125	135	144	160*
5			100*	120	137	151	162	171
6				127	146	163	176	188
7				140*	154	172	188	201
8					160*	180	197	212

Table 8.5.19

Density 600 f_b 0.25		f_p 0.45		γ_m 3.5		$\phi1$ 0.00 $\phi2$ 0.00 γ_f 1.2	$\phi3$ 0.00	$\phi4$ 0.00 Limit 2025

Height	Length							
	1	2	3	4	5	6	7	8
1	44	61	69					
2		86	106	119	127	134		
3		99	128	148	163	174	183	190
4			141	168	188	204	217	228
5			151	182	207	227	244	257
6				192	221	245	265	282
7				200	232	259	282	301
8					241	271	296	318

Table 8.5.20

Density 600 f_b 0.25		f_p 0.45		γ_m 3.5		$\phi1$ 1.00 $\phi2$ 1.00 γ_f 1.2	$\phi3$ 1.00	$\phi4$ 1.00 Limit 2250

Height	Length							
	1	2	3	4	5	6	7	8
1	31	43	60*					
2		62	76	85	100*	120*		
3		71	91	106	117	125	140*	160*
4			101	120	135	147	157	164
5			108	130	149	164	176	186
6				138	159	177	192	204
7				144	167	187	204	219
8					174	195	214	231

Table 8.5.21

Density 600 f_b 0.25		f_p 0.45		γ_m 3.5		$\phi1$ 0.00 $\phi2$ 0.00 γ_f 1.2	$\phi3$ 0.00	$\phi4$ 0.00 Limit 2025

Height	Length							
	1	2	3	4	5	6	7	8
1	47	65	74					
2		93	114	128	137	144		
3		106	137	159	175	187	197	204
4			152	180	202	220	233	244
5			162	195	222	244	262	277
6				206	237	263	284	302
7				215	249	278	303	324
8					259	291	318	342

Table 8.5.22

Density 600 f_b 0.25	Wind 750 f_p 0.45			γ_m 3.5			$\phi1$ 1.00 $\phi2$ 1.00 γ_f 1.2	$\phi3$ 1.00 $\phi4$ 1.00 Limit 2250
Height				Length				
	1	2	3	4	5	6	7	8
1	33	46	60*					
2		66	81	91	100*	120*		
3		76	98	114	126	135	141	160*
4			109	129	145	158	168	177
5			116	140	160	176	189	200
6				148	171	190	206	219
7				154	180	201	219	235
8					186	210	230	248

Table 8.5.23

Density 600 f_b 0.25	Wind 900 f_p 0.45			γ_m 3.5			$\phi1$ 0.00 $\phi2$ 0.00 γ_f 1.2	$\phi3$ 0.00 $\phi4$ 0.00 Limit 2025
Height				Length				
	1	2	3	4	5	6	7	8
1	52	71	81					
2		102	125	140	150	157		
3		117	150	174	192	205	215	224
4			166	198	222	240	256	268
5			177	214	244	267	287	303
6				226	260	288	312	331
7				235	273	305	332	355
8					283	318	348	374

Table 8.5.24

Density 600 f_b 0.25	Wind 900 f_p 0.45			γ_m 3.5			$\phi1$ 1.00 $\phi2$ 1.00 γ_f 1.2	$\phi3$ 1.00 $\phi4$ 1.00 Limit 2250
Height				Length				
	1	2	3	4	5	6	7	8
1	37	51	60*					
2		72	89	100	107	120*		
3		83	107	125	138	147	155	161
4			119	142	159	173	184	193
5			127	154	175	193	207	219
6				162	187	208	225	240
7				169	197	220	240	257
8					204	230	252	272

Table 8.5.25

Density 600 f_b 0.25	Wind 550 f_p 0.60			γ_m 3.5			$\phi1$ 0.00 $\phi2$ 0.00 γ_f 1.2	$\phi3$ 0.00 $\phi4$ 0.00 Limit 2025
Height				Length				
	1	2	3	4	5	6	7	8
1	37	53	61					
2		73	91	104	112	120*		
3		82	108	127	141	152	161	168
4			118	142	161	176	189	199
5			125	153	175	194	210	223
6				160	186	208	227	242
7				166	194	219	240	258
8					201	227	259	271

Table 8.5.26

Density 600 f_b 0.25	Wind 550 f_p 0.60	γ_m 3.5	$\phi1$ 1.00 $\phi2$ 1.00 γ_f 1.2	$\phi3$ 1.00 $\phi4$ 1.00 Limit 2250

Height	Length							
	1	2	3	4	5	6	7	8
1	26	40*	60*					
2		52	65	80*	100*	120*		
3		60*	77	91	101	120*	140*	160*
4			84	102	116	127	140*	160*
5			100*	109	126	140	151	161
6				120*	134	150	164	175
7				140*	140*	158	173	187
8					160*	164	181	196

Table 8.5.27

Density 600 f_b 0.25	Wind 650 f_p 0.60	γ_m 3.5	$\phi1$ 0.00 $\phi2$ 0.00 γ_f 1.2	$\phi3$ 0.00 $\phi4$ 0.00 Limit 2025

Height	Length							
	1	2	3	4	5	6	7	8
1	40	57	66					
2		79	99	113	122	129		
3		89	117	138	154	165	175	182
4			128	155	175	192	205	216
5			136	166	191	211	228	243
6				174	202	226	246	264
7				181	211	238	261	280
8					218	247	272	294

Table 8.5.28

Density 600 f_b 0.25	Wind 650 f_p 0.60	γ_m 3.5	$\phi1$ 1.00 $\phi2$ 1.00 γ_f 1.2	$\phi3$ 1.00 $\phi4$ 1.00 Limit 2250

Height	Length							
	1	2	3	4	5	6	7	8
1	28	41	60*					
2		56	71	80	100*	120*		
3		64	84	99	110	120*	140*	160*
4			92	111	126	138	148	160*
5			100*	119	137	152	165	175
6				125	145	163	178	191
7				140*	152	171	188	203
8					160*	178	197	213

Table 8.5.29

Density 600 f_b 0.25	Wind 750 f_p 0.60	γ_m 3.5	$\phi1$ 0.00 $\phi2$ 0.00 γ_f 1.2	$\phi3$ 0.00 $\phi4$ 0.00 Limit 2025

Height	Length							
	1	2	3	4	5	6	7	8
1	43	62	71					
2		85	107	121	131	138		
3		96	126	148	165	178	188	196
4			138	166	188	206	220	232
5			146	178	205	227	245	261
6				187	217	243	265	283
7				194	227	255	280	301
8					235	265	292	316

Table 8.5.30

Density 600 f_b 0.25		Wind 750 f_p 0.60		γ_m 3.5		$\phi1$ 1.00 $\phi2$ 1.00 γ_f 1.2		$\phi3$ 1.00 $\phi4$ 1.00 Limit 2250

Height	Length							
	1	2	3	4	5	6	7	8
1	31	44	60*					
2		61	76	86	100*	120*		
3		68	90	106	118	128	140*	160*
4			99	119	135	148	159	168
5			104	128	147	163	177	188
6				134	156	175	191	205
7				140*	163	184	202	218
8					169	191	211	229

Table 8.5.31

Density 600 f_b 0.25		Wind 900 f_p 0.60		γ_m 3.5		$\phi1$ 0.00 $\phi2$ 0.00 γ_f 1.2		$\phi3$ 0.00 $\phi4$ 0.00 Limit 2025

Height	Length							
	1	2	3	4	5	6	7	8
1	47	68	78					
2		93	117	132	144	152		
3		105	138	162	181	195	206	215
4			151	182	206	226	242	255
5			160	195	224	249	269	286
6				205	238	266	290	310
7				212	249	280	307	330
8					257	291	320	346

Table 8.5.32

Density 600 f_b 0.25		Wind 900 f_p 0.60		γ_m 3.5		$\phi1$ 1.00 $\phi2$ 1.00 γ_f 1.2		$\phi3$ 1.00 $\phi4$ 1.00 Limit 2250

Height	Length							
	1	2	3	4	5	6	7	8
1	34	48	60*					
2		66	83	95	103	120*		
3		75	99	116	130	140	148	160*
4			108	130	148	162	174	184
5			114	140	161	179	194	206
6				147	171	192	209	224
7				152	179	202	222	239
8					185	210	231	251

Tables 8.5.33 to 8.5.48 inclusive — three sides vertical

```
* * * * * * * *
*
*
*
*
*
*
* * * * * * * *
```

Table 8.5.33

Density 600 f_b 0.25	Wind 550 f_p 0.45		γ_m 3.5		$\phi 1$ 0.00 γ_f 1.2	$\phi 2$ 0.00	$\phi 3$ 0.00 Limit 1350	
Height	1	2	3	Length 4	5	6	7	8
1	56	67	72					
2		109	123	132	137	141		
3		138	159	175	186	194	199	204
4			188	208	225	237	246	253
5			209	235	255	272	285	296
6				257	280	300	317	331
7				274	302	324	343	361
8					319	345	366	385

Table 8.5.34

Density 600 f_b 0.25	Wind 550 f_p 0.45		γ_m 3.5		$\phi 1$ 1.00 γ_f 1.2	$\phi 2$ 1.00	$\phi 3$ 1.00 Limit 1500	
Height	1	2	3	Length 4	5	6	7	8
1	40	48	60*					
2		78	88	94	100*	120*		
3		97	115	126	133	138	142	160*
4			134	151	162	170	176	181
5			150	169	185	197	206	213
6				185	204	219	231	240
7				198	220	237	252	263
8					233	252	269	283

Table 8.5.35

Density 600 f_b 0.25	Wind 650 f_p 0.45		γ_m 3.5		$\phi 1$ 0.00 γ_f 1.2	$\phi 2$ 0.00	$\phi 3$ 0.00 Limit 1350	
Height	1	2	3	Length 4	5	6	7	8
1	60	73	78					
2		118	134	143	149	153		
3		150	173	191	202	211	217	221
4			204	226	244	258	268	275
5			228	255	277	296	310	321
6				279	305	326	345	360
7				298	328	352	373	392
8					347	375	398	419

Table 8.5.36

Density 600 f_b 0.25	Wind 650 f_p 0.45		γ_m 3.5		ϕ_1 1.00 γ_f 1.2	ϕ_2 1.00	ϕ_3 1.00 Limit 1500	
Height	1	2	3	Length 4	5	6	7	8
1	43	52	60*					
2		85	96	102	106	120*		
3		106	125	137	145	150	154	160*
4			146	164	176	185	192	197
5			163	184	201	214	224	231
6				202	222	238	251	261
7				215	239	258	273	286
8					253	274	293	308

Table 8.5.37

Density 600 f_b 0.25	Wind 750 f_p 0.45		γ_m 3.5		ϕ_1 0.00 γ_f 1.2	ϕ_2 0.00	ϕ_3 0.00 Limit 1350	
Height	1	2	3	Length 4	5	6	7	8
1	65	78	84					
2		127	144	154	160	164		
3		161	186	205	217	226	233	238
4			219	243	263	277	287	296
5			245	274	298	318	333	345
6				300	327	350	370	387
7				320	352	378	401	421
8					373	403	427	450

Table 8.5.38

Density 600 f_b 0.25	Wind 750 f_p 0.45		γ_m 3.5		ϕ_1 1.00 γ_f 1.2	ϕ_2 1.00	ϕ_3 1.00 Limit 1500	
Height	1	2	3	Length 4	5	6	7	8
1	46	56	60*					
2		91	103	109	114	120*		
3		114	134	147	155	161	166	169
4			157	176	189	199	206	212
5			175	198	216	230	240	248
6				217	238	256	269	280
7				231	256	277	294	307
8					272	295	314	331

Table 8.5.39

Density 600 f_b 0.25	Wind 900 f_p 0.45		γ_m 3.5		ϕ_1 0.00 γ_f 1.2	ϕ_2 0.00	ϕ_3 0.00 Limit 1350	
Height	1	2	3	Length 4	5	6	7	8
1	71	86	92					
2		139	158	168	175	180		
3		176	204	224	238	248	255	260
4			240	266	288	303	315	324
5			268	300	326	348	365	378
6				328	358	384	406	424
7				350	386	414	439	462
8					408	441	468	493

Table 8.5.40

Density 600 f_b 0.25	Wind 900 f_p 0.45		γ_m 3.5		$\phi 1$ 1.00 γ_f 1.2	$\phi 2$ 1.00	$\phi 3$ 1.00 Limit 1500	
Height	1	2	3	Length 4	5	6	7	8
1	51	61	65					
2		100	113	120	125	128		
3		125	147	161	170	177	182	185
4			172	193	207	218	226	232
5			191	217	237	252	263	272
6				237	261	280	295	307
7				254	281	303	322	337
8					298	323	344	362

Table 8.5.41

Density 600 f_b 0.25	Wind 550 f_p 0.60		γ_m 3.5		$\phi 1$ 0.00 γ_f 1.2	$\phi 2$ 0.00	$\phi 3$ 0.00 Limit 1350	
Height	1	2	3	Length 4	5	6	7	8
1	53	65	70					
2		103	119	128	134	138		
3		130	151	168	179	188	194	199
4			177	197	214	228	238	246
5			196	222	242	259	273	284
6				241	265	284	301	316
7				256	284	307	325	342
8					298	325	346	365

Table 8.5.42

Density 600 f_b 0.25	Wind 550 f_p 0.60		γ_m 3.5		$\phi 1$ 1.00 γ_f 1.2	$\phi 2$ 1.00	$\phi 3$ 1.00 Limit 1500	
Height	1	2	3	Length 4	5	6	7	8
1	37	46	60*					
2		74	85	91	100*	120*		
3		91	109	121	129	134	140*	160*
4			126	142	155	164	171	176
5			139	160	175	188	197	205
6				173	192	207	220	230
7				184	206	223	238	251
8					217	237	253	268

Table 8.5.43

Density 600 f_b 0.25	Wind 650 f_p 0.60		γ_m 3.5		$\phi 1$ 0.00 γ_f 1.2	$\phi 2$ 0.00	$\phi 3$ 0.00 Limit 1350	
Height	1	2	3	Length 4	5	6	7	8
1	58	71	76					
2		112	129	139	145	150		
3		141	165	182	195	204	211	216
4			193	215	233	247	258	267
5			214	242	263	281	297	309
6				262	288	309	327	344
7				278	309	333	353	372
8					324	353	376	396

Table 8.5.44

Density 600		Wind 650				$\phi 1$ 1.00	$\phi 2$ 1.00	$\phi 3$ 1.00
f_b 0.25		f_p 0.60		γ_m 3.5		γ_f 1.2		Limit 1500

Height	Length							
	1	2	3	4	5	6	7	8
1	41	50	60*					
2		80	92	99	103	120*		
3		99	118	131	140	146	151	160*
4			137	155	168	178	186	191
5			152	174	191	204	215	223
6				189	209	225	239	250
7				200	224	243	259	272
8					236	258	276	291

Table 8.5.45

Density 600		Wind 750				$\phi 1$ 0.00	$\phi 2$ 0.00	$\phi 3$ 0.00
f_b 0.25		f_p 0.60		γ_m 3.5		γ_f 1.2		Limit 1350

Height	Length							
	1	2	3	4	5	6	7	8
1	62	76	82					
2		121	138	149	156	161		
3		152	177	196	210	219	227	232
4			207	231	250	266	277	287
5			229	260	282	302	319	332
6				282	310	332	352	369
7				299	331	358	380	399
8					348	379	404	426

Table 8.5.46

Density 600		Wind 750				$\phi 1$ 1.00	$\phi 2$ 1.00	$\phi 3$ 1.00
f_b 0.25		f_p 0.60		γ_m 3.5		γ_f 1.2		Limit 1500

Height	Length							
	1	2	3	4	5	6	7	8
1	44	54	60*					
2		86	99	106	111	120*		
3		106	127	141	150	157	162	166
4			147	166	181	191	199	206
5			163	186	205	219	231	240
6				203	224	242	257	268
7				215	240	261	278	293
8					254	277	296	313

Table 8.5.47

Density 600		Wind 900				$\phi 1$ 0.00	$\phi 2$ 0.00	$\phi 3$ 0.00
f_b 0.25		f_p 0.60		γ_m 3.5		γ_f 1.2		Limit 1350

Height	Length							
	1	2	3	4	5	6	7	8
1	68	83	90					
2		132	152	163	171	176		
3		166	194	215	230	240	248	254
4			227	253	274	291	304	314
5			251	284	309	331	349	364
6				309	339	364	385	404
7				327	363	392	416	438
8					382	415	443	467

Table 8.5.48

Density 600 f_b 0.25	Wind 900 f_p 0.60			γ_m 3.5	$\phi1$ 1.00 γ_f 1.2	$\phi2$ 1.00	$\phi3$ 1.00 Limit 1500	
Height	Length							
	1	2	3	4	5	6	7	8
1	48	59	64					
2		94	108	116	122•	125		
3		117	139	154	164	172	177	181
4			161	182	198	210	218	225
5			178	204	224	240	253	262
6				222	246	265	281	294
7				236	263	285	304	321
8					278	303	324	343

8.6 Design to CP 121

The previous part of this Chapter, *Sections 8.1 to 8.5*, dealt with the mathematical solutions to the design of plain masonry walls subject to lateral loading. It is possible to produce lateral design load tables based on the recommendations of BS 5628 (*Sections 8.4 and 8.5*) but even so it is still necessary to determine a number of basic items such as the design wind pressure, the type of support conditions, and so on, before they can be used. However, by imposing certain conditions it is possible to simplify the sizing of a wall subject to lateral wind pressure even further. Such an approach is given in CP 121[8.3] which provides simple area/thickness rules applicable to buildings up to and including four storeys.

The general approach given in CP 121 is explained in this Section, although it should be noted that CP 121 is currently being revised and will also include allowance for openings which it currently does not.

Clause 3.2.2.2 of CP 121 starts by stating that non-loadbearing walls should be designed on engineering principles — which may now be taken to mean BS 5628. However, providing the building and walls comply with the following conditions, then the walls may be proportioned directly from simple rules.

The restrictions applied are:

(1) the building is not more than four storeys;

(2) the actual thickness in solid walls is not less than 90 mm;

(3) in double leaf (cavity) walls, the actual thickness of each leaf is not less than 90 mm, the cavity width does not exceed 100 mm, and metal ties are used and spaced in accordance with Table 3.11 except that butterfly ties may only be employed in cavities not exceeding 60 mm in width in Zones 1, 2 and 3;

(4) the walls are supported on any three edges;

(5) the walls are free from any doors, windows or other openings unless intermediate supports are provided as shown in Figure 8.25;

(6) the mortar is not below designation (iii).

To produce simple rules it is necessary to assume certain general exposure conditions. Therefore, to cover for the rather exposed site it is stated that the recommendations may not apply to walls in buildings on hill-tops or exposed coastal sites, or in valleys known to produce wind funnelling. In these situations, advice should be taken as to whether the site may be treated as being in the next higher exposure Zone. In this event reference may be made to CP3:Chapter V:Part 2 for guidance. It is also fairly obvious that any support must be sufficient to carry the transmitted load without undue deflection. Unfortunately no values are given for the wind pressure in each Zone and therefore those given later may be of use. Characteristic loads of connections are given in *Chapter 3*. The approach used in CP 121 is in three stages as follows:

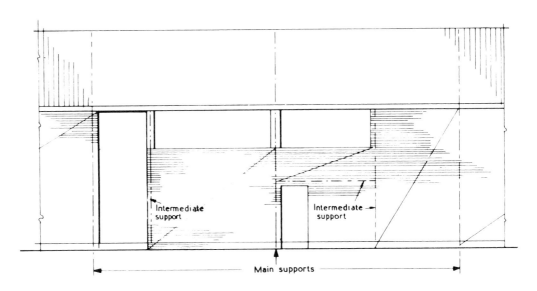

Figure 8.25 Intermediate supports

STAGE ONE
Determine the exposure Zone from Figure 8.26 appropriate to the position at which the building is to be located.

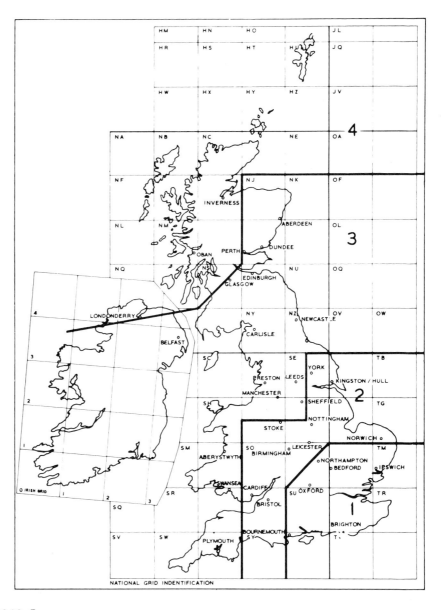

Figure 8.26 Exposure zones

Determine the number of sides on which the wall is supported and whether the supports are pinned or fixed (see Figures 8.27 to 8.30). Where the conditions for assessing a fixed or pinned support are not met, the edge should be regarded as being free.

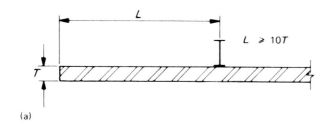

(a)

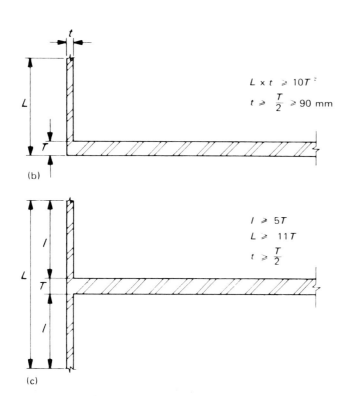

(b)

(c)

Figure 8.27 Fixed support conditions in solid walls

STAGE THREE

From the exposure Zone and support conditions determine the permitted area/thickness from Table 8.3 checking that the distance between the supports does not exceed forty times the total thickness of the masonry in the wall.

Figures 8.27 to 8.30 indicating pinned and fixed supports may also be of use in assessing support conditions when designing in accordance with BS 5628. In addition, by considering typical low rise buildings and the basic wind speeds in the various exposure Zones, it is possible to show that the dynamic wind pressure for the four Zones applicable to buildings up to four storeys will be in the following general region:

Zone 1   0.55 kN/m^2

Zone 2   0.65 kN/m^2

Zone 3   0.75 kN/m^2

Zone 4   0.90 kN/m^2

Further consideration of recent wind surveys suggests that the Zones may need to be modified as shown by the dotted lines in Figure 8.26.

Free standing walls

CP 121 also provides useful information on the sizing of free standing walls. It is stated that straight non-loadbearing walls, whether external or internal, subject to wind pressures, should, unless stability calculations are carried out, have height to thickness ratios

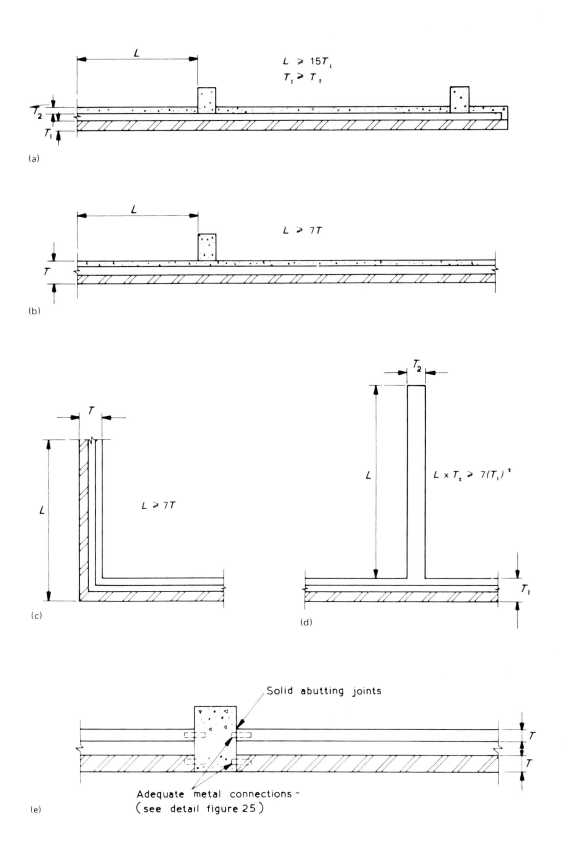

$L \geqslant 15T_1$
$T_1 \geqslant T_2$

(a)

$L \geqslant 7T$

(b)

$L \geqslant 7T$

(c)

$L \times T_1 \geqslant 7(T_1)^2$

(d)

Solid abutting joints

Adequate metal connections –
(see detail figure 25)

(e)

Figure 8.28 Fixed support conditions in cavity walls

not exceeding those given in Table 8.4, if there is no horizontal damp-proof course or if there is a horizontal damp-proof course which can develop tension vertically across it.

137

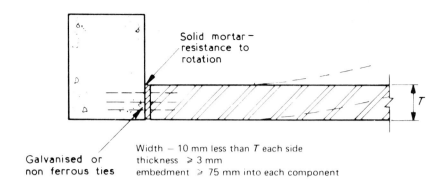

(a)

Solid mortar – resistance to rotation

Width – 10 mm less than T each side
thickness $\geqslant$ 3 mm
embedment $\geqslant$ 75 mm into each component

Galvanised or non ferrous ties

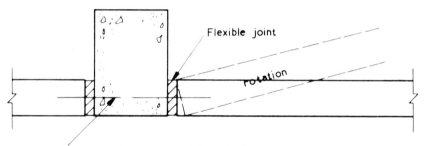

Tie

(b)

Figure 8.29 Details of fixed support conditions to columns

Flexible joint

rotation

Tie greased or wrapped in polythene

Figure 8.30 Details of pinned support conditions to columns

Table 8.3 Maximum area of certain walls (m²)

Zone number	Fixed on three sides	Pinned on one or more of the three supported sides
(i) 120 mm thick solid walls or double leaf (cavity) walls		
1	16	12
2	13.5	10.5
3	11	9
4	9	7.5
(ii) 190 mm thick solid walls		
1	27	22
2	23	18
3	18	14
4	13	10
(iii) 90 mm thick solid walls		
1	8	6
2	7	5.5
3	6	5
4	5	4

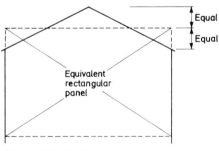

Equal

Equal

Equivalent rectangular panel

Figure 8.31 Gable walls

Note: For the purpose of this table, pitched gable ends are supported on all sides, may be regarded as rectangular, and the height should be measured to half way up to triangular portion, as illustrated in Figure 8.31.

138

Table 8.4 Height to thickness ratio related to wind speed

Design wind speed m/s	Wind pressure N/m²	Height to thickness ratio
up to 20	Up to 285	not exceeding 10
28	575	7
34	860	5
38	1150	4

Intermediate values may be interpolated

The Code indicates that if there is a horizontal damp-proof course near the base of the wall which is not capable of developing tension vertically, the minimum wall thickness should be the greater of that calculated from either:

(1) the appropriate height/thickness ratio given in Table 8.4 reduced by 25% and the height from the level of the damp-proof course;

or

(2) the appropriate height/thickness given in Table 8.4 and the height from the lower level at which the wall is restrained laterally.

There is also a comment to the effect that it may be necessary to decrease the height to thickness ratios quoted in Table 8.4 when the units weigh less than 960 kg/m³.

A particular point is made that low walls should be designed to adequately resist any force which may be expected to be exerted on them, and parapets, balustrades, canopy walls or walls to areas where access other than maintenance is envisaged should be designed for loads not less than those given in CP3:Chapter V:Part 1:Section 8. It is also pointed out that stability may be provided by designing adequate lateral support to the top of such walls; this could consist of a capping rail of wood or metal of adequate transverse strength or of reinforcement in horizontal joints, in either case securely fixed at both ends to an element of structure capable of resisting the forces involved without exceeding the limits of stress allowed for the particular material. When a wall is too long for this method, or other circumstances would render the method inappropriate, vertical supports should be provided at intervals; in some cases it may only be necessary to fix these at the floor if the fixing is sufficiently secure.

In the particular case of free standing parapet walls to areas where no access other than for normal maintenance is envisaged, the height to thickness ratio should not exceed six.

8.7 References

8.1   The Building Regulations 1972 (and amendments 1976). HMSO, London.

8.2   BRITISH STANDARDS INSTITUTION. CP 111: 1970 *Structural recommendations for loadbearing walls.* BSI, London. pp 40

8.3   BRITISH STANDARDS INSTITUTION. CP 121: Part 1: 1973 *Code of Practice for walling.* Part 1: *Brick and block masonry.* BSI, London. pp 84

8.4   BRITISH STANDARDS INSTITUTION. BS 5628: Part 1: 1978 *Code of Practice for the structural use of masonry.* Part 1: *Unreinforced masonry.* BSI, London. pp 40

8.5   ISAACS, D V. An interim analysis of the strengths of masonry block walls in respect to lateral loading. *Special Report No 1*, Commonwealth Experimental Building Station. June 1948.

8.6   BRITISH CERAMIC RESEARCH ASSOCIATION. *Technical Notes 226, 242* and *248.* BCRA, 1974/1975.

8.7   ANDERSON, C. Lateral loading tests on concrete block walls. *The Structural Engineer, Vol 54*, No 7, July 1976.

8.8   FISHBURN, C C. Effects of mortar properties on strength of masonry. *Monograph 36.* United States Department of Commerce. National Bureau of Standards, Washington. 20 November 1961. pp 1—45

8.9   JOHANSEN, K W. Yield-line formulae for slabs. Eyre & Spottiswoode Publications Limited, Leatherhead, 1972. Publication No 12.044. pp 106

8.10 JONES, L L. Ultimate load analysis of reinforced and pre-stressed concrete structures. Chatto and Windus, London, 1962.

8.11 JONES, L L, AND WOOD, R H. Yield-line analysis of slabs. Thames and Hudson, Chatto and Windus, London, 1967.

8.12 COMITE EUROPEAN DU BETON. *Bulletin D'Information No 35.* CEB, 1962.

8.13 SINHA, B P. A simplified ultimate load analysis of laterally loaded orthotropic model brickwork panels of low tensile strength. *The Structural Engineer, Vol 56B*, No 4, 1978. pp 81—84

8.14 SINHA, B P. An ultimate load analysis of laterally loaded brickwork panels. *The International Journal of Masonry Construction, Vol 1*, No 2, 1980. pp 57—61

8.15 HELLERS, B B, AND JOHANSON, B. Horizontally loaded masonry. *Report No BER 730637-7*, Swedish State Committee for Building Research, Malmo.

8.16 CAJDERT, A. Laterally loaded masonry walls. Chalmers University of Technology, Division of Concrete Structures, 1980. Publiction No 80: 5. Goteburg, Sweden.

9

Reinforced masonry

9.1 Introduction

Reinforced masonry has been widely used in countries which experience seismic problems. In the UK it has been used for large laterally loaded wall panels, localized reinforcement of buildings, and for many years to build retaining walls up to 3 m high, particularly agricultural silage retaining walls. The design of such walls was based on an adaptation of reinforced concrete design to reinforced masonry contained in CP 111:Part 2:1970[9.1], but this Code is not strictly applicable to this type of construction and, if used, can result in over-design and uneconomic sections.

Recognizing the need for more realistic information, a programme of research into the behaviour of reinforced concrete blockwork was commenced in 1972. The result of this research has been presented in reports[9.2—9.5], papers[9.6, 9.7] and *The Structural Engineer*[9.8]. The section of CP 111 dealing with unreinforced masonry has been revised and issued as BS 5628:Part 1:1978[9.9]. Work has been completed on the draft of Part 2 of this Code[9.10], which will deal with reinforced masonry but publication will inevitably take a few years. This Chapter is, therefore, intended to provide an interim design procedure for both vertically and horizontally reinforced concrete blockwork subject to lateral loading, and is based on British research evidence as well as consideration of foreign codes. Recommendations are also given on the method of construction and the detailed design of a silage retaining wall. Simplified design charts applicable to cantilevered walls and information on loadings from stored agricultural materials are also included.

It must be realized that while the lateral load capabilities of reinforced masonry are much greater than those for unreinforced walls, there is little to be gained in terms of axial load carrying performance. For completeness, however, an outline design method is provided for axial and combined loads, using an approach similar to that which may be adopted for Part 2 of BS 5628.

9.2 Design information available

The current UK design guide is CP 111[9.1], which, although strictly speaking is not intended as a design basis for laterally loaded retaining walls, is the only indigenous information designers have on which to base their calculations. Now that BS 5628:Part 1 is available it is possible to adapt the characteristic masonry stresses permitted in this document, but as yet no further guidance is available. In the USA[9.11], Canada[9.12], and New Zealand[9.13] the incidence of seismic problems has led to much greater development of Codes of Practice dealing with reinforced masonry, and reference has been made to these. While the Codes of these countries differ in detail they tend to follow similar procedures and for comparison purposes the ACI[9.11] document has been used. The comparison of allowable stresses in CP 111 and the three overseas guides have been summarized in Table 9.1. Some modifications have been made to the stresses to allow for differences in the test procedures for concrete blocks in accordance with work published in *Magazine of Concrete Research*[9.14].

Table 9.1 Comparison between various Codes of Practice for reinforced blockwork (all stresses and moduli in N/mm²)

Code and country of origin		UK — CP 111:Part 2:1970 with Amendment Slip No. 1	USA — Report on Concrete Masonry Structures (ACI)	CANADA — National Building Code of Canada Section 4.4	NEW ZEALAND — New Zealand Standard Model Building By-Laws
Unit strength		7.0 / 14.0 / 21.0 / 28.0 / 35.0	7.0* / 14.0 / 21.0 / 28.0 / 35.0	7.0* / 14.0 / 21.0 / 28.0 / 35.0	7.0* / 14.0 / 21.0 / 28.0 / 35.0
Equivalent prism strength			7.43 / 14.85 / 22.28 / 29.71 / 37.14	7.43 / 14.85 / 22.28 / 29.71 / 37.14	7.43 / 14.85 / 22.28 / 29.71 / 37.14
Test conditions		Unit test only — nett area (tested hollow)	Prism test — nett area (core filled) unit test — nett area	Prism test } Nett area; Unit test } (core filled)	Prism test — nett area (tested unit of minimum standard hollow)
Basic or average compressive strength of masonry	(a) unit		6.0 / 9.5 / 11.75 / 14.0	9.5 / 11.56 / 14.0 / 15.18	14.85 / 22.28 / 29.71 / 37.14
	(b) prism		7.43 / 14.85 / 22.28 / 29.71	14.85 / 22.28 / 29.71 / 37.14	
(1) Permissible axial compressive strength	(a) unit	0.76 / 1.25 / 1.70 / 2.1 / 2.5	1.35 / 2.13 / 2.63 / 3.14	2.14 / 2.60 / 3.15 / 3.42	1.73 / 1.73 / 1.73 / 1.73
	(b) prism		1.67 / 3.33 / 5.0 / 6.67	3.34 / 5.01 / 6.68 / 8.36	2.67 / 4.01 / 5.35 / 6.69
(2) Permissible flexural compressive stress	(a) unit	1.01 / 1.67 / 2.27 / 2.8 / 3.33	1.98 / 3.14 / 3.88 / 4.62	3.14 / 3.81 / 4.62 / 5.01	2.76 / 2.76 / 2.76 / 2.76
	(b) prism		2.45 / 4.90 / 6.30 / 6.30	4.90 / 7.35 / 9.80 / 12.26	4.90 / 7.35 / 9.80 / 12.26
Ratio Row 2 / Row 1		1.333	1.470	1.465	1.595
Permissible shear stress	(a) unit	Varies as to the amount of dead load: shear 0.10 — 0.50 as D.L. 0 — 2.50	0.22 / 0.28 / 0.31 / 0.34	0.19 / 0.23 / 0.28 / 0.30	0.35 / 0.35 / 0.35 / 0.35
	(b) prism		0.25 / 0.35 / 0.35 / 0.35	0.30 / 0.35 / 0.35 / 0.35	0.41 / 0.41 / 0.41 / 0.41
Permissible tensile stress in masonry	(a) bed joint	0.07	0.27	0.25	0.07
	(b) perpend joint	0.14	0.54	0.50	0.07
Permissible bond stress	(a) plain bar	0.56	—	0.55	0.41 (0.55**)
	(b) deformed bar	0.56	1.12	1.10	0.83 (1.10**)
Permissible steel tensile stress	(a) M.S.	140	140	124	124
	(b) H.Y.S.	210	170	166	138
Modulus of elasticity	(a) steel	—	210 000	200 000	
	(b) masonry (unit)	—	6000 / 9500 / 117 500 / 14 000	9 500 / 11 560 / 14 000 / 15 180	10 350 / 10 350 / 10 350 / 10 350
	(c) masonry (prism)	—	7430 / 4000 / 14 000 / 14 000	14 850 / 20 700 / 20 700 / 10 700	14 850 / 22 280 / 29 710 / 37 140
Modular ratio	(a) unit	35 / 30 / 27 / 24 / 21	35 / 22 / 18 / 15	21 / 17 / 14 / 12	— / —
	(b) prism		28 / 15 / 15 / 15	13.5 / 9.5 / 9.5 / 9.5	

*Allowable stresses for unit strengths below 105 N/mm² are not defined in these documents
**Derived from prism strength

9.3 Results of Cement and Concrete Association research

The programme of research and experimental details has been reported elsewhere[9.2—9.8] so that consideration is only given to the results of the flexural tests and their implications for the design procedure.

To compare the measured ultimate bending moments recorded during the tests with a theoretical design procedure a method of design, similar to CP 110[9.15]. was adopted. In this procedure a stress block equal to 0.6 of the nett compressive strength of the unit is adopted, and the depth of the stress block is limited to $0.5d$. A fuller description of the derivation of the design equations is given in *Section 9.9*, but they may be stated as follows:

$$M_u = \left(\frac{0.225}{\gamma_{mb}}\right) f_m b d^2 \quad\dots\dots\dots\dots\dots\dots(1)$$

$$M_u \quad \left(\frac{f_y}{\gamma_{ms}}\right) A_s z \quad\dots\dots\dots\dots\dots\dots(2)$$

$$z = \left(1 - \frac{0.72\,\gamma_{mb}\,F_y\,A_s}{f_m b d}\right)\dots\dots\dots\dots\dots(3)$$

Where:

M_u = the ultimate resistance moment, which is the lesser of those resulting from equations (1) and (2)

A_s = the area of tension reinforcement

b = the width of the section

d = the effective depth to the tension reinforcement

f_y = the characteristic strength of the reinforcement

f_m = the nett block strength

z = the lever arm

γ_{ms} = the partial factor of safety for steel

γ_{mb} = the partial factor of safety for blockwork

To compare the moment carried by the section (remembering that failure in all but a few cases was dictated by yielding of the steel), equation (1) was modified to eliminate the partial factors of safety for materials and the yield stress of the reinforcement was employed.

The predicted moments derived from the above equations are compared in *Interim Technical Note 6*[9.16] with the measured moments, and Table 9.2 presents some of the results contained therein. To aid comparison, the ratio of the measured value to predicted value is also presented. It is apparent that the limit state formulae give a good indication of the behaviour of the reinforced blockwork sections.

The validity of the design procedure having been established, it is now possible to compare the working moments CP 111 would permit for these sections with those using the design formulae above, incorporating the various partial factors of safety. This has been done in Table 3 and results are shown for $\gamma_{mb} = 1.5$, as would be employed for concrete, and for $\gamma_{mb} = 2.5$, which is the value, as discussed later, suggested for reinforced concrete blockwork in flexure. It is clear from Table 9.3 that in all but a few isolated instances the CP 111:1970 theory predicts that the concrete block should be the weak link in the section, whereas the CP 110 theory predicts control by the steel in nearly all cases. Since the validity of the CP 110 theory has been demonstrated, it is clear that the CP 111:1970 design method can be very conservative.

It is apparent that a reinforced block wall section will not develop the calculated ultimate bending moment if the ultimate anchorage bond strength of the reinforcement to the infill is not adequate to prevent bond failure. Bond tests have, therefore, been carried out and the results are presented in *Interim Technical Note 6* together with the results for concrete (from CP 110) of the grade equivalent to the infill mix. The CP 110 values are ultimate stresses and not characteristic stresses, and therefore include a partial factor of safety for the material. Some information has also been obtained on shear failure, and the results are presented in *Interim Technical Note 6* together with the ultimate shear stress from CP 110 for a 30 N/mm² concrete, remembering again that the

Table 9.2 A comparison between the measured and predicted moments of experimental sections

Type of specimen	Specimen no.	Moments of experimental sections		
		measured (kN m)	predicted (kN m)	$\dfrac{\text{measured}}{\text{predicted}}$
Vertically reinforced (3.0 × 0.6 × 0.2 m)	1	10.5	8.8	1.2
	2	9.5	8.8	1.1
	3	15.7	12.9	1.2
	4	10.9	9.5	1.1
	5	9.1	8.8	1.0
	6	16.3	12.9	1.3
	7	16.3	12.9	1.3
	8	22.7	19.7	1.2
	9	15.5	13.1	1.2
	10	22.5	19.7	1.2
	11	13.4	13.5	1.0
	12	21.6	22.0	1.0
	13	9.8	9.4	1.0
	14	14.8	16.0	0.9
	15	8.4	8.9	0.9
	16	57.8	46.3	1.2
	17	59.2	46.3	1.3
	18	60.3	46.3	1.3
	19	12.9	12.4	1.0
	20	34.2	32.6	1.1
Horizontally reinforced (shallow slot) (0.6 × 3.0 × 0.2 m)	21	15.4	10.9	1.4
	22	20.8	22.8	0.9
	23	6.2	6.6	0.9
	24	5.8	6.3	0.9
	25	24.3	24.8	1.0
	26	8.7	9.0	1.0
	27	8.7	9.8	0.9
Horizontally reinforced (deep slot) (0.6 × 3.0 × 0.2 m)	28	40.7	34.7	1.2
	29	51.7	43.2	1.2
	30	51.7	43.2	1.2
Vertically reinforced (2.4 × 0.4 × 0.4 m)	31	61.3	53.7	1.1
	32	80.9	85.1	1.0
	33	85.2	85.1	1.0
Vertically reinforced (2.9 × 0.66 × 0.42 m)	34	59.5	45.9	1.3
	35	83.5	58.5	1.4
	36	93.8	58.5	1.6
	37	58.8	43.3	1.4
	38	58.8	43.3	1.4
Bond-beam or lintel (2.8 × 0.2 × 0.2 m)	39	21.3	23.8	0.9
	40	20.9	17.5	1.2
	41	10.3	10.9	0.9
	42	20.9	17.2	1.2
	43	14.2	10.8	1.3
	44	24.1	23.0	1.0
	45	13.5	10.8	1.3
	46	23.5	23.0	1.0
	47	19.9	17.4	1.1
	48	11.4	10.8	1.1
	49	24.9	20.0	1.2
	50	16.7	10.3	1.6

former has effectively to be modified by a material factor so that ultimate strengths may be compared. More recent research on the shear behaviour of reinforced concrete blockwork has been presented by Rathbone[9.17].

Table 9.3 A comparison of design moments from CP 111[1] with those from CP 110[15] theory

Wall no.	Design moment to CP 111 (kN m)		Ultimate moment from CP 110 theory (kN m) $\gamma_{ms} = 1.15$, $\gamma_r = 1.6$			
			$\gamma_{mb} = 1.5$		$\gamma_{mb} = 2.5$	
	Based on steel stress*	Based on block stress†	steel*	block†	steel*	block†
1	(3.8)‡	2.0	3.9	(8.1)	3.6	(4.8)
2	(3.8)	2.0	3.9	(8.1)	3.6	(4.8)
3	(5.5)	3.6	5.7	(16.1)	5.4	(9.6)
4	(5.5)	3.6	5.7	(16.1)	5.4	(9.6)
5	(3.8)	2.0	3.9	(8.1)	3.6	(4.8)
6	(5.5)	3.6	5.7	(16.1)	5.4	(9.6)
7	(6.6)	2.4	6.4	(8.1)	(5.5)	4.8
8	(9.3)	4.2	9.4	(15.6)	8.5	(9.4)
9	(6.6)	2.4	6.4	(8.1)	(5.5)	4.8
10	(9.3)	4.2	9.4	(15.6)	8.5	(9.4)
11	5.6	5.6	5.9	(31.0)	5.8	(18.6)
12	(9.5)	6.5	10.1	(30.2)	9.6	(18.1)
13	(3.9)	3.1	4.1	(15.6)	4.0	(9.4)
14	(6.7)	3.7	7.1	(15.6)	6.6	(9.4)
15	(3.9)	3.1	4.1	(15.6)	4.0	(9.4)
16	(21.2)	7.1	22.6	(29.3)	(19.4)	17.6
17	(21.2)	7.1	22.6	(29.3)	(19.4)	17.6
18	(21.2)	7.1	22.6	(29.3)	(19.4)	17.6
19	5.6	5.6	5.9	(31.0)	5.8	(18.6)
20	(14.2)	6.5	15.8	(30.2)	14.5	(18.1)
21	(4.7)	3.0	4.9	(19.2)	4.8	(11.5)
22	(11.4)	2.4	12.2	(19.2)	10.4	(11.5)
23	2.6	(3.0)	2.8	(19.2)	2.8	(11.5)
24	2.6	(3.0)	2.8	(19.2)	2.8	(11.5)
25	(10.5)	4.9	11.1	(37.0)	10.7	(22.2)
26	3.9	(6.3)	4.1	(38.7)	4.0	(23.2)
27	3.9	(6.3)	4.1	(38.7)	4.0	(23.2)
28	(15.8)	4.9	15.9	(35.9)	14.8	(21.5)
29	(25.2)	5.1	23.5	(35.9)	20.9	(21.5)
30	(25.2)	5.1	23.5	(35.9)	20.9	(21.5)
31	(22.6)	18.9	25.9	(156.9)	25.1	(94.1)
32	(38.3)	26.6	44.2	(196.3)	42.8	(117.8)
33	(38.3)	26.6	44.2	(196.3)	42.8	(117.8)
34	(25.4)	6.3	(24.4)	24.3	(19.0)	14.6
35	(48.5)	7.3	(32.6)	24.3	10.8	(14.6)
36	(48.5)	7.3	(32.6)	24.3	10.8	(14.6)
37	(31.9)	15.5	(23.7)	18.0	(11.6)	10.8
38	(31.9)	15.5	(23.7)	18.0	(11.6)	10.8
39	(14.6)	1.5	(12.8)	12.4	(9.8)	7.4
40	(9.5)‡	1.6	9.5	(12.8)	(8.2)	7.7
41	(5.4)	1.6	5.9	(13.2)	5.5	(7.9)
42	(9.5)	1.5	9.3	(11.9)	(8.0)	7.1
43	(5.4)	1.6	5.9	(12.2)	5.4	(7.3)
44	(14.6)	1.5	(12.4)	11.5	(9.2)	6.9
45	(5.4)	1.6	5.8	(12.2)	5.4	(7.3)
46	(14.6)	1.5	(12.4)	11.5	(9.2)	6.9
47	(9.6)	1.5	9.3	(11.9)	(8.0)	7.1
48	(5.5)	1.6	5.8	(12.3)	5.4	(7.4)
49	(11.2)	1.7	10.7	(13.1)	(9.1)	7.8
50	(6.2)	1.4	6.3	(10.1)	5.7	(6.0)

*i.e. assuming that block stress does not control.
†i.e. assuming that steel stress does not control.
‡Figures in parentheses denote that stresses do not control the design moment.

9.4 Selection of a design method

It has been demonstrated, both by the Cement and Concrete Association's research work in comparing a limit state approach with the CP 111 elastic design method and by comparison of the ACI 531 elastic design method with the CP 111 elastic design (Section 10.9), that CP 111 is very conservative and results in uneconomic sections. Since the recommendations of CP 111 for unreinforced masonry have already been rewritten in limit state terms, it would be appropriate to consider a limit state approach for reinforced masonry.

The choice is between using a compressive strength for the stress block of 0.6 nett block strength as determined by research or adapting the BS 5628:Part 1 characteristic strengths for unreinforced masonry to some rectangular or rectangular parabolic stress block. For example, the rectangular stress block of intensity $1.1 f_k$ could be used from BS 5628:Part 1 and this is compared with the $0.6 f_m$ approach in Figure 9.1, for a block with 45% voids (55% solid), which is fairly typical, together with a γ_{mb} of 2.5. The design procedure using a $0.6 f_m$ stress block limited to a depth of 0.5 d provides the most favourable prediction of flexural behaviour and is hence used in this section. The alternative approach of deriving some stress block to suit the characteristic strengths and providing a reasonable prediction of behaviour for a wide range of masonry materials has been taken by the Committee responsible for production of BS 5628:Part 2, and this is briefly reviewed later in this Chapter. Referring again to Figure 9.1, it should be noted that BS 5628 incorporates a cut-off point for a 21 N/mm² unit strength which limits the maximum permitted bending moment — as an interim measure this limit has been included in the design method described.

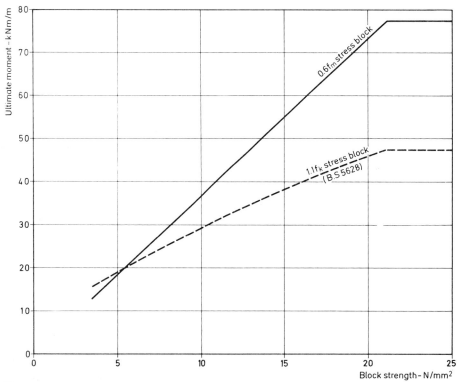

Figure 9.1   Comparison of ultimate moments (0.6 f_m — 1.1 f_k stress block)

9.5 Selection of an appropriate value for γ_{mb} — the partial factor of safety for masonry strength

Attention must now be paid to the selection of an appropriate value for the partial factor of safety for masonry strength, γ_{mb}. BS 5628 currently indicates for unreinforced blockwork, values of γ_{mb} ranging from 2.5 to 3.5, depending upon the level of control exercized over block manufacture and the degree of site supervision during construction. To aid comparison the ultimate resistance moments predicted by the proposed design methods and methods derived from BS 5628, assuming failure to be controlled by block strength, are given in relation to the moments of resistance based on the prism and unit tests, in accordance with the ACI design and the CP 111 method, for various areas of steel and for a 7 N/mm² block (50% voids) in Figure 9.2. For the purpose of this Figure,

146

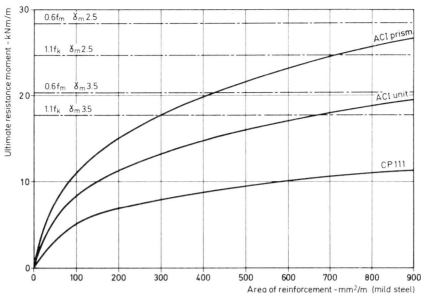

Figure 9.2   Comparison of ultimate moment controlled by block (ACI/CP 111
0.6 f$_m$ – 1.1 f$_k$ stress block)

the ultimate resistance moments determined from the CP 111 and ACI methods are taken as the predicted moments multiplied by 1.6, the most common value of γ_f, the partial factor of safety for load.

Table 9.4 Proposal for relating γ_{mb} to manufacturing and construction control

		Category of construction control	
		Special	Normal
Category of manufacturing control of structural units	Special	2	2.3
	Normal	2.2	2.5

The ACI design method, based on prism specimens, is more akin in philosophy to the test approach taken in BS 5628. Furthermore, BS 5628 and CP 111 both stipulate that the infill concrete should have a strength not less than the nett block strength, whereas no such limitations are placed on the ACI design procedure. Therefore, certainly for the 7 N/mm² block commonly used in agricultural work, there is little difference in the results given by the 0.6 f_m stress block method, the BS 5628 method or the ACI approach, and the value for γ_{mb} of 2.5 seems entirely appropriate. In addition it is quite justified that the behaviour of reinforced masonry in flexure should be governed by different values of γ_{mb} to the behaviour of unreinforced walls in compression because the modes of failure are quite different. The ultimate moment of resistance as controlled by the reinforcement is, of course, determined with respect to a partial factor of safety of only 1.15. Applying the same procedure for the determination of γ_{mb} in BS 5628 to the reinforced case then the values of γ_{mb} in Table 9.4 appear to be appropriate. However, for the purpose of this interim design guide only a γ_{mb} of 2.5 has been employed.

9.6 Other design parameters

Mention has already been made of some of the research results produced by the Cement and Concrete Association. While it is beyond the scope of this book to report these results in detail, they have been used to form the basis of the following recommendations.

9.6.1 Ultimate anchorage bond strength

The ultimate anchorage bond strength should be calculated in accordance with the procedure outlined in CP 110 and should not exceed 1.2 N/mm² for a plain bar in tension or 1.7 for a deformed bar in tension. The CP 110 procedure may also be used for determining the lap of bars, etc.

9.6.2 Curtailment and anchorage of reinforcement

The general recommendations given in CP 110 should be followed when curtailing any bars in reinforced blockwork. Where the loading is substantially uniformly distributed the simplified curtailment rules may also be used. It is also considered appropriate to allow the use of the simplified rules for cantilevered walls subject to triangular loading, i.e., from stored agricultural materials, since the moments and shear forces decline at a faster rate. Walls subject to rectangular/triangular loading, such as exerted by silage or granular material with surcharge, should be examined under the general curtailment recommendations. Walls designed to span horizontally shall be provided with reinforcement having hooked or bent ends to provide adequate anchorage at the support. Although the curtailment rules simplify design it will generally be desirable to check the curtailment position in greater detail since this will usually result in lower cut-off points and will ease construction.

9.6.3 Shear strength

The design shear stress (V) in reinforced concrete blockwork should be limited so that:

$$v \leqslant \frac{v_c}{\gamma_{mv}}$$

$$\text{when } v = \frac{V}{bd}$$

where:

v = design shear force due to load

v_c = characteristic shear stress (given in Table 9.5)

b = breadth of the member

d = effective depth to the reinforcement

γ_{mv} = partial factor of safety for material strength in shear

For the purpose of the interim design recommendations given in this Handbook γ_{mv} should be taken as 2.5.

Table 9.5 Characteristic shear strength in blockwork

$100 \frac{A_s}{bd}$	Characteristic shear strength N/mm²
0.25	0.5
0.50 1.00 2.00	0.70

9.6.4 Deflection and cracking

Based on the research information available to date it is proposed that the serviceability limit states will be satisfied if:

(1) The deflection is limited to not more than $h/200$ where h is the distance between supports or between a support and its free edge in the case of a cantilevered wall. The crack width should then be limited to less than 0.3 mm. The approach used in the handbook to CP 110[9.18] may be used to calculate the deflection — the modulus of elasticity for the blockwork being typically 15 kN/mm² and for the steel 200 kN/mm².

(2) The ratio of the effective thickness does not exceed 40. The recommendations given

in BS 5628 should be used for determining effective length and thickness. For plain single leaf walls this means that the serviceability limit states will be satisfied provided that the thickness is not less than $L/40$ when spanning between single supports, and $L/20$ for a cantilevered wall.

(3) In cases where the area of reinforcement is greater than 1% of the effective area the engineer must ensure that the serviceability limit states are met. For the purpose of this interim design the maximum area of reinforcement has been limited to 1% of the effective area of the section.

9.6.5 Reinforcement

There should only be one reinforcing bar in each core (apart from that required for laps) and reinforcement should be provided in at least every other core. There should also be a minimum amount of main tensile reinforcement of not less than 0.15% and horizontal reinforcement of not less than 0.05% of the cross sectional area of the members. The size of the main reinforcement should be not less than 10 mm. The minimum area of horizontal reinforcement is applicable to mild steel reinforcement or an equivalent area of high yield reinforcement.

The characteristic tensile strength of the reinforcement should be taken as 250 N/mm^2 in the case of mild steel reinforcement and 410 N/mm^2 in the case of high yield reinforcement.

9.6.6 Durability

To provide adequate durability in the reinforcing steel all reinforcement should be sufficiently embedded in infill concrete or mortar. The overall cover to reinforcement (disregarding applied surface finishes) and the cover to the interior faces of the masonry should be as given in Table 9.6. In the case of galvanized or austinitic stainless steel reinforcement or mild steel reinforcement with a stainless steel coat a lesser cover may be appropriate.

Table 9.6 Minimum cover in reinforced concrete blockwork to main reinforcement

Condition of exposure	Minimum cover (mm) to:	
	outer face of block	internal face of block (core)
Severe: below damp-proof course and buried masonry	75	30
Normal: exposed masonry above damp-proof course	50	25
Mild: protected* masonry	25	10

*The term 'protected' is to be taken as meaning surfaces which are protected against weather or aggressive conditions, except for brief periods of exposure to normal weather conditions during construction, and to surfaces which are protected by an impervious coating that can be readily inspected, as in the case of storage walls. These figures may be reduced by 5 mm for secondary reinforcement.

9.6.7 Provision of movements

To reduce the risk of shrinkage and thermal cracking it is recommended that contraction joints be provided at approximately 9 m centres. Where the joints are sealed it will be advisable to provide dowels to restrict lateral movement between adjacent panels but *designed* to permit movement within the plane of the wall. A detail of a typical dowelled joint is shown in Figure 9.3. Expansion joints should be considered in walls greater than about 30 m in length.

9.6.8 Infill concrete and mortar

The design recommendations given in this document are only applicable for the following mortars and infill concrete.

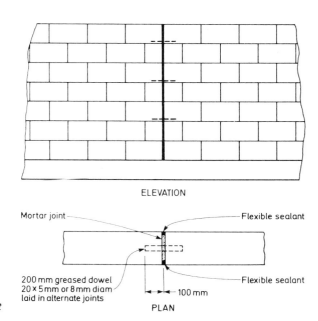

ELEVATION

Mortar joint ——— ——— Flexible sealant

200 mm greased dowel
20 x 5 mm or 8 mm diam
laid in alternate joints

——— Flexible sealant

|← →|← 100 mm

PLAN

Figure 9.3   Vertical control joint

Mortars   Mortars shall be cement:lime:sand of designation (i) or (ii) as given in CP 121.

	cement	hydrated lime	sand
i.e. designation (i)	1	0—¼	3
designation (ii)	1	½	4—4½

Infill concrete   Concrete used to fill the cores of hollow blocks should have proportions by weight as follows:

Ordinary Portland Cement	Sand BS 882	Aggregate 10 mm maximum size
1	2½—3	2

Sufficient water should be added to obtain a concrete with a slump in the region of 150—200 mm, depending upon the absorption of the masonry and the method of placing.

9.6.9 Construction

It is suggested that a construction sequence using full height pours (maximum 3 m) should be employed. The system of numerous laps, requiring blocks to be continuously lifted over lengths of reinforcement, is not recommended.

In the high lift system the wall is built to its full height (maximum 3 m), clean out holes are left at the bottom and the reinforcement is threaded down into the cores and located in position before filling. Any mortar which extrudes into the cores should be cut off during construction and remaining extrusions removed by rodding (mortar falling to the bottom of the cores may be taken out from the clean out holes). A simple method of providing clean out holes is to support the first row of blocks at their ends on either concrete bricks or cut portions of solid blocks.

9.7 Summary of design recommendations and design tables and charts

Notation

A_s area of tension reinforcement

b breadth of member

d effective depth to reinforcement

f_g gross block strength

f_m nett block strength

f_y characteristic strength of reinforcement

150

t thickness of member

V design shear force

v design shear stress

v_c characteristic shear stress

γ_{mb} partial safety factor for masonry strength in bending

γ_{mv} partial safety factor for masonry strength in shear

Ultimate resistance moment when controlled by concrete

$$M_{uc} = \frac{0.225\,f_m bd^2}{\gamma_{mb}}$$

Ultimate resistance moment when controlled by reinforcement

$$M_{us} = 0.87\,f_y\,A_s\left(\frac{1 - 0.72\,\gamma_{mb}\,f_y\,A_s}{f_m\,bd}\right)d$$

Nett block strength

$$f_m = \frac{f_g}{(1-v)}$$

$$= \frac{f_b}{0.55}\ \text{for a block with 45\% area of voids}$$

Partial safety factor for masonry strength in bending

$$\gamma_{mb} = 2.5$$

Characteristic strength of reinforcement

$$f_y = 250\ \text{N/mm}^2\ \text{mild steel reinforcement}$$
$$410\ \text{N/mm}^2\ \text{high yield steel reinforcement}$$

Minimum percentage of reinforcement (mild steel or equivalent high yield)

$$\left.\begin{array}{l} A_s \not> 0.01\,bd \\ \not< 0.0015\,bt \end{array}\right\}\ \text{main reinforcement}$$
$$\not< 0.0006\,bt\quad \text{secondary reinforcement}$$

Minimum cover to main reinforcement*

Condition of exposure	Minimum cover (mm) to:	
	outer face of block	internal face of block (core)
Severe: masonry below damp-proof course or otherwise buried	75	30
Normal: exposed masonry above damp-proof course	50	25
Mild: protected masonry	25	10

*These figures may be reduced by 5 mm for secondary reinforcement.

Ultimate anchorage bond stress

1.7 N/mm² for deformed bars
1.2 N/mm² for plain bars

Bond and curtailment requirements as CP 110.

Shear stress

$$v \leqslant \frac{V_c}{\gamma_{mv}}$$

$100\dfrac{A_s}{bd}$	Characteristic shear stress (v_c) N/mm²
0.25	0.50
0.50	
1.00	0.70
2.00	

when $v = \dfrac{V}{bd}$ partial safety factor for masonry in shear, $\gamma_{mv} = 2.5$

Slenderness

$$\frac{\text{effective length}}{\text{effective thickness}} > 40 \text{ i.e. } \frac{L}{40} \text{ between simple supports}$$

$$\frac{L}{20} \text{ for a cantilever}$$

alternatively check deflection and cracking.

Mortar

1 : 0—¼ : 3 or 1 : ½ : 4—4½ to CP 121

Infill concrete

1 : 2½—3 : 2 sand BS 882 — aggregate 10 mm

Movement joints

Construction joints approximately 9 m intervals.
Expansion joints in excess of 30 m.

For Design Charts see Figures 9.4 to 9.10 and Tables 9.7, 9.8 and 9.9.

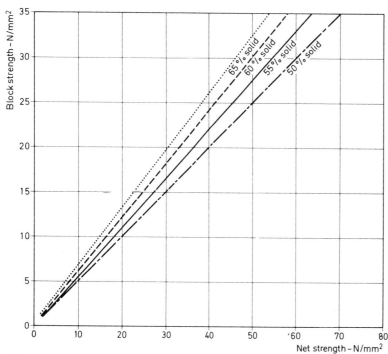

Figure 9.4   Net compressive strength of hollow blocks with different percentages of solid material

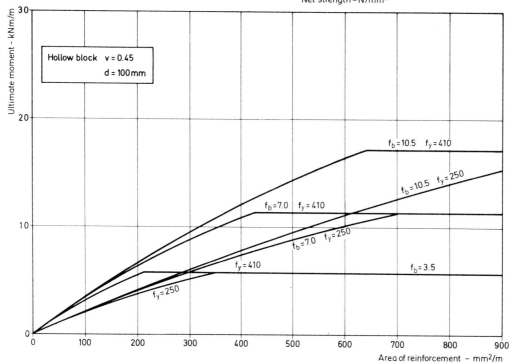

Figure 9.5   Design chart for reinforced hollow blockwork (d = 100 mm)

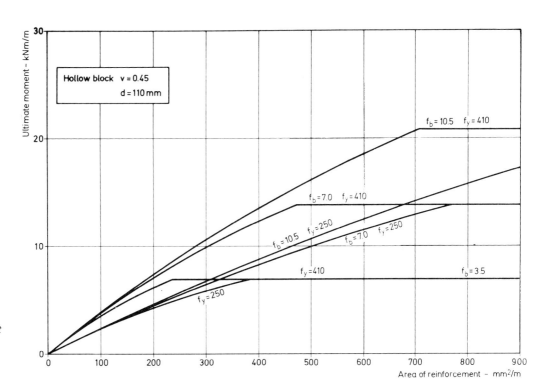

Figure 9.6 Design chart for reinforced hollow blockwork (d = 110 mm)

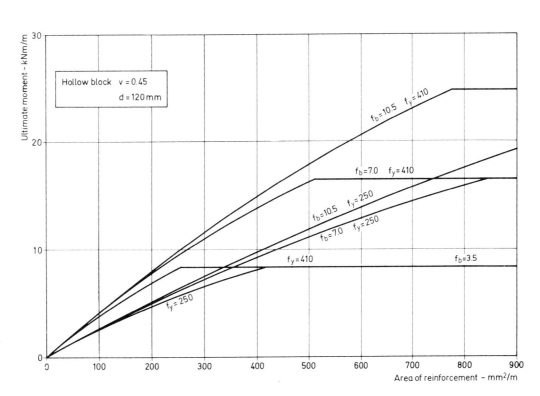

Figure 9.7 Design chart for reinforced hollow blockwork (d = 120 mm)

Table 9.7 Sectional area of reinforcement per metre width

Spacing in mm	Size of reinforcing steel			
	10 mm	12 mm	16 mm	20 mm
200	393	565	1005	1571
225	349	503	894	1396
400	196	283	503	785
450	174	251	447	698
1 No	78.5 mm^2	113 mm^2	201 mm^2	314 mm^2

153

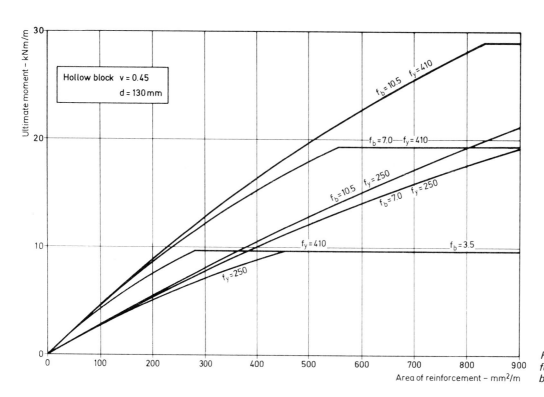

Figure 9.8   Design chart for reinforced hollow blockwork (d = 130 mm)

Table 9.8

Bars per block	Reinforcement areas mm² per m	
	length of block mm	
	390	440
1:10	196	174
1:12	282	251
2:10	392	349
1:10, 1:12	478	425
1:16	502	446
2:12	565	502
1:10, 1:16	698	621
1:12, 1:16	785	697
2:16	1005	893

Table 9.9 Cross sectional areas of groups of bars (mm²)

Bar size (mm)	Number of bars									
	1	2	3	4	5	6	7	8	9	10
6	28.3	56.6	84.9	113	142	170	198	226	255	283
8	50.3	101	151	201	252	302	352	402	453	503
10	78.5	157	236	314	393	471	550	628	707	785
12	113	226	339	452	566	679	792	905	1020	1130
16	201	402	603	804	1010	1210	1410	1610	1810	2010
20	314	628	943	1260	1570	1890	2200	2510	2830	3140
25	491	982	1470	1960	2450	2950	3440	3930	4420	4910
32	804	1610	2410	3220	4020	4830	5630	6430	7240	8040
40	1260	2510	3770	5030	6280	7540	8800	10 100	11 300	12 600

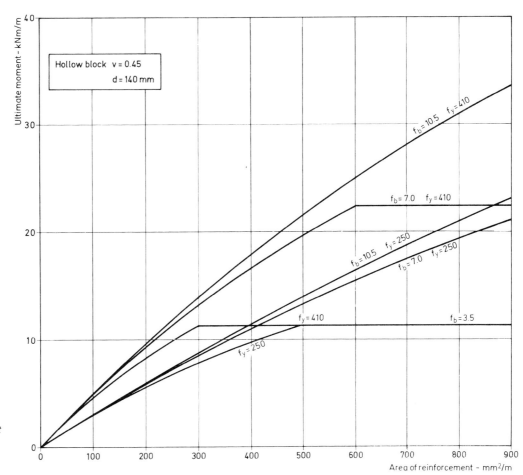

Figure 9.9 Design chart for reinforced hollow blockwork (d = 140 mm)

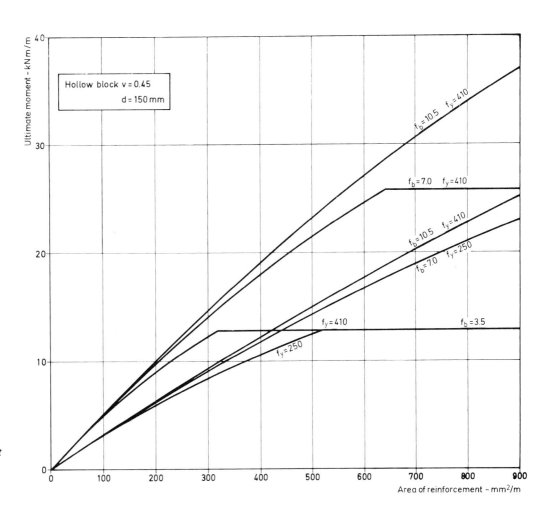

Figure 9.10 Design chart for reinforced hollow blockwork (d = 150 mm)

155

9.8 Design example — silage wall

This design example is of a 2.35 m high, 215 mm thick reinforced blockwork silage wall for a Class 2 structure as defined in BS 5502[9.19]. Silage is to be compacted by a wheeled tractor weighing 5 to 6 tonnes, drainage is to be provided.

9.8.1. Density of materials

Silage (mean) = 400 kg/m^3 + 72 kg/m^3 per metre depth
Blockwork   = 2200 kg/m^3
Concrete   = 2350 kg/m^3

9.8.2 Loading from silage

Characteristic imposed loading from silage where moisture content of cut grass at time of ensiling ≤ 80% and gross vehicle compacting weight ≤ 6 tonne Q_k = 3.5 + 3.5x kN/m^2 per metre depth, where x is the depth in metres below the rolled surface of the ensiled material.

In addition two 3 kN loads applied 2 m apart, 0.6 m below the rolled level, to represent the tractor loading. The point loads for this design are considered as being distributed to the base of the wall, as shown below.

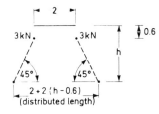

The hollow blocks are to be supported on 100 mm high concrete bricks at their ends. The infill concrete will carry the moment below that point. Therefore, the moment applied to the blockwork should be calculated 2.25 m from the top of the wall. The moment acting on the 2.35 m high wall is taken by normal reinforced concrete design to CP 110, with a characteristic strength of 20 N/mm^2.

9.8.3 Design moment

From BS 5502, the design imposed load for a Class 2 structure

$$= \gamma_f \, \gamma_c \, Q_k = 1.6 \times 0.925 \times Q_k = 1.48 \, Q_k$$
(γ_c is classification factor)

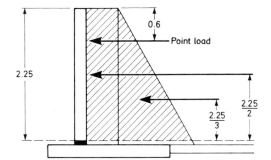

Figure 9.11 Loading applied to wall (vertical dimensions in m, horizontal pressure in kN/m²)

From Figure 9.11 it may be seen that the design moment applied to the blockwork is given by:

$$M = 1.48 \left(\frac{3.5 \times 2.25^2}{2} \right) + \left(\frac{3.5 \times 2.25^2}{6} \right) + \left(\frac{6(2.25 - 0.6)}{2(2.25 - 0.6) + 2} \right)$$

$$= 1.48 \, (8.86 + \ 6.64 + 1.87)$$

M = 25.71 kN/m   Neglecting the effect of self weight.

156

9.8.4 Design of blockwork

Thickness of wall = 215 mm
Design resistance moment of blockwork

$$M_u = \frac{0.225}{\gamma_{mb}} f_m b d^2$$

Hence nett block strength required

$$f_m = \frac{M_u \ \gamma_{mb}}{0.225 b d^2}$$

Since the wall is to retain silage, the inside surface must be rubbed and filled and painted with two coats of bituminous or chlorinated rubber paint. The exposure of the inside face may be considered to be 'mild' and the reinforcement should be provided with 10 mm cover within the core and at least 25 mm to the exposed face.

A hollow 215 mm block will have a shell thickness of about 45 mm. Allowing for 10 mm internal cover the effective depth

$$d = 215 - 45 - 10 - \text{(bar radius, assuming 16 mm bars)}$$
$$= 152 \text{ mm}$$

Using $\gamma_{mb} = 2.5$, the required nett block strength

$$f_m = \frac{25.71 \times 2.5 \times 10^6}{0.225 \times 1000 \times (152)^2}$$

$$= 12.36 \text{ N/mm}^2$$

A 215 mm hollow block to BS 2028, 1364 can contain up to 50% voids; however, design on the assumption of only 45% voids

$$f_g = 12.36 \ (1-0.45) = 6.80 \text{ N/mm}^2$$

Therefore select as 7 N/mm² block $f_m = 12.73$ N/mm²

$$M_u = \frac{0.225}{2.5} \ . \ 12.73 \ (152)^2 \ \frac{1000}{10^6} = 26.47 \text{ kN/m}$$

9.8.5 Design of reinforcement

$$M_u = 0.87 \, f_y \, A_s \, z$$

$$\text{where } z = \left(1 - \frac{0.72 \ \gamma_{mb} \, f_y \, A_s}{f_m b d} \right) d$$

$$\text{i.e. } M_u = 0.87 \, f_y \, A_s \left(1 - \frac{0.72 \ \gamma_{mb} \, f_y \, A_s}{f_m \, b d} \right) d$$

using high yield reinforcement with $f_y = 410$ N/mm² and putting $M_u = M$

$$A_s^2 \left(\frac{0.87 \times 0.72 \times 2.5 \times 410^2}{12.73 \times 1000} \right) - 0.87 \times 410 \times 152 \, A_s + 25.71 \times 10^6 = 0$$

i.e. $20.68 \, A^2 - 54 \ 218 \, A_s + 25.71 \times 10^6 = 0$

$$A_s = \frac{54 \ 218 \pm \sqrt{54 \ 218^2 - 4 \times 20.68 \times 25.71 \times 10^6}}{2 \times 20.68}$$

$$= \frac{54 \ 218 \pm 28 \ 511}{41.36} = 622$$

Hence $A_s = 622$ mm² per metre. (Check minimum required $\dfrac{0.15 \times 215 \times 10^3}{100} = 323$ mm² per metre)

9.8.6 Detailing

It is possible to satisfy the steel requirements by providing Y12 and Y16 bars alternately at 225 mm centres (giving 628 mm² per metre), but it is more convenient to use Y16 bars only, which gives 893 mm² per metre.

Provide Y16 as starter bars with Y12 lapped on for the full height of the wall.
For Y12 at 225 mm centres,

A_s = 502 mm² per metre

$$M_u = 0.87 \times 410 \times 502 \left(1 - \frac{0.72 \times 2.5 \times 410 \times 502}{12.73 \times 1000 \times 152} \right) \times 152 \times 10^{-6}$$

$$= 22 \text{ kN/m}$$

Try moment in wall at 2 m down (i.e., the change point from 12 to 16 mm bars)

$$M = 1.48 \left(\frac{3.5 \times 2^2}{2} + \frac{3.5 \times 2^3}{6} + \frac{6(2 - 0.6)}{2(2 - 0.6) + 2} \right) = 19.86 \text{ kN/m}$$

This is acceptable.

9.8.7 Anchorage length of 12 mm bar

$$A_s = 113 \text{ mm}^2$$

Taking the anchorage bond stress as 1.7 N/mm², the anchorage length

$$= \frac{410 \times 113 \times 0.87}{1.7 \times 3.142 \times 12} = 629 \text{ mm}$$

This bar is lapped with a bar of larger diameter; therefore increase length by 25% 629 × 1.25 = 786 mm
Allowing for error in cutting and placing bars, provide a lap length of 900 mm
Consider lap from base:
The moment at the curtailment position, i.e. 2.35 − 0.9 = 1.45 m down

$$M = 1.48 \left(\frac{3.5 \times 1.45^2}{2} + \frac{3.5 \times 1.45^3}{6} + \frac{6(1.45 - 0.6)}{2(1.45 - 0.6) + 2} \right) = 10.12 \text{ kN/m}$$

Moment of continuing reinforcement = 21.65 kN/m. This is greater than twice the moment at the curtailment position. Twelve bar diameter above the change point = 0.35 × 12 × 0.016 = 0.55 m. Therefore, curtailment at 900 mm from the base is acceptable according to CP 110, Clause 3.11.7.1.

9.9 Loading data

9.9.1 Horizontal reinforcement

Minimum horizontal (mild steel) reinforcement required

$$= \frac{0.5 \times 215 \times 1000}{100}$$

$$= 108 \text{ mm}^2 \text{ per metre}$$

Therefore, use two R6 bars every other course (or equivalent steel strength in high yield reinforcement).

9.9.2 Design moments

From Figure 9.12 it may be calculated that the design moment at the base of the wall, per metre, is

$$M = 1.48 \left(\frac{3.5 \times 2.35^2}{2} + \frac{3.5 \times 2.35^3}{6} + \frac{6(2.35 - 0.6)}{2(2.35 - 0.6) + 2} \right)$$

$$= 21.65 \text{ kN/m}$$

Considering the detail on Figure 9.13, and ignoring the supporting brick, the effective

158

design moment on the concrete infill

$$M = 28.33 \times \frac{450}{350}$$

$$= 36.4 \text{ kN/m}$$

From CP 110, the design moment of resistance as controlled by the concrete

$$M_u = 0.15\, f_{cu}\, bd^2$$

$$= 0.15 \times 20 \times 1000 \times 152^2 \times 10^{-6}$$

$$= 69.31 \text{ kN/m}$$

The design moment of resistance as controlled by the reinforcement

$$M_u = 0.87\, f_y A_s z$$

$$\text{where } z = \left(1 - \frac{1.1\, f_y A_s}{f_{cu} bd} \right) d$$

$$= \left(1 - \frac{1.1 \times 410 \times 893}{20 \times 1000 \times 152} \right) \times 152$$

$$= 132 \text{ mm}$$

Therefore:

M_u (reinforcement) $= 0.87 \times 410 \times 893 \times 132 \times 10^{-6} = 42.0 \text{ kN/m}$

Moment at base is therefore acceptable.

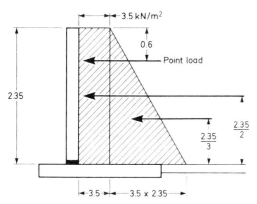

Figure 9.12 Loading applied at base (vertical dimensions in m, horizontal pressure in kN/m²)

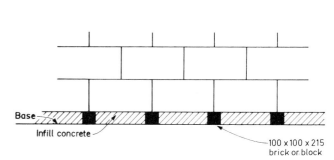

Figure 9.13 Support of block wall

9.9.3 Shear

Horizontal force due to tractor is conceived as two 3 kN loads (Figure 9.14).

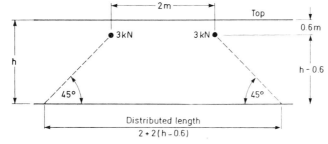

Figure 9.14 Distribution of point load

Effective shear at base above brickwork

$$= \frac{6}{2(1.65) + 2}$$

$$= 1.13 \text{ kN/m}$$

Horizontal force due to uniform pressure

$$= 3.5 \times 2.25 = 7.88 \text{ kN/m}$$

Horizontal force due to triangular pressure

$$= 3.5 \times \frac{2.25^2}{2} \text{ kN/m}$$

Total shear force

$$= 1.13 + 7.88 + 8.86$$

$$= 17.87 \text{ kN/m}$$

Ultimate shear force

$$V = 17.87 \times 1.6 \times 0.925$$

$$= 26.45 \text{ kN/m}$$

Hence, design shear stress

$$v = \frac{26.45 \times 10^3}{1000 \times 152}$$

$$= 0.17 \text{ N/mm}^2$$

$$A_s = 893 \text{ mm}^2 \text{ per metre}$$

Therefore

$$\frac{A_s}{bd} = \frac{100 \times 893}{1000 \times 152}$$

$$= 0.59$$

Therefore characteristic shear strength

$$f_v = 0.70 \text{ N/mm}^2$$

Thus

$$\frac{f_v}{\gamma_{mv}} = \frac{0.70}{2.5}$$

$$= 0.28 \text{ N/mm}^2$$

Therefore

$$v_h < \frac{f_v}{\gamma_{mv}}$$

Thus the wall has adequate resistance to shear.

9.9.4 Stability

Consider stability with and without tractor load, taking the tractor as weighing 5 tonnes.
Horizontal point load

$$= 2 \times 3 \text{ kN}$$

This load is distributed as shown in Figure 9.14, thus the effective point load is

$$\frac{6}{2 (1.98) + 2} = 1.0 \text{ kN/m}$$

Horizontal force due to uniform pressure

$$= 3.5 \times 2.35$$

$$= 8.23 \text{ kN}$$

Horizontal force due to triangular pressure

$$= 3.5 \times \frac{2.35^2}{2}$$

$$= 9.66 \text{ kN}$$

160

Mean shear strength of silage

$$= 3.75 + 0.75 \times 2.35$$
$$= 5.51 \text{ kN/m}^2$$

Mean shear force

$$= 5.51 \times 2.35$$
$$= 12.95 \text{ kN}$$

Mean silage density

$$= 400 + 72 \times 2.35$$
$$= 569 \text{ kg/m}^2$$

Check stability with base as positioned in Figure 9.15.

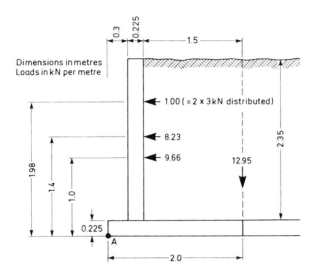

Figure 9.15

Consider overturning moment about point A in Figure 9.15

Element	Force	F	$\bar{y}$	$F\bar{y}$
Silage	tractor effect	1.0	1.98	1.98
	uniform load	8.23	1.4	11.52
	triangular load	9.66	1.0	9.66
	Total (with tractor)	18.89		23.16
	(without tractor)	17.89		21.18

Element	Force	W	$\bar{x}$	$W\bar{x}$
Wall	$0.215 \times 2.35 \times 2200 \times \dfrac{9.81}{1000}$	10.90	0.4	4.36
Floor slab	$2.0 \times 0.225 \times 2350 \times \dfrac{9.81}{1000}$	10.37	1.0	10.37
Silage (self weight)	$1.5 \times 2.35 \times 569 \times \dfrac{9.81}{1000}$	19.68	1.27	24.99
Silage (shear force)	5.51×2.35	12.95	2.0	25.90
Tractor	$\dfrac{5000}{2\,(1.98) + 2} \times \dfrac{9.81}{1000}$	8.23	1.27	10.45
	Total (with tractor)	62.13		76.07
	(without tractor)	53.90		65.62

Stability against overturning

$$= \frac{W\bar{x}}{F\bar{y}}$$

With tractor, stability

$$= \frac{76.07}{23.16} = 3.28$$

161

Without tractor, stability

$$= \frac{65.62}{20.18} = 3.25$$

Both acceptable, since greater than 1.4 as required by BS 5502.

9.9.5 Bearing pressure

Equivalent eccentricity of vertical force from point A

$$= \frac{W\bar{x} - F\bar{y}}{W}$$

With tractor, eccentricity

$$= \frac{76.07 - 23.16}{62.13}$$

$$= 0.85 \text{ m}$$

Eccentricity from centre of base:

$$e = 1.0 - 0.85$$

$$= 0.15 \text{ m}$$

Since this is within mid-third of base, bearing pressure

$$= \frac{W}{A} \pm \frac{We}{Z}$$

$$= \frac{62.13}{1.0 \times 2.0} \pm \frac{62.13 \times 0.15 \times 6}{1.0 \times (2-0)^2}$$

$$= 45.05 \text{ and } 17.08 \text{ kN/m}^2$$

Without tractor, the equivalent eccentricity of vertical force from point A

$$= \frac{65.62 - 21.18}{53.90} = 0.82 \text{ m}$$

Eccentricity from centre of base:

$$e = 1.0 - 0.82$$

$$= 0.18 \text{ m}$$

This is again inside the mid-third; therefore the bearing pressure

$$= \frac{53.9}{1.0 \times 2.0} \pm \frac{53.9 \times 0.18 \times 6}{1.0 \times (2-0)^2}$$

$$= 41.5 \text{ and } 12.4 \text{ kN/m}^2$$

The pressure is reasonable for a shallow base on most types of ground.

9.9.6 Resistance to sliding

Factor of safety against sliding

$$= \frac{WC_f}{F}$$

Consider coefficient of friction:

$C_f = 0.55$

With tractor, resistance to sliding

$$= \frac{62.13 \times 0.55}{18.89}$$

$$= 1.81$$

162

Without tractor, resistance to sliding

$$= \frac{53.90 \times 0.55}{17.89}$$

$$= 1.66$$

The safety factor against sliding is therefore greater than 1.4, as required by BS 5502. The stability may also be improved by passive resistance in front of the base.

9.9.7 Design of base

Thickness = 225 mm
Concrete strength = 25 N/mm^2
Minimum cement content = 350 kg/m^3
Design moment is as given at the base of the wall:

$$M = 28.33 \text{ kN/m}$$

Cover to reinforcement must be 40 mm; therefore

$$d = 185 \text{ mm}$$

By comparison with the wall design, the base is adequate with 16 mm high yield reinforcement. (Actual reinforcement required = 445 mm^2 per metre).

9.9.8 Anchorage

Anchorage length of bar will exceed length to first bend; therefore, check bearing stress in bend as in CP 110 Clause 3.11.6.8:

$$\frac{E_{bt}}{r\phi} \leqslant \frac{1.5 f_{cu}}{1 + 2\phi/a_b}$$

Therefore, the required internal radius

$$r = F_{bt} \frac{1 + 2\phi/a_b}{1.5 f_{cu}}$$

$$= \frac{0.87 \times 410 \times 201(1 + 2 \times 16/225)}{1.5 \times 16 \times 25}$$

$$= 136 \text{ mm}$$

Bend bars to radius of 125 mm, since stress in bar will be less than 410 N/mm^2. Total anchorage length required

$$= \frac{410 \times 201 \times 0.87}{2.2 \times 3.142 \times 16} = 648 \text{ mm}$$

Anchorage length of bend

$$= 24 \text{ bar diameters}$$

$$= 484 \text{ mm}$$

Provide normal 3 diameter radius at remaining bends. Distribution reinforcement required in base

$$= 0.12\% \times 1000 \times 225$$

$$= 270 \text{ mm}^2 \text{ per metre}$$

Use R12 bars at 400 mm centres (A_s = 283 mm^2 per metre).

9.9.9 Shear on base

From Figure 9.16 maximum pressure on the base at point B

$$= (45.05 - 17.08)\frac{1.5}{2.0} + 17.08$$

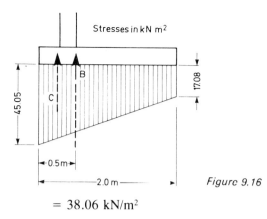

Figure 9.16

$$= 38.06 \ \text{kN/m}^2$$

Therefore, shear force on base

$$= \frac{(38.06 + 17.08) \ 1.5}{2} - (19.68 + 12.95 + 8.23)$$

$$= 41.36 - 40.86 = 0.5 \ \text{kN/m}$$

Maximum pressure on the base at point C

$$= (45.05 - 17.08) \frac{0.3}{2} + 17.08$$

$$= 40.85$$

Shear force on base at C

$$= \frac{(45.05 + 40.85)}{2} \times 0.3$$

$$= 12.9 \ \text{kN/m}$$

Reinforcement in base

$$A_s = 893 \ \text{mm}^2 \ \text{per metre}$$

$$\frac{100A_s}{bd} = \frac{100 \times 893}{1000 \times 185} = 0.48$$

From Table 5 of CP 110, ultimate shear stress

$$v_c = 0.50 \ \text{N/mm}^2$$

From Table 14,

$$\xi_s = 1.05$$

$$\xi_s v_c = 1.05 \times 0.50$$

$$= 0.52 \ \text{N/mm}^2$$

Shear stress

$$\frac{V}{bd} = \frac{12.9 \times 10^3}{1000 \times 185}$$

$$= 0.07 \ \text{N/mm}^2$$

Therefore no shear reinforcement is required.

9.9.10 Tractor load

The 5 tonne tractor load was taken for stability since it gives the most critical condition. However, the applied moment is applicable to the case of a 6 tonne tractor and therefore the design is adequate for tractors up to this gross weight.

9.9.11 Drainage

To comply with the loading criteria used in this design, drainage should be provided within 500 mm of the inside wall face.

164

9.9.12 Protection of masonry

The blockwork must be rubbed and filled with a 1:1 cement:sand slurry which is allowed to cure and then painted with two coats of chlorinated rubber or bituminous paint.

9.9.13 Detail drawing

Figure 9.17 gives the total design requirements for the 2.35 m high concrete blockwork silage retaining wall.

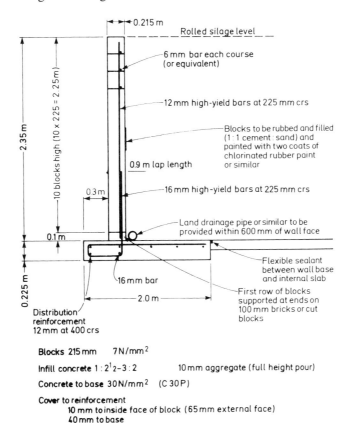

Blocks 215 mm   7 N/mm²

Infill concrete 1 : 2¹⁄₂-3 : 2   10 mm aggregate (full height pour)

Concrete to base 30 N/mm²   (C 30 P)

Cover to reinforcement
    10 mm to inside face of block (65 mm external face)
    40 mm to base

Figure 9.17   Design requirements for a 2.35 m high concrete blockwork retaining wall

9.10 Design moments for cantilever walls

To simplify the design of cantilever walls for Class 2 structures in BS 5502, Figure 9.18 is provided, which shows design moments plotted against height for various density/ pressure coefficient curves, including that of silage, for a Class 1 or Class 2 structure. These curves correspond to different values of the density of the stored material multiplied by κ, the pressure coefficient for granular materials.

$$\kappa = \frac{(\cos \phi)^2}{(a + 1)}$$

where $a = \sin^2 \phi - \frac{1}{2} \tan \phi \sin^2 \theta$
in which ϕ = angle of slope of bank of retained material
θ = angle of internal shear resistance
In the case of a level fill, where $\theta = 0$,

$$\kappa = \frac{1 - \sin \theta}{1 + \sin \theta}$$

In the particular case of an inclined fill, where $\phi = \theta$,

$$\kappa = \cos^2 \theta$$

The curves have been plotted for moments about the footing. If the blocks are laid on 100 mm bricks or blocks then the moment required for design purposes is found by using the wall height − 0.1 m.

165

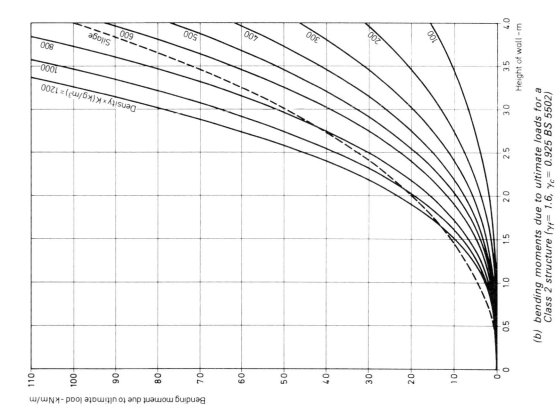

(b) bending moments due to ultimate loads for a Class 2 structure (γ_f= 1.6, γ_c= 0.925 BS 5502)

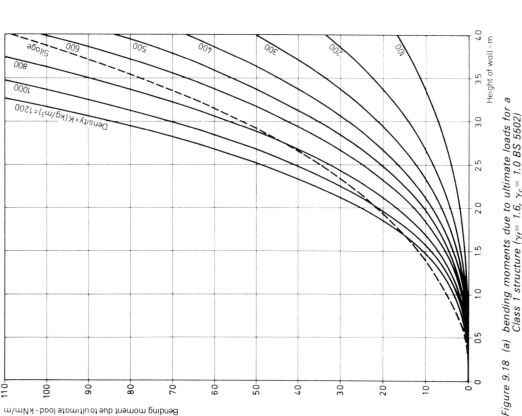

Figure 9.18 (a) bending moments due to ultimate loads for a Class 1 structure (γ_f= 1.6, γ_c= 1.0 BS 5502)

166

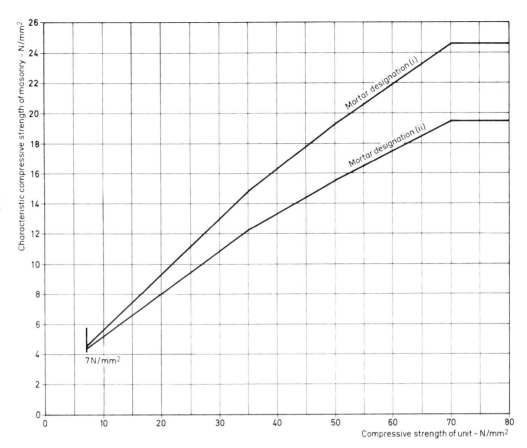

Figure 9.19 Characteristic compressive strength, f_k, of block masonry constructed with solid blocks having a ratio of height to least horizontal dimension of 1.0

Table 9.10 Characteristic compressive strength of masonry, f_k, in N/mm² when constructed with solid blocks having a ratio of height to least horizontal dimension of 1.0

Mortar designation	Compressive strength of unit (N/mm²)						
	7	10	15	20	35	50	70 or greater
(i)	4.4	5.7	7.7	9.5	14.7	19.3	24.7
(ii)	4.1	5.4	6.8	8.2	12.1	15.7	19.4

9.11 Summary of draft of BS 5628 issued for public comment

The following section provides a resume of the approach given in the draft version of BS 5628[9.10] issued for public comment. It must be remembered that this approach has no official status at this time and will certainly be amended before publication. An important point to consider is that the document is intended to relate to all types of masonry and some of the values quoted are not necessarily as advantageous to concrete masonry as those given earlier in the Chapter.

The approach to bending which has been adopted in the draft Code has been developed from the simplified approach presented in CP 110:Part 1:1972. One benefit of this approach is that many engineers will be familiar with CP 110 and hence the change, where appropriate, to reinforced masonry design, will be comparatively simple.

In a paper by Roberts and Edgell[9.20] the background to the design for bending incorporated in the draft has been discussed. A rectangular stress block has been assumed with an intensity of f_f/γ_{mm} taken over the whole compression zone, where f_f is the characteristic compressive strength of reinforced masonry in bending, and γ_{mm} is the partial safety factor for compressive strength of masonry. The value of f_f is determined by multiplying the appropriate value of f_k, the characteristic masonry strength, by 1.2. This factor has been the subject of some debate and may not be justified in the published Code for all types of masonry. The factor of 1.2 was introduced to obtain realistic estimates of the ultimate bending moment capacity of reinforced hollow concrete block-work members. A new addition to the Code is a table and graph (Table 9.10 and Figure 9.19 herein) giving the characteristic strength of units with a height to thickness ratio of 1.0 (i.e., a typical hollow block).

167

While the draft recognizes two levels of *manufacturing* control of structural units, normal or special, only one level of *construction* control is recognized, essentially the special category.

No attempt has been made to reproduce the full content of the draft, but rather to extract sufficient salient features to enable the designer to apply the basic principles to reinforced blockwork through the examples provided. Particular attention should be paid to the need to update this section when Part 2 of BS 5628 is published.

9.11.1 Materials and components for reinforced masonry

9.11.1.1 Structural units Blocks and concrete bricks should comply with BS 6073[9.21]. The minimum compressive strength of the unit should usually be 7 N/mm² for blocks and 20 N/mm² for concrete bricks. The designer may employ lower strength units only if he is confident of the behaviour of that particular type of unit. Attention is also drawn to the durability requirements of CP 121 which specify minimum strengths required for different conditions of exposure.

9.11.1.2 Reinforcement and wall ties These should comply with the requirements of CP 110 and BS 5628:Part 1.

9.11.1.3 Cements, aggregates and sands These should meet the requirements of BS 5628:Part 1 but masonry cement and high alumina cement must not be used.

9.11.1.4 Mortars Mortars should be mixed and used to comply with CP 121:Part 1[9.22] or BS 5390[9.23]. The proportions of the materials required are given in Table 9.11. When testing is required Appendix A1 of BS 5628:Part 1 should be followed. Ready mixed mortars should comply with BS 4721.

Table 9.11 Requirements for mortar

Mortar designation	Type of mortar (proportion by volume)		Mean compressive strength at 28 days	
	Cement: lime:sand	Cement:sand with plasticizer	Preliminary (laboratory) tests	Site tests
			N/mm²	N/mm²
(i)	1:0—¼:3	—	16.0	11.0
(ii)	1:½:4—4½	1:3—4	6.5	4.5

9.11.1.5 Concrete infill Concrete infill should be one of the following mixes:
(1) 1:¼:3:2, cement:lime:sand:10 mm aggregate, proportioned by volume of dry materials — Materials should preferably be weigh batched;
(2) a prescribed or designed mix of grade 25 or better in accordance with BS 5328[9.24] with a nominal maximum size of aggregate of 10 mm;
(3) a prescribed or designed mix of grade 25 or better in accordance with BS 5328[9.24] with a nominal maximum size of aggregate of 20 mm.

Each of these mixes should have a slump between 75 mm and 175 mm. Mixes (1) and (2) should be used for filling spaces with a minimum dimension of 50 mm. Mix (3) may be used for filling spaces with a minimum dimension of 100 mm.

9.11.1.6 Colouring agents and admixtures Colouring agents and admixtures should comply with the requirements of BS 5628:Part 1. The use of calcium chloride or admixtures based on calcium chloride is not permitted in mortars or concretes.

9.11.2 Reinforced masonry subjected to bending

9.11.2.1 Introduction This section contains simple rules for the design of reinforced concrete blockwork subjected to bending only, e.g., beams, slabs, retaining walls.
(N.B. Ignore axial thrust if not greater than $0.1 f_k$ times cross sectional area, otherwise use section on combined loads.)

9.11.2.2 Effective span The effective span of an element should be taken as follows:

Simply supported member: the smaller of the distances between centre of supports *or* the clear distance between supports plus the effective depth

Continuous member: the distance between centres of supports

Cantilever: the length to the face of the support plus half its effective depth, unless it forms the end of a continuous beam where the length to the centre of the support should be used.

9.11.2.3 Effective span/effective depth ratio For walls designed to resist lateral loading only, the ratio of effective span to effective depth should not exceed the values given in Table 9.12.

Table 9.12

End condition	Ratio
Simply supported	35
Continuous	45
Cantilever with up to 0.5% reinforcement	18

9.11.2.4 Assumptions

(1) plane sections remain plane;

(2) rectangular stress block in masonry of width f_f/γ_{mm} where $f_f = 1.2\ f_k$;

(3) strain in outermost compression fibre at failure is 0.0035;

(4) tensile strength of masonry and concrete infill ignored;

(5) stresses in reinforcement as shown in Table 9.13;

(6) depth of compressive stress block does not exceed half effective depth.

Table 9.13 Characteristic tensile strength of reinforcing steel

Designation	Nominal sizes (mm)	Characteristic strength (N/mm^2)
Hot rolled steel grade 460/425 (BS 4449)	Up to and incl. 16	460
	Over 16	425
Hot rolled steel grade 250 (BS 4449)	All sizes	250
Cold worked steel grade 460/425 (BS 4461)	Up to and incl. 16	460
	Over 16	425
Hard drawn steel wire and fabric (BS 4482 and BS 4483)	Up to and incl. 12	485

9.11.2.5 Design formulae For singly reinforced sections with a ratio of span to effective depth of the member greater than 1.5 the design moment of resistance would be taken as the lower of:

$$M_d = 0.375 \frac{f_f\, bd^2}{\gamma_{mm}}$$

$$M_d = \frac{A_s f_y z}{\gamma_{ms}}$$

$$\text{where } z = d\left(1 - \frac{0.5 A_s f_y \gamma_{mm}}{bd\, f_f\, \gamma_{ms}}\right) \not> 0.95d$$

where:

M_d = design moment of resistance

b = the width of the section

169

d = effective depth

f_y = characteristic tensile strength of the reinforcement

f_f = characteristic flexural compressive strength of masonry ($= 1.2\,f_k$)

z = lever arm

γ_{mm} = partial safety factor for masonry strength

γ_{ms} = partial safety factor for reinforcement strength

In the case of a reinforced hollow block member where the reinforcement is placed so that the section can act as a flanged beam, the width of the flanges should be taken as the rib width plus 12 times the thickness of the flange, t_f, but not more than the spacing of the ribs. This is shown in Figure 9.20. The design moment may be taken as the lesser of:

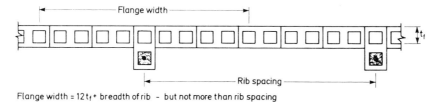

Flange width = 12 t_f + breadth of rib – but not more than rib spacing

Figure 9.20 Recommended flange width for reinforced hollow block walls

$$M_d = \frac{f_f}{\gamma_{mm}}\, b t_f \left(d - \frac{t_f}{2} \right)$$

$$M_d = \frac{f_f}{\gamma_{ms}}\, A_s \left(d - \frac{t_f}{2} \right)$$

where t_f = flange thickness and is the lesser of $0.5d$ at the level considered or the actual thickness of the masonry between the ribs.

Alternatively, design charts may be used as illustrated in Figure 9.21.

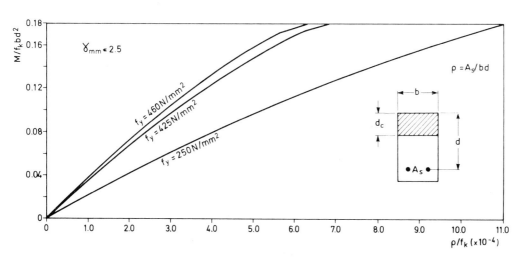

Figure 9.21 (a) design chart for singly reinforced rectangular members subjected to flexure ($\gamma_{mm} = 2.5$)

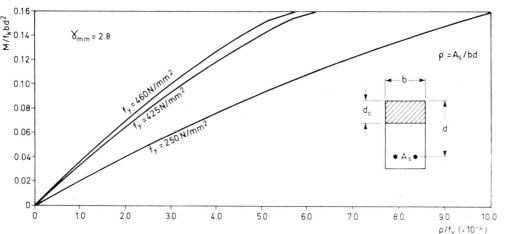

(b) design chart for singly reinforced rectangular members subjected to flexure ($\gamma_{mm} = 2.8$)

170

9.11.2.6 Shear resistance of flexural elements The shear stress, v, resulting from design loads at any cross section should be calculated from:

$$v = \frac{V}{bd}$$

where:

V = shear force due to design loads

b = width of section

d = effective depth (use actual thickness between ribs for flanged members if this is less than the effective depth)

Where the calculated shear stress is less than the characteristic shear strength of masonry (f_v) divided by the partial safety factor γ_{mv} shear reinforcement is not generally needed. Beams of major importance should have nominal links provided.

9.11.3 Design of reinforced masonry subjected to axial compressive loading only

This procedure applies only to walls and columns subjected to vertical loading for which the resultant eccentricity does not exceed 0.05 times the thickness of the member in the direction of the eccentricity.

9.11.3.1 Lateral support A lateral support must be capable of transmitting to the elements of construction that provide lateral stability to the structure as a whole, the sum of the following design lateral forces:

(1) the simple static reactions to the total applied design horizontal forces at the line of lateral support; and

(2) 2.5% of the total design vertical load that the wall or column is designed to carry at the line of vertical support; the elements of construction that provide lateral stability to the structure as a whole need not be designed to support this force.

However, the designer should satisfy himself that loads applied to lateral supports will be transmitted to the elements of construction providing stability. Further guidance on lateral supports and enhanced lateral supports is given in BS 5628:Part 1: Clause 28.

9.11.3.2 Effective height Effective height should be determined by analysis or be taken from Table 9.14.

Table 9.14 Effective height of walls and columns

End conditions	Effective height (h_{ef})
Wall with lateral supports at top and bottom which provide enhanced resistance to lateral movement	$0.75h$
Wall with lateral supports at top and bottom which provide simple resistance to lateral movement	h
Column with lateral supports restricting movement in both directions at top and bottom	h in respect of both directions
Column with lateral supports restricting movement in one directions only at top and bottom	h in respect of restrained direction $2h$ in respect of unrestrained direction

9.11.3.3 Effective thickness (t_{ef}) For a single leaf wall the effective thickness should be taken as the actual thickness. The effective thickness of a reinforced cavity wall should be taken as the overall thickness for cavity widths up to 100 mm. The contribution of a cavity width over 100 mm should not be considered.

9.11.3.4 Limiting slenderness ratio The slenderness ratio should not exceed 27.

9.11.3.5 Reduction for slenderness The capacity reduction factor (β) by which the design strength of a wall or column is to be reduced to allow for the effects of slenderness may be taken from Table 9.15.

171

Table 9.15 Capacity reduction factors for reinforced blockwork

Slenderness ratio $\dfrac{h_{ef}}{t_{ef}}$	β
0	1.00
6	1.00
8	1.00
10	0.97
12	0.93
14	0.89
16	0.83
18	0.77
20	0.70
22	0.62
24	0.53
26	0.45
27	0.40

9.11.3.6 Design strength   The design axial load resistance (N_d) of a wall or column is given by:

$$N_d = \beta \left[\frac{f_k A_m}{\gamma_{mm}} + \frac{0.8 f_y A_s}{\gamma_{ms}} \right]$$

where:

β = capacity reduction factor

f_k = characteristic compressive strength

A_m = horizontal cross sectional area of masonry

γ_{mm} = partial safety factor for masonry

f_y = characteristic tensile strength of reinforcement

A_s = cross sectional area of reinforcement

γ_{ms} = partial safety factor for steel

9.11.4 Columns subjected to a combination of vertical loading and bending

Since the same basic stress block was employed for reinforced masonry as for reinforced concrete it is possible to use the same Load — Moment interaction diagrams to design members subjected to combinations of loading. It is important to note that the area of steel and cover must be the same on each face. The procedure is described for both short and slender columns.

9.11.4.1 Short columns   Calculate the following:

$$\frac{N}{b\,t\,f_k} \quad \text{and} \quad \frac{M}{bt^2 f_k}$$

where:

M = design moment

N = axial design load

b = the breadth of the section

t = overall thickness of the section in the plane of bending

f_k = the characteristic compressive strength of masonry

172

Then for a known f_y and d/t ratio it is possible to determine from the interaction curve the figure value ρ_1/f_k where $\rho_1 = A_s/bt$ and hence determine the percentage of reinforcement required. Alternatively use the design formulae provided in the draft Code.

9.11.4.2 Slender columns Here the design is essentially the same as for short columns except that account must also be taken of the additional moment induced by the vertical load, due to lateral deflection, which may be taken to be:

$$\frac{N\, h_{ef}^2}{2000\, b}$$

where:

N = axial design load

h_{ef} = the effective height in mm of the column

b = the dimension in mm of the column in the plane of bending

This additional moment must be added to the design moment and the resulting value used in the equation given for short columns. The percentage of steel can then be determined from the interaction curve. Alternatively use the design formulae provided in the draft Code. These are presented in Figure 9.22.

Figure 9.22 (a)

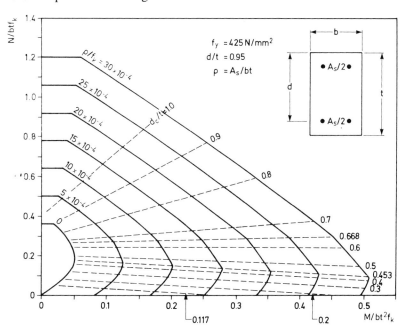

Figure 9.22 Design charts for symmetrically reinforced rectangular columns

Figure 9.22 (b)

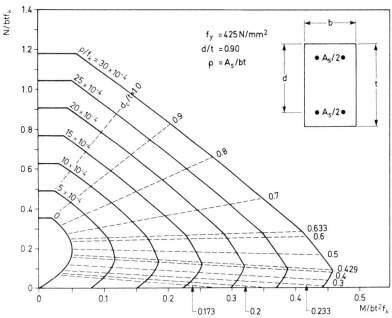

Figure 9.22 (c)

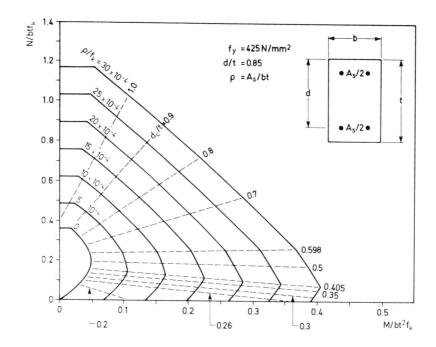

Figure 9.22 (d)

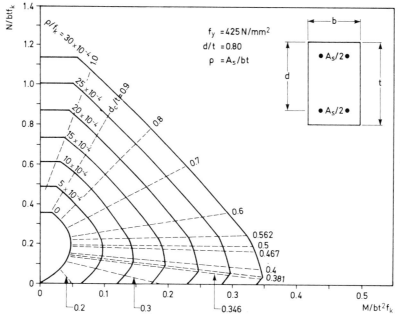

Figure 9.22   Design charts for symmetrically reinforced rectangular columns

Figure 9.22 (e)

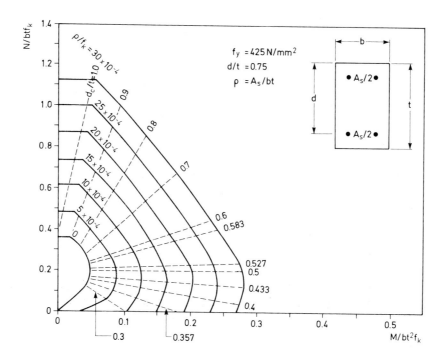

9.11.5 Characteristic shear strength of reinforced masonry, f_v

For hollow block and filled cavity reinforced masonry the characteristic shear strength should be taken from Table 9.16.

Table 9.16

$100\dfrac{A_s}{bd}$	Up to 0.15	0.5	1.0	1.5	2.0
f_v	0.35	0.45	0.55	0.60	0.65

9.11.6 Characteristic anchorage bond strength

The characteristic anchorage bond strength (f_b) between mortar and steel should be taken as:

(a) for plain bars 1.5 N/mm² in tension or compression

(b) for deformed bars 2.0 N/mm² in tension or compression

The characteristic anchorage bond strength between concrete infill and steel should be taken as:

(a) for plain bars 1.8 N/mm² in tension or compression

(b) for deformed bars 2.5 N/mm² in tension or compression

9.11.7 Partial safety factor

9.11.7.1 Loads   As Part 1 of BS 5628

9.11.7.2 Materials   Only two values of the partial safety factor (γ_{mm}) for strength are used with reinforced masonry. These values reflect the category of manufacturing control of the structural units, only the special category of construction control from Part 1 is recognized.

Table 9.17

Category of manufacturing control of structural units	Special	2.5
	Normal	2.8

9.11.7.3 Other partial safety factors

Table 9.18

Masonry in shear	γ_{mv}	2.5
Bond between concrete infill or mortar and steel	γ_{mb}	1.5
Steel	γ_{ms}	1.15

9.11.8 Detailing

9.11.8.1 Minimum area of main reinforcement   The area of main reinforcement in all reinforced masonry members based on the effective depth times the breadth of the section including concrete in cores or pockets, should not be less than:

0.2% for mild steel

0.15% for high yield steel.

9.11.8.2 Minimum area of secondary reinforcement in floors and slabs   In all walls and slabs designed to span in one direction only, the area of secondary reinforcement provided should not be less than 0.05% based on the effective depth times the breadth of the section.

9.11.8.3 Columns The designer should consider whether links are necessary in masonry columns. If required they should not be less than 6 mm in diameter. The spacing of these links should not exceed the lesser of:

(1) the least lateral dimensions of the column;

(2) 50 × link diameter;

(3) 20 × main bar diameter.

9.11.8.4 Curtailment, anchorage, etc. Other reinforcement details should generally conform with CP 110.

9.11.8.5 Cover to reinforcement This section has been considered in some detail in the draft Code. Nominal cover is that used in design and indicated on the drawings and is that cover which should be provided to all main reinforcement. Details of nominal cover are given in Table 9.19 (disregarding applied surface finishes) for the exposure conditions defined in the Table — the distance from the inner face of the masonry being as shown in Figure 9.23.

Table 9.19 Nominal cover to reinforcement (mm)

Exposure conditions	To inner face	Joint reinforcement
(1)	20	25
(2)	30	50
(3)	50	25*

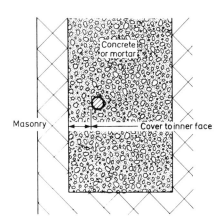

Figure 9.23 *Position of reinforcement in relation to surrounding of masonry*

*Austenitic stainless steel only

Definition of Exposure Conditions

(1) Masonry completely protected against weather, or aggressive conditions, except for a brief period of exposure to normal weather conditions during construction, internal work, and to surfaces which are protected by an impervious coating that can readily be inspected.

(2) Masonry sheltered from severe rain and against freezing while saturated with water, external work, buried masonry and masonry continuously submerged in fresh water.

(3) Masonry exposed to driving rain and freezing whilst wet, subjected to heavy condensation or corrosive fumes, exposed to alternate wetting and drying or continuously submerged in salt water or moorland water.

Minimum cover to secondary reinforcement may be taken as the nominal cover reduced by the diameter of the secondary reinforcement, but must not be less than the diameter of such reinforcement.

Reinforcement in joints between units should be galvanized, resin coated galvanized, stainless steel coated or stainless steel. The cover of mortar or concrete around any part of all reinforcement should not be less than one quarter of the diameter of the bar and in no case less than 3 mm thick.

The nominal cover required in Table 9.19 for given exposure conditions may be reduced by one category when galvanized steel to BS 729[9.25] is employed. Where austenitic stainless steel is employed nominal cover may be reduced in all cases to condition (1).

9.11.8.6 Site factors The organization of work on a reinforced masonry scheme should ideally follow Civil or Structural Engineering practice and be carefully supervized. Particular care will be needed to ensure the correct placement of steel and infilling concrete while maintaining the necessary cover. Figure 9.24 illustrates a scheme using reinforced hollow block masonry, while Figure 9.25 shows reinforced cavity blockwork.

9.12 Design examples using the information in *Section 9.11*

9.12.1 Example 1

Design a 2.6 m high retaining wall 215 mm thick to resist a moment at the base of 29 kN per metre. Although the exposure condition is fairly severe the surface of the wall is to be rubbed and filled and treated with two coats of bituminous paint. The exposure condition for calculating cover has therefore been considered as moderate. A mortar designation

Figure 9.24 Reinforced hollow block masonry in the USA

Figure 9.25 Reinforced cavity blockwork in the USA

(i) will be employed. Take $f_y = 425$ N/mm^2.

Neglect the self weight of the wall.

Consider also the effect of shear force due to design load of 30 kN per metre at the base by calculating the design shear stress comparing with the characteristic shear stress.

9.12.2 Solution 1

The ratio of span to effective depth of this wall should be checked:

effective span = length to face of support + ½ effective depth

$$= 2.6 + \frac{150}{2} = 2.68 \text{ m}$$

$$\frac{\text{span}}{\text{effective depth}} = \frac{2.68}{0.15} = 17.9 \quad \text{Therefore: OK } (< 18)$$

For the masonry:

$$M_d = 0.375 \frac{f_t\, bd^2}{\gamma_{mm}}$$

Therefore:

$$f_t = \frac{M_d \gamma_{mm}}{0.375\, bd^2} = \frac{29 \times 10^6 \times 2.5}{0.375 \times 10^3 \times 150^2} = 8.6 \text{ N/mm}^2$$

For the steel:

$$z = d\left(1 - \frac{0.5\, A_s\, f_y\, \gamma_{mm}}{bd\, f_t\, \gamma_{ms}}\right)$$

$$M_d = \frac{A_s\, f_y\, z}{\gamma_{ms}} \quad \text{i.e. } z = \frac{M_d\, \gamma_{ms}}{A_s\, f_y}$$

Therefore:

$$\frac{29 \times 10^6 \times 1.15}{A_s\, 425} = 150\left(1 - \frac{0.5\, A_s\, 425\ 2.5}{10^3\ 150\ 8.6\ 1.15}\right)$$

Therefore: $A_s^2 - 2793\, A_s + 1\,460\,000 = 0$

Hence: $A_s = 697$ mm^2 per m.

Check minimum quantity required =

$$\frac{0.15 \times 215 \times 1000}{100} = 323 \text{ mm}^2 \text{ per m.}$$

Therefore: need to provide 697 mm^2 per m.

1 No. Y16 bar in each core provides 893 mm^2 per m.

Use 10.5 N/mm^2 blocks, which if 60% solid, gives $f_t = 10.3$ N/mm^2 (8.6 N/mm^2 required)

9.12.2.1 Detailing It is possible to calculate the change point for providing, say 16 mm ϕ starter bars to lap with 12 mm ϕ bars which run for the full height of the wall. The required anchorage length should also be calculated.

9.12.2.2 Horizontal steel The minimum horizontal steel required (mild steel)

$$= \frac{0.05 \times 215 \times 1000}{100} = 108 \text{ mm}^2 \text{ per metre}$$

Therefore use two R6 bars every other course (= 126 mm^2 per m)

9.12.2.3 Shear Design shear stress = 30 kN

Therefore

$$v = \frac{V}{bd} = \frac{30 \times 10^3}{10^3 \times 150} = 0.13 \text{ N/mm}^2$$

$$\frac{A_s}{bd} = \frac{100 \times 893}{1000 \times 150} = 0.66$$

Therefore: Characteristic shear strength $f_v = 0.48$ N/mm^2

Thus

$$\frac{f_v}{\gamma_{mv}} = \frac{0.48}{2.5} = 0.19 \text{ N/mm}^2$$

Therefore the wall has adequate resistance to shear.

9.12.3 Example 2

Calculate the axial load capacity of a 2.8 m high wall built with 390 × 190 × 190 mm two core hollow blocks of mortar designation (i). The blocks have a strength of 21 N/mm^2 and are 60% solid. Each core contains one 12 mm ϕ high yield steel reinforcing bar. Simple lateral support is provided at the top and bottom of the wall. Take $f_y = 460$ N/mm^2.

178

9.12.4 Solution 2

Since lateral support is provided the effective height may be considered as the actual height. For a single leaf wall effective thickness is equal to the actual thickness.

$$\text{Thus the slenderness ratio} = \frac{2.8}{0.19} = 14.7$$

Thus from Table 9.10 $\beta = 0.87$

For a 21 N/mm² block, 60% solid f_k 14.7 N/mm²

Design axial load capacity Nd per m length,

$$= \beta \left[\frac{f_k A_m}{\gamma_{mm}} + \frac{0.8 f_y A_s}{\gamma_{ms}} \right]$$

$$= 0.87 \left[\frac{14.7 \times 190 \times 10^3}{2.5} + \frac{0.8 \times 460 \times 565^*}{1.15} \right] 10^{-3}$$

$$= 0.87 \left[1117.2 + 180.8 \right] = 1129 \text{ kN}$$

*N.B. 226 mm² A_s per 400 mm $= 566$ mm² per m run.

9.12.5 Example 3

Design for moderate conditions of exposure a 6 m high column subjected to an axial load of 400 kN and a moment of 40 kN/m. The column is to be 390 × 390 mm in section and will be built from 390 × 190 × 190 mm two core hollow blocks with a block strength of 15 N/mm² and which are 55% solid. A mortar designation (i) will be employed. Lateral supports are to be provided which restrict movement in both directions at the top and bottom of the column. Take $f_y = 460$ N/mm².

9.12.6 Solution 3

Lateral support is provided $h_{ef} = h$

Therefore: Slenderness ratio $= \dfrac{6}{0.39} = 15.4 < 27 \therefore$ OK

The slenderness ratio is greater than 12 and must therefore be designed as a slender column with due account taken of the additional moment induced by the vertical load due to lateral deflection. This may be taken as:

$$\frac{N h_{ef}^2}{2000b} = \frac{400(6)^2}{200 \times 0.39} = 18.4 \text{ kN/m}$$

$$\text{Thus } \frac{N}{bt f_k} = \frac{400 \times 10^3}{390 \times 390 \times 12.1} = 0.22$$

$$\text{and } \frac{M}{bt^2 f_k} = \frac{40 + 18.4 \times 10^6}{390 \times (390)^2 \times 12.1} = 0.08$$

Moderate exposure conditions apply, therefore cover to the outside of the bar = 50 mm. Thus for (say) a 20 mm diameter bar

$d = 390 - 60 = 330$ m

therefore

$$\frac{d}{t} = \frac{330}{390} = 0.85$$

From the interaction diagram for $f_y = 460$ N/mm²

$\dfrac{\rho_1}{f_k} = 4 \times 10^{-4}$ Therefore $A_s = \rho_1 bt = 4 \times 10^{-4} \times 12.1 \times 390 \times 390 = 736$ mm²

Therefore: Require 1 No. 16 mm ϕ bar in each core.

9.12.7 Example 4

Design for moderate conditions of exposure a 4.6 m high column subjected to an axial load of 300 kN and a moment of 25 kN/m. The column is to be 390×390 mm in section and will be built from $390 \times 190 \times 190$ mm two core hollow blocks with a block strength of 7 N/mm² and which are 55% solid. Lateral supports are provided such that movement in both directions at the top and bottom of the column is restricted. Take $f_y = 460$ N/mm².

9.12.8 Solution 4

Lateral support is provided. Therefore $h_{ef} = h$

$$\text{Therefore: Slenderness ratio} = \frac{4.6}{0.39} = 11.8$$

Therefore: A short column.

$$\frac{N}{bt\, f_k} = \frac{300 \times 10^3}{390 \times 390 \times 6.8} = 0.30$$

$$\frac{M}{bt^2\, f_k} = \frac{25 \times 10^6}{390 \times (390)^2 \times 6.8} = 0.062$$

Assume 10 mm ϕ steel therefore with moderate exposure conditions

$$d = 390 - 55 = 335 \text{ mm}$$

Therefore:
$$\frac{d}{t} = \frac{335}{390} = 0.86$$

From interaction diagram for $f_y = 460$ N/mm²

$$\frac{\rho_1}{f_k} = 2 \times 10^{-4} \quad \text{Where } \rho_1 = \frac{A_s}{bt}$$

Therefore: $A_s = 2 \times 10^{-4} \times 6.8 \times 390 \times 390 = 207$ mm²

Therefore: Require 1 No. 8 mm ϕ bar in each core.

9.12.9 Example 5

Design a flanged retaining wall shown below to resist a moment of 30 kN/m. The wall will be subjected to severe conditions of exposure. Take $f_y = 425$ N/mm².

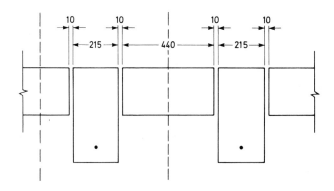

9.11.10 Solution 5

The distance between centres of reinforcing steel

$$= 440 + 10 + 10 + \frac{2(215)}{2} = 675 \text{ mm} .$$

The effective depth to (say) 20 mm diameter steel

$$= 440 - 75 - 10 = 355 \text{ mm}$$

The effective thickness is the lesser of the actual thickness

$$= 215 \text{ mm or } 0.5\, d = 177 \text{ mm}$$

Thus for the masonry:

$$M_d = \frac{f_f}{\gamma_{mm}} b\, h_f \left(d - \frac{h_f}{2} \right)$$

Therefore: $f_f = \dfrac{M_d\ \gamma_{mm}}{b\, h_f \left(d - \dfrac{h_f}{2}\right)} = \dfrac{30 \times \times 10^6 \times 2.5}{(675 \times 177)\left(355 - \dfrac{177}{2}\right)} = 2.36 \text{ N/mm}^2$

For the steel:

$$M_d = \frac{f_y}{\gamma_{ms}} A_s \left(d - \frac{h_f}{2} \right)$$

Therefore: $A_s = \dfrac{M_d\ \gamma_{ms}}{f_y \left(d - \dfrac{h_f}{2}\right)} = \dfrac{30 \times 10^6 \times 1.15}{425 \left(355 - \dfrac{117}{2}\right)} \times 305 \text{ mm}^2$

Therefore require a 20 mm ϕ bar in each flange, and minimum block strength permitted for conditions of exposure, normally 7 N/mm².
(Check minimum percentage of steel = 114 mm²).

9.13 References

9.1 BRITISH STANDARDS INSTITUTION. CP 111: Part 2: 1970 *Structural recommendations for loadbearing walls*. Part 2: *Metric units*. BSI, London. pp 40

9.2 ROBERTS, J J. The behaviour of vertically reinforced concrete blockwork subject to lateral loading. Cement and Concrete Association, London, 1975. Publication No 42.506. pp 13

9.3 ROBERTS, J J. Further work on the behaviour of reinforced concrete blockwork subject to lateral loading. Cement and Concrete Association, Slough, 1980. Publication No 42.531. pp 43

9.4 RATHBONE, A J. The behaviour of reinforced concrete blockwork beams. Cement and Concrete Association, Slough, 1980. Publication No 42.540. pp 23

9.5 ROBERTS, J J. The development of an electrical-resistance technique for assessing the durability of reinforcing steel in reinforced concrete blockwork. Cement and Concrete Association, Slough, 1980. Publication No 42.532. pp 19

9.6 ROBERTS J J. The development of a technique for investigating the durability of reinforcing steel in reinforced concrete blockwork. *Proceedings of the North American Masonry Conference*, Colorado, 1978.

9.7 ROBERTS, J J. Recent research on reinforced concrete blockwork. Paper presented at the BCS/ISE/C&CA Symposium *CP 110 — The Next Stage: the development of a draft code for reinforced and prestresssed masonry*. Cement and Concrete Association, London, May 1979.

9.8 CRANSTON, W B AND ROBERTS, J J. The structural behaviour of concrete masonry — reinforced and unreinforced. *The Structural Engineer, Vol 54*, No 11, November 1976. pp 423—436

9.9 BRITISH STANDARDS INSTITUTION. BS 5628: Part 1: 1978 *Code of Practice for the structural use of masonry*. Part 1: *Unreinforced masonry*. BSI, London. pp 40

9.10 BRITISH STANDARDS INSTITUTION. Document 81/10350 *Draft for public comment of British Standard Code of Practice for the structural use of masonry*. Draft Part 2: *Reinforced and prestressed masonry*. BSI, London, April 1981. pp 81

9.11 AMERICAN CONCRETE INSTITUTE. ACI Committee 531. Concrete masonry structures — design and construction. *Proceedings of the American Concrete Institute, Vol 67*, No 6, June 1980. pp 442—460

9.12 NATIONAL RESEARCH COUNCIL OF CANADA. National Building Code of Canada, Section 4.4: *Plain and reinforced masonry*. 1977.

9.13 NEW ZEALAND INSTITUTE. New Zealand Standard Model Building By-Laws Chapter 9: *Design and construction*. Division 9.2: *Masonry*. NZI, Wellington, July 1964.

9.14 ROBERTS, J J.The effect of different test procedures upon the indicated strength of concrete blocks in compression. *Magazine of Concrete Research, Vol 25*, No 83, London, June 1973. pp 87—98

9.15 BRITISH STANDARDS INSTITUTION. CP 110: Part 1: 1972 *The structural use of concrete*. Part 1: *Design, materials and workmanship*. BSI, London. pp 156

9.16 TOVEY, A K, AND ROBERTS, J J. Interim design guide for reinforced concrete blockwork subject to lateral loading only. *Interim Technical Note No 6*, Cement and Concrete Association, Slough, April 1980. pp 44

9.17 RATHBONE, A J. The shear behaviour of reinforced concrete blockwork beams. *Paper presented at the Symposium on the draft of BS 5628: Part 2*. The Institute of Structural Engineers, London, 8 July 1981. pp 17—28

9.18 BATE, S C C, *et al*. Handbook on the Unified Code for structural concrete (CP 110: 1972). Eyre & Spottiswoode Publications Limited, Leatherhead, 1972. Publication No 14.005. pp 153

9.19 BRITISH STANDARDS INSTITUTION. BS 5502: 1978 *Code of Practice for the design of buildings and structures for agriculture*. BSI, London.

9.20 ROBERTS, J J, AND EDGELL, G J. The approach to bending. *Paper presented at the Symposium on the draft of BS 5628: Part 2*. The Institution of Structural Engineers, London, 8 July 1981. pp 12—16

9.21 BRITISH STANDARDS INSTITUTION. BS 6073: 1981 *Precast concrete masonry units*. Part 1: *Specification for precast* concrete masonry units (pp 12) and Part 2: *Method for specifying precast concrete masonry units* (pp 8). BSI, London.

9.22 BRITISH STANDARDS INSTITUTION. CP 121: 1973 *Code of Practice for walling.* Part 1: *Brick and block masonry.* BSI, London. pp 84

9.23 BRITISH STANDARDS INSTITUTION. BS 5390: 1976 *Code of Practice for stone masonry.* BSI, London. pp 40

9.24 BRITISH STANDARDS INSTITUTION. BS 5328: 1976 *Methods for specifying concrete.* BSI, London. pp 16

9.25 BRITISH STANDARDS INSTITUTION. BS 729: 1971 *Hot dip galvanized coatings on iron and steel articles.* BSI, London. pp 16

10

Concentrated loads

10.1 Background

The concept of allowing increased stresses under localized situations is not new. CP 111:1970 allowed stresses to exceed the basic permissible stresses by up to 50% provided they were of a *purely local nature, as at girder bearings, etc.* There is little published information to support the use of this single figure and, in fact, evidence from unpublished work casts doubt on the validity of the 50% allowance when considering loads applied to the ends of a wall and certain edge conditions.

Experimental evidence shows that compressive failure in concrete and brick masonry is preceded and accompanied by the development of vertical splitting cracks in the units. In concrete the stiff aggregate particles attract load and, because of the random arrangement of the particles, lateral tensile stresses are set up in the cementing matrix. In masonry there is the added complication of the weaker mortar joints which tend to *squeeze out* and thereby add to the lateral stresses inflicted on the cementing matrix.

The case for allowing increased stresses under a localized bearing may be illustrated by considering the simple case of a bearing in the centre of a square block of concrete as shown in Figure 10.1. The general form of failure as shown in sketch (b) is to split the block into four parts. By considering section A—A in sketch (c) it is seen that the lateral compressive stresses acting on the cone must be several times the tensile strength of the block since the area to be split is much larger than that of the cone. A significant triaxial stress field develops in the concrete under the localized bearing area enhancing its resistance to vertical stress.

In the case of an edge loading the form of failure will differ depending on whether the element bearing on the edge of the member is able to move laterally as well as downwards or is constructed only to move downwards. The former gives rise to a *sliding wedge* type of failure (Figure 10.2(a)) whereas the latter tends to have a *slip circle* failure (Figure 10.2(b)). Research carried out on the two types of failure, although limited, indicates that the *slip circle* failure will give higher results than the *sliding wedge*. More extensive research conducted on concrete shows that at least a 25% enhancement is feasible with the *sliding wedge* type of failure. Since it is difficult to predict the exact type of failure it

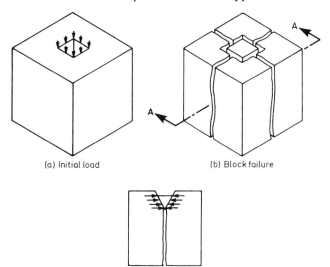

(a) Initial load   (b) Block failure

(c) Section A-A showing wedge and splitting

Figure 10.1 Bearing failure in concrete: (a) initial load (b) block failure (c) section A–A showing wedge and splitting

is reasonable to adopt the 25% enhancement for a continuous edge loading.

In the case of a part edge loading, as shown in Figure 10.3, an effective wedge forms with rupture planes along the sides of the area. Since the total rupture length is longer than the loaded length, it is reasonable to expect some additional enhancement over the normal edge condition. The additional enhancement will vary according to the ratio of the loaded length to the rupture length. However, by controlling the loaded length a standard enhancement may be specified. This has been done in the Code by allowing for a 50% enhancement for edge loading conditions where the loaded length is restricted to eight times the width of the bearing. When the load is applied over the full width of the supporting member some enhancement in stress may again be expected but since the load has a smaller area to dissipate into than in the case of the edge loading, some restriction in the extent of loaded area must be applied. If the load is applied over a length of wall equal to, say, ten times the thickness of the wall then it is probable, most engineers would agree, that an enhancement in stress should not be

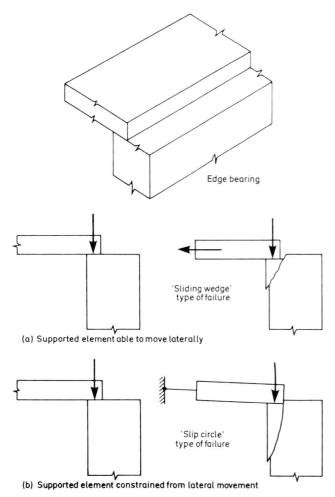

Edge bearing

'Sliding wedge' type of failure

(a) Supported element able to move laterally

'Slip circle' type of failure

(b) Supported element constrained from lateral movement

Figure 10.2 Modes of failure in edge bearing: (a) supported element able to move laterally (b) supported element constrained from lateral movement

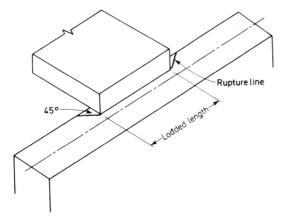

Rupture line

45°

Loaded length

Figure 10.3 Concentrated edge loading

may be expected where the bearing length is about six times the wall width. BS 5628 refers to $6x$ and it appears therefore that this should be related instead to $6t$. Loads on the end of a wall may be dealt with in a similar way but in this instance an enhancement to 1.5 f_k would apply to a bearing length of $2t$ and 1.25 f_k to a length of $3t$.

The enhanced stresses permissible at localized bearing situations allow a heavy beam load to be carried. It is still necessary, however, to ensure that the section of wall is not overstressed at a lower level where the strength is controlled by the capacity reduction factor β. This situation is covered in the Code in Clause 34(b) and is dealt with in detail later.

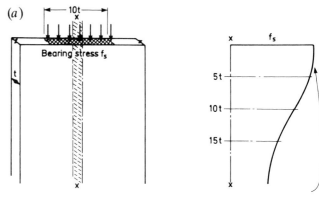

Figure 10.4 (a) Wide bearing width. Intensity of vertical stress hardly changes in this area and therefore if enhanced bearing stresses permitted failure could be expected in main body of wall
(b) Narrow bearing width. Intensity of stress falls rapidly and thus enhanced bearing stress acceptable

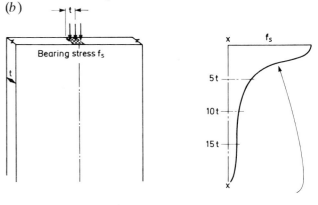

10.2 Code recommendations

Clause 34 indicates that increased local stresses may be permitted beneath the bearing of a concentrated load of a purely local nature, such as beams, columns, lintels, and so on, provided that the element applying the load is sensibly rigid, or that a suitable spreader is introduced. No guidance is given as to what is considered to be a sensibly rigid beam or suitable spreader and this must therefore be left to the engineer's judgement. Concrete beams or concrete encased steel beams will generally be regarded as rigid so that the stresses beneath the beam can be regarded as being uniformly distributed. In addition, any concrete bearing pad whose length is not greater than, say, twice its height can also be expected to impart a uniform stress to the masonry since the applied load can be distributed at an

permitted. This may be seen by considering Figure 10.4(a) which illustrates that the reduction in stress as the load dissipates downwards into the wall is not too rapid, and a normal type of wall failure can initiate in the region of t to $3t$ down from the load. If on the other hand the loaded length of wall is equal to, say, its thickness then the reduction in vertical stress is much more rapid and enhanced bearing stresses are acceptable as wall failure is unlikely to occur except at a very high enhanced stress. Test evidence is limited but an enhancement of 50% would appear to be reasonable in cases where the loaded length is not greater than four times the wall width, since under this condition the rupture length is some 50% longer than the loaded length. By interpolation a 25% enhancement in bearing stress

184

angle of 45° through it (Figure 10.5)*.

Reinforced spreader beams of a shallower section than shown in Figure 10.5 can be used but some care needs to be taken since the stress distributed beneath the bearing may not be exactly uniform (Figure 10.6), the reason being that the beam theoretically does not act until it has deflected so that a non-uniform stress distribution may occur. It is difficult to be precise on this point but a reinforced spreader, whose length is not greater than, say, four times its height, is likely to impart a reasonably uniform stress to the masonry (Figure 10.6). The reference in the Code that *concentrated loads may be assumed to be uniformly distributed over the area of the bearing* (except bearing type 3) is reasonable if the above guidelines are followed but consideration should be given to the development of non-uniform stresses where the spreader is shallow.

bearing is longer than three times the wall thickness. Where the bearing is longer than $3t$ then no enhancement is permitted and the bearing stress must be limited to f_k. However in cases where the bearing is long there will be a tendency for non-uniform stress distribution to occur as indicated in Figure 10.10. This is due to deflection of the lintel and rotation at the bearing. Again it is difficult to be precise but it is reasonable to consider a uniform stress in cases where the bearing length of a reinforced concrete beam or lintel is not greatly in excess of three times its depth (Figure 10.10).

10.6 Stresses at a distance below bearing

Although enhanced stresses are permitted directly

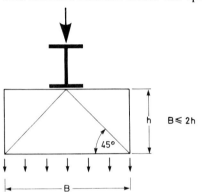

Figure 10.5 Rigid bearing pad

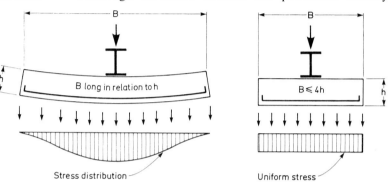

Figure 10.6 Stress distribution under reinforced spreader

10.3 Permitted bearing stress

The enhanced stress permitted in BS 5628 under beam bearings depends on the position and size of the bearing with respect to the wall and basically follows the technical reasoning explained at the beginning of the Chapter. In effect the local load combined with stresses due to other loads should be checked directly beneath the bearing and at a distance below the bearing.

10.4 Directly beneath bearing

The stress directly beneath the bearing should be controlled so that the stresses do not exceed $1.25\ f_k/\gamma_m$ where the bearing is of a type within those shown in Figure 10.7 (bearing type 1, Figure 4(a) BS 5628) or $1.5\ f_k/\gamma_m$ where the bearing is of a type within those shown in Figure 10.8 (bearing type 2, Figure 4(b) BS 5628). The conditions for enhanced stresses as shown in Figures 10.7 and 10.8 are also repeated in tabular form in Figure 10.9 which may be easier to follow in certain cases.

10.5 End bearing

In the particular case of beams spanning in the plane of the wall some care needs to be exercized when the

beneath a localized bearing, such as beam bearings or spreaders, it is necessary to check the stresses at a lower level to ensure that the lower part of the wall is not overstressed. The stresses need to be checked at a distance $0.4\ h$ below the bearing, which in effect is at the top of the central fifth zone of the wall where the additional eccentricity is assumed to be at a maximum (See Appendix B of BS 5628). Since the capacity reduction factor β is determined with respect to this position, it follows that the stresses resulting from the local load with any stresses due to other loads need to be controlled so that they do not exceed:

$$\frac{\beta f_k}{\gamma_m}$$

where f_k is the characteristic strength of the masonry
γ_m is the partial safety factor for the material
β is the capacity reduction factor

For checking the stresses at a lower level the localized bearing stresses may be considered to be distributed at an angle of 45° from the edges of the bearing. Thus, in the situation as shown in Figure 10.11, the reaction of the beam of width B is spread over a length of wall equal to $0.8\ h + B$. The stresses resulting from this spread of load are then added to any stress also acting along that length of wall, for example, as may be applied from loads above the beam level. The combined stresses must be checked to ensure that they do not exceed $\beta f_k/\gamma_m$, i.e. the general stress capacity of the wall.

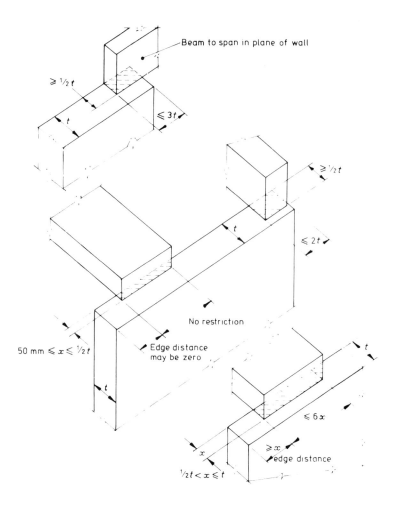

Figure 10.7 Concentrated loads. Bearing type 1. Local design strength $\dfrac{1.25\ f_k}{\gamma_m}$

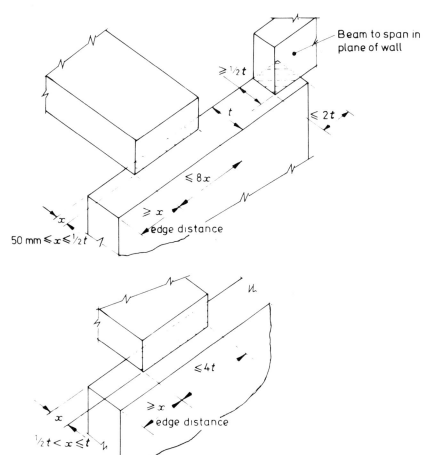

Figure 10.8 Concentrated loads. Bearing type 2. Local design strength $\dfrac{1.5\ f_k}{\gamma_m}$

186

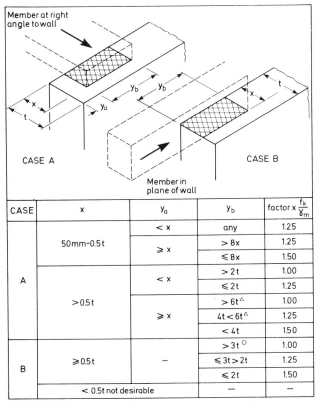

CASE	x	y_a	y_b	factor $\times \dfrac{f_k}{\gamma_m}$
A	50mm–0.5t	< x	any	1.25
		≥ x	> 8x	1.25
			≤ 8x	1.50
	>0.5t	< x	> 2t	1.00
			≤ 2t	1.25
		≥ x	> 6t △	1.00
			4t < 6t △	1.25
			< 4t	1.50
B	≥0.5t	—	> 3t ○	1.00
			≤ 3t > 2t	1.25
			≤ 2t	1.50
	< 0.5t not desirable		—	—

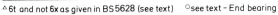

△ 6t and not 6x as given in BS 5628 (see text)   ○ see text – End bearing

Figure 10.9   Conditions for enhanced stresses

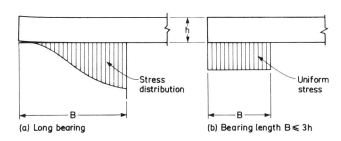

Figure 10.10   Stress distribution at beam ends: (a) long bearing (b) bearing length < 3h

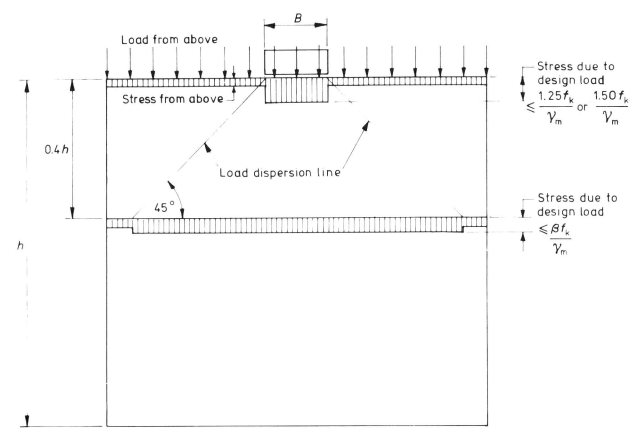

Stress due to design load to be compared with design strength as indicated above.

Figure 10.11   Load distribution for bearing types 1 and 2

187

10.7 End spreader in plane of wall

In the particular case of a spreader beam located at the end of a wall and spanning in its plane (Figure 10.12) the distribution of stress under the spreader may be derived from an acceptable elastic theory. Providing the stress is derived by some elastic analysis the maximum stress which occurs under the loading edge of the spreader as a result of the load applied directly to the spreader combined with stresses due to other loads are allowed to reach a value of $2 f_k/\gamma_m$.

As with the general bearing conditions mentioned previously, the stresses must be checked at a distance of $0.4\,h$ below the bearing, where the stress must not exceed $\beta f_k/\gamma_m$. For this type of spreader, however, the load from the supported beam should be taken as being distributed at an angle of 45° from the edge of the beam (Figure 10.5) rather than from the edge of the spreader as occurs in Figure 10.13.

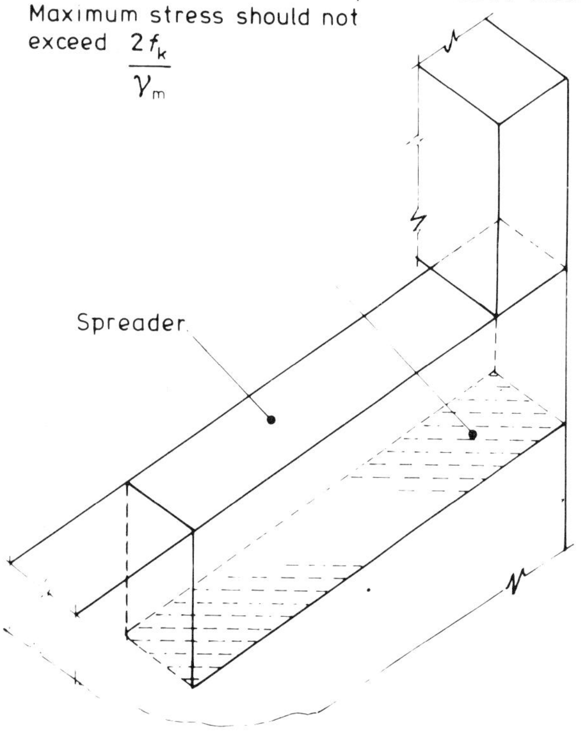

Figure 10.12 Concentrated loads. Bearing type 3

10.8 Design of spreader

The Code gives no details on design of the spreader and determining the distribution of the bearing stresses. The stress distribution, providing the elasticity of the beam and masonry are known, can be determined by finite element methods or by use of analysis of beams on elastic foundations. The latter method would give rise to the indicative shape of the stress diagram as shown in Figure 10.13 which is explained fully by Timoshenko[10.1].

The design solution for long spreader beams is rather complex and as a degree of uncertainty may occur even after a stress distribution has been derived, it has been decided not to go into the detailed method

188

of design for such spreaders, which in any case may be limited and not very practical. However, the simple case of short spreaders is outlined below since they are often found but, as shown, may not always reduce the bearing condition (Figure 10.15).

With concentrated loads applied to the extreme end of a wall by a stiff beam or perhaps a column (Figure 10.14) the stress may be checked by assuming a rectangular stress block and comparing the values with the enhanced stress permitted for the appropriate bearing condition (type 1 or 2). In certain areas the stress may reach a value whereby it exceeds the enhanced value permitted for localized conditions, in which case a spreader or stronger unit will be required to reduce the stress to an acceptable level. In some instances it may be possible to reduce the stress to an acceptable level by introducing a short spreader so that the load may be distributed linearly. Consider, for example, a situation where a column rests on the end of a wall (Figure 10.16) such that the direct stress assuming a rectangular stress block, produces a stress of $1.5\,\dfrac{f_k}{\gamma_m}$ from which:

$$P = \frac{1.5\, f_k\, b\, t}{\gamma_m}$$

If a spreader were introduced of length $2b$ (Figure 10.17) and the stresses determined as in the typical case of a foundation design, the eccentricity of load is outside the mid-third of the section, thus giving rise to a triangular stress distribution of which the maximum intensity of stress (ignoring adhesion between spreader and mortar):

$$f = \frac{2P}{3\left(\dfrac{b}{2}\right)t}$$

which gives: $P = \dfrac{3\, b\, t\, f}{4}$

Now, since the load P must balance:

$$\frac{3\, b\, t\, f}{4} = \frac{1.5\, f_k\, b\, t}{\gamma_m}$$

hence $f = \dfrac{2\, f_k}{\gamma_m}$

which means the spreader designed in this way does not appear to ease the situation. $2 f_k/\gamma_m$ is the maximum permitted when determined by elastic analysis. This approach uses the typical assumption of the load P being applied axially. In practice, however, and using the limit state concept for the stress block in the column and spreader, it is possible to consider that the load in ultimate terms could be transmitted to the spreader by a stress block concentrated to the rear of the column as shown in Figure 10.18. However, it is important to realize that this condition can only occur where the column is held in position at the top and prevented from rotating, whereas with beams rotation will generally occur, and the load will not be applied in this manner.

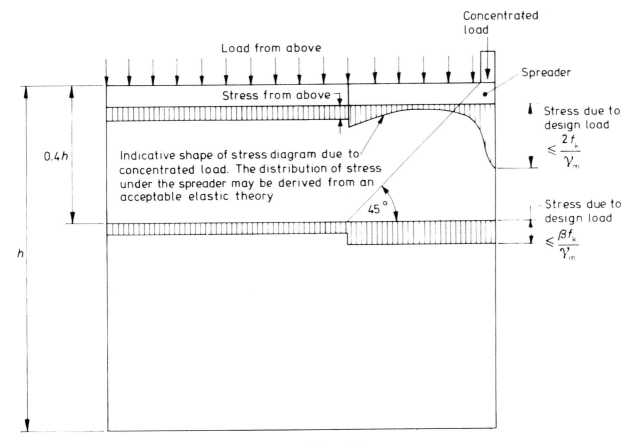

Stress due to design load to be compared with design strength as indicated above.

Figure 10.13   Load distribution for bearing type 3

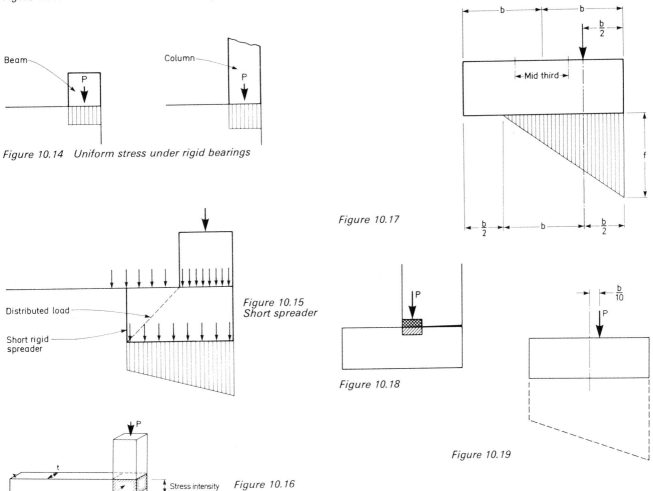

Figure 10.14   Uniform stress under rigid bearings

*Figure 10.15
Short spreader*

Figure 10.16

Figure 10.17

Figure 10.18

Figure 10.19

The width of the stress block could be determined and the stress under the spreader checked with a revised eccentricity of load. Assuming, for example,

189

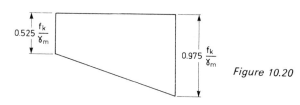

Figure 10.20

that the force P could be carried by the concrete on a stress block of width $b/5$ this would give an eccentricity of $e = b/10$ (Figure 10.19).

Taking

$$P = 1.5 \frac{f_k}{\gamma_m} b t$$

$$A = 2 bt$$

$$Z = \frac{(2b)^2 t}{6}$$

results in a stress diagram with a lower value of 0.525 f_k/γ_m and upper value of 0.975 f_k/γ_m (Figure 10.20).

10.9 References

10.1 TIMESHENKO. Strength of materials — Part II — Chapter 1. Van Nostrand Reinhold Co, New York, 1958. pp 1—25

10.2 WILLIAMS, A. The bearing capacity of concrete loaded over a limited area. Cement & Concrete Association, London, 1979. Publication No 42.526. pp 70

11

Composite action

11.1 Introduction

There are several papers dealing with the subject of composite action of brick masonry walls supported on both reinforced concrete and steel beams and references 11.1 to 11.3 are typical examples. A paper by Levy and Spira[11.4] gives experimental results together with a method of analysis[11.5] for concrete masonry walls, both with and without openings, when strengthened by reinforced concrete elements. Other work on composite action, some of which remains unpublished, is being carried out. The most recent paper[11.8] gives a graphical solution of composite wall beams.

Unfortunately, no method of analysis has been fully developed in this country to an extent whereby it can be given total authority and included in a British Standard Code of Practice. This Chapter sets out to review the principles of composite construction, to outline the basic recommendations made in the documents referred to and to make a few additional comments for consideration. It is important to emphasize that the published work should be consulted so that the range of walls that were tested and the limitations imposed on any design recommendations made are clearly understood.

11.2 Treatment of composite action in published work

The traditional method of designing a beam to support a loading from a triangular section of masonry, as

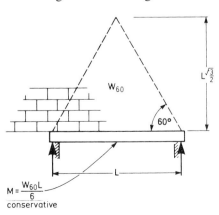

Figure 11.1 Commonly assumed design loading from non-loadbearing wall

$$M = \frac{W_{60}L}{6}$$
conservative

shown in Figure 11.1, is a conservative approach, at least when it is only self weight of the wall that is being considered. The assumption that any superimposed load that is applied above the apex of the triangle (Figure 11.2) is distributed by some arch action to the supports, thus leaving the moment applied to the beam unaltered, is considered by many to be questionable. This method, as indicated by Wood[11.1] when applied to a 225 mm brick wall of span 3.25 m and height 3.25 m gives bending moments based on the total load as follows:

Superimposed load:	0	10 tonne	20 tonne	30 tonne
Bending moment	$\dfrac{WL}{12}$	$\dfrac{WL}{42}$	$\dfrac{WL}{72}$	$\dfrac{WL}{102}$

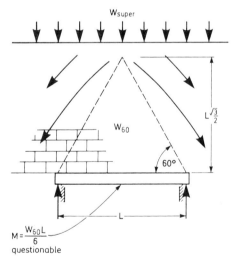

Figure 11.2 Design loading sometimes considered for load-bearing wall

From test results it was concluded that at low loads this approach over-predicts the bending moment applied to the beam but insufficient data exists to give confidence to the moment predicted under higher loads. Since the simple approach appears unreliable, Woods[11.1] proposes two methods of design. The first (Figure 11.3) is to adopt an equivalent bending moment on the basic span of either $\dfrac{WL}{50}$ where openings occur towards the beam supports, or $\dfrac{WL}{100}$ where there

191

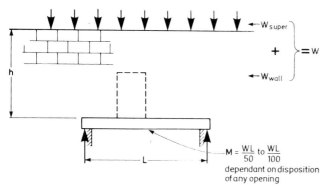

Figure 11.3 Equivalent bending moment method (Woods[11.1])

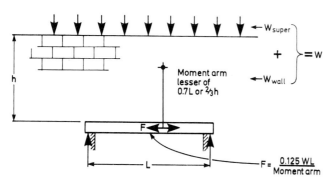

Figure 11.4 Moment arm method (Woods[11.1])

are no openings or where openings occur at mid-span. The second method, Figure 11.4, which is only applicable to walls without openings, is to consider the wall and beam as a composite deep beam which is taken to have an internal moment arm of either $0.7L$ or $\frac{2}{3}h$, whichever is the lesser. (L is the effective span, h is the height of the wall.) Sufficient reinforcement needs to be provided to balance the moment produced from considering the total loading applied to a simply supported beam. In both methods the design proposals are only applicable for cases where the height of the wall is not less than $0.6L$, where other limiting conditions are also imposed.

The work by Colbourne[11.2] deals with the problem in a more analytical way by deriving equilibrium equations which were used in a computer programme to predict stresses in the wall and supporting beam. Further work on composite action between brick walls and their supporting beams was carried out by Burhouse[11.3]. This work compares experimental values of the internal moment arm method with the theoretical values calculated in accordance with the method proposed by Colbourne[11.2]. The experimental results for the limited cases investigated appear to give good agreement with moment arm predicted by Colbourne. The results indicate that the method proposed by Wood over-estimates the moment arm, although it is fair to say that Wood did propose limited steel stresses. Davies and Ahmed used a modified finite element programme in conjunction with some practical cases to develop an approximate method for analysing composite wall beams[11.7]. Further work by the same authors has simplified the approximate solution to a simple graphical approach[11.8] so that it may be used as the basis for a design procedure.

11.3 The principle of composite action

The experimental data indicates that when a wall (subject to self weight and any applied load at its top) is supported by a beam, some form of composite action takes place. This composite action tends to reduce the distribution of load transmitted to the beam but in so doing increases the stresses in the wall at the support, as shown in Figure 11.5. In many of the experimental cases it was the increased stresses in the masonry near the supports that resulted in failure. The beam itself would take some of the moment but would tend to act more as a tie resisting thrust from the arch.

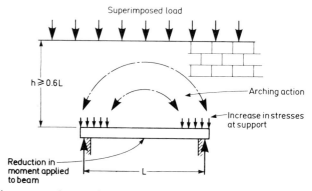

Figure 11.5 Composite action of wall and beam

One of the more recent proposals[11.6] for the design of composite action between a wall and its supporting member suggests that it could be analogous with that of a beam on an elastic foundation. This report indicates that the relative stiffness parameters of the wall and beam could be an important factor in determining the stress distribution in the wall and the forces applied to the beam.

The influence of the stiffness of the beam is illustrated in the following Figures. In Figure 11.6 where the beam is slender (i.e., greater deflection), then the vertical stresses from the wall would be carried over a short length of wall. This would result in higher bearing stresses than would result with a stiff beam, shown in Figure 11.7, since the contact length would be greater. Conversely, since more load is applied towards mid-span with the stiffer beam the bending moment will be higher than for the more slender beam.

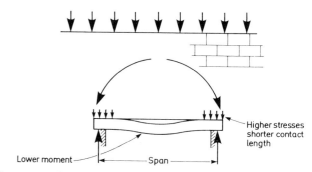

Figure 11.6 Slender beam condition

The difficulty, particularly when load is applied at beam level, is to ensure that the beam has sufficient capacity to carry the moments but is stiff enough to prevent the masonry from being over-stressed in the region of the beam supports. It is not proposed to go

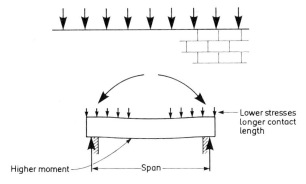

Figure 11.7 Stiff beam condition

into any further detail in this book with the relative stiffness approach since this is still under consideration and could eventually form the basis of Code recommendations for composite construction of masonry walls and their supporting beams. However, the mathematical solution given by Spira and Levy[11.4, 11.5] and Davies and Ahmed[11.7, 11.8] may be of use in estimating the forces and contact stress acting on the wall.

11.4 Limitations of design

There are several limitations imposed upon the published design recommendations and readers should fully understand these before attempting composite design. A few of the most common limiting parameters determined from experimental results are as follows:

(1) Nearly all the design recommendations indicate that to achieve composite action the height of the wall should be not less than 0.6 of the span ($h > 0.6L$);

(2) Although composite action can be used to reduce the reinforcement in the supporting beams, the loading on the wall in such circumstances should be less than the design load permitted by the structural masonry codes.

In the case of a slender wall (Figure 11.8) the critical stresses within the wall are controlled by the slenderness factor (β in BS 5628). A similar concept of indicating that the beam should carry a loading equal to $\dfrac{\beta f_k t}{\gamma_m}$ per metre on a simple span could be considered, but since the purpose of the β factor is to prevent critical stresses being reached within the mid-height of the wall it is reasonable to suggest that some degree of arch (and hence reduced contact length) is permissible since the stress at the base of the wall could be allowed to reach a maximum of $\dfrac{f_k}{\gamma_m}$ (Figure 11.9).

From Figure 11.9 it may be seen that the contact length L_c to prevent stresses occurring in excess of those permissible is found from the following:

$$L_c \geqslant \frac{L \beta \dfrac{f_k}{\gamma_m} t}{2 \dfrac{f_k}{\gamma_m} t} \qquad .. \qquad .. \qquad .. \quad (1)$$

$$L_c \geqslant \frac{L\beta}{2}$$

Taking the contact length L_c as so determined suggests a moment applied to the beam:

$$M = \frac{\beta^2 f_k t L^2}{\gamma_m \ 8} \qquad .. \qquad .. \qquad .. \quad (2)$$

Now since the design load $W = \dfrac{\beta f_k t L}{\gamma_m}$

$$M = \left(\frac{\dfrac{WL}{8}}{\beta}\right) .. \qquad .. \qquad .. \quad (3)$$

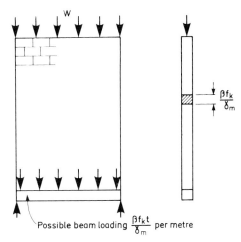

Figure 11.8 Full design stress reached in slender wall

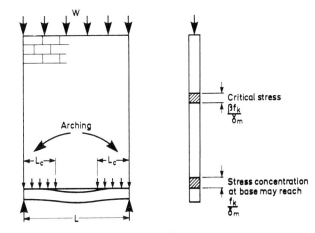

Figure 11.9 Arching in slender wall

Should the loading on the wall in either case, or in a short wall, be less than the maximum design capacity then the following moment may be similarly deduced:

$$M = \frac{\dfrac{WL}{8} \dfrac{W}{W}}{\beta \ W_u} .. \qquad .. \qquad .. \quad (4)$$

the term $\dfrac{W}{W_u}$ simply indicates the ratio between the design load applied to the ultimate capacity.

The predicted bending moments in relation to the ratio $\dfrac{W}{W_u}$ for various capacity reduction factors (β) are

193

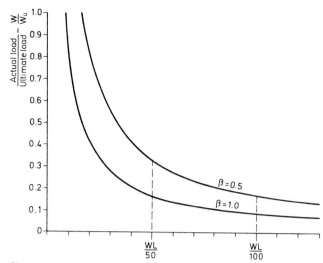

Figure 11.10 *Relationship between actual load and ultimate load capacity of wall to bending moment predicted by equation (4)*

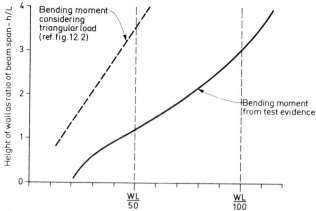

Figure 11.11 *Possible bending moment in beam due to self weight of wall (Woods[11.1])*

plotted in Figure 11.10. From this Figure it can be seen that the actual design load must be considerably less than the ultimate capacity of the wall when designing the beam to bending moments between $\frac{WL}{50}$ to $\frac{WL}{100}$.

The bending moment induced while constructing the wall must be considered. There could be a situation where the imposed load is so small that the moment from composite action is less than the moment required to support the masonry during construction.

The work by Wood[11.1] showed that the stresses induced in the beam during construction were equivalent to the beam carrying a bending moment of between $\frac{WL}{20}$ and $\frac{WL}{30}$. Thus after the walling had reached a height equal to about 0.7 of the span, the stresses due to the additional courses were similar to applying a superimposed load to the completed wall. At low loads this gave equivalent moments in the order of $\frac{WL}{300}$ or less. Assuming that the results by Wood[11.1] are typical, then Figure 11.11 could be considered as indicating the moments that might be expected to result from the self weight of the wall. The dotted line represents the equivalent moment considering the normal triangular load as in Figure 11.1.

11.5 References

11.1 WOOD, R H. Studies in composite construction. Part 1: The composite action of brick panel walls supported on reinforced concrete beams. *National Building Studies Research Paper No 13*, HMSO, London, 1952.

11.2 COLBOURNE, J R. Studies in composite construction: an elastic analysis of wall beam structures. *Building Research Station Current Paper 15/69*. BRS, May 1969.

11.3 BURHOUSE, P. Composite action between brick panel walls and their supporting beams. *Building Research Station Current Paper 2/70*. BRS, January 1970.

11.4 LEVY, M, AND SPIRA, A. Experimental study of masonry walls strengthened by reinforced concrete elements. International Association for Bridge and Structural Engineering, Publications, 1975. Vol 35—ii. pp 113—132

11.5 LEVY, M, AND SPIRA, A. Analysis of composite walls with and without openings. International Association for Bridge and Structural Engineering, Zurich, 1973. Mémoires Abhandlugen Publications 33—1.

11.6 BRITISH STANDARDS INSTITUTION. Technical Committee. Unpublished work dealing with composite construction between masonry and supporting beams.

11.7 DAVIES, S R, AND AHMED, A E. An approximate method for analysing composite wall beams. *Proceedings of the British Ceramic Society*. BCS, London 1978. No 27. pp 305—321.

11.8 DAVIES, S R, AND AHMED, A E. A graphical solution of composite wall beams. *The International Journal of Masonry Construction*, No 1, 1980. United Trade Press Ltd, London. pp. 29—33

11.6 Bibliography

WOOD, R H, AND SIMMS, L G. A tentative design method for composite action of heavily loaded brick panel walls supported on reinforced concrete beams. *Building Research Station Current Paper 26/69*. BRS, 1969.

ROSENHAUPT, S. Stress in point supported composite walls. *Proceedings of American Concrete Institute, Vol 61*. 1964.

COULL, A. A composite action of walls supported on beams. *Building Science, Vol 1*, 1966.

YETTRAM, A, AND HIRST, M. An elastic analysis for the composite action of walls supported on simple beams. *Building Science, Vol 6*, 1971.

MALE, D, AND ARBON, P. A finite element study of composite action of walls supported on simple beams. *Building Science, Vol 6*, 1971.

STAFFORD SMITH, B. The composite behaviour of infilled frames, tall buildings. *Proceedings of Symposium on Tall Buildings*, 1966. Pergamon Press, Oxford, 1967.

BURHOUSE, P. Composite action between brick panel walls and their supporting beams. *Proceedings of the Institution of Civil Engineers, Vol 43*, 1969.

STAFFORD SMITH, B, KHAN, M A H, AND WICKENS, H G. Test on wall-beam structures. *Proceedings of the British Ceramic Society, No 27*, London, 1978. pp 289—304

STAFFORD SMITH, B. AND RIDDINGTON, J R. The composite behaviour of masonry walls on steel beam structures. *Proceedings of First Canadian Masonry Symposium*, University of Calgary, Calgary, Alberta, Canada, 1976.

12

The thermal performance of masonry walls

12.1 Background to the Regulations

In January 1975 Part F of the Building Regulations for England and Wales[12.1] was amended. The amendment reduced the maximum permissible thermal transmittance value (U value) for external walls of dwellings from 1.7 W/m² °C to 1.0 W/m² °C. Part F applies only to dwellings and the reduction in U value was basically intended to reduce the incidence of condensation, but obviously fuel conservation was also achieved. During the last few years it became clear, because of the increase in the cost of fuel, that measures would be required to reduce fuel consumption in all heated buildings. One implementation of this policy was the introduction of Part FF to the Building Regulations. This extended thermal insulation requirements to all heated buildings (dwellings are still covered by Part F) with a floor area greater than 30 m², and came into operation on 1 June 1979. Previously the Building Regulations contained no thermal requirements for these buildings and certain multi-use buildings and buildings which, by reason of the proposed use, require only minimal heating, are given special consideration. Purpose Group III (buildings which comprise one or more dwellings) are exempt from Part FF but are still required to satisfy the requirements of Part F. Similar requirements are given in the Building Standards (Scotland Consolidation) Regulations[12.2] and in the Building Regulations (Northern Ireland)[12.3]. There are currently no thermal requirements in the Building (Constructional) By-Laws[12.4] that apply in Inner London, although this situation is not expected to continue for much longer.

Since the introduction of Part FF designers have become used to the need to achieve good standards of thermal insulation particularly when designing walls to achieve a thermal transmittance value of 0.6 W/m² °C. Thus the introduction of more stringent requirements in Part F of the Regulations, on 1 April 1982, did not require new methods of construction, but served to bring the requirements for dwellings into line with those for other buildings.

12.2 Requirements of Part F

Part F of the Regulations, which essentially applies only to dwellings, is a prescriptive requirement. The opaque parts of the external wall are required to have a thermal transmittance value of not more than 0.6 W/m² °C. Additional clauses deal with walls adjoining ventilated and partially ventilated spaces.

The permitted area of single-glazed window openings should not be greater than 12% of the area of perimeter wallings. The area of perimeter walling is measured internally between finished floor and ceiling levels and includes all openings. In the case of double and treble glazing, the permitted area may be doubled or trebled respectively.

If walls with a U value better than 0.6 W/m² °C are used, the area of the window openings may be increased to the point where the calculated rate of heat loss through the total area of external walls and window openings does not exceed the calculated rate of heat loss which would result if the external walls had a U value of 0.6 W/m² °C and the window area limitations (i.e., 12% of perimeter wall for single glazing) were applied. The U value of single glazing is taken as 5.7 W/m² °C, double glazing as 2.8 W/m² °C and treble glazing 2.0 W/m² °C.

The lintel, jamb or sill used in conjunction with an opening can be considered either as part of the wall or as part of the opening. Clearly if it is considered as part of the wall the maximum U value must not exceed 0.6 W/m² °C.

12.3 Requirements of Part FF

Part FF3 of the Regulations requires only that a building, or part of a building, be so designed that the structure provides *adequate* resistance to the loss of heat to reduce the consumption of energy. It is to Part FF4 that reference must be made to establish which measures are deemed to satisfy the requirements of FF3. Generally, Part FF4 requires a U value of 0.6 W/m² °C for external walls, roofs and exposed floors on the majority of buildings, with a U value of 0.7 W/m² °C allowed for factory and warehouse buildings. In addition to the requirements for walls, floors and roofs, restrictions are made in respect of the amount of glazing permitted. Full details of the requirements for U values and glazing are given in Tables 12.1 and 12.2

Table 12.1 Maximum percentage of window openings and rooflight openings permitted by Regulation FF4(a)(i)

Openings	Purpose groups* II or III	Purpose groups* IV, V or VII	Purpose groups* VI or VIII
Window	25	35	15
Rooflight	20	20	20

Table 12.2 Maximum U value of walls, floors and roofs as required by Regulation FF4(b)(i)

Element of building	Maximum U value of every part of element W/m² °C	
	Purpose groups* II, III, IV, V or VI, or (if for storage) VIII	Purpose groups* VI or (if for storage) VIII
External wall (other than any such wall enclosing a ventilated space or a partially heated space)	0.6	0.7
Internal wall exposed to a ventilated space	0.6	0.7
Floor having its under-surface exposed to the external air or to a ventilated space	0.6	0.7
Roof (other than a roof over a ventilated space or a partially heated space) including (a) any ceiling to the roof; or (b) any roof space and any ceiling below that space	0.6	0.7

*Purpose groups:
I   small residential   IV office   VII assembly
II institutional   V shop   VIII storage and general
III other residential   VI factory

It is important to note that as an alternative to meeting the prescribed limits on maximum percentage area of glazing, it is permitted (Clause FF4 (a)(ii)) to calculate the total rate of heat loss in W/m² °C through all window and rooflight openings and to demonstrate that (as a result of using double glazing, for example), the total heat loss is not greater than would have occurred with single glazing meeting the prescribed limits. Similarly, (Clause FF4 (b)(ii)) the requirements may be satisfied by showing that the total heat loss through the walls, floors and roofs does not exceed that which would have been obtained had all the elements complied with the requirements of Table 12.2. There is thus some scope for trading off building elements, such as greatly increasing the roof insulation, so that a walling material not having a U value as good as 0.6 W/m² °C may be used. Conversely, better wall performance

196

could be traded against a lesser roof performance. It is not possible under Part FF4 to trade glazing performance with that of opaque wall, floor or roof.

The heat flow rate through an element is given by the following expression:

$$Q = A_e U (T_i - T_o) \qquad .. \qquad .. \qquad .. \quad (12.1)$$

where:

A_e = the area of the element

U = thermal transmittance of element

T_i = inside temperature

T_o = outside temperature

When sharing off between various elements the term $(T_i - T_o)$ may be disregarded since it is a constant. Thus the maximum permitted heat flow through the opaque elements (walls, roofs, floors) may be written as follows:

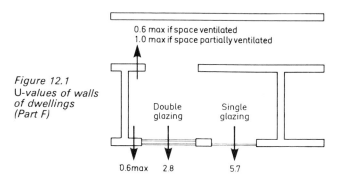

Figure 12.1
U-values of walls
of dwellings
(Part F)

$$Q_{o(max)} = 0.6^* A_{wo} + 0.6^* A_r + 0.6^* A_f \quad .. \quad (12.2)$$

where:

A_{wo} = area of opaque wall

A_r = area of opaque roof

A_f = area of opaque exposed floor (if any)

Similarly, the heat flow through the opaque parts of the actual structure may be written as:

$$Q_{o \, (actual)} = A_{wo} U_w + A_r U_r + A_f U_f \, .. \qquad .. \quad (12.3)$$

where:

A_{wo}, A_r and A_f are as previously

U_w = actual U value of wall element

U_r = actual U value of roof element

U_f = actual U value of floor element (if any)

Now, to satisfy FF4 (b)(ii), i.e. when U values through elements are other than 0.6 or 0.7, as appropriate, then:

$$Q_{o \, actual} \leq Q_{o \, (max)} \quad .. \qquad .. \qquad .. \qquad .. \quad (12.4)$$

hence:

$$A_{wo} U_w + A_r U_r + A_f U_f \leq A_{wo} 0.6^* + A_r 0.6^* + A_f 0.6^* \, .. \qquad .. \qquad .. \qquad .. \qquad .. \quad (12.5)$$

*For buildings of purpose groups VI, of storage VIII, replace 0.6 with 0.7

and when there is no exposed floor:

$$A_{wo} U_w + A_r U_r \leqslant A_{wo} 0.6 + A_r 0.6$$

thus:
$$U_w \leqslant \frac{A_{wo} 0.6 + A_r 0.6 - A_f 0.6}{A_{wo}}$$

$$\leqslant 0.6 + \frac{A_r}{A_{wo}} (0.6 - U_r) \quad .. \quad .. \quad (12.6)$$

hence the required U value of a wall can be determined from a known roof insulation. Similarly

$$U_r \leqslant \frac{0.6 + 0.6 U_w}{\left[\dfrac{A_r}{A_{wo}} \right]} \quad .. \quad .. \quad (12.7)$$

Where, for example, separate parts of the wall have different U values, it will be necessary to return to formula (12.5) and add additional terms, such as: $A_{wo1} U_{w1} + A_{wo2} U_{w2}$, and so on.

Example 1 (Figure 12.2): The following example outlines the method of redistribution of insulation applied to an office block. The office under consideration has a wall area of 900 m² and an opaque roof area of 360 m². The requirements of FF3 would be satisfied by provision of a U value of 0.6 W/m² °C for the wall and roof elements. In this instance it has been decided to insulate the roof to a U value of 0.3 W/m² °C so that the level of insulation required in the walls must be determined as follows:

Roof area = 360 m²

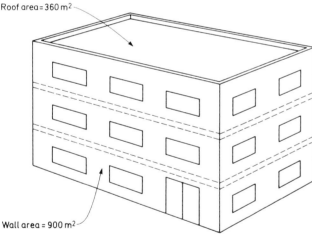

Wall area = 900 m²

Figure 12.2 Example 1

Area of roof: $A_r = 360$ m²

Area of wall: $A_w = 900$ m²

U value of roof: $U_r = 0.3$ W/m² °C

from formulae (12.6) the required U value of the wall is:

$$U_w \leqslant 0.6 + \frac{360}{900} (0.6 - 0.3)$$

$$\leqslant 0.72 \text{ W/m}^2 \text{ °C}$$

Example 2 (Figure 12.3): The insulation requirements for the storage structure (Purpose group III) as shown in Figure 12.3 would be satisfied by providing the walls and roof with a U value of 0.7 W/m² °C. However, in this instance the wall is bridged by columns ($U =$

2.0 W/m² °C). If the roof were maintained at 0.7 W/m² °C, what insulation would the walls need to have?

Since
$$Q_o \leqslant Q_{o\,(max)}$$

then $A_{wo1} U_{w1} + A_r U_r \leqslant (A_{w1} + A_{w2}) 0.7 + A_r 0.7$
if A_{w1} = area of wall
A_{w2} = area of columns

then U value of wall:

$$U_w \leqslant \frac{(A_{w1} + A_{w2}) 0.7 + A_r 0.7 - A_r U_r - A_{w2} U_{w2}}{A_{w1}}$$

$$\leqslant \frac{404 \times 0.7 + 520 \times 0.7 - 520 \times 0.7 - 4 \times 2}{400}$$

$$\leqslant 0.69 \text{ W/m}^2 \text{ °C}$$

If the roof insulation were increased to 0.45 W/m² °C, then the insulation of the wall would only need to be:

$$U_w \leqslant \frac{404 \times 0.7 + 520 \times 0.7 - 520 \times 0.45 - 4 \times 2}{400}$$

$$\leqslant 1.0 \text{ W/m}^2 \text{ °C}$$

Total roof area = 520 m²

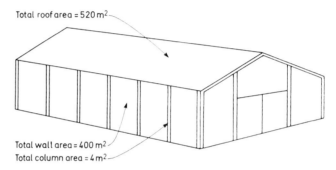

Total wall area = 400 m²
Total column area = 4 m²

Figure 12.3 Example 2

The percentage of glazing in the wall and roof may be determined in a similar manner. The corresponding formulae are:

$$Q_{g\,(max)} = 5.7 \frac{W_{max}}{100} A_{wall} + \frac{R_{max}}{100} A_{roof}$$

where

$Q_{g\,(max)}$ = maximum permissible heat flow through glazing

W_{max} = maximum permissible percentage of window glazing

R_{max} = maximum permissible percentage of roof-light glazing

A_{wall} = total area of wall including windows

A_{roof} = total area of roof including rooflights

and $Q_g = U_{aw} A_{aw} + U_{ar} A_{ar}$

where

Q_g = actual heat flow through glazing

U_{aw} = actual U value of windows

U_{ar} = actual U value of rooflights

197

A_{aw} = actual area of windows

A_{ar} = actual area of rooflights

To satisfy Part FF4 (a)(ii): $Q_g \leqslant Q_{g\,(max)}$

12.4 Condensation

Condensation problems may occur when high insulating materials are used on a building, particularly when the insulation is placed on the inside. Guidance on the problems of condensation and how to assess whether condensation may occur is given in BRE Digest 110[12.5] and in BS 5250[12.6] (although this Code is specific to domestic rooms). It should also be noted that the minimum standard of insulation of roofs in heated buildings is already controlled by the Thermal Insulation (Industrial Buildings) Act, 1957[12.7], although the requirements of Part FF are more severe.

12.5 Deemed-to-satisfy construction

The amendment to the Building Regulations contains schedules giving some general deemed-to-satisfy constructions for walls, floors and roofs for a variety of materials. The purpose of *Section 12.6: Typical constructions* is to illustrate typical constructions and provide a general picture of the various ways in which concrete masonry may be used to meet the requirements. The details provide an indication of the levels of insulation which may be achieved and the approximate thickness of the various constructions.

12.6 Typical constructions

General information is given against each of the constructions, where necessary including a note of some of the items to be considered by the architect during design and construction. Of necessity this article has treated each element of the building separately, but consideration must be given to ensuring the continuity of insulation between walls, floors and roofs to obviate cold bridging in buildings. Other forms of cold bridge, such as dense concrete and steel lintels, also need to be considered.

The values taken for the thermal resistances of various components are presented in a later section. In the case of added insulation materials, a standard value for expanded polystyrene has been adopted for situations where a range of added insulants might potentially be employed. Since the thermal conductivity of different types and grades of insulation materials varies widely, the designer should carry out his own calculations to verify the thermal transmittance of his construction using given proprietary materials. Thermal resistances of blocks and bricks also need to be checked with manufacturers.

Regulation FF4(b) specifies in generic terms a number of insulating materials and deemed-to-satisfy provisions of various constructions. It is also important to ensure that other properties such as durability are suitable. For simplicity, masonry walling is grouped into three categories:

(1) cavity walls with clear cavity — using standard thickness masonry — increasing block thickness

(2) cavity walls with filled cavity;

(3) solid walls

Figure 12.4 illustrates typical constructions. Manufacturers will, however, produce individual data illustrating exactly what can be achieved with their particular products. The thermal insulating blocks referred to in the text are those which were initially developed for use in dwellings and typically have a thermal resistance between 0.445 m² °C/W and 0.625 m² °C/W. This group includes normal density autoclaved aerated concrete blocks and solid lightweight aggregate concrete blocks. Foam or similarly filled aggregate blocks may also provide a good thermal resistance but the revised CIBS[12.8] method for determining the thermal resistance of foam or similarly filled blocks gives lower results than those previously employed, particularly in the case of foam filled dense aggregate blocks. A further development has been the introduction of thermal insulating facing blocks which provide good insulation without the need for rendering or other coverings. Recent developments in block types include those made with lower density materials than were previously available. Blocks in the form of autoclaved aerated concrete with densities as low as 475 kg/m³ are already available, and further developments can be expected with lightweight aggregate blocks. An alternative approach has been to develop blocks which can be provided with integral bonded insulation on one face. In the following sections various thermal transmittance values are shown to indicate the effect of changing the thermal resistance of the block in the range 0.445 m² °C/W to 0.625 m² °C/W. Reference should be made to the manufacturer for information on each particular type of block.

12.6.1 Cavity walls with clear cavity

12.6.1.1 Standard thickness masonry Details are given in this section of the level of insulation that may be achieved with masonry commonly used in the cavity walls of dwellings (now required to have a U value not exceeding 0.6 W/m² °C). The exact U value of the various constructions will obviously depend on the products used. The values given against each construction are those which will typically be achieved using standard bricks and 100 mm thermal insulating blocks currently available.

To achieve the required level of thermal insulation many constructions require a 25 mm thick cavity insulation bat. Usually these are attached to the inner leaf, but this may be dictated by condensation considerations and the properties of the particular material being used. In some circumstances insulation can be added to

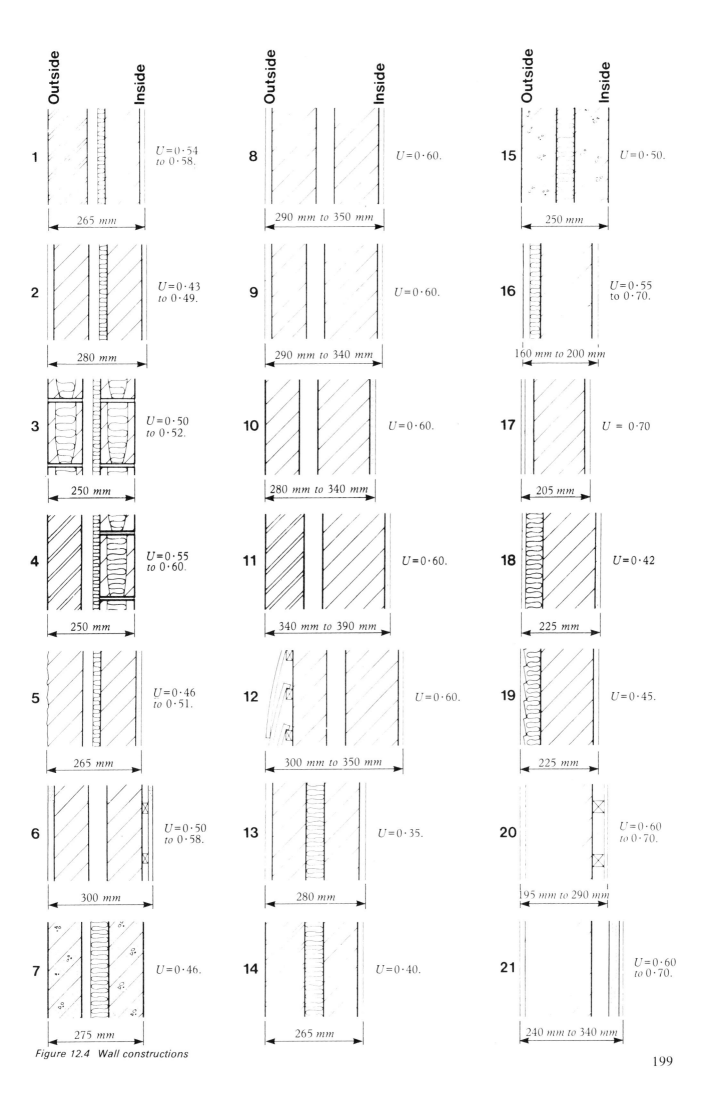

Figure 12.4 Wall constructions

199

the inside of the inner leaf, i.e., beneath plasterboard. However, before doing so, the designer should carefully consider the potential problems of interstitial condensation.

(1) *Facing brick or block* (Figure 12.4(1)): This construction uses a 25 mm cavity bat, a drained cavity maintaining resistance to rain penetration. It is very important to check for secure fixing of bats during construction. If allowed to fall forward, rain penetration may occur. The U value of this construction will improve to between 0.45 — 0.48 when plasterboard on battens is used. For a facing brick a 30 mm bat would be needed to achieve 0.7.

(2) *Rendered double leaf block, cavity bat* (Figure 12.4(2)): Modifying the previous design to include a rendered thermal insulating block on the external leaf gives an improved thermal transmittance value. The precautions mentioned in (1) need to be applied when bats are positioned, although in this instance the render coat reduces the problems of rain penetration due to misplaced bats. Obviously any render should be applied carefully. Two leaves of blocks improve insulation from (1) so it is possible to use 90 mm thick blocks and increase the clear cavity to 45 mm or 50 mm, giving a U value typically between 0.46 — 0.5. The use of plasterboard on battens produces a U value of about 0.4.

(3) *Fair faced blocks* (Figure 12.4(3)): The illustration shows foam filled facing blocks. If unfilled blocks are used, the cavity bat will need to be increased in thickness to between 35 mm — 40 mm but the overall size of the construction and clear cavity should be maintained using 90 mm blocks. All concrete blocks should be protected from rain by covering the stacked blocks on site, but this is particularly important when foam filled blocks are used. Though some potential problems with condensation and pattern staining have been envisaged with this type of block, no actual problems have been recorded. The cavity prevents any direct cold bridging to the outside. In areas of severe exposure the ability of the wall to resist rain penetration should be checked with the manufacturer and good workmanship ensured. There may be cost savings from eliminating finishing trades but a high standard of blocklaying will be required.

(4) *Facing brick, bat, dense fair faced thermal insulating block* (Figure 12.4(4)): This construction is similar to the previous wall except that the outer leaf is replaced with a facing brick. Again it is important to ensure that the foam filled blocks are protected during construction.

(5) *Lightweight thermal insulating facing block* (Figure 12.4(5)): An interesting construction is the use of exposed aggregate or stone finish thermal insulating facing blocks with an inner leaf of standard thermal insulating blocks. A U value of about 0.5 is achieved but it should also be noted that it is possible to achieve U values of 0.6 or 0.7 without the cavity bat when plasterboard or lightweight plaster is used internally. A good standard of blocklaying

will be required for facing work, care will need to be taken to maintain joint thickness and specials may be required. Where facing blockwork is required internally, it is possible to build two leaves of thermal facing blocks.

(6) *Rendered double leaf block, clear cavity* (Figure 12.4(6)): Where it is desired to retain the full nominal cavity, two leaves of thermal insulating blocks with foil-backed plasterboard on battens may be used to provide a construction having a U value better than 0.6. Double leaf block walls provide a great deal of flexibility since the same construction using plasterboard on dabs provides a U value between 0.58 — 0.69; using lightweight plaster 0.60 — 0.72; and dense plaster 0.63 — 0.74. As with all masonry construction, the actual thermal resistance will depend on the particular block used; as thermal insulating blocks are developed further even better results may be expected. For brick outerleaf, U value is between 0.66 — 0.72. Plasterboard may be more prone to damage than traditional plastering and may cause difficulties in heavy fixings. As an alternative to rendering, tile hanging or some other form of cladding may be employed, further improving the thermal performance.

(7) *Double leaf dense facing block* (Figure 12.4(7)): Where it is desired to retain a cavity and to use two traditional leaves of dense facing blocks or bricks, it will usually be necessary to increase the cavity to 75 mm. The illustration indicates the U value to be expected with a 50 mm bat. It is possible to achieve a U value of 0.6 W/m² °C using a 25 mm bat and retaining a clear cavity of 40 — 50 mm, which is more likely to provide an efficient barrier to rain penetration in more severe conditions. A construction using 90 mm thick leaves will provide a U value of 0.5 and be within the traditional wall thickness expected for a cavity wall.

12.6.1.2 Increasing block thickness All but one of the constructions in the previous section required the use of additional insulation to achieve U values of 0.6 W/m² °C and 0.7 W/m² °C. In some situations it may not be appropriate to reduce the effective clear cavity by using a bat, and the following constructions are designed to retain a full 50 mm wide cavity using blocks thicker than the standard 100 mm. Thicknesses widely available are 140 mm, 190 mm and 215 mm, but some manufacturers can provide others.

(1) *Rendered double leaf block* (Figure 12.4(8)): When employing dense plaster on a double leaf wall, a block between 106 mm and 135 mm is required to achieve a U value of 0.6. With lightweight plaster the required thickness is between 100 — 129 mm; with plasterboard on dabs 96 — 122 mm and with plasterboard on battens a thickness between 73 — 94 mm (i.e., as shown in Figure 12.4(6), a thickness with the standard 100 mm blocks may be used). To achieve a U value of 0.7, the required block thickness will be about 20% less.

(2) *Rendered double leaf block* (Figure 12.4(9)): When it is necessary to increase the block thickness to achieve the necessary level of insulation it is advantageous to increase only the inner leaf rather than both leaves. The main advantages are that the loadbearing capacity of the wall is increased and better use is made of the insulation since there is a greater amount of material in a protected situation. Using a 140 mm inner leaf in conjunction with a 100 mm outer leaf will produce a *U* value typically between 0.54 — 0.65 using dense plaster; 0.53 — 0.63 using lightweight plaster; 0.51 — 0.61 using plasterboard on dabs and 0.45 — 0.52 using plasterboard on battens.

(3) *Facing thermal insulating block* (Figure 12.4(10)): If a lightweight facing thermal insulating block is used and the nominal 50 mm clear cavity is required then the inner leaf of insulating block will have to be increased to between 130 — 190 mm. Again, very good loadbearing potential is achieved because of the thickness of the inner leaf.

(4) *Facing brick cavity wall* (Figure 12.4(11)): This construction is similar to Figure 12.4(10). Due to the difference in insulation between a lightweight facing thermal insulating block and the facing brick, the inner leaf is increased to between 190 — 240 mm. An inner leaf of between 185 — 235 mm would be required when using dense plaster, and 175 — 225 mm for lightweight plaster. Using one of the new 475 kg/m³ autoclaved aerated concrete blocks an inner leaf thickness of 130 — 150 mm would be required, depending upon the internal finish.

(5) *Tile hung double leaf block* (Figure 12.4(12)): This construction is similar to Figure 12.4(9) with the outer render coat replaced by tile hanging. A 100 mm block on the inner leaf provides a *U* value between 0.49 — 0.68; a 140 mm block can have a value as low as 0.43. When using this type of construction, consideration should be given to the possible damage or displacement of tiles, particularly those for use at ground and first floor level. Other forms of cladding, such as weatherboarding, may be used as an alternative to tiles.

12.6.2 Cavity walls with filled cavity

One way of achieving a *U* value less than 0.6 W/m² °C with standard thickness masonry in a cavity wall is to use cavity fill material. This is by no means a straightforward solution, however, and many factors have to be borne in mind. Although it is always desirable, when using bricks or blocks as the outer leaf of a cavity wall, to ensure good workmanship and supervision, this becomes essential when cavity fill is employed. For an injected fill, the installers are expected to satisfy themselves that the wall is in a suitable condition before filling, although this is often very difficult to do. In new construction, on the other hand, if the wall is constructed with full width insulation slabs, the construction can be inspected as the slabs are positioned. A number of cavity fill materials are available including urea formaldehyde foam, blown-in mineral fibre, expanded polystyrene in the form of beads or foam, and polyurethane foam. Cavity slab insulation materials include resin-bonded rock wool fibres and glass fibres, and expanded polystyrene.

When using a cavity fill material it is important to remember that the outer leaf will be colder and remain wetter than with an unfilled cavity, and thus the outer leaf must be checked for susceptibility to frost damage. Concrete masonry materials are generally not prone to frost damage but manufacturers' experience should be sought, especially in the colder regions of the country; clay facing bricks are also at risk.

(1) *Rendered double leaf block* (Figure 12.4(13)): The construction shows a good level of insulation to be achieved with two leaves of thermal insulating blocks. The rendering assists resistance to rain penetration. Tile hanging instead of render would give a *U* value of 0.34.

(2) *Facing brick or block* (Figure 12.4(14)): A similar *U* value would be obtained if a facing block replaced the brick outer leaf. Currently, the incidence of rain penetration problems for filled cavity walls is quoted by the manufacturers as less than 1%, and this is supported by the Building Research Establishment.

(3) *Double leaf facing block* (Figure 12.4(15)): Good workmanship should be ensured to help resist rain penetration and the type of block used in areas of high exposure to rain given careful consideration (check with manufacturers). Some savings in cost may be achieved by not needing to provide finishes, but a high standard of blocklaying is required. A similar *U* value will be achieved with two leaves of concrete brickwork.

12.6.3 Solid walls

The previous constructions were all based on the traditional cavity wall. Though solid walls used in the past were beset by problems of condensation and dampness, there does seem some merit in basically re-examining solid forms of construction, particularly as much higher insulation is now required and there is an increased use of external insulation systems and internal dry linings. Compared with internal insulation and some other methods of improving wall performance, the use of an external insulation system offers the following advantages:

(a) the thermal capacity of the walling material is utilized and the comfort of the occupants thereby improved. Maximum use is made of the structure to reduce solar gain, maintain night time temperatures and generally reduce temperature variations;

(b) cold bridging problems are avoided;

(c) there is no loss of internal space;

(d) the acoustic performance is not degraded due to longitudinal vibration as might be the case with some lightweight lining systems;

(e) potential interstitial condensation problems are largely avoided;

(f) the fire hazard is potentially much less than in the case of a corresponding internal insulation system in terms of rate of heat build-up;

(g) the exterior protection provided to the insulation should ensure a better resistance to rain penetration than conventional solid wall constructions.

Against these advantages must be set the obvious limitations of the type of finish and appearance given to the building, and in some circumstances the vulnerability of particular systems to vandalism.

There are basically three types of system:

(a) lightweight renders;

(b) rigid insulation panels;

(c) flexible insulation mats.

The lightweight renders are thermally less efficient than the other techniques, but are likely to be cheaper and may be used in marginal cases where the additional insulation provided by the render is sufficient to give an acceptable U value.

The following constructions are typical examples of external insulation systems applied to concrete blocks, although they may be applied to almost any rigid substrate. While render is shown as the finishing coat because it is a comparatively cheap solution, claddings could also be used. Additional savings may occur since the overall construction is likely to be reduced in thickness and it is generally cheaper to construct solid walls than cavity walls.

(1) *Externally insulated* (Figure 12.4(16)): The thickness of insulation may be increased very easily. Satisfactory levels of insulation are given by a construction from as little as 160 mm in overall thickness, a saving in thickness compared with the cavity walls. Careful detailing is necessary around openings and roof level. The rendered outer coat and the insulation provide an extremely good barrier to rain and thus, in combination with the wall, are likely to provide a weathertight construction. Consideration should be given to thickness of render to give adequate impact resistance if used at ground level. Cladding may also be used to protect the insulation. The illustration shows 25 mm of insulation; if this is increased to 50 mm there is approximately a 30% improvement in U value. A 100 mm leaf would be suitable for insulating and cladding but consideration must be given to its lateral stability. Increasing to 140 mm would improve its insulation, stability and loadbearing capacities.

(2) *Lightweight renders* (Figure 12.4(17)): The exact U value will depend on the applied density and thickness of render. Some manufacturers suggest thicknesses up to 100 mm. The resistance of proprietary systems to impact damage varies considerably and, in some cases, a strong decorative finish

will be needed. The substrate should be prepared as for a traditional render.

(3) *Rigid panels* (Figure 12.4(18)): The rigid panel form of external insulation is attached to the substrate either by mechanical fixings or adhesives. The adhesive methods are widely used in other countries, although in the UK preference seems to be given to the mechanical fixings. The panels need to be bonded together with a fibre reinforcing mat or similar and need to be protected with a render or cladding. A grc render can be used to provide the necessary impact protection. Expanded polystyrene boards need to be *aged* to reduce shrinkage movement and the surface of the board needs to be of a roughened texture so that render may be easily applied.

(4) *Flexible insulants* (Figure 12.4(19)): With this system the insulation is usually supplied attached to a metal carrier and breather paper. Mechanical fixings are invariably used and again the insulation has to be protected by a render or cladding. When fixing, care needs to be taken not to compress the insulant. A scratch render coat will probably be required to reduce *bounce* in the metal carrier before the main coats are applied.

(5) *Rendered thermal insulating block* (Figure 12.4(20)): When external insulation is omitted, a block about 225 mm in thickness is required to achieve a U value of 0.6 even when foil-backed plasterboard on battens is used. A 190 mm block would give a U value of less than 0.7 (145 mm is the minimum to achieve 0.7). The external render will assist in preventing rain penetration. Experience indicates that the construction should be suitable for moderate exposure and, depending on the type of block and thickness, also for severe exposure. Special consideration should be given to detailing at floor level to avoid problems of rain penetration. The use of tile hanging or one of the proprietary cladding panels will considerably improve thermal insulation.

(6) *Posted construction* (Figure 12.4(21)): An interesting adaptation of the solid wall is the posted construction which is ideally suited for single storey structures. In this method the outer solid wall (fair faced or rendered) is used as the loadbearing member and a non-loadbearing isolated studding, supported by a sleeper wall, is provided internally. The *cavity* is thus completely unbridged and allowed to drain freely at ground level. The plasterboard and studding may be replaced by proprietary partitioning with a consequent increase in insulation. Because of the completely clear cavity (no problems of dirty ties) this construction is suitable even for the most severe conditions of exposure. It is, in fact, a traditional Scottish construction not commonly found in England and Wales. When used on multi-storey structures, attention must be given to the detailing at floor levels to reduce rain penetration problems.

12.7 An explanation of λ, R and U values

Whilst it is not within the scope of this book to go deeply into the thermal performance of buildings, the designer should at least be aware of the factors which will influence the flow of heat through the fabric. This is of particular importance in meeting either prescriptive requirements of regulation (i.e., the element must have a thermal transmittance value equal to or better than the specified value) or functional requirements (i.e., the resistance to the passage of heat must be *adequate*). It is apparent that a temperature difference across a building element such as a wall will give rise to a flow of heat through the element, and it is the function of insulation to resist this flow of heat. The process by which heat flows through a material is called conduction and, because air is a poor conductor, insulants tend to comprise of materials in which a lot of air is trapped. Convection will occur in the air within a building due to changes in density because of temperature variations and will lead to heat transfer at various points within the structure. Finally, it should be noted that all bodies emit energy in the form of radiation, the amount of radiation depending upon the temperature of the body and the type of surface.

12.7.1 Thermal conductivity

The ability of a material to conduct heat is known as its thermal conductivity or λ value*. The thermal conductivity of any given material is usually given as the heat flow (W) per unit area (M^2) when there is a temperature difference of 1°C across a 1 m thickness of the material (i.e., λ − W/m² °C). The thermal conductivity of most materials will alter with density, porosity and moisture content. Rain penetration or condensation could result in sufficient moisture being present in the fabric of a building to significantly reduce the thermal conductivity of the material. Standard moisture contents and corrections for masonry are given in *Section 12.11* on standard thermal resistance values. The reciprocal of the thermal conductivity is known as the thermal resistivity and indicates the ability of the material to resist the flow of heat (m² °C/W).

12.7.2 Thermal resistance

The thermal resistance is a convenient way of measuring the resistance to heat flow of a material or several materials combined. The thermal resistance or *R* value of a slab of homogeneous material is obtained by dividing its thickness (*l*) by its thermal conductivity (λ), i.e., $R = l/λ$ m² °C/W. It is apparent that doubling the thickness of the given material will double the thermal resistance.

12.7.3 Thermal transmittance

The thermal transmittance (*U* value) is the rate of heat flow through unit area of the element when a unit temperature difference exists between the air on each side. The *U* value takes into account, as well as the resistance offered by the fabric, the outside and inside surface resistance.

$$\text{Thus: } U = \frac{1}{\Sigma R} \text{ W/m}^2 \text{ °C}$$

Standard resistance values for a range of material and surface resistances are given in a later section. Since notionally the *U* value provides a direct comparison of the heat flow through a wall or other element, it is the figure used to compare the performance of different constructions and to make energy use calculations.

12.8 Calculation methods for multi-slotted blocks

When, in January 1975, Part F of the Building Regulations was amended requiring the external walls of dwellings to meet a *U* value of 1.0 W/m² °C, not all blocks then in use as the inner leaf to a brick outer leaf were sufficiently good insulators to comply with the mandatory requirements. To improve thermal resistance, some manufacturers incorporated slots into their blocks.

Reference to *Chapter 4* will indicate that the standard thermal conductivity test in BS 874[12.12] is a test on a solid layer of material and thus there is no way to test the performance of a multi-slotted block without testing walls in the way described in the next section — a non-standard procedure for which few test rigs are yet available. It has, therefore, been necessary to rely on calculation methods to assess the thermal performance of blocks. Several different assumptions may be made with the result that a number of methods of calculation are possible, as illustrated in Figure 12.5.

Method 1: Assessing the average *U* value of the wall by determining the *U* values of the differing cross sections and proportioning them to their respective areas

Method 2: Assessing the average *U* value of the wall by determining the average conductance of the leaf to the centre line of the cavity with a value for finishes incorporated into the basic formula (the method given in DoE circular BRA/668/68[12.9])

Method 3: As *Method 2* but with the resistance of the finishes added after the conductance of the leaf has been determined

Method 4: Assessing the average *U* value of the wall by determining the average surface to surface conductance of the bridged and unbridged sections (the upper limit of the revised CIBS guide)

Method 5: Assessing the average *U* value of the wall by summing the equivalent resistance of the various core and solid strips (the lower limit of the revised CIBS guide and also given by ASHRAE[12.10])

---

*Previously referred to as κ value

203

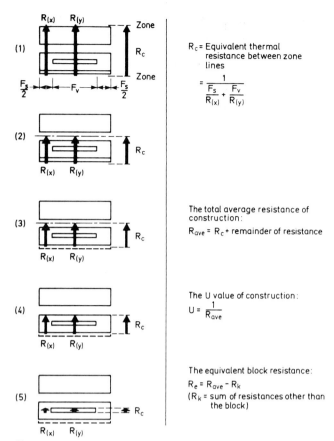

R_c = Equivalent thermal resistance between zone lines

$$= \frac{1}{\dfrac{F_s}{R_{(x)}} + \dfrac{F_v}{R_{(y)}}}$$

The total average resistance of construction:

$R_{ave} = R_c +$ remainder of resistance

The U value of construction:

$$U = \frac{1}{R_{ave}}$$

The equivalent block resistance:

$R_e = R_{ave} - R_k$
(R_k = sum of resistances other than the block)

Figure 12.5 Basic heat flow concept used

12.8.1 Multi-slotted blocks

Because of the variations which occur it is difficult to determine the precise thermal resistance value of a slotted block and, therefore, for the purpose of consistency one method of calculation only should be adopted. The average of *Method 4* and *Method 5* is that contained in the revised CIBS guide and has been adopted by DoE.

12.9 Foam-filled blocks

In the absence of measured values obtained by testing wall panels in a thermal transmittance rig, the DoE have accepted calculations based on *Method 2,* as used for multi-slotted blocks. However, the revised CIBS guide which uses the mean of *Method 4* and *Method 5* gives lower results and may become a DoE accepted method. This latter method gives better agreement with test results than the resistance obtained from *Method 2.* In this case the thermal resistance of the air pocket is replaced by the thermal resistance t_b/λ of the insulating material.

When considering the use of foam or other insulant filled blocks, a number of factors need to be considered including condensation risk, fire resistance, durability of the wall and properties of the foam, especially in damp conditions.

12.9.1 Condensation risk

Theoretically the presence of high insulation foam materials may lead to condensation within the inner leaf of a cavity wall. This problem will generally only be significant if condensation occurs within the foamed layer, thereby reducing the value of the insulation and possibly causing deterioration of the foam.

12.9.2 Fire resistance

The protection afforded to the insulant by the block will give adequate performance for most low rise applications but each manufacturer will have particular recommendations for the blocks he produces, bearing in mind the insulating material and class of aggregate employed.

12.9.3 Durability of the wall

In an outer leaf situation water will invariably penetrate the block and reduce the insulation value of some materials, possibly affecting their durability. Although most concrete blocks themselves are not likely to suffer from frost attack, a poorly graded sand used to make the mortar could be excessively permeable and suffer frost damage.

12.9.4 Properties of the foam

Some foam materials are closed cell and do not take up water and therefore change the thermal insulation provided, whereas some materials do take up water and hence reduce the level of insulation. Furthermore, some materials will deteriorate in the presence of moisture. The designer must clearly satisfy himself as to the adequacy of the materials which he proposes to use.

Additional factors to be considered relate to the method of providing the insulation, which may range from spraying in situ to the insertion of rigid panels into the finished blocks. In both cases, the insulation needs to be so well located that it will not be lost or left out during transporting and laying.

12.10 Test methods for walling

Whilst it is beyond the scope of this manual to go too deeply into methods of test for assessing the U value or conductance of a wall, the reader should be aware of the test methods available. Essentially there are two techniques which may be employed:

(1) a guarded hot-box rig in which the energy required to maintain a temperature differential across a wall (all extraneous heat losses having been excluded) is measured;

(2) placing a heat flow meter on the wall to measure the amount of flow of heat per unit area.

A typical hot box-rig, as based on ASTM[12.11], is shown in Figure 12.6. It should be noted that this is not a standard method of test in the UK and rig designs and operating parameters differ which is likely to lead to differences in results obtained. The test result would also include the effect of the mortar joints — this is normally excluded from the calculation method. As far

Figure 12.6 A hot box rig capable of measuring the thermal transmittance value of 2 m × 2 m wall panels

as the use of heat flow meters is concerned, the principal drawback seems to be that the meters themselves modify the passage of heat through the wall. *U* value measurement may be made by modifying the flow of air across a wall to give the appropriate standard resistances and by measuring the air temperature on either side of the wall. Alternatively, the surface temperature may be measured and the conductance of the wall determined.

12.11 Standard thermal resistances used in Section 12.6

Thermal resistances used to determine *U* values given	m² °C/W
Thermal insulation blocks per 100 mm thickness	0.445 — 0.625
Dense solid facing blocks per 100 mm thickness	0.100
Brickwork (105 mm)	0.125
Dense plaster (13 mm)	0.026
Lightweight plaster (13 mm)	0.08
Plasterboard (10 mm) on dabs including air space	0.14
Foil-backed plasterboard (10 mm) on battens including air space	0.41
Cavity insulation bats and fill (per mm)	0.028
Structural concrete depending on type (per 100 mm)	0.07 — 0.5
Inside/outside surface resistance: walls	0.018
roofs	0.15
floors	0.19

Table 12.3 Standard moisture contents for protected and exposed masonry

Material	Moisture content by volume/(%)	
	Protected	Exposed
Brickwork	1.0	5.0
Concrete work	3.0	5.0

Protected covers internal partitions, inner leaves separated from outer leaves by a continuous air space, masonry protected by tile hanging, sheet cladding or other such protection, separated by a continuous air space.

Exposed covers masonry directly exposed to rain, unrendered or rendered.

Example: For a typical brick-cavity-block construction the brickwork is considered to have a moisture content of 5% and the blockwork 3%.

Table 12.4 Correction factors to obtain the new λ value of a material after a change in its moisture content

Measured moisture content by volume (%)	Factor for material at standard moisture contents		
	1% mc	3% mc	5% mc
0.5	1.12	1.39	1.52
1.0	1.00	1.23	1.35
1.5	0.93	1.14	1.25
2.0	0.88	1.08	1.18
2.5	0.84	1.03	1.13
3.0	0.81	1.00	1.10
4.0	0.78	0.96	1.05
5.0	0.74	0.91	1.00

Example: The λ value at 3% is 1.23 × (λ at 1%)

Table 12.5 Thermal conductivities of homogeneous masonry

Material and standard moisture content (% by volume)	Bulk dry density (kg/m³)	Thermal conductivity* Protected	Thermal conductivity* Exposed
	400	0.15	0.16
	500	0.16	0.18
	600	0.19	0.20
	700	0.21	0.23
Concrete blockwork and brickwork	800	0.23	0.26
	900	0.27	0.30
	1000	0.30	0.33
(Aerated concrete and	1100	0.34	0.38
dense and lightweight aggregate concrete)	1200	0.38	0.42
	1300	0.44	0.49
	1400	0.51	0.57
	1500	0.59	0.65
Note:	1600	0.66	0.73
For foamed slag aggregate concrete	1700	0.76	0.84
multiply by 0.75	1800	0.87	0.96
	1900	0.99	1.09
	2000	1.13	1.24
	2100	1.28	1.40
	2200	1.45	1.60
	2300	1.63	1.80
	2400	1.83	2.00
	1200	0.31	0.42
	1300	0.36	0.49
	1400	0.42	0.57
	1500	0.48	0.65
Fired clay brickwork	1600	0.54	0.73
	1700	0.62	0.84
	1800	0.71	0.96
	1900	0.81	1.09
	2000	0.92	1.24

*The thermal conductivity of masonry may be taken to be as given for the particular dry density of the material and its position. Alternatively, it may be determined in accordance with BS 874[12.12] Brickwork is considered to have a standard λ value of 0.84 and thickness of 105 mm giving a thermal resistance of 0.125.

Protected refers to internal partitions, inner leaves separated from outer leaves by a continuous air space, masonry protected by tile hanging, sheet cladding or other such protection, separated by a continuous air space. *Exposed* refers to masonry directly exposed to rain, unrendered or rendered. The standard thermal conductivities apply to the standard moisture contents in the first column and represent typical values. They are given for a range of densities and it is not implied that the materials are available at all the densities indicated. These values assume mortar joints of similar thermal conductivity and density as those of the bulk material. Typical mortars for walling may be expected to have a density in the range 1600 — 1800 kg/m³.

Table 12.6 Inside surface resistance, R_{si}

Building element	Heat flow direction	Surface resistance/(m² K/W) High emissivity	Surface resistance/(m² K/W) Low emissivity
Walls	Horizontal	0.12	0.30
Ceilings on roofs, flat or pitched and floors	Upward	0.10	0.22
Ceilings and floors	Downward	0.14	0.55

Note: *Surface emissivity:*
Most materials have a high emissivity. Air spaces lined with low emissivity material such as aluminium foil have a much higher resistance because radiation is largely prevented. However, high emissivity should be assumed unless the air space is known to be lined with such a material.

Table 12.7 Outside surface resistance, R_{so}, for stated exposure

Building element	Emissivity of surface	Surface resistance for stated exposure/(m² K/W) Sheltered	Normal	Severe
Wall	High	0.08	0.06	0.03
	Low	0.11	0.07	0.03
Roof	High	0.07	0.04	0.02
	Low	0.09	0.05	0.02

The outside surface resistance for *standard U* values is based on a wind speed at roof surface of 3 m/s. This corresponds to the values of outside surface resistance to *normal* exposure given above.

The effect of differing exposures is usually ignored for opaque structures. However, for glazing, the exposure must be taken into account. The exposure conditions are defined thus:

sheltered — up to third floor of buildings in city centres;

normal — most suburban and rural buildings and fourth to eighth floors of buildings in city centres;

severe — buildings on coastal or hill sites, floors above fifth in suburban or rural districts and floors above the ninth in city centres.

Table 12.8 Standard thermal resistances for unventilated divided air spaces for horizontal heat flow, e.g., voids in blocks, R_a

Thickness of air space/mm	Thermal resistance/(m² K/W) for air space of stated width/mm 200 or greater	100	50	20	10 or less
5	0.10	0.10	0.11	0.11	0.11
6	0.11	0.12	0.12	0.12	0.13
7	0.12	0.12	0.13	0.13	0.14
8	0.13	0.13	0.13	0.14	0.15
10	0.14	0.14	0.15	0.16	0.17
12	0.15	0.16	0.16	0.18	0.19
15	0.16	0.17	0.18	0.19	0.21
20	0.17	0.18	0.19	0.22	0.24
25 or more	0.18	0.20	0.21	0.24	0.27

Table 12.9 Standard thermal resistances for unventilated air spaces, R_v

Type of air space		Thermal resistance/(m^2 K/W) for heat flow in stated direction		
Thickness	Surface emissivity	Horizontal	Upward	Downward
5 mm	High	0.10	0.10	0.10
	Low	0.18	0.18	0.18
25 mm or more	High	0.18	0.17	0.22
	Low	0.35	0.35	1.06
High emissivity plane and corrugated sheet in contact		0.09	0.09	0.11
Low emissivity multiple foil insulation with air space on one side		0.62	0.62	1.76
5 mm gap behind normal plaster plasterboard*		0.08		
20 mm gap behind foil-backed plasterboard		0.35		

Linear interpolation is permissible for air spaces in blocks intermediate between those given in the Table.

*The reduction in resistance of the 5 mm air space behind plasterboard on dabs is due to the bridging effect of the dabs.

The increase in resistance of the 20 mm air space behind foil-backed plasterboard is due to the reflective nature of the foil.

Table 12.10 Standard thermal resistance of ventilated air spaces, R_v

Type of air space (thickness 25 mm minimum)	Thermal resistances (m^2 K/W)
Air space between asbestos cement or black metal cladding with unsealed joints, and high emissivity lining	0.16
Air space between asbestos cement or black metal cladding with unsealed joints, and low emissivity surface facing air space	0.30
Loft space between flat ceiling and unsealed asbestos cement sheets or black metal cladding pitched roof	0.14
Loft space between flat ceiling and pitched roof with aluminium cladding instead of black metal or low emissivity upper surface on ceiling	0.25
Loft space between flat ceiling and pitched roof lined with felt or building paper	0.18
Air space between tiles and roofing felt or building paper	0.12
Air space behind tiles on tile hung wall*	0.12
Air space in cavity wall construction	0.18

*For tile hung wall or roof, the value includes the resistance of the tiles.

Table 12.11 Typical thermal conductivity and thermal resistance of other common building materials

Material	Thermal conductivity W/m K	Typical thickness mm	Thermal resistance m^2 K/W
Dense plaster	0.50	13	0.026
Lightweight plaster	0.16	13	0.08
Plasterboard*	0.16	9.5	0.06
External render	0.70	18	0.026
Cavity insulation bats	0.035	25	0.714
Cavity insulation fill	0.040	50	1.25

The above values are often used but should be amended where necessary.

*When using plasterboard, the resistance of the air pocket between the material and the block may be allowed for (see Table 12.10). Thus the resistance of plasterboard on dabs (5 mm gap) = 0.06 for the plasterboard plus 0.08 for the air pocket = 0.14 m^2 K/W.

12.12 Worked example

Given the following construction, calculate the U values of the wall:

Construction: A rendered double leaf cavity wall using bricks externally and plasterboard on dabs on the inner leaf

Outside surface resistance	Table 12.7	R_{so}	= 0.06
18 mm external render	Table 12.11	R_1	= 0.026
Resistance of brickwork	Table 12.5	R_2	= 0.125
Resistance of cavity	Table 12.10	R_{v1}	= 0.180
Resistance of 100 mm block (say)		R_b	= 0.349
Resistance of air pocket between plasterboard and inner leaf	Table 12.9	R_{v2}	= 0.080
9.5 mm plasterboard	Table 12.11	R_3	= 0.060
Inside surface resistance	Table 12.6	R_{si}	= 0.12

Therefore: R = 1.000

$$U = \frac{1}{\Sigma R} = \frac{1}{1.000} = 1.0 \text{ W/m}^2 \text{ °C}$$

12.13 References

12.1 The Building Regulations 1976. HMSO, London.

12.2 The Buildings Standards (Scotland Consolidation) Regulations, 1981. HMSO, London.

12.3 The Building Regulations (Northern Ireland) 1977. HMSO, London.

12.4 London Building Acts 1930—1939. London Building (Constructional) By-Laws 1972 and 1974 (with subsequent amendments). Greater London Council.

12.5 BUILDING RESEARCH ESTABLISHMENT. BRE Digest 110: *Condensation*. BRE, Garston.

12.6 BRITISH STANDARDS INSTITUTION. BS 5250: 1975 *Code of basic data for the design of buildings: the control of condensation in dwellings*. BSI, London. pp 28

12.7 Thermal Insulation (Industrial Buildings) Act, 1957. HMSO, London.

12.8 CHARTERED INSTITUTE OF BUILDING SERVICES. CIBS Guide, Section A3: *Thermal properties of building materials*. CIBS, London, 1980.

12.9 DEPARTMENT OF THE ENVIRONMENT. DoE Circulars reference BRA/668/68, 14 September and 30 November, 1976.

12.10 AMERICAN SOCIETY OF HEATING, REFRIGERATING AND AIR-CONDITIONING ENGINEERS. Guide and data book. ASHRAE, New York, 1965.

12.11 AMERICAN SOCIETY OF TESTING MATERIALS. ASTM: C236—66: *Standard method of test for thermal conductance and transmittance of built up sections by means of the guarded hot-box*. ASTM, 1976.

12.12 BRITISH STANDARDS INSTITUTION. BS 874: 1973 *Methods of determining insulating properties, with definitions of thermal insulating terms*. BSI, London. pp 40

13

The resistance of concrete masonry to rain penetration

13.1 Introduction

The ability of a building to resist the ingress of rain and air penetration will depend not only upon the materials used but on the construction and skill of the designer and the workforce, and on the orientation, size and location of the building. It is possible to assess the degree of exposure by the use of the driving rain index and the direction of the prevailing weather can be judged by use of the driving rain roses. BRE Digest No. 127[13.1] covers the procedure for using these aids, but for a simple assessment Figures 13.1 and 13.2 show the driving rain index and roses for the United Kingdom. It should be noted that the local conditions will modify the level of exposure to which a building is subjected

quite markedly, and to allow for this fact CP 121:Part 1:1973[13.2]* suggests that the exposure grading of a site should be decided by the following rules:

(1) sheltered conditions in districts where the driving rain index is three or less, excluding areas that lie within 8 km of the sea or large estuaries, where the exposure should be regarded as moderate;

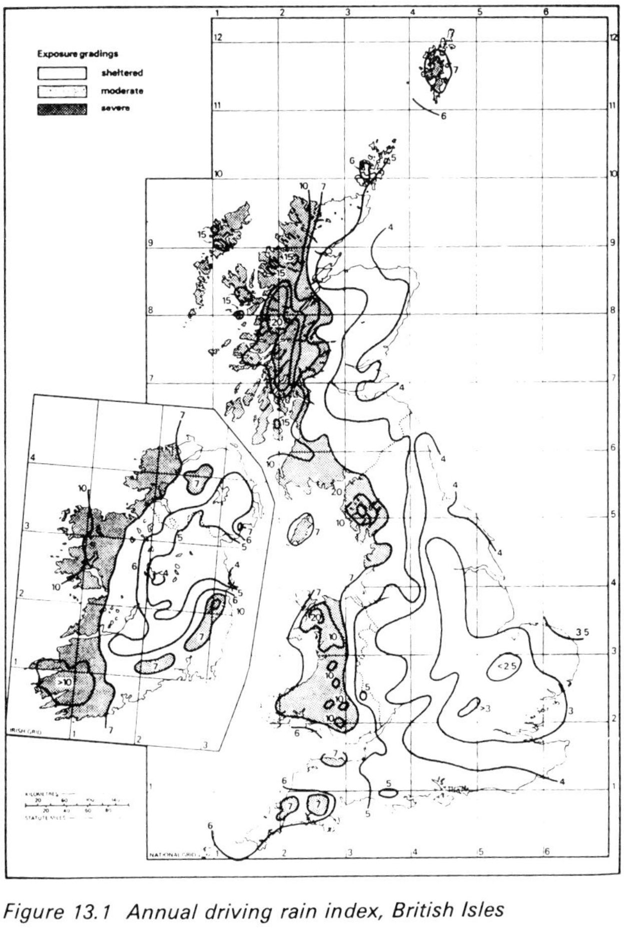

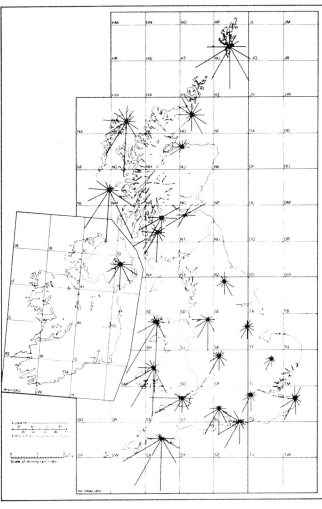

Figure 13.2 Annual relative driving rain index for each of eight wind directions at 20 stations

*CP 121 is currently being revised. A Draft for Development on the assessment of exposure to rain penetration is to be issued by the British Standards Institution.

Figure 13.1 Annual driving rain index, British Isles

(2) moderate conditions in districts where the driving rain index is between three and seven except in areas which have an index of five or more and which are within 8 km of the sea or large estuaries in which the exposure should be regarded as severe;

(3) severe conditions in areas with a driving rain index of seven or more;

(4) in areas of sheltered or moderate exposure, high buildings which stand above their surroundings, or buildings of any height on hill slopes or hill tops, should be regarded as having an exposure one grade more severe than indicated by the maps.

13.2 Standard method of test for walling

The rain penetration testing of masonry walling is covered by BS 4315:Part 2:1970[13.3]. This method of test involves subjecting a wall panel to a static pressure differential whilst water is applied intermittently. The procedure is intended to simulate wind driven rain. A typical rain penetration rig complying with BS 4315:Part 2:1970 is shown in Figures 13.3 and 13.4. A centrifugal mounted externally to the pressure box produces a pressure differential of 500 N/m² (500 Pa). Water is applied to the top of the wall by means of a sparge bar at a rate of 25 ml/min for every 10 mm of test area. The test should typically last for 48 hours.

BS 4315 indicates three means of assessing the performance of a wall:

(1) by using time lapse photography to record areas of dampness as the test progresses;

(2) by measuring the change of weight of the wall and hence the water take up;

(3) by collecting the amount of water passing through the wall.

Unfortunately, BS 4315 does not give any guidance on the interpretation of the results. If a cavity wall is built under laboratory conditions, for example, it is fairly clear that water penetration to the inner leaf is unlikely. In practice, however, a fairly permeable outer leaf may result in high water loads on standard details and may highlight workmanship faults. Some observations on the interpretation of results of tests on concrete block masonry are given in the next section.

13.3 The suitability of various wall types to different exposure conditions

The cavity wall was developed as a simple method to produce rain resistant walling even when permeable masonry was employed. There is no doubt that given perfect workmanship a cavity wall should prevent rain penetration completely. Rain can, of course, penetrate through a single leaf of brick or block masonry by passing through the unit itself, through the mortar, or through any hair cracks which may be present between the unit and mortar, and it is possible for all three of these mechanisms to operate. Providing that the cavity is not bridged, the water may pass into the inner face of

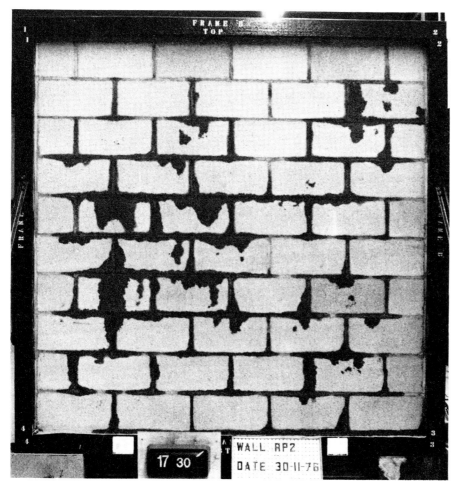

Figure 13.3 *Wall panel in position against the pressure box*

Figure 13.4 Control equipment for pressure box

the outer leaf and so run down to the cavity tray or below the damp-proof course, as the case may be. This is assuming that the cavity tray is able to cope with the water load placed on it and that provision is made to allow the water to drain from the wall.

In practice, the present levels of workmanship on site mean that particular care needs to be taken in the selection of components. The following factors should be taken into account:

(1) wall ties and cavity trays are frequently found in practice to be extensively bridged with mortar droppings and other debris;

(2) perpend joints are often not properly filled but

Table 13.1 Examples of the suitability of external walls for the exclusion of rain under various conditions of exposure

Exposure	Wall type	Construction		Minimum thickness
SEVERE	Single leaf	Wall clad externally by tile hanging, slate hanging, and so on		—
		Rendered blockwork	Hollow blocks of dense or lightweight aggregate concrete with horizontal bed joint in two separate strips	200 mm (8 in.)
			Solid aerated concrete blocks	250 mm (10 in.)
MODERATE	Single leaf	Brickwork	Rendered	225 mm (9 in.)
			Unrendered perforated through-the wall brick (such as V-63) with horizontal bed joint in two separate strips	225 mm (9 in.)
		Rendered blockwork	Fired-clay hollow blocks with horizontal bed joint in two separate strips	150 mm (6 in.)
			Dense or lightweight aggregate concrete or solid aerated concrete blocks	200 mm (8 in.)
		Unrendered blockwork	Specially designed fired-clay hollow blocks with horizontal bed joint in two separate strips	150 mm (6 in.)
			Dense or lightweight aggregate hollow blocks with horizontal bed joint in two separate strips	200 mm (8 in.)
SHELTERED	Single leaf	Brickwork	Unrendered	337.5 mm (13½ in.)
		Rendered blockwork	Solid or hollow block of fired-clay or concrete	100 mm (4 in.)

The table is given for general guidance only; the following factors are assumed to affect rain penetration: thickness, materials, use of rendering, special design and type of bed joint. Thicknesses less than those given may be suitable for some non-domestic construction, such as factory walls. Guidance for construction other than that mentioned below may be derived from experience or tests measuring resistance to rain penetration.

merely pointed up;

(3) coursing is sometimes lost resulting in wall ties which slope towards the inside of the wall.

It is apparent, therefore, that where local conditions are likely to be severe it terms of rain penetration, careful attention needs to be paid not only to careful site supervision but also to the choice of units so that potential leakage is minimized. Particular care may need to be taken where it is planned to fill or partially fill the cavity with an insulating material. Consideration should, of course, also be given to the use of cavities wider than 50 mm. Rendering of the outer leaf will considerably reduce the potential water load and this form of construction is, therefore, particularly suitable in exposed areas where insulation is to be contained within the wall.

It is possible to build a satisfactory solid wall which will adequately resist severe exposure, but the units themselves need to be resistant to moisture penetration and the use of shell bedding may have to be considered. As with cavity walls, a rendering coat will significantly improve the performance of a wall, or a cladding system such as tile hanging will greatly increase the rain resistance of a cavity wall. Some solid wall constructions such as those with a posted lining are also suitable for use in exposed conditions.

Table 13.1, extracted from CP 121:Part 1:1973 indicates the suitability of various masonry constructions for a given level of exposure.

13.4 The suitability of various unit types

Using a BS 4315 test rig a number of rain penetration tests have been carried out on concrete masonry walls[13.4]. Unfortunately, it is not possible to relate standard block parameters, such as strength or density, to the subsequent behaviour of a wall built from the units. The following are comparisons of the performance of similar open textured facing blocks, considering:

(1) two different types of block from each manufacturer (Figures 13.5, 13.6 and 13.7);

(2) three different manufacturers for each type of block (Figures 13.8 and 13.9);

(3) the repeatability of the construction and test procedure for two of the panels tested.

A summary of the details of the blocks used for each of the above walls is presented in Tables 13.2 and 13.3.

The comparison between the two different types of block for each manufacturer in Figures 13.5, 13.6 and 13.7 shows that manufacturers 1 and 2 produce solid-with-voids blocks which perform better than their respective true solid blocks. The reverse is true for the hollow blocks of manufacturer 3, although there is very little difference between the two and neither performs well. In practice, it has been found that the use of solid-with-voids blocks to form the outer leaf of a cavity wall in areas of high exposure can lead to water build up in the cores and subsequently delay drying out. It is also possible that this water build up can increase

Table 13.2 Block properties

| Block type * | Result of compression tests | | | Void content (%) | Material density (kg/m³) |
	Block strength (N/mm²)	Standard deviation (N/mm²)	Coefficient of variation (%)		
1 (swv)	12.8	0.40	3.15	19.5	2007
1 (ts)	14.8	1.69	11.41	0	2008
2 (swv)	17.7	1.18	6.67	19.8	2124
2 (ts)	22.8	1.90	8.34	0	2095
3 (h)	14.1	0.80	5.63	29.2	2075
3 (ts)	20.8	1.58	7.57	0	2008

Table 13.3 A summary of the time lapse photography results

| Wall number | Block type * | Time for 80% wetted area (hours) | % wetted area at | | | Final % wetted area |
			6 hours	12 hours	24 hours	
1	1 (swv)	21.0	17	51	84	93
2	1 (ts)	11.4	37	83	97	100
3	2 (swv)	48.0	16	35	62	70
4	2 (ts)	2.2	97	98	98	100
5	3 (h)	3.2	97	98	100	100
6	3 (ts)	3.2	97	98	100	100
7	2 (ts)	1.4	91	93	97	97
8	1 (swv)	25.5	29	61	79	95

*the number refers to the manufacturer
(swv) = solid-with-voids
(ts) = true solid
(h)   = hollow

the pressure differential across the wall and hence lead to more leakage.

Of the three different voided blocks, it can be seen from Figure 13.8 that those from manufacturer 3 performed best. In Figure 13.9 it is apparent that the true solid block from manufacturer 1 was the best of the three. Tables 13.2 and 13.3 indicate that in terms of strength and density each group of blocks is very similar and thus these parameters are not good indicators of performance.

The results of two pairs of panels (each pair of identical construction) are presented in Figure 13.10. It is apparent that there is good agreement between the results of the identical panels, one pair of which was built with true solid blocks and one pair with solid-with-voids blocks. Note that it is not possible to carry out repeat tests on the same panels — concrete blockwork walls improve with repeated testing due to internal efflorescence and autogenous healing. This effect has been reported widely in practice, where improvement is also aided by the deposition of dirt in the pores of the blocks.

The results shown in Figure 13.11 indicate that providing the wall does not reach 80% wetted area in the first four or five hours of test, the amount of water passing through a saturated wall is dependent on the area of dampness determined by testing to BS 4315. This must bring into question the usefulness of testing to BS 4315 for concrete block masonry for longer than

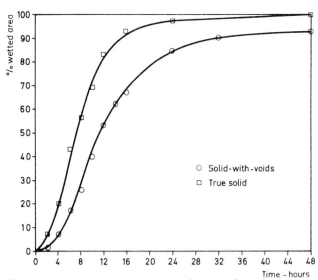

Figure 13.5 Percentage wetted area for manufacturer 1

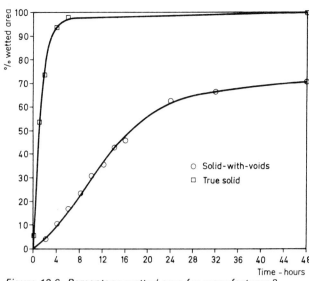

Figure 13.6 Percentage wetted area for manufacturer 2

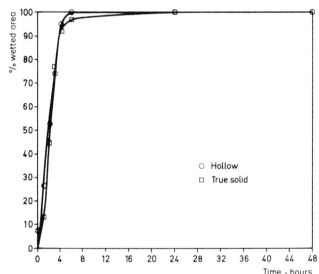

Figure 13.7 Percentage wetted area for manufacturer 3

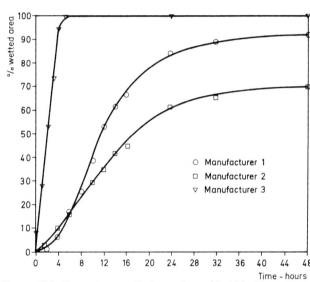

Figure 13.8 Percentage wetted area for voided blocks

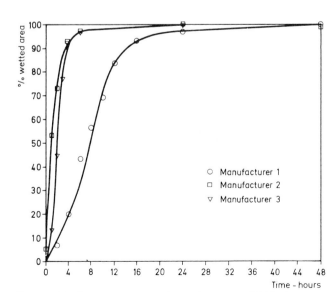

Figure 13.9 Percentage wetted area for true solid blocks

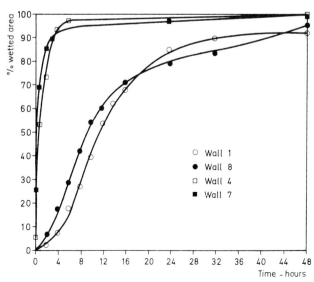

Figure 13.10 Percentage wetted area for repeatibility tests

213

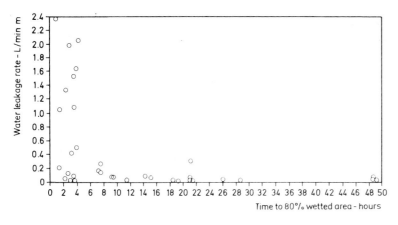

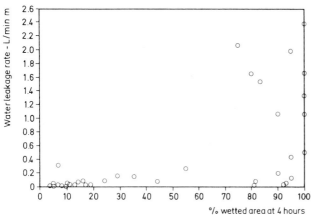

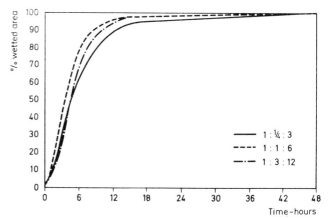

Figure 13.11 Water leakage rate through the fully saturated wall against the time taken for the dry wall to reach 80% wetted area

Figure 13.12 Water leakage rate through the fully saturated wall against the percentage wetted area at four hours

Figure 13.13 Percentage wetted area against time for three walls constructed using different grades of mortar but otherwise identical

four to five hours, since it is the quantity of water which is able to pass through the outer leaf of the cavity wall that is of prime importance. It seems fair to speculate that the greater the amount of water passing through the outer leaf, the greater the chance of water crossing to the inner leaf via some defect. An alternative approach to determine acceptable performance would, perhaps, be to record percentage dampness at four hours and set an arbitrary maximum value. Figure 13.12 shows that if the area of dampness at four hours is below 75%, the flow rates for water through saturated walls are low and not very dependent upon the area of dampness.

Further limitations of the usefulness of damp area assessment are shown in Figure 13.13, which indicates the effect of mortar designation on otherwise identical walls. It is apparent that the differences between the areas of dampness are not significant, but when fully saturated the flow rates for walls built with 1:¼:3, 1:1:6 and 1:3:12 (cement:lime:sand) mortars were 0.091, 0.268 and 0.154 litres/minute respectively, i.e., nearly three times as much water passing through the worst in relation to the best, but all giving almost identical time/percentage dampness curves. It must be pointed out, however, that all the suggestions made to date for acceptable performances relate only to the laboratory tests. A paradox exists that even blocks which perform quite badly in the laboratory are known to perform adequately in practice. One reason is doubtless the tendency for the performance of concrete block masonry walls to improve with time.

It has already been indicated that the open textured type of unit is generally the most susceptible to rain penetration. At the other end of the scale, units with very dense faces, as in the case of many bricks, can give rise to a great deal of run-off down the face of the wall due to low absorption of the unit. The presence of so much water running down the face of the wall highlights any fine cracks which may tend to form between the unit and the mortar making the ingress of water by this path more likely. The use of the weakest grade of mortar practicable must be recommended to limit the size of any potential shrinkage cracks. With all types of masonry construction the use of deeply recessed or raked back joints often gives rise to problems. Mortar joints should be flush and lightly tooled.

13.5 Particular problems due to detailing and specification faults

The following section is not intended to be a fully comprehensive list of problems, rather an indication of some of the pitfalls which can occur in practice:

(1) *Lintel masked with block strips* This design detailing fault has occurred where facing blockwork has been employed and it was required to maintain the blockwork appearance over the face of a concrete lintel, as illustrated in Figure 13.14. If the window is set too far forward, water can penetrate through the porous block and behind the window frame.

(2) *Parapet design* There are a number of parapet details in use, but some points to note regarding concrete masonry are as follows:

(a) unless a purpose made, dense impermeable

coping is to be employed the coping stone should be laid on a damp-proof membrane extending the full width of the cavity;

(b) where a stepped damp-proof course is positioned, the damp-proof course material should be carried right through the face of the blockwork;

(c) particular care will be needed in the execution of joints in the damp-proof course at corners, and so on;

(d) the junction of the roof membrane with the stepped tray should be carefully considered.

(3) *Stepped trays* Where a wall intersection requires a stepped damp-proof course consideration should be given to providing purpose made preformed stepped trays to avoid the problems of carrying out such work on site.

(4) The damp-proof course material should always pass through the wall, material *stuck* to the surface of the blockwork is unlikely to be satisfactory.

(5) In areas of high exposure, blocks containing a void may allow water to build up in the cores and hence give rise to differential drying and weathering.

(6) Particular attention should be paid to site supervision so that perpends, and such like, are properly filled.

(7) The grade of sand used should be carefully considered so that potential frost attack is obviated in areas of high exposure where walls may remain wet for long periods.

(8) The cavity must be kept clear of mortar droppings and other debris.

13.6 Remedial measures

Where a problem of rain penetration exists, it is important to establish the factors which are contributing to the ingress of water. A detailed examination of the walling should be carried out with due regard to the factors highlighted in *Section 13.5*. Joints around windows, doors, and so on, provide obvious local defects for the ingress of water, but if rain penetration appears to be through the wall itself, then a more thorough examination will be necessary. External examination will determine whether the mortar joint has been properly pointed and whether cracks have developed between the mortar and the unit. By drilling 10 — 12 mm diameter holes through the mortar joint it will be possible to insert an optical probe through the wall and examine the cavity for bridged wall ties and other defects which will need to be remedied. If, as a result of investigation, it is concluded that too much water is passing through the masonry, there are a range of options available. A render coating or paint system will be an effective method of reducing rain penetration through the wall, but will change the appearance of the

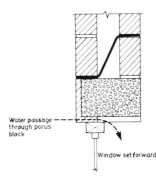

Figure 13.14 Leakage past lintel masked with block slips

building and will represent a substantial additional cost. A variety of colourless treatments are available but careful consideration will be required to ensure that the particular proprietary system will work with the type of unit used in the wall. Most colourless treatments have a limited life but this can be offset by the ability of concrete masonry to improve in terms of rain resistance with age.

Methods of assessing the effectiveness of masonry waterproofing materials have been described in NBS Technical Note 883[13.3], by the National Bureau of Standards in the USA. Although it is not intended to describe the test procedures contained therein in detail, the following criteria were considered in making the tests on the waterproofing materials:

(1) the material should produce a surface resistance to water penetration;

(2) the material must be sufficiently permeable to water vapour to prevent accumulation of moisture in the wall;

(3) the material should be resistant to the formation of efflorescence.

Any assessment of a waterproofing product for use as a remedial measure with a given type of walling material should be made with the above points in mind. It should also be noted that the presence of high water content in the masonry can give rise to frost damage of the mortar, particularly in poorly graded or batched mortar, and a check should be made as to the soundness of the mortar, especially in vulnerable joints such as cavity trays in exposed parapets.

13.7 References

13.1 BUILDING RESEARCH ESTABLISHMENT. BRE Digest 127, BRE, Garston.

13.2 BRITISH STANDARDS INSTITUTION. CP 121: Part 1: 1973 *Code of Practice for walling.* Part 1: *Brick and block masonry.* BSI, London. pp 84

13.3 BRITISH STANDARDS INSTITUTION. BS 4315: Part 2: 1970 *Methods of test for resistance to air and water penetration.*

Part 2: *Permeable walling constructions (water penetration).* BSI, London. pp 16

13.4 ROBERTS, J J. Rain penetration problems with concrete blockwork. *Chemistry and Industry,* London, March 1980.

13.5 NATIONAL BUREAU OF STANDARDS. *Technical Note 883.* NBS, Washington, USA, 1978.

14

Sound insulation

14.1 Introduction

The general subject of sound insulation is so complex that an in depth study is outside the scope of this handbook. It is, however, possible to outline the principal objectives of sound insulation and to give general guidance on the sound performance properties of concrete masonry walls.

Sound insulation may be split into two basic parts:

(1) the control of sound between two separate locations, i.e., control of sound between, say, one room and another;

(2) the control of sound within a given location, i.e., control of the sound within a room itself.

More attention will be given to the former since although masonry can be used to aid acoustical control of internal sound, it is better known for its ability to act as a sound separater. The information given, particularly with respect to the sound insulation values of different constructions, is for general guidance and the performance of individual manufacturers' materials may differ from those given.

It is difficult to define sound insulation but it can be considered as the control of noise between the source and the listener. In CP 3:Chapter 3[14.1] *noise* is referred to as *unwanted sound* and it can, therefore, be said that this whole subject simply revolves around the control of unwanted sound. Noise, apart from being most annoying, can under certain conditions, induce stress, damage hearing and will most certainly disturb concentration, thereby affecting not just a person's well being but also their working efficiency. For these and other reasons it is desirable to reduce noise to a minimum wherever possible.

Figure 14.1 indicates the decibel scale of sound intensities from various sources. It is desirable for separating walls between dwellings, and indeed walls between individual rooms of all types of buildings, to possess adequate sound insulation. The sound insulation between dwellings is a mandatory requirement but in other situations, apart from the possible requirements imposed by the Factory Inspector or the local authority, there is seldom any requirement for the con-

trol of noise between adjacent rooms and in many cases this is solely the responsibility of the designer.

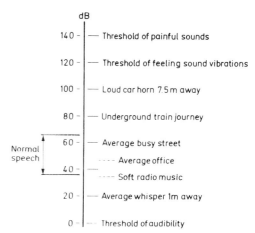

Figure 14.1 Decibel scale of sound intensities

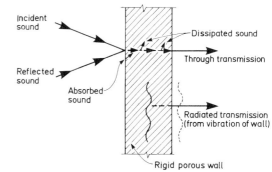

Figure 14.2 Sound transmission

14.2 Sound absorption and sound transmission

The control of sound in buildings is dealt with in detail in CP 3:Chapter 3. In simple terms, to prevent an excessive level of noise occurring within a building, it is necessary to consider two properties of the construction material: (a) sound absorption and (b) sound transmission, as shown in Figure 14.2.

14.2.1 Sound absorption

The sound absorption of a masonry wall is the measure of its ability to reduce the reflection of incidental sound. Masonry is often covered by some decorative material such as plaster and is rarely called upon to act as an absorbent at the surface of the wall. It is important that the units are not of the no-fines type of concrete, since the high permeability of the material will lower its expected insulation[14.6]. Lightweight aggregate masonry can reduce the reflection of sound by absorbing some of the sound into its porous surface[14.2, 14.3, 14.4]. The absorption characteristic of lightweight concrete is one of the reasons for the indicated improvement in the sound transmission associated with cavity walls built with this type of unit above that which might be expected from consideration of the mass law. Absorbents may be classified into several types, but with masonry materials these fall into two areas: (a) porous material and (b) cavity resonators. Masonry is not a true surface absorbent in the same way as soft felts but the slightly open texture of the surface of facing units can reduce reflected sound more than a hard, dense, flat surface such as plain concrete or steel sheeting. Hollow concrete blocks with slots or holes in one face can act as cavity resonators and again reduce reflected sound. Most cavity resonators, including those formed of hollow concrete blocks, are only efficient over a narrow band of frequencies and since sound source often covers a wide frequency range this particular form of absorbent is only useful where a noise peak occurs within a close band of frequencies, for example, with certain mechanical plant.

It has been suggested[14.5] that masonry cavity resonators can be designed to act over a broad range of frequencies and considerably reduce the reflected sound and pressure levels in situations where noisy machinery is being used. Such walls have been used adjacent to highways in an attempt to reduce the effect of traffic noise and to reduce the sound from large power transformers[14.9].

14.2.2 Sound transmission

Sound may be transmitted from one location to another in a number of ways as illustrated in Figure 14.3. The two principal sources of sound transmission are: (a) direct transmission and (b) flanking transmission. Both are equally important because adequate sound insulation will be difficult to achieve if one or other of these factors is neglected. It is important to emphasize that the potential sound insulation of, say, a 225 mm separating wall may not be realized if little attention is given to the question of flanking sound. Flanking sound is defined as any sound which travels from the source to the receiving room by paths other than through the separating element. The figures illustrate the general areas where loss of sound insulation may occur but other factors such as cracks or poorly filled perpend joints may explain why one building behaves differently to an otherwise identical building. Unfilled joints have been shown by Levitt[14.6] to reduce the sound insulation of masonry walls by some 3 decibels.

14.3 Sound tests

14.3.1 Assessment of sound insulation

Since the sound insulation between one building and another is not only dependent on the separating element but also on its associated structure, it has in the past been necessary to test a structure rather than just the dividing wall in a normal laboratory situation. However, recent tests[14.13] have shown that it is possible to obtain close agreement between a structure and a newly designed test chamber[14.14]. The sound insulation achieved with walls of lightweight masonry in the new test chamber are reported in a recent CIRIA publication[14.16]. A number of field measurements have also been reported by the Building Research Establishment[14.10, 14.11, 14.12]. Testing the wall in a normal acoustic chamber gives an indication of the potential sound insulation of the wall, but consideration must be given to the possible effects of flanking transmission and workmanship.

14.3.2 Measurement of sound transmission

The measurement of sound transmission is covered by BS 2750:1980: *Methods of measurement of sound insulation in buildings and of building elements. Parts 1 to 8*[14.7]. The sound insulation of a wall is generally referred to as being the average reduction in sound as measured between two opposite faces of the wall over a frequency range from 100 — 3150 Hz. A typical result of a test is plotted in Figure 14.4, together with the grade curve as contained in the Building Regulations. In accordance with the Building Regulations, if the test result does not fall below the grade curve by an aggregate deviation of more than 23 dB then the structure is deemed-to-satisfy the requirement that the wall and its associated structure provide adequate resistance to the transmission of airborne sound. It will be seen that the grade curve runs from 40 dB at 100 Hz to 56 dB at 1600 Hz and beyond. This gives a total or aggregate of 792 dB over the 16 different frequencies and an average value of 49.5 dB over the range covered. Since the permitted total tolerance is −23 dB, the mean permissible total can be considered to be 769 dB which gives an average value of 48 dB. Providing there is no serious loss of sound insulation due to flanking transmission or defects of workmanship, a wall which notionally indicates an average insulation in the region 48 dB or better, i.e., by laboratory test or by reference to the mass law, is likely to be acceptable as providing adequate sound insulation for the separating wall of a residential building.

Unfortunately the simple method of assessing sound insulation based on the average decibel reduction over the frequency range 100 — 3150 Hz does not always give a reliable indication of the sound performance of the wall since it is possible for a low value of insulation at one frequency to be offset by a high value at another frequency. In addition this method does not take into account the subjective aspects of insulation.

An attempt to take into account the subjective aspects of sound insulation is made in the Building Regulations[14.17] by adopting a maximum adverse aggre-

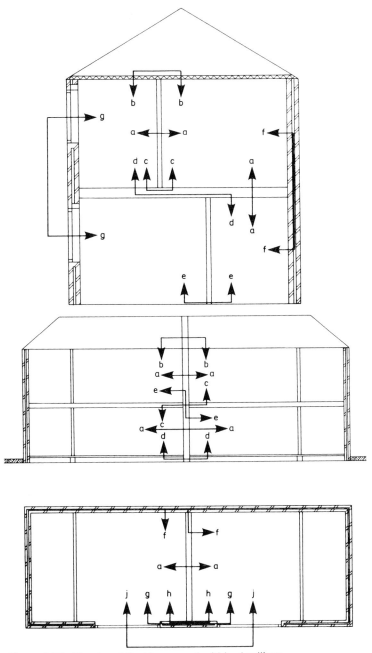

Figure 14.3 Direct and flanking sound within dwellings

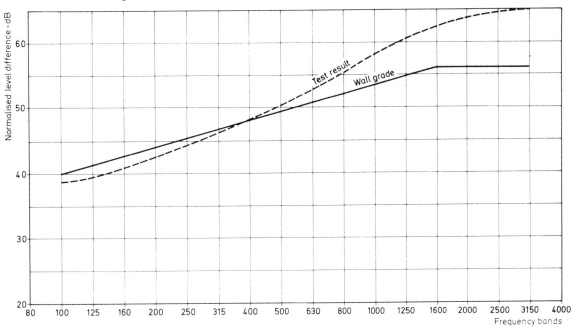

Figure 14.4 Typical curve for airborne sound insulation compared with separating wall grade

219

gate deviation approach. The BS 5821:1980[14.15] method of rating sound insulation in building elements also attempts to take into account the subjective aspects of sound insulation. This latter method is more appropriate to a variety of building types unlike the Building Regulations which only apply to dwellings.

14.4 Mass law

An indication of the sound insulation performance of a wall may be estimated by reference to what is known as *mass law*. In simple terms the mass law states that there is a relationship between the mass of a wall and its sound insulation, the typical relationship commonly taken being shown in Figure 14.5. This law indicates that a wall of a given mass will provide a certain defined average decibel reduction and that walls of similar mass will behave in the same way. In practice, however, this is not absolutely correct, since there are several factors which affect the sound insulation of an element, such as stiffness, permeability, absorption characteristics, and so on, all of which are variables, so that two walls being of the same mass but of different dimensions or elasticity may well perform differently. Despite the variations which can occur between different walls, the mass law is nevertheless a most valuable aid in estimating the likely performance of a wide range of wall constructions.

passage of air (see *Permeability*) then CP 3:Chapter 3 indicates that it is likely to perform in a similar way to that of an impervious solid wall of the same mass.

Permeability Walls can only be expected to perform as indicated by the mass law if they are relatively impervious to the passage of air. Thus, solid concrete blocks and bricks can be expected to perform as the mass law suggests, but some open textured, permeable, unfinished concrete block walls may fall short of the expected insulation since sound can travel through the fine pores of the material[14.6] (see *Section 14.2.1*). For this reason it is often necessary to seal masonry walls with plaster for them to perform to their maximum efficiency. This will also assist in reducing the effect of unfilled mortar joints. Sealing with two coats of cement based paint has been shown to be effective in an open textured wall (both solid and hollow units) enabling it to perform as expected from the mass law. The effect of using plasterboard on separating walls has been rather varied which may be due to the permeability characteristics of the wall and workmanship factors. Thus plastered walls have tended to be regarded as being more reliable than walls with plasterboard finish, although this was not the case with the recent tests reported by CIRIA[14.16].

Single leaf/cavity walls The sound insulation of a single leaf masonry wall, as previously explained, is largely

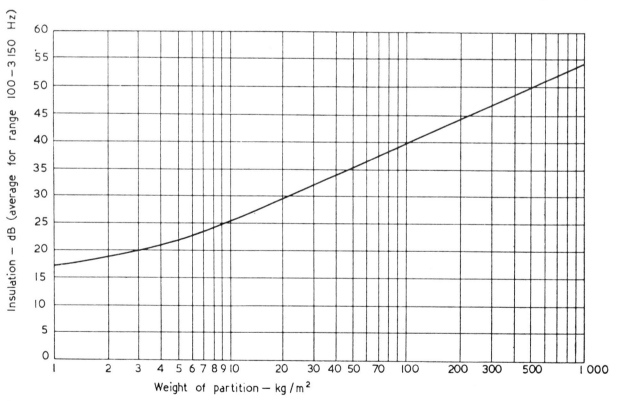

Figure 14.5 Mass Law – decibel reduction

It is important to note that the mass law applies basically to solid, relatively impervious, well constructed, single leaf walls. The typical variations to these three basic points are dealt with as follows:

Solid/hollow units Where a wall is built from hollow blocks, providing it is still relatively impervious to the

related to its surface mass, provided that there are no direct air paths through the wall.

With cavity walls it is indicated that the sound insulation is related not only to the surface mass but also to the width of the cavity and the rigidity and spacing of the wall ties. A cavity wall with a 50 mm nominal cavity with leaves connected by wire ties may be expected to have a resistance to sound transmission similar to that of a solid masonry wall of the same surface mass. An improvement in the resistance to sound transmission can be achieved by lowering the coupling effect between the leaves, i.e., by widening the cavity or by omitting the ties. As an example, using Schedule 2 of the Building Regulations as a basis, a cavity wall having a 75 mm cavity and built with lightweight concrete block leaves connected by wire ties at standard spacings may have an improvement of up to 4 decibels over that expected from a single leaf wall of similar surface mass. Some of this improvement may be due to the lightweight concrete which gives better energy dissipation within the cavity. Some published results[14.6, 14.10], however, show that the results may be rather variable. A similar improvement in the resistance to sound transmission can also be expected to occur, whatever the unit, where the leaves are isolated from each other, i.e., no ties[14.6, 14.16].

Although no general figures can be quoted, it has been found that increasing the number of ties or using more rigid ties will reduce the resistance to sound transmission through the wall.

Walls with openings Where a gap or hole occurs in masonry walls, such as a window or door opening, there will be sound transmitted through the opening independent of the basic performance of the wall, resulting in a loss of insulation disproportionate to the small area of the opening compared to the area of the wall. An estimate of the value of sound insulation of a wall with an opening may be made by reference to Figure 14.6 which indicates the theoretical loss of sound insulation of a non-uniform partition. Insulation values for doors and windows may be found in CP 3:Chapter 3[14.1], but typical values are 15 dB for light doors and 20 dB and 40 dB for single and double glazing respectively. A typical 225 mm concrete brick wall will have an average sound insulation in the order of 50 dB, but with 50% single glazing (20 dB) the difference in insulation is 50 − 20 = 30 dB and the ratio of area is 1:1 which indicates that the basic wall insulation will be lowered by some 26 dB. Thus the expected sound insulation of the

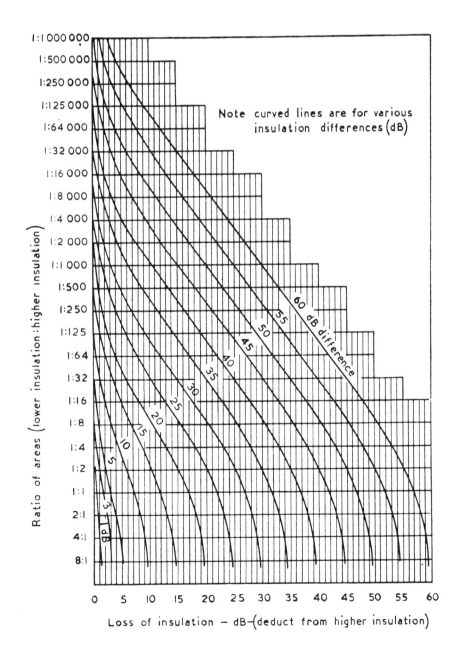

Figure 14.6   Nett sound reduction of non-uniform wall

wall will be 50 − 26 = 24 dB. If double glazing were used (40 dB) the difference in insulation becomes 10 dB for the same area ratio 1:1 which indicates a loss in insulation of some 6 dB and hence the sound insulation of the wall will be 50 − 6 = 44 dB.

14.5 Statutory regulations

There are various statutory regulations within the British Isles laying down requirements for sound insulation between residential buildings. The Building Regulations require that the separating wall between dwellings and its associated structure shall provide adequate insulation which is deemed to be satisfied if a test shows the construction or a similar structure to be within an aggregate of 23 dB adverse deviation to a grade curve (see p. 219) or that the walls comply with Schedule 12 of the Regulations. The other statutory regulations differ slightly in their application but are all likely to be satisfied by a separating wall which complies with the Building Regulations. Satisfying the regulations by test was dealt with in principle on p. 218. The Schedule 12 walls which are deemed-to-satisfy the Building Regulations are indicated in Figure 14.7. The value of mass required as shown in Figure 14.7 should be taken as the total mass of the wall including the weight of mortar and plaster. It is also generally acceptable to consider the density of material at 3% moisture content by volume, i.e., dry density of material plus 30 kg/m³. For the construction to be deemed-to-satisfy according to the Regulations, the walls shown in Figure 14.7 must adjoin or be positioned next to the flanking wall as shown in Figure 14.8(a). For the constructions shown in Figure 14.7 to satisfy Regulation G1(1) of the Building Regulations there are certain additional requirements concerning their relationship to the adjacent or surrounding structure which are also illustrated.

The separating wall has to extend at least 460 mm from the external face of the flanking wall as shown in Figure 14.8(a). An alternative is to tie the separating wall to one leaf of the external wall, as indicated in Figure 14.8(b), that has a mass of 120 kg/m² including plaster, mortar, etc. It is usual to tie the inner leaf to avoid problems with rain penetration and condensation. The length of the wall x that is required depends on the size of the opening adjacent to the separating wall and is shown in Figures 14.8(c) and (d).

In the case of a staggered dwelling, the Department of the Environment indicates[14.8] that a stagger of not less than 915 mm, as shown in Figure 14.8(e), would be considered to give equivalent separation. Where the separating wall has a cavity consideration should be given to the prevention of convection within the cavity as indicated in Figure 14.8(f).

The third means of providing adequate flanking resistance is by extending the separating wall to the outer face of a lightweight external wall (Figure 14.8(g)) and tying this to concrete floors as shown in Figure 14.8(h).

14.6 Estimation of the sound insulation of walls

Adopting the concept of the mass law, together with the information given previously on the effect of cavities and permeability on the sound insulation of a wall, Figure 14.9 may be used to estimate the basic potential sound insulation (sound reduction) of a wall. The mass given relates to the dry density of the wall with allowance being made in the position of the sloping line to cater for the effect of mortar joints and moisture within the wall in service. The basic insulation, as shown in Figure 14.9, may then be modified by the accompanying factors, to give an indication of the potential sound insulation of the wall. Alternatively, an indication of the sound reduction of the wall construction may be determined from Figure 14.5 by including the mass of all wall components, i.e., units, mortar, plaster, and so on. It is important to note the possible significant effect which flanking transmission may have on the actual structure (see *Section 14.2.2*).

When using Figure 14.9 it should be noted that:

(1) The Figure applies to walls which are plastered or have two coats of cement based paint. Plasterboard may give similar results but some loss in insulation might be expected, particularly with open textured permeable units as compared to a plastered wall.

(2) The Figure may be modified typically by:

   (a) − 3 dB — for untreated walls

   (b) + 4 dB — for cavity walls of lightweight blocks

   (c) + 4 dB — for an isolated cavity (i.e., no ties)

Where an estimation of the sound insulation is to be made using the basic mass law shown in Figure 14.5, the mortar and render may be taken to have a density of 1800 kg/m³, lightweight plaster 800 kg/m³ and dense plaster 1500 kg/m³.

Table 14.1 Typical noise reduction coefficients*

Material	Coefficient
Lightweight aggregate block	0.45**
Dense aggregate block	0.27**
Autoclaved aerated concrete block	0.20**
Plaster	0.03
Concrete	0.02
Glass	0.02

*Noise reduction coefficient is taken as average of noise absorption coefficient over the frequency range 250, 500, 1000 and 2000 Hz.

**Actual value will depend on block type and surface texture (typical variation ± 10%). Paint will reduce the values by 10% to 90% dependng on type, method of application, and number of coats.

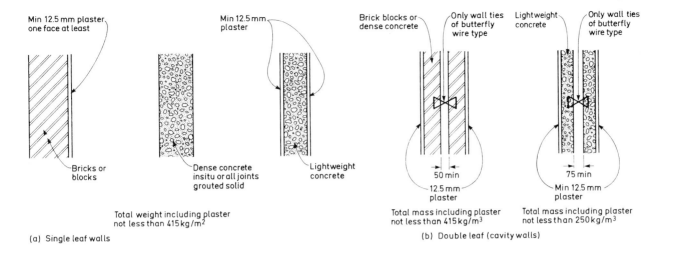

Figure 14.7 Deemed-to-satisfy walls (Building Regulations): (a) single leaf (b) double leaf (cavity)

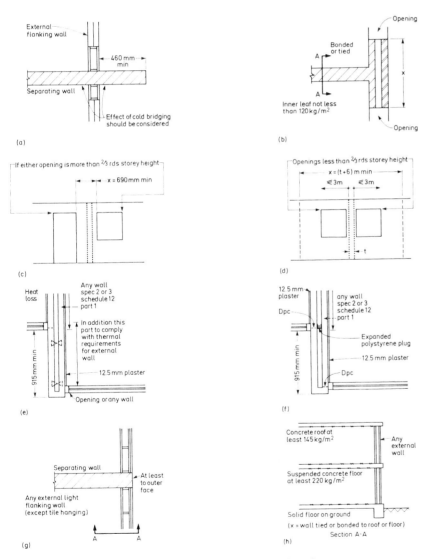

Figure 14.8 Flanking requirements of G2(2) Building Regulations

223

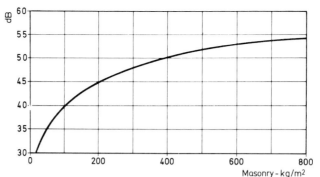

Figure 14.9   Approximate relationship between sound insulation and block weight

14.7 References

14.1 BRITISH STANDARDS INSTITUTION. CP 3: Chapter 3: 1972 *Code of basic data for the design of buildings.* Chapter 3: *Sound insulation and noise reduction.* BSI, London. pp 112

14.2 LENCHUK, P. Noise. How to control it in structures. Florida Concrete and Products Association Inc, Florida, 1970. pp 1—21

14.3 TOENNIES, H. Sound reduction properties of concrete masonry walls. National Concrete Masonry Association, Arlington, 1955, pp 1—24

14.4 COPELAND, R E. Controlling sound with concrete masonry. *Concrete Products, Vol 68,* July 1965.

14.5 DIEHL, G M. *Compressed Air Magazine.* USA, 1976.

14.6 LEVITT, M, LEACH, C H C, AND WILLIAMSON, J J. Factors affecting the sound insulation of lightweight aggregation concrete block walls. *Precast Concrete, Vol 2,* No 1, March 1971. pp 161—169

14.7 BRITISH STANDARDS INSTITUTION. BS 2750: 1980 *Methods of measurement of sound insulation in buildings and of building elements.* Part 1 to 8. BSI, London.

14.8 DEPARTMENT OF THE ENRIVONMENT. Technical Information Notes — Parts F and G — Thermal and sound insulation. DoE, 1974.

14.9 Tuning concrete masonry for transformer enclosures. Project Review. Concrete Masonry Association of Australia.

14.10 SEWELL, E C, ALPHEY, R S, SAVAGE, J E and FLYNN, S J. Field measurements of the sound insulation of plastered cavity masonry walls. *BRE Current Paper CP 4/80*

14.11 SEWELL, E C, ALPHEY, R S, SAVAGE, J E and FLYNN, S J. Field measurements of the sound insulation of plastered solid blockwork walls. *BRE Current Paper CP 5/80*

14.12 SEWELL, E C, ALPHEY, R S, SAVAGE, J E and FLYNN, S J. Field measurements of the sound insulation of dry-lined masonry party walls. *BRE Current Paper CP 6/80.*

14.13 JONES, R D, AND CLOUGH, R H. Sound insulation of house separating and external walls (with lightweight masonry for thermal insulation). *CIRIA Project Record 278,* 1980.

14.14 JONES, R D. A new laboratory facility for the determination of the airborne sound insulation of party walls. *Applied Acoustics, Vol 9,* No 2, 1976. pp 119—130

14.15 BRITISH STANDARDS INSTITUTION. BS 5821: 1980 *Method for rating sound insulation in buildings and of building elements.* BSI, London. pp 8

14.16 JONES, R D, AND CLOUGH, R H. Sound insulation of house separating and external walls (with lightweight masonry for thermal insulation). *CIRIA Report 88,* 1980.

14.17 The Building Regulations 1976 (amended 1978). HMSO, London.

14.8 Bibliography

BUILDING RESEARCH ESTABLISHMENT. BRE Digest 96: *Sound insulation and new forms of construction.* BRE, 1971.

BUILDING RESEARCH ESTABLISHMENT. BRE Digest 102: *Sound insulation of traditional dwellings: 1.* BRE, 1971.

BUILDING RESEARCH ESTABLISHMENT. BRE Digest 103: *Sound insulation of traditional dwellings: 2.* BRE, 1971.

BUILDING RESEARCH ESTABLISHMENT. BRE Digest 128: *Insulation against external noise — 1.* BRE, 1971.

BUILDING RESEARCH ESTABLISHMENT. BRE Digest 129: *Insulation against external noise — 2.* BRE, 1971.

CHARTERED INSTITUTE OF BUILDING SERVICES. *Guide Book A3: Sound and vibration.* CIBS. pp A1—11, A1—17

Sound absorption of concrete block walls. *Concrete building and concrete products, Vol. 43,* No 1, January 1968. pp 13, 15 & 16

Concrete masonry cuts noise nuisances. *Contract Journal, Vol 252,* No 4882, 19 March 1973. pp 39

15

Fire resistance

15.1 Basic principles

One very important aspect to be considered by the designer is the fire resistance of the structure. This subject is quite complex and forms a major part of the various statutory requirements.

The main objectives of structural fire precautions are that the building should not collapse and that the occupants should be protected from smoke and fire until they can be safely evacuated. The four basic principles to follow are that the building should be designed:

(1) so that the materials used in construction do not assist in rapid development of the fire;

(2) to contain the fire within confined limits both within the building and between buildings;

(3) to provide structural elements with sufficient fire resistance according to the type and size of the building;

(4) to provide a means of escape for the occupants.

Regulations covering all these aspects may be found in Parts E and EE of the Building Regulations[14.1], and similarly in the Building Standards (Scotland)[14.2], the London Building Acts[14.3], and the Building Regulations (Northern Ireland)[14.4]. In addition the rules of the Fire Officer's Committee[14.5] and the Fire Officer's Committee of Ireland are often adopted for insurance purposes.

15.2 Elements of structure

The British Standard covering tests for fire resistance of materials is BS 476[14.6], which has several parts dealing with ignitability, flame spread, etc., but only Part 8 is generally applicable to masonry walls. Concrete bricks and blocks are essentially non-combustible material and it is generally only necessary to determine the fire resistance of the wall or element. Where blocks contain some form of combustible material in cores or voids to provide extra insulation then additional tests may be necessary.

A significant number of tests to BS 476:Part 1:1953 and BS 476:Part 8:1972, carried out in conjunction with national research projects and sponsored work by manufacturers, have shown that concrete brick and block walling is capable of notional fire resistance periods of between half-an-hour to six hours and of providing several hours protection to other structural elements. The notional fire resistance period of a wall or construction is an indication that it is able to satisfy conditions for stability, integrity and insulation for the period specified and is obtained by testing in accordance with a standard time-temperature curve, as shown in Figure 15.1. In this context, *stability* means that the wall does not collapse, *integrity* means that the wall does not develop cracks through which flames can pass, and *insulation* means that the wall does not transmit sufficient heat to ignite flammable materials in

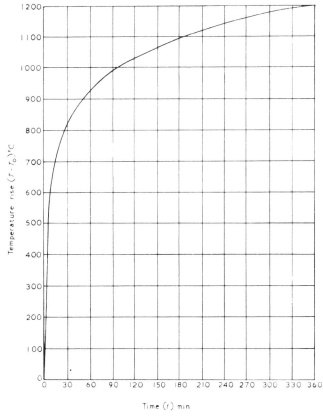

Figure 15.1 Standard time-temperature curve given in BS 476: Part 8: 1972[15.6]

contact with the side remote from the fire. The criteria of failure for each condition is as follows:

Stability In a non-loadbearing wall which carries only its self weight during the fire test, the stability period is taken as the time taken to collapse. A loadbearing wall is required to support the test load during the prescribed heating period and also 24 hours after the end of the heating period. However, should collapse occur during heating or during the reload test, the notional maximum period for stability for such a specimen should be construed as 80% of the time to collapse or the duration of heating if failure occurs in the reload test.

Integrity The integrity period is taken to be the time until cracks occur which are large enough to allow flame or hot gases through in sufficient quantity to cause cotton wool pads to ignite.

Insulation The insulation period is taken to be the time period until any point on the surface remote from the fire reaches a temperature greater than 180°C or the mean surface temperature exceeds 140°C.

The notional fire resistance of a wall is the period during which the wall fulfils all the relevant requirements. The typical grading periods are ½, 1, 1½, 2, 3, 4 and 6 hours. A test can be terminated at any time before failure occurs if it is expedient to do so. Thus, if a loadbearing wall has stability failure of 140 minutes, an integrity failure of 120 minutes and an insulation failure of 140 minutes, the wall would be given a notional fire resistance period of two hours. In certain cases where one or more of the three conditions can be relaxed, the fire resistance period of the wall may not necessarily be controlled by the lowest of the test conditions. The notional fire resistance periods, however, given in the Regulations and in CP 121[14.7] always cover for all three test conditions.

The insulation criteria of BS 476:Part 8 requires that the surface temperature of the unexposed face of the wall should not exceed a certain maximum and mean value. This temperature is set so that in normal circumstances it would not be high enough to ignite combustible material. It should be noted, however, that temperature beneath highly insulated materials in close contact with the wall may be much higher than the BS limits due to the reduced heat losses from the face. In situations where this is likely to be a problem then advantage may be taken of the better insulating properties of lightweight aggregate and aerated concrete block walls since, although they may be classified as having the same notional fire resistance period as dense walls (the stability and integrity controlling), the improved insulation would result in lower unexposed surface temperatures. For further information on this aspect either the Fire Research Station or individual manufacturers should be consulted.

Concrete brick and block walling may be used to provide fire resistant structural elements and also the means of providing effective and economical compartmentation to both new and existing buildings. Concrete masonry walling being non-combustible does not produce smoke or toxic gases and, therefore, attention has only to be focused towards decorative coverings such as paints, etc., applied to the surface of the wall. Another application is the upgrading or protection of elements with a comparatively poor fire resistance, such as steel stanchions.

The performance of a given wall is complex since it depends upon a number of factors, the notable items being:

(1) the type of unit, e.g., solid, hollow or aerated;

(2) the type of aggregate*, e.g. Class 1 or Class 2;

(3) the thickness of the wall;

(4) whether the wall is loadbearing or non-loadbearing;

(5) the type of finishes, e.g., none, cement-gypsum plaster, etc.

It is necessary to consider these various factors when determining the type of wall required. It is clearly an advantage to be able to produce a wide range of constructions which can be offered to suit any one particular problem.

The details given in Figures 15.2, 15.3 and 15.4 provide a brief indication of the performance and applicability of walls and constructions using concrete bricks and blocks based on information extracted from the Building Regulations. More extensive information may be found in the deemed-to-satisfy schedules of the individual controlled Standards and CP 121. In particu-

Construction	Performance (hours)	Required thickness (T)-mm	
		Loadbearing	Non-loadbearing
Solid concrete bricks	1	100	75
	2	100	100
	4	200	170
Solid concrete blocks. Class(1) aggregate	1	100	75
	2	100	75
	4	150	100
Aerated concrete blocks	1	100	50
	2	100	62
	4	180	100
Solid concrete bricks or blocks	1	100	75
	2	100	75
	4	100	75

Figure 15.2 Fire resistance of independent walling (walls finished with 12.5 mm cement/sand/gypsum – sand plaster)

*Class 1 aggregate: air-cooled blast furnace slag, foamed or expanded slag, sintered pulverized fuel ash, crushed brick, expanded clay or shale, well burnt clinker, pumice and limestone.
Class 2 aggregate: all gravels and crushed natural stones except limestones.

lar, information on fire resistance periods up to six hours is given in both CP 121[14.7] and in the Fire Officers' Committee Regulations[14.5].

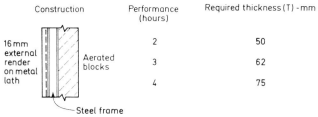

Figure 15.3 Fire resistance of non-loadbearing composite walls

Construction	Performance (hours)	Required thickness (T) - mm
16 mm external render on metal lath — Aerated blocks — Steel frame	2	50
	3	62
	4	75

15.3 Construction

It is important that walls should be correctly constructed so that full benefit is obtained of their strength, sound and thermal insulation, fire resistance and so on. For this purpose the recommendations given in CP 121: Part 1: *Brick and block walling* should be followed and adequate specifications provided. The details given are applicable to walls with mortared joints. Some concrete blocks may contain tongue and grooved ends and to maintain fire performance and sound insulation, it is

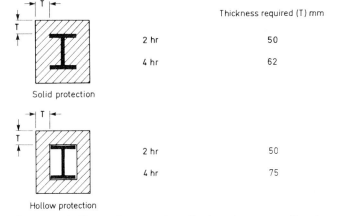

Construction	Performance	Minimum column dimensions	
		Built into wall	Free standing
	1 hr	75*	200
	2 hr	100*	300
600 min	4 hr	180*	450

*In order to effect reduction in column size a wall of appropriate fire resistance must be used

Construction	Performance	Thickness required (T) mm
Solid protection	2 hr	50
	4 hr	62
Hollow protection	2 hr	50
	4 hr	75

Figure 15.4 Fire resistance of walling used as protection to other structural elements

Note: The above examples are related to steel stanchions weighing less than 45 kg/m and for solid concrete blocks of foamed slag or pumic aggregate. Horizontal joint reinforcement is also required and is given in the Building Regulations

important that these joints should be filled with mortar and not left butted together.

15.4 References

15.1 The Building Regulations 1976 (amended 1978). HMSO, London.

15.2 The Building Standards (Scotland Consolidation) Regulations 1971 (with subsequent amendments). HMSO, London.

15.3 London Building Acts 1930—1939. London Building (Constructional) By-Laws 1972 and 1974 (with subsequent amendments). GLC, London.

15.4 The Building Regulations (Northern Ireland) 1977. HMSO, London.

15.4 BRITISH STANDARDS INSTITUTION. Rules for the construction of grades 1 and 2. Fire Officers Committee and Fire Officers Committee of Ireland. London, 1978. pp 30

15.5 BRITISH STANDARDS INSTITUTION. BS 476: Part 1: 1953 *Fire tests on building materials and structures* and BS 476: Part 8: 1972 *Test methods and criteria for the fire resistance of elements of building construction* (pp 16). BSI, London.

15.7 BRITISH STANDARDS INSTITUTION. CP 121: Part 1: 1973 *Code of Practice for walling*. Part 1: *Brick and block masonry*. BSI, London. pp 84

15.5 Bibliography

Apart from the references (15.1—15.7) given, further information on fire resistance of walling may also be found in the following:

BRITISH STANDARDS INSTITUTION. CP 111: Part 2: 1970 *Structural recommendations for loadbearing walls. Part 2: Metric Units*. BSI, London. pp 40

MALHOTRA, H L. Fire Note No 6: *Fire resistance of brick and block walls*. HMSO, London, 1966.

DAVEY, N, AND ASHTON, L A. Investigations on building fires. Part V: Fire tests on structural elements. *National Building Studies Research Paper No 12*. HMSO, London, 1953.

FISHER, R W, AND SMART. P M T. Results of fire resistance tests on elements of building construction. Volumes 1 and 2. BRE Reports — HMSO, London, 1975 and 1976.

READ, R E H, ADAMS, F C. AND COOKE. G M E. Guidelines for the construction of fire resisting structural elements. HMSO, London, 1980. pp 37

16

Movement in masonry

16.1 Introduction

This Chapter, which deals with the general subject of
movement in masonry, covers the technical background
to the subject and gives general recommendations for
the practical accommodation of movement in masonry.
Due attention should also be paid to the requirements
of *Chapter 6*. Although this handbook is predominantly
concerned with concrete masonry, it is recognized that
concrete units and fired-clay bricks are often used in
the same structure, so that some information has also
been included dealing with the use of the latter.

16.2 Technical background

An indication of the various factors which affect
movement in masonry, together with typical values for
unrestrained free thermal and moisture movement, are
presented in this Chapter in the manner which is probably to be adopted for the revision to the Code of Practice for walling, CP 121 (likely to be BS 5628:Part 3). It
is expected that this method of presentation will provide the designer with a clearer indication of the factors
affecting movement, but it should be noted that it is
almost impossible to determine mathematically, with
any degree of certainty, the extent of movement that
will actually occur. The determination of movement is a
complex problem and not merely a summation or sub-
traction of extremes of individual values of thermal and
moisture movement, creep, deflection, and so on. For
example, as a material expands due to increase in
temperature, it will also shrink as moisture is lost. In
addition each movement will be controlled to some
extent by the degree of restraint to which the masonry
is subjected and its orientation and location within the
structure. The clauses which follow indicate the various
individual movements separately, in such a way as to
show not only the general range of values for different
materials, but also the implication of other important
factors which need to be considered in an attempt to
estimate the likely movement within a given construction.

16.3 Thermal movement

From Figure 16.1 it can be seen that the total range of
free movement due to thermal effect, which is generally
reversible, is equal to the temperature range multiplied
by the appropriate coefficient of thermal expansion.
However, the movement that actually occurs within a
wall after construction depends not only on the range of
temperature but also on the initial temperature of the
units as laid and on their moisture content. This will
vary with the time of year and the weather conditions
during the construction period and may, with some
materials, be influenced by the age of units. For example, certain steam or similarly cured units have
sufficient strength to be delivered relatively fresh from
the curing chamber, but are likely to have a higher
initial temperature than air cured units. To determine
the effective free movement that could occur, therefore, some estimation of the initial temperature and
temperature range must be made. The effective free
movement, so derived, must still be modified to allow
for the effects of restraints.

Table 16.1 indicates typical ranges of coefficients of
thermal movement and some estimation must be made
of the actual value for the material being used, although
most manufacturers should be able to supply more precise values for their own materials. For further information on coefficients of thermal expansion for various
materials, together with examples of service temperature ranges of materials, reference should be made to
BRE Digest 228[16.1].

**Table 16.1 Coefficient of linear thermal movement of
units and mortar**

Materials	Coefficient of linear thermal movement $\times 10^{-6}$ per °C
Fired-clay bricks and blocks (depending on type of clay)	4—8
Concrete bricks and blocks (depending on aggregate and mix)	7—14
Calcium silicate bricks	11—15
Mortars	11—13

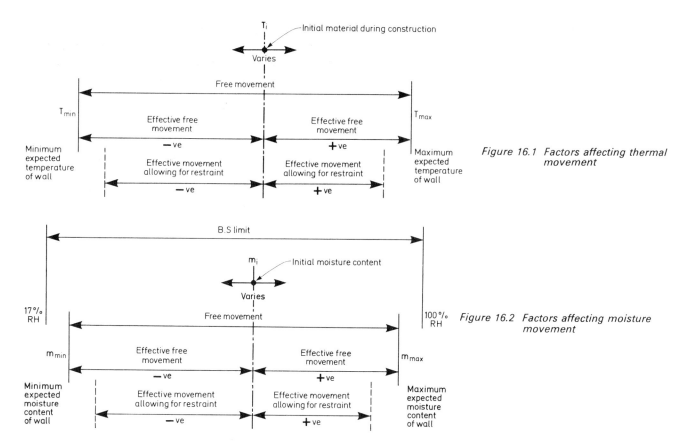

Figure 16.1 Factors affecting thermal
movement

Figure 16.2 Factors affecting moisture
movement

The differences between mortars and units can largely be neglected when considering movement along the wall, since the effect of such differences will be controlled by the adhesion of the mortar to the units. Some slight adjustment may be necessary for brick walls due to the greater quantity of mortar present. The units do not restrain the mortar in the vertical direction and therefore the movement in the height of the wall may be determined by multiplying the dimensions of the units and the mortar by the respective coefficients.

16.4 Moisture movement

The movement occurring in a wall as a result of changes in moisture content is basically controlled in the same way as thermal movement outlined above, except that in this instance attention needs to be given to minimum, initial and maximum moisture content rather than temperatures (Figure 16.2).

The values shown in Table 16.2 represent the maximum permitted shrinkage laid down by BS 6073 for concrete units. These limits are basically for quality control purposes and do not represent practical conditions. The BS test, which is currently being reviewed, determines the shrinkage of concrete bricks and blocks between saturation and oven conditions at a relative humidity of approximately 17%, whereas in practice a wall is seldom totally saturated and usually operates in relative humidity conditions between 50 and 85%. Thus the free movement will normally be less than the BS limit (see also BRE Digest 228[16.1]).

From Figure 16.2 it can be seen that the effective movement within a wall is related to the moisture content of the units at the time of laying and it is clear that keeping the units as dry as possible before and during

Table 16.2 Maximum permitted shrinkage of concrete masonry units

Material	Shrinkage (%)
Concrete bricks and dense and lightweight aggregate blocks	0.06
Autoclaved aerated concrete blocks	0.09

construction will reduce subsequent movement. The effective free movement will need to be modified to take restraints into account, but it should be noted that such restraints, particularly at the end of a wall, are likely to increase the tensile stresses in the wall.

The free moisture movement of fired-clay units is generally less than 0.02% and is usually neglected. Attention should be given to the long term movement of fired-clay units due to adsorption of moisture, as the adsorption gives rise to long term expansion, and care should, therefore, be taken when concrete and clay units are used together as, for example, in a cavity wall. Consideration should be given to the effects of differential movement. With this in mind it should also be noted that wire ties have greater flexibility than flat twisted ties. The total long term unrestrained expansion is typically 0.10% but a lower value may be appropriate, depending upon the type of clay.

The free moisture of mortar is similar to that of concrete units, although the effective free movement is likely to be greater, since initial moisture loss will not take place, as shown in Figure 16.3. Typical shrinkage values are given in Table 16.3, although the actual values will depend upon the constituents of the mortar, the mix proportions and the relative humidity. For convenience the lower values in the Table may be taken to apply to mortars in external walls and the higher to mortars in internal walls. Reversible movement of internal walls may generally be neglected since they are unlikely to become wet after initial drying out.

Figure 16.3 Moisture movement of mortars

Table 16.3 Shrinkage of mortars

Initial drying shrinkage (%)	Subsequent reversible movement (%)
0.04—0.10	0.03—0.06

Additional shrinkage of concrete units and mortar can occur as a result of carbonation. The extent of carbonation and the subsequent movement depend on the permeability of the concrete and on the relative humidity. In dense units and in autoclaved units, carbonation shrinkage may be neglected since it is extremely small. In unprotected open textured units and mortar, the shrinkage due to carbonation will still be relatively small and may be neglected for most purposes since such movement is unlikely to exceed 0.2 to 0.3 of the initial free movement.

16.5 Determination of total movement within a wall

To determine the movement likely to take place in a wall it is necessary to combine the individual effective movements due to thermal, moisture and other effects. However, the effective thermal and moisture movements are not directly additive since a wall is unlikely to be at both its maximum temperature and its saturated condition at the same time, so that to estimate the possible maximum movement it is necessary to consider carefully the temperature range over which the moisture movement occurs and make some attempt to combine the thermal and moisture movements on a rational basis rather than just considering the extremes. Since there are so many variables involved, it is extremely difficult to determine with any degree of certainty the actual movement that will occur. This Section basically outlines the factors that affect movement and in general it is simpler to adopt standard rules rather than try to estimate movement. It is hoped that the presentation of the factors in this Section will be of use in instances where some attempt has to be made to mathematically determine the effective movement that may occur.

With fired-clay walls long term expansion usually predominates and a simple solution would be to adopt the effective global movement coefficients to be given in the revision to CP 121. With concrete masonry the movement is small and predominantly controlled by the effects of shrinkage and thermal contraction. It is usual to provide 10 mm movement joints at nominal spacings as indicated in *Section 16.6* instead of trying to determine the actual movement that may occur and hence determine optimum movement joint spacings. There is no proven mathematical method for determining the

optimum spacing of movement joints but readers may find the paper by Copeland[16.2] of some assistance in this respect. This paper is based upon unpublished experimental data by R.W. Carlson and T.J. Reading to determine stress distribution curves that occur in walls with varying length and height. In effect the approach suggested by Copeland is simply to determine the ratio of the effective maximum strain that is likely to occur in the wall, as a result of contraction, to the ultimate strain capacity of the wall. This is then related to a panel size in which the Carlson/Reading curves give a ratio of average stress to maximum stress at the centre line of the panel of the same height to length ratio. This gives rise to the following formula:

$$P_m \leqslant \frac{e_u}{R\,(e_d + e_{temp})}$$

where P_m = ratio average stress : maximum stress (Figure 16.4)

e_u = ultimate tensile strain

e_d = drying shrinkage

e_{temp} = temperature contraction

R = factor for degree of restraint

Following the general approach indicated for determination of movement within a wall, this could be rewritten as meaning:

$$P_m = \frac{\text{ultimate strain capacity}}{\text{effective strain}}$$

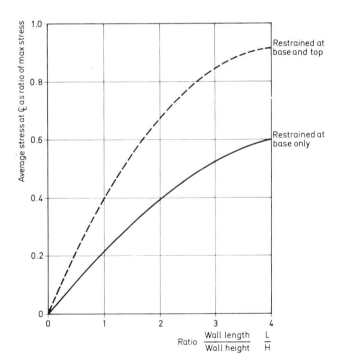

Figure 16.4 Relationship between average stress and maximum stress of walls of various L/H

If this approach is examined with regard to a concrete masonry wall constructed of average units and subject to average weather conditions the following result is found:

Average drying shrinkage = 0.07%

Effective shrinkage, say 50%, giving $e_d = 0.0035$

231

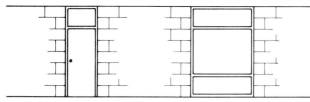

Figure 16.5

Average coefficient of temperature contraction 10×10^{-6} per °C

Effective temperature contraction 20°C giving $e_{\text{temp}} = 0.0002$

Average ultimate strain capacity $e_{\text{u}} = 0.0002$

Taking a value of $R = 0.9$ to allow for the effect of relaxation at damp-proof course (or alternatively this factor could be taken to allow for the fact that the shrinkage and temperature effects are not directly additive), this gives:

$$\frac{e_{\text{u}}}{R\,(e_{\text{d}} + e_{\text{temp}})} = \frac{0.0002}{0.9\,(0.0035 + 0.0002)} = 0.4$$

Figure 16.4 indicates that the ratio of length to height for a wall free at the top should not exceed about 2, i.e.,

$L/h \leqslant 2$. Taking a typical storey height of 3 m gives the well known recommendation for spacing movement joints in concrete masonry at approximately 6 m centres.

The method outlined by Copeland makes a few assumptions which may not be technically correct and suggests that some additional modifications may be necessary to cope with the mass effect of the wall, but there is little published information on the ultimate strain capacity of concrete masonry. However, Copeland's paper is one of the few which tries to deal with the subject in mathematical terms and, together with the suggested approach for determining effective movement, may help to reinforce the engineering judgement upon which this subject must still heavily rely.

16.6 Accommodation of movement

Defects such as cracking are undesirable and difficult to deal with after the event, and it is most important to consider provision for movement at the design stage.

The effects of movement may be reduced by:

(1) designing the building to use discrete panels of masonry;

(2) providing movement joints (control joints);

(3) using the correct mortar;

(4) keeping the units and wall protected during construction;

(5) providing local bed joint reinforcement;

(6) designing to maintain bond pattern.

These factors are considered in more detail, as follows:

Discrete panels: One way of ensuring that the masonry is able to accommodate small seasonal movements is to design the building so that the masonry is separated into discrete panels, for example by use of feature panels at window openings and storey height door openings. This is illustrated in Figure 16.5 and also in the accompanying photographs. In this design the length of masonry panel should be limited to around 6 m and ideally its length should not be greater than about twice its height.

Movement joints: The provision of movement joints (control joints) has the same effect as the discrete panel method in that joints divide the wall into defined lengths which are able to accommodate the strains arising from temperature and moisture variations. This method is suitable in situations where long walls of masonry occur. The distance between the control joints should not normally exceed about 6 m, but since there are wide variations in the physical properties between different concrete units, some variation of joint spacing is acceptable, although it should be noted that the risk of cracking may be greater where the length of panel exceeds about twice its height. Joint spacing towards 7.5 m may be acceptable for autoclaved dense aggregate units and for certain internal applications. It is, however, always desirable to consult with individual manufacturers before extending joint spacings.

Control joints may be of two types (see Figure 16.6), i.e., contraction joints or expansion joints. Generally the contraction type joints which are able to open to allow the tensile strains within the wall to be accommodated are suitable, although such joints may have weak mortar within the vertical joint and for some low strength units an infill fibre board material would be

better. In some instances, particularly on internal walls, a dry butt joint can be used. Expansion joints will generally only be required where the length of a wall exceeds 30—50 m. These joints must have compressive (not fibre board) material within the joint. The contraction joint with fibre material will also tend to allow a small amount of expansion to take place and thereby only one type of joint is necessary. The small expansive movement that occurs in the short distance of around 6 m generally means that fibre material is acceptable. All such joints should not be bridged by any service or tie which would prevent free movement occurring. Short flat ties may be used to aid stability of walls at contraction joints providing the wall is still free to move longitudinally, but great care should be taken at expansion joints since any tie must be of a type that would tolerate free compressive movement. This is extremely difficult to achieve in practice and the stability of the walls is best achieved in some other way, for example, by providing top support and sizing the wall accordingly. A small factor, but one that is nevertheless important, is that the sealant used must be capable of accommodating the expected movement of the joints. This is not usually a problem in concrete masonry, since the joints do not generally exceed 6—8 m and most sealants can accommodate the movement occurring in this length of wall.

The reference to the notional 6 m length applies to walls without end restraint, i.e., the distance between free joints. In the case of a wall which is visibly within this distance, such as a gable wall, it must be noted that the restraint which occurs at the return will limit the ability of the wall to shorten and, thereby, increase the tensile stresses within the wall. In the case of a gable wall or a panel between a control joint and a corner restraint, therefore, the effective length should be considered to be some 25—50% greater than the visual length. When this effective length is much in excess of the notional spacing given previously then joints in the case of the gable, or closer joints in the case of the corner situation, or the provision of bed joint reinforcement, should be considered. In the particular case of a very rigid vertical support, as in tying to a column, an effective length of twice the visual length should be taken.

In addition to the general rule of spacing joints at certain notional centres, the provision of control joints should also be considered at positions where concentration of changes in stress may occur. Examples of this

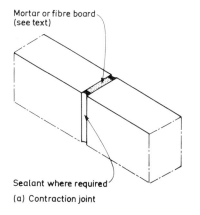

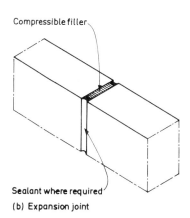

Figure 16.6   Movement joints:
(a) contraction joint
(b) expansion joint

233

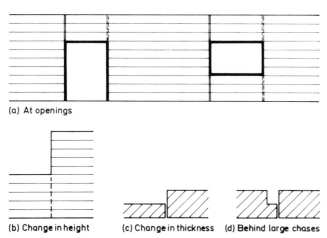

(a) At openings

(b) Change in height   (c) Change in thickness   (d) Behind large chases

Figure 16.7 Movement joint locations: (a) at openings (b) change in height (c) change in thickness (d) behind large chases

are given below, some of which are illustrated in Figure 16.7:

(1) change in height;

(2) change in thickness;

(3) at large chases;

(4) at expansion or contraction joints in a building or floor slab;

(5) at window and door openings;

(6) at change in direction.

The use of control joints at changes in direction, unlike most other points, needs little more explanation. Joints are not generally provided in the extreme corner of external wall returns. It is, in fact, usual to aid stability by placing any control joints required at this location, a short distance from the external corner but within the limit previously given. Similarly, short walls of, say, less than 2—3 m that intersect other walls, will not specifically require a joint at the intersection, although in facing work it will be necessary to provide a joint at that position to maintain the bonding pattern along the main wall (see Figure 16.10). Such joints can also reduce the amount of cutting required and ease construction by avoiding the need to form toothing for partition walls which may be built later. Provision of movement joints along and at the ends of walls supported by long span floors or beams will often be beneficial in reducing the effect of any deflection which may occur. Movement joints should be built into the wall during construction and run for the full height of the masonry. The designer is advised against the use of sawn joints since unless very great care is taken they will be ineffective. It is not usual to continue the joints below the ground floor damp-proof course since the amount of movement below this level is minimal. However, in the case of a sloping site where the damp-proof course is well above ground level, the control joint should be continued down to ground level.

For aesthetic reasons, the designer may wish to conceal joints as much as possible and this can be achieved by placing the joints at the position of down pipes, by matching the sealant with the mortar and units and by using stack bonded walls.

Specification of mortar: It is important to note that mortar influences the way in which a wall accommodates movements. A masonry wall built with a relatively low strength mortar is better able to accommodate the stresses developing in a wall as a result of movement than a wall with a very strong mortar, as the weaker mortar relieves the stresses that may otherwise cause problems. As a result it may be taken that the general recommendations on the accommodation of movement, and hence control joint spacings, apply to situations where the most appropriate mortar is employed — namely a mortar of designation (iii). Where stronger mortars are required for structural or durability reasons, then some modification to the recommendations may be necessary. Higher strength mortars can normally be tolerated in vertically reinforced walls due to the presence of the reinforcement.

Storage and protection of masonry: For cracking to occur within a masonry wall tensile stresses must be present. These stresses chiefly occur as a result of moisture loss, differential movement and thermal contraction. Since excessive shrinkage could obviously cause problems the British Standard for concrete blocks and bricks, BS 6073[16.3], lays down certain maximum drying shrinkage values for the units. This reduces the risk of excessive shrinkage occurring but it will be quite apparent that the higher the moisture content at the time of laying, the greater the shrinkage will be, and to reduce subsequent shrinkage it is desirable to protect units from the rain while they are stored and during construction. As thermal contraction can also set up tensile stresses it is important that units are not used hot from an autoclave or curing chamber.

Reinforcement: The use of bed joint reinforcement was mentioned in the section dealing with the provision of control joints. Bed joint reinforcement can be used to modify joint spacings and to assist in situations where high stress concentrations occur as, for example, at window openings (Figure 16.8). The reinforcement should be of the tram-line type, preferably with an effective diameter of between 3—5 mm, with a cover of at least 20 mm from the face of the mortar and should be galvanized where it is to be used in wall which is exposed to the weather. Such reinforcement should extend at least 600 mm past the opening. Reinforcement may also be used to increase the distance between movement joints, and care should again be taken whenever spacings in excess of about 6 m are used. The provision of reinforcement will not ensure that cracking does not occur but it will considerably lessen the risk.

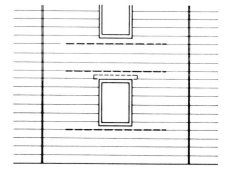

Figure 16.8 Bed joints at openings

Little research evidence is available to support the use of reinforcement to control cracking and the only information that can be offered is that issued by the National Concrete Masonry Association of America which is given in Table 16.4. The advice is apparently based more on practical experience than mathematics and hence needs to be used with some degree of caution, particularly with regard to the suggestion that no reinforcement is required for cases where $L/h \leqslant 2$*.

Table 16.4 Movement joint spacing for reinforced walls

Ratio of panel length to height $\dfrac{L}{h}$	Vertical spacing of joint reinforcement mm	Maximum length regardless of height m
2	None*	12
2½	600	14
3	400	16
4	200	18

The reinforcement should consist of two parallel mild steel bars of nominal size 3—5 mm diameter, or equivalent strength in high yield bars

Bonding pattern: Although maintaining the bond pattern is an automatic criterion for facing work, it is often found that little attention is paid to this aspect in work that is to be rendered or plastered. This may seem to be of little consequence but in practice the lack of initial design, together with poor workmanship, can result in a series of virtually aligning perpend joints as depicted by Figure 16.9, with the result that the wall is considerably weakened and cracking is more likely to occur.

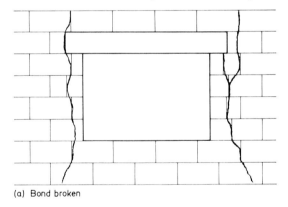

(a) Bond broken

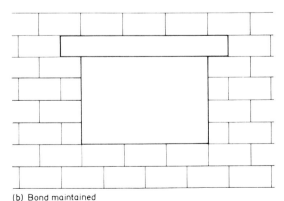

(b) Bond maintained

Figure 16.9 Maintaining bond pattern: (a) bond broken (b) bond maintained

*It is suggested for conditions where $\leqslant 2$, that, due to mass effects, some reinforcement may be required when movement joints are spaced at centres exceeding 6 m.

Similarly it is of benefit to design the building so that wherever possible lintels can be supported by a full length block.

Wall bonding: With concrete masonry it is common practice not to bond intersecting walls together by toothing one wall into the other. The intersection of such walls, as explained in the section dealing with the accommodation of movement, is often a desirable location at which to incorporate either a contraction or expansion joint. Even if a true movement joint is not required it will often be beneficial to use a tied butt joint at such locations since this considerably reduces the amount of cutting and enables the bond pattern of the passing wall to be maintained (Figure 16.10). If the intersection is not required to act as a full movement joint it may be tied with either lengths of expanded metal or strips of steel in each course. It is important, however, to ensure that such joints are not confused with movement joints. Tied joints of this form will not generally allow movement to take place, particularly in the example shown in Figure 16.11 and, therefore, care should be taken in the location of such joints. Joints tied with expanded metal are not as rigid as steel strips. A simple approach would be to not use fully tied joints unless the length of the wall from the intersection does not exceed 2 m. In many instances it will be safer to provide actual movement joints at all locations and design the panels to have adequate stability in some other way, for example, by providing support to the top of the intersecting wall.

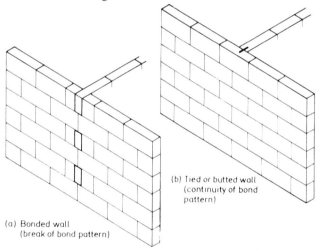

(b) Tied or butted wall (continuity of bond pattern)

(a) Bonded wall (break of bond pattern)

Figure 16.10 (a) bonded wall (break of bond pattern) (b) tied or butted wall (continuity of bond pattern)

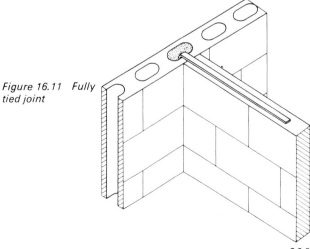

Figure 16.11 Fully tied joint

16.7 Differential movement

In addition to the general points made previously, to assist in reducing the occurrence of cracking particular attention should be given to the effects of differential movements between various materials. The differential movement between the various types of concrete masonry, i.e., dense aggregate, lightweight aggregate and autoclaved aerated concrete blocks and concrete bricks, will generally be fairly small, but consideration should nevertheless be given to the possible effects of this differential movement. In most instances with cavity walls this movement between inner and outer leaves can be accommodated by the flexibility of the wall ties.

Butterfly and double triangular wire ties are more flexible than flat twisted ties and are thus better at accommodating any differential movement which may occur. This aspect is particularly important where more substantial differential movement may occur, as for example when one leaf is of fired-clay masonry and the other is of concrete masonry. It is essential that the effects of differential movement are considered since serious problems may otherwise arise. In principle the wall details should be checked to ensure that any differential movement is free to take place. An example of a detail which has caused problems in the past is illustrated in Figure 16.12, where (a) shows the basic wall detail and (b) indicates the effect that the differential

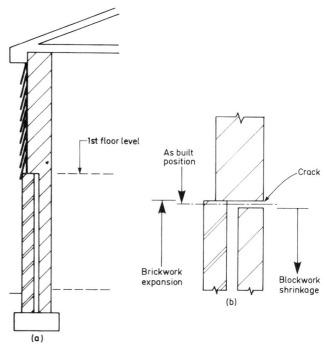

Figure 16.12 Differential movement problem

movement could have on the wall. When designing with both fired-clay and concrete masonry the essential point to remember is that fired-clay walling has a general tendency to an expansive movement while concrete masonry has a tendency to shrink.

16.8 References

16.1 BUILDING RESEARCH ESTABLISHMENT. BRE Digest 228: *Estimation of thermal and moisture movements and stresses*. Part 2. BRE, 1979. pp 8

16.2 COPELAND, R E. Shrinkage and temperature stresses in masonry. *Journal of the American Concrete Institute*, 1957.

16.3 BRITISH STANDARDS INSTITUTION. BS 6073: 1981 *Precast concrete masonry units*. BSI, London.

16.9 Bibliography

BESSEY, G E. Shrinkage and expansion in brickwork and blockwork, causes and effects. *Journal of the British Ceramic Society, Vol 6,* No 2, 1969.

BRITISH STANDARDS INSTITUTION. BRE Digest 227 and 229: *Estimation of thermal and moisture movements and stresses* (Parts 1 and 3). BRE, 1979. pp 8

ALEXANDER, S J, AND LAWSON, R M. Design for movement in buildings. Technical Note 107, CIRIA, London, 1981. pp 54

17

Specification and workmanship

17.1 Object of specifications

This section deals with specifications for concrete masonry and indicates the main design and workmanship aspects that need to be covered. It is important that masonry, particularly where it has been designed structurally in accordance with either CP 111 or BS 5628, should be built correctly. Indeed, both Codes of Practice and the Statutory Instruments indicate that materials, components and workmanship should comply with the appropriate recommendations of CP 121. The Code of Practice CP 121 provides the designer and contractor with a lot of practical information on the subject of construction with masonry. Although it is generally indicated that work should comply with the recommendations of CP 121, it is not practical to refer to this as the sole contract document for masonry, since the clauses of the Code are not always explicit, and there are often several recommended alternatives to a particular item. The Code does not necessarily cover all possible acceptable ways of dealing with any particular problem. In addition the Code explains general recommendations and not necessarily mandatory items; use is therefore made of the word *should* and not *shall*.

The object of the specification is to ensure that the most important aspects of design and workmanship are simply, clearly and explicitly stated. Thus CP 121 provides the designer with extremely useful information on materials, design and workmanship for masonry. The recommendations given may be used or developed for design purposes and can also form the basis for production of the contract specifications.

There are several ways of tackling the question of specifications — they can be individually written for each contract or a general office specification can repeatedly be used. The latter method, which unfortunately is most common, can lead to serious problems since such specifications are often noticeably out of date and can contain errors which are repeated on each and every contract, but due to the pressure of work in the design office, often insufficient time is available to take the former approach. One approach to this problem is the use of a standard specification document such as the National Building Specification[7.1] which is in essence a very comprehensive series of standard specification clauses to cover most building trades and operations. The NBS, in particular, was written in very clear, simple and explicit terms and has the major advantage that the text is continually being revised and updated as codes change. When using this form of specification the designer can quickly select the clauses most appropriate, so that the bulk of specifications can be compiled with comparative ease, allowing more time to deal with clauses of particular importance. The outcome of using such standard specifications is that time is available to compile individual specifications for each contract.

Another important factor is that the specification should be correct, which is sometimes difficult to ensure with the normal office specification and again, an advantage of texts such as NBS is that the designer can confidently rely on the accuracy of the wording in the general specification clause and has only to check that any insertions, such as dimensions, reference numbers, etc., have been written correctly.

It was suggested at the beginning of the Chapter that specifications should ideally be simple, clear and explicit. Often it is found that the specification is far too long and too complex and that the principal point to be made is lost in a long meaningless passage. It may be more difficult to write short specifications than long specifications that effectively say no more, but the shorter the specification is the more likely it is to be clear, understandable, and therefore, the simpler it will be to read and to be followed. The small additional effort is worthwhile from every point of view.

One way in which a specification may be simplified is considered in the following text, which is not uncommonly found and which will have a degree of familiarity:

The coarse aggregate shall be clean, natural or crushed stone complying with BS 882 and shall be free from chalk, clay, organic or other deleterious material. The particles shall be well and evenly graded to conform to the limits given in Table 1 of BS 882 for the maximum size aggregate appropriate to the concrete mix

A great deal of this text is simply repeating that which is already a stated requirement within the British Standard, in that the comments regarding *free from chalk*, and such like, are part of the British Standard, so why repeat it? With this in mind, it can be seen that the wording could adequately be reduced to:

> *The coarse aggregate shall comply with the requirements of BS 882 and be graded in accordance with Table 1*

Examining the British Standard further, it will be found that only graded aggregate is covered by Table 1. Additionally reference to BS 882 can only mean that the aggregate must comply with its requirements. Adopting the technique used for the National Building Specification, the specification could be reduced to a very clear, simple and explicit form such as:

> *Coarse aggregate : to BS 882, graded*

which, after all, is the importance of the clause.

The accuracy of a specification is something else to be considered, as errors can occur in any specification, but they are far easier to find when the specification is uncluttered. It will have been noted from the materials section that BS 2028[7.2] and BS 1180[7.3] have been replaced by BS 6073[7.4]. Apart from a general update of the masonry standard, one major reason for the revision was to simplify it by deleting or amending items which had caused confusion in the past. This has resulted in BS 6073 being divided into two parts — Part 1: *Specification for precast concrete masonry units* and Part 2: *Method for specifying concrete masonry units*.

The following example, which starts by considering a requirement based on the previous standard (BS 2028:1364), illustrates this attempt to simplify Specifications and shows the ease with which errors in the specification may be noticed and corrected.

Requirements: Fair faced blocks for painting, strength 7 N/mm², size 390 × 190 × 100 mm, completely solid.

Specification: Concrete blocks to BS 2028:1364
Type: A solid to be painted
Strength: 7 N/mm²
Size: 390 × 190 × 100 mm

The error here lies in the fact that a fair faced finish is required and yet the specifier has simply indicated any Type A block to be used. It is possible that the specifier mistakenly assumed that Type A meant facing block, which of course it did not. In addition the old definition of *solid* allowed up to 25% voids which may mean that the specifier may not get completely solid blocks as originally required. With the specification in this simple form it would be easy to check. With a little more thought, the architect or specifier would be sure of the required finish by specifying the block by name, i.e.:

Specification: Concrete blocks to BS 2028:1364

Type: "Super face", no void, solid

Strength: 7 N/mm²

Manufacturer: Quality Block Company Limited

This example, apart from indicating an incorrect specification, shows why reference to types A, B and C have not been retained and why the definition of *solid*

has been amended in BS 6073. Part 2 of BS 6073 is thus the section to which the designer should refer when specifying or ordering masonry units. Appendix A: BS 6073 indicates the information to be given by the purchaser with his enquiry or order, and the essential topics to be considered when writing the specification. The previous example can now be completed by writing the specification in terms of BS 6073:

> Concrete blocks to BS 6073:Part 1
>
> Size: 390 × 190 × 100 mm
>
> Type: Solid
>
> Properties: Super face
>
> Manufacturer: Quality Block Company Limited

To summarize, when specifications are written it is desirable that they are not over-wordy, thereby losing the impact of the clause, and it is essential that they are correct.

17.2 Cross referencing specification/drawings

Having developed simple and correct specifications, a very useful exercise is to cross reference them with the drawings and to schedule the various types of wall specifications at the beginning of the masonry section. An illustration of a completed schedule page is given in Table 17.1. From a quick reference to this schedule the contractor is able to identify the position and various types of wall on the project. It is also simple to determine the various types of mortar, and such like, required. The type numbers can be used on the drawings as shown in Figure 17.1 to directly correspond to the specification for the wall.

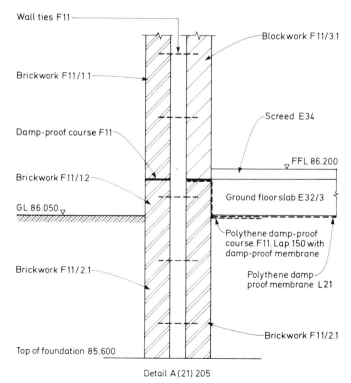

Detail A (21) 205

Figure 17.1 Use of type numbers on drawings

Table 17.1 Completed schedule — brick/block walling

	Use or location	Brick/block	Mortar F11:Y	Bond F11:3	Jointing/pointing F11:4
Type F11/1.1	External leaf above damp-proof course	Facing bricks F710 F725	Group 3 coloured for pointing	Stretching ⅓ lap	Flush pointing
Type F11/1.2	External leaf below damp-proof course	ditto	Group 3 sulphate-resisting cement coloured for pointing	ditto	ditto
Type F11/1.3	Screen walls above damp-proof course	ditto	Group 3 coloured for pointing	Flemish garden wall	ditto
Type F11/1.4	Screen walls below damp-proof course	ditto	Group 3 sulphate-resisting cement coloured for pointing	ditto	ditto
Type F11/2.1	External walls below ground	Common bricks F605	Group 1 sulphate-resisting cement	Stretching	—
Type F11/2.2	Screen walls below ground	ditto	ditto	English	—
Type F11/2.3	Manholes	Engineering bricks F810	ditto	English garden wall	Flush jointing
Type F11/3.1	Inner leaf and partitions, factory	Fair faced blocks F150	Group 3	Stretching ½ lap	Pail handle jointing
Type F11/3.2	Inner leaf, offices	Thermal blocks F160	ditto	ditto	For plaster
Type F11/3.3	Partitions, offices	Common blocks F125	ditto	ditto	ditto

17.3 Items for specification and general specification clauses

The essential information to be given when ordering concrete masonry units, as recommended by BS 6073:Part 2, is as follows:

Item	Information
Quantity	Number of units or area of walling
Size	*Work* size required, given in terms of length, height and thickness
Strength	(a) for blocks less than 75 mm, no compressive strength need be specified
	(b) for blocks equal to or greater than 75 mm, the compressive strength required in N/mm^2
	(c) for bricks, the compressive strength required in N/mm^2 or *special purpose bricks* where a minimum strength of 40 N/mm^2 and 350 kg/m^2 cement is required
Type	(a) for blocks, the type of units required, i.e., solid, cellular or hollow
	(b) for bricks, the type of units required, i.e., solid, perforated, hollow or cellular, or for special use 'fixing bricks'
Materials	To specify to the manufacturer whether any particular material is to be included or restricted
Specials	(a) whether special shape units, such as quoin or cavity closure blocks, are required
	(b) can also be used to indicate whether any special requirements with regard to tolerances are required
Properties	The manufacturer shall be informed of any requirements with regard to colour, texture, thermal properties, etc.
Quality control	If special category quality control in accordance with the recommendations of BS 5628 is required, this must be conveyed to the manufacturer
Identification	Where additional means of identifying the masonry units are required
Handling	To convey to the manufacturer any special handling requirements, such as palletization, strapping, mechanical off-loading, and so on.

It is unlikely that all these requirements will need to be covered in each specification clause and it is, therefore, necessary to be selective. It may also be necessary to include reference to the *Manufacturer* in the specification and perhaps the location of particular units within the structure if not covered by use of a schedule as adopted by NBS. Thus, a general specification clause for normal blocks could read as follows:

Concrete blocks to BS 6073

Size: $390 \times 190 \times 100$ mm

Strength: 3.5 N/mm²

Type: Solid

A specification for facing blocks could be:

Concrete blocks to BS 6073

Size: $390 \times 190 \times 100$ mm

Strength: 7 N/mm²

Type: Solid

Materials: No calcium chloride

Properties: Buff fair faced

Manufacturer: Modern Block Company Limited

Most fair faced blocks are produced to tolerances well within the British Standard values. If special or specific requirements on tolerances are needed they must be discussed and agreed with the manufacturer.

The previous information in this Chapter has hopefully given some indication as to how to tackle the general topic of specifications. It is not appropriate in this handbook to attempt to cover all the possible specifications which could be required for a masonry contract. Instead a series of basic points and some main specifications have been included as being the topics most likely to be required. The specifications themselves are not intended to be for simple extraction and are at times more wordy than is necessary. The clauses are provided as a check list of the most important features that need to be considered for specification, and guidance notes are provided for particular points.

17.3.1 Items for specification

To write a specification the designer needs to understand the material, whether it is clay brick, concrete brick or block, plastic, timber, and so on. For concrete masonry some of the most important items to be considered are given below. Specification of units may also need to take account of the following:

Materials	Autoclaved aerated concrete
	Lightweight aggregate concrete
	Dense aggregate concrete
Blocks	Standard blocks
	Facing blocks
	Thermal blocks
	Special blocks — quoin blocks, etc.

Bricks	Standard bricks
	Facing bricks
	Fixing bricks
	Special purpose bricks
Block materials	Use and durability
Block strength	2.8 to 35 N/mm² strength
Brick strength	7 to 40 N/mm² strength, use and durability
Block forms	Solid
	Hollow
	Cellular
Brick forms	Frogged
	Unfrogged
Performance requirements	Thermal insulation
	Fire resistance
	Sound insulation
	Rain resistance
Other aspects	Weight
	Speed of construction
	Handling
	Identification

Specifications for design and workmanship may need to take account of:

Standard work	Mortar mixes
Facing work	Joint profile
Control joints	Handling of blocks
Stability	Storage of materials
Bonding	Rendering
Wall ties	Testing
Cutting and chasing	

17.3.2 Specification clauses

17.3.2.1 Materials and properties

(1) Concrete blocks
All blocks to comply with BS 6073:Part 1 and any additional requirements as specified

(a) Standard blocks
The concrete blocks ....(location) shall be ....(description or manufacturer's designation), to be obtained from .... (manufacturer), or other equal approved, and be ....(solid, cellular, hollow) having a minimum compressive strength of .... N/mm² in the following size(s) ....

A standardized method of specifying precast concrete masonry units is given in BS 6073:Part 2. The basic items which should be given in any specification for concrete masonry units are the size and compressive strength, where this is required to be greater than the minimum average permitted by Part 1 (2.8 N/mm²). This should be followed where necessary by details of any additional or specific requirements relating to such things as type, materials, shape, density, colour, and so on, and whether the units are to be of special category (BS 6073:Part 2). Refer to CP 121 for recommendations on minimum quality of units for durability.

The purpose of including the reference to (location) is simply to indicate that it is of benefit to make it quite clear where each type of unit is located. It would not strictly form part of the specification clause. The (description or manufacturer's designation) may need to be included, particularly where special requirements such as thermal and/or sound insulation are required. In some instances the manufacturer's designation may automatically cover the question of (solid, cellular, hollow), but in situations such as for reinforced work it is essential to specify hollow. When non-loadbearing partition blocks are required (less than 75 mm thick) the information could be reduced to:
The concrete blocks . . . .(location) *shall be obtained from* . . . .(manufacturer), *or other equal approved, and be* . . . .(solid, cellular) *in the following size(s)* . . . .

(b) Facing blocks
The facing blocks . . . .(location) *shall be* . . . .(description or manufacturer's designation), *obtained from* . . . .(manufacturer), *or other equal approved, and be* . . . .(solid, cellular, hollow) *having an average compressive strength of* . . . . .N/mm² *in the following size(s)* . . . .*and comply with the approved sample panels located at* . . . .

The same guidance notes as previously used similarly apply to this clause, except that emphasis in this instance is also on facing units. The inclusion of reference to the sample panel is simply to indicate the importance of this and it would generally form a separate clause. The purpose of the sample panel(s) is to establish such physical factors as range of sizes and variations in colour, texture, pattern and so on. The panel must be of sufficient size and contain normal and corner blocks, etc., for these factors to be established. The panel(s) are also used to indicate the acceptable workmanship and therefore should also be of such configuration as to fairly cover intricacies of the work.

(c) Special blocks
Special blocks shall be to drawing(s) . . . .*and be within the following tolerances* . . . .
The inclusion of tolerances in this clause is to bring to the readers attention the fact that BS 6073 basically applies to normal rectangular units. Generally it will not be necessary to bother with tolerances since the manufacturer will adhere to the Standard as far as is practicable. If for very high quality work it is felt necessary to specify tolerances for special blocks, such as corner blocks, then it is advisable to discuss the matter first with the manufacturer, since such blocks may be manufactured on differ-

ent machinery to normal blocks. In addition a method of measurement may also be necessary, particularly for blocks with exposed aggregate or split faces.

(2) Concrete bricks
All bricks to comply with BS 6073:Part 1
The general clauses for concrete bricks are liable to be similar although not containing as much data, since units will generally be solid (with or without frogs) and the strength designation is also used to define durability — see CP 121.

(3) Mortars

(a) Materials for mortar

(i) Cement
The cement for mortar shall be to BS . . . .
For guidance on cements for mortars see *Chapter 3* and CP 121. Ordinary Portland cement to BS 12 will be the most commonly used, although Portland blast furnace cement (BS 146) and masonry cement (BS 5224) are also acceptable. Sulphate-resisting Portland cement (BS 4027) may also be used but the subject of sulphate attack should be carefully considered before specifying this cement (see *Section 3.4.2* and CP 121).

(ii) Lime
The lime for mortar shall be to BS 890
Building limes normally used for mortar are non-hydraulic (calcium) limes or semi-hydraulic (calcium) and magnesium limes.

(iii) Sand
The sand for mortar shall be to BS 1200
Other sands, apart from sands to BS 1200, can produce acceptable mortars but this needs to be checked with local experience. It should be noted that very finely graded sands can result in mortars more friable and permeable than would normally be accepted.

(iv) Water
The water shall be from normal mains supplies or approval obtained before use
Where the quality of supply is doubtful the water should be tested in accordance with BS 3148.

(v) Admixtures
Admixtures may be used subject to approval in writing. Calcium chloride shall not be permitted
Before approving the use of an admixture the architect should first check the appropriate manufacturer's recommendations and then ask the contractor to submit evidence of satisfactory performance of the admixture when used correctly, and details of the arrangements for the use of admixtures. The architect should also confirm in his written approval the agreed procedure for use.

(b) Preparation of mortars

(i) Recommended mortar
Mortar . . . .(location) *shall be* . . . .
(mix proportions) *by* . . . . (weight/volume) *of dry materials*

In specifying the mortar mix consideration should be given to its strength, durability and ability to accommodate movements. Attention is drawn to CP 121. The most common mortar for both concrete blockwork and brickwork is of designation (iii), i.e., 1 : 1 : 5 — 6 or equivalent. Sand proportions should be specified as a single value or grading conditions specified — see also CP 121. Where special category construction is to be used in accordance with BS 5628 then appropriate clauses for strength and sampling will need to be included. Volume proportions will be the norm but increased accuracy will result when batching is by weight.

(ii) Equivalent mortar mixes
Alternative mortar mixes may be used subject to written approval
The contractor's proposed alternative mix should be assessed by the designer for compliance with strength, durability and so on, prior to written approval being given to the equivalent mortar mix. Guidance on equivalent mixes is given in CP 121.

(iii) Batching of mortars
Measure materials accurately to specified mix proportions either by weight or gauge boxes

(iv) Mixing of mortars
The mortar shall be mixed by machine and be used within two hours of mixing. Mortars, except coloured mortars, may be retempered during the two hour period
Retempering of coloured mortars may alter colour.

(4) Concrete for core filling

(a) Materials

(i) Cement

The cement for concrete shall be to BS ....
In normal circumstances use Ordinary Portland cement complying with BS 12.

(ii) Fine and coarse aggregates
Fine aggregate shall comply with BS .... Coarse aggregate shall comply with BS ....
The type of aggregate should be specified according to the performance requirements. Generally this will mean using an aggregate smaller than that used for the concrete block. Relevant British Standards include BS 882, BS 1165 and BS 3797.

(iii) Water
The water shall be from normal mains supply or approval obtained before use.
Where the quality of supply is doubtful water should be tested in accordance with BS 3148.

(iv) Admixtures
Admixtures may be used subject to approval in writing.
Before approving the use of an admixture the architect should first check the appropriate manufacturer's recommendations and then ask the contractor to submit evidence of satisfactory performance of the admixture when used correctly, and details of the arrangements for the use of the admixtures. The architect should also confirm in his written approval the agreed procedure for use. Calcium chloride must never be used in reinforced masonry.

(b) Preparation of concrete

(i) Recommended mix
Concrete for core filling shall be ....(strength and/or proportions) with a slump of .... mm.
The concrete should be specified by the designer to satisfy the performance requirements of the wall, e.g., strength, sound insulation, thermal insulation and so on. A typical general mix for such purposes is 1 : 2½—3 : 2 with a slump of 125 mm.

(ii) Alternative mix
Alternative concrete mixes may be used subject to written approval.

(5) Reinforcement, wall and bonding ties

(a) Reinforcement
The reinforcement for ....(location) shall be ....(type/size) to BS ....
For type indicate type of reinforcement (mild steel, high yield steel, etc.). For size indicate length and diameter (reference to drawing/schedule often required). Reinforcement for cores should generally not exceed 16 mm.

(b) Bed joint reinforcement
The bed joint reinforcement for .... (location) shall be ....(type/size/reference number) and comply to ....(BS or other).
For type indicate mild steel, high yield steel, etc. For size indicate length, diameter (reference to schedule) and for proprietary bed joint reinforcement indicate width and/or manufacturer's reference number and manufacturer.

(c) Bonding ties
Metal strips or mesh for bonding .... (location) shall be ....(material and BS) of dimension ....
The particular bonding tie to be specified must take account of the conditions of exposure to which it will be subjected. Such ties, when used at control joints, should not affect the performance of joints. Quote dimensions or refer to drawing.

(d) Wall ties
Wall ties shall be ....(description) to ....(BS or other)
The particular wall tie to be specified must take account of the conditions of exposure, sound insulation and structural requirements to which it will be subjected. Butterfly ties to BS 1243 will be the most common tie for concrete masonry. Where stiff ties are needed for special structural requirements, additional consideration should be given to the question of accommodation of movements (*Chapter 16*) and its effect on sound insulation (*Chapter 14*).

(6) Handling

(a) Cement
Cement should be stored in dry conditions and be used in order of delivery

(b) Sand
Store sands separately according to type, prevent contamination

(c) Metals
Ties should be stored to prevent metal becoming rusty and contaminated
Reinforcement to be free from loose mill scale and rust

(d) Blocks
Facing blocks shall be carefully unloaded to avoid damage. All blocks to be stacked on prepared level areas to avoid ground contamination. Stacks to be covered to prevent saturation and facing blocks to be protected to avoid becoming stained or marked
Covering and protection of blocks is desirable to minimize effects of subsequent shrinkage, loss of bond and maintain appearance.

(7) Testing

(a) General
Independent testing of blocks shall be carried out strictly in accordance with Clause 13 of BS 6073:Part 1

(b) Special category manufacturing control
Quality.control and compliance procedure shall be in accordance with Clause 6.5 of BS 6073:Part 1

17.3.2.2 Workmanship

(1) General

(a) Dimensions
All blockwork shall be set out and built to the respective dimensions, thickness and height indicated
When detailing, consideration should be given to the size and position of openings to allow for a full unit to be positioned correctly directly beneath a lintel bearing.

(b) Uniformity
All work to be plumbed and levelled as the work proceeds

(c) Bond
The work shall be built to the bond indicated on the drawings or schedule. Where no bond is indicated, the units shall be laid in stretcher bond, half lap. Where possible the coursing to be arranged to allow a full block to be positioned directly beneath a lintel bearing
The purpose of arranging a full block beneath a lintel is to reduce vertical alignments of perpend joints which may induce cracking.

(d) Cutting
Blocks used for facing shall be cut with a masonry saw. Where cut wet they shall be allowed to dry before use

(e) Chases
Chasing shall be as indicated on the drawings and carried out with a chasing tool unless otherwise approved
General chasing should not be permitted as this may affect the serviceability of the wall (CP 121).

(f) Weather
Protect units separated from stacks before use. Take precautions during cold weather to prevent frost damage to fresh mortar. Brace constructions to prevent damage by winds or other causes
The general precaution during cold weather is to either stop laying when the air temperature is close to freezing, at say 3°C or less, or ensure a minimum temperature of 4°C in the work when laid and thereafter prevent the mortar from freezing until hardened. Problems can still exist even when initial air temperatures are above 3°C if overnight temperatures are expected to be low, or the units are very cold (CP 121).

(g) Laying
All units to be laid and adjusted to final position while mortar is still plastic

(2) Mortar joints

(a) Bedding
Units shall be laid on a . . . .(full, shell mortar bed). Vertical joints shall be filled. Joints to be nominally . . . . .mm thick
Most masonry will normally be laid on a full bed of mortar of normal thickness 10 mm. Shell bedding is used occasionally in an attempt to improve the rain resistance of single leaf walls but it will reduce the loadbearing capacity of the wall.

(b) Joint types

(i) Facing work
Joints for . . . .(location) shall be . . . .(specified profile).
The tooling of joints shall be carried out to the specified profiles while the mortar is thumb-print hard

(ii) Standard work
Joints shall be . . . .(struck or raked) for . . . .(plastering, rendering, etc.) at . . . . (location)
Advice as to whether the wall needs to be struck or raked can be obtained from the block manufacturer.

(c) Excess mortar
Any mortar which extrudes from the joints of fair faced units shall be cut away and not smeared onto the face of the block

(d) Reinforced walls
The cores shall be kept clear and clean of mortar droppings and any extruding mortar shall be removed while soft. Clean out holes to be provided at the bottom of core

243

A simple method for providing for clean out is to sit the ends of the first row of blocks on bricks.

(3) Control joints
Control joints shall be constructed as indicated on the drawings. Expansion joints shall be cleaned out to ensure the mortar does not bridge the joint
Attention is drawn to *Chapter 16* and CP 121 with reference to thermal and other movements. It is important that control joints should be clearly drawn to show positions and details of any ties.

(4) Double leaf (cavity) walls

(a) Wall ties
The walls shall be built with cavities of the width shown on the drawings and tied together with ties embedded in the mortar at least 50 mm spaced in accordance with the following table:

Least leaf thickness (mm)	Cavity width (mm)	Spacing of ties	
		Horizontally (mm)	Vertically (mm)
75	50 — 75	450	450
90 or more	50 — 75	900	450
90 or more	75 — 100	750	450
90 or more	100 — 150	450	450

The spacing may be varied providing that the number of ties per unit area is maintained. Additional ties shall be provided in every course within 225 mm of openings and on each side of control joints. Ties shall be laid falling to the external leaf

(b) Cavities
The cavity and ties shall be kept clean and any extruding mortar shall be struck off flush. No cavity shall be sealed off until instructed.

(c) Weepholes (cavity walls)
Weepholes 10 mm wide by 75 mm high shall be provided at not more than 900 mm centres through the vertical mortar joints of the outer leaf, at ground level and at positions where the cavity is bridged
Weepholes enable the water which penetrates the outer leaf to escape.

(5) Partitions
Partitions shall not be built on suspended slabs until after the props have been removed
Allowance may need to be made for the deflection of the slab or beam.

(6) Reinforcement

(a) Reinforcement
The reinforcement shall be of the size and number as shown on the drawings and be positioned accurately, to maintain the specified cover
Reference should be made to *Chapter 9* for the recommended cover.

(b) Bed joint reinforcement
Bed joint reinforcement shall have a side cover of not less than . . . ., *be continuous except at*

control joints or where otherwise indicated, and be located as shown on the drawings

(7) Core filling
Cores shall be filled in lifts not exceeding . . . .*(height). The concrete to be fully compacted by tamping.*
To ensure that the cores can be cleaned and the concrete fully compacted the designer should, before allowing or specifying lifts in excess of 450 mm, insert additional clauses or confirm in writing to the contractor the agreed procedure for core filling. Full height filling, maximum 3 m, will ease construction and reduce costs.

(8) Lintels
Concrete block lintels shall be positioned and reinforced as shown on the drawings and filled with concrete as specified. Block lintels are to be propped during construction. All lintels shall have a minimum bearing length of . . . .*mm*
Where lintels other than block lintels are to be used, they should be specified in this section. The bearing length will depend on structural requirements. A nominal minimum length of 150 mm is reasonable.

(9) Protection

(a) Stability
Precautions shall be taken to ensure stability of walls during backfilling and concreting operations

(b) Finished work
The tops of constructed walls shall be protected from rain and in addition fair faced work shall be protected against staining from construction activities

(10) Making good
At the completion of the work all temporary holes in mortar joints of fair faced work shall be filled with mortar and suitably tooled. Any damaged blockwork shall be repaired with approved materials or replaced

17.3.2.3 Related work The following items, although not part of the masonry, are connected with masonry construction and should, unless included in the masonry section, be adequately covered elsewhere in the main specification.

(1) Sealing
Joints around door and window frames, control joints, abutting joints at external columns and other joints where sealing is indicated shall be brush painted with . . . .(type or name) *primer and filled with* . . . .(type, colour or name) *sealant to manufacturer's recommendations*
It is important to ensure that the specified sealant is suitable for the particular width and tolerance of the joint to be sealed.

(2) Flashing
Wall flashings shall be built into or secured to the masonry as shown on the drawings and be provided with . . . .*mm laps*

It is important that to ensure the flashings are effective they should be clearly detailed. The use of certain dissimilar materials can cause problems (attention is drawn to CP 121).

(3) Damp-proofing

(a) Damp-proof courses
Horizontal damp-proof courses shall be positioned so as to fully cover the thickness, be laid on an even bed of fresh mortar and covered by mortar so as to maintain regular joint thickness. While exposed, they shall be protected from damage. Stepped damp-proof courses at openings shall extend beyond the end of the lintel by at least 100 mm. Vertical damp-proof courses shall be of ....(width) and be fixed so as to separate the inner and outer leaves of the wall. The material for damp-proof courses shall comply with BS 743
Particular care is to be taken in detailing and positioning of damp-proof courses and attention is drawn to CP 121 and BRE Digest 77.

(b) Tanking
Tanking and water-proofing of basement walls or retaining walls shall be carried out to the details as shown on the drawings and all materials are to be used in accordance with the manufacturer's recommendations

(4) Backfilling
Backfilling shall not be placed against concrete masonry walls within ....days of completion of the construction. Vehicles shall not be closer to the wall than a distance equal to the height of the wall

(5) Painting
Painting shall not commence until the surface of the walls has been allowed to dry out and has been cleaned down to remove all dust, dirt and mortar dabs. Where efflorescence occurs, it shall be removed with a cloth or stiff brush prior to painting
For guidance on painting of walls see BRE Digests 197, 198 and 163. Recommendations on the painting of buildings are given in CP 231. Paint for use directly in contact with masonry needs to be alkali resistant.

(6) Rendering
Newly applied rendering, including stipple and spatter-dash coats, shall be kept damp for the first three days. A second coat shall be not applied until the previous layer has hardened for seven days. The surface of the rendering shall be finished as specified. The block surface and subsequent rendering coats may be damped sufficiently to control suction but not saturated. Rendering shall not be applied to frost bound walls or during frost conditions. Any rendering shall be discontinuous at control joints
The type of rendering and preparation required should be related to the background material and exposure conditions. Clauses given here are of a general nature. As many materials exist it is suggested that the manufacturer of the blocks or BS 5628 should be referred to and suitable clauses specified. General advice is that each subsequent coat should not be thicker than that which precedes it. Designation (iii) renders are usually adequate for most purposes. Strong renders should be avoided.

(7) Plastering
Before plastering, all dirt, dust and efflorescence shall be removed. The walls shall be treated and plastered in accordance with the manufacturer's recommendations. Any plastering shall be discontinuous at control joints
As many materials exist it is suggested that the manufacturer of the blocks or BS 5492 should be referred to and suitable clauses specified.

(8) Wall tiling
Before tiling all walls shall be allowed to dry to the level recommended by the tiling manufacturer. Movement joints shall be provided at control joints and other locations recommended by the tiling manufacturer
As many materials exist it is recommended that the manufacturer of the blocks or BS 5385 should be referred to.

The documents referred to in the previous specifications and guidance notes are as follows:

BRITISH STANDARDS

BS 12	Ordinary and rapid hardening Portland cement
BS 146	Portland — blastfurnace cement
BS 743	Materials for damp-proof courses
BS 882	Aggregates from natural sources for concrete
BS 890	Building limes
BS 1165	Clinker aggregates for concrete
BS 1200	Sands for mortar for plain and reinforced brickwork, block walling and masonry
BS 1243	Metal ties for cavity wall construction
BS 3148	Methods of tests for water for making concrete
BS 3797	Lightweight aggregates for concrete
BS 4027	Sulphate resisting Portland cement
BS 4551	Methods of testing mortars and specification for mortar testing sand
BS 5224	Masonry cement
BS 6073	Precast concrete masonry units Part 1: Specification for precast concrete masonry units Part 2: Method of specifying precast concrete masonry units

CODES OF PRACTICE

CP 111	Structural recommendations for loadbearing walls
CP 121	Walling Part 1: Brick and block masonry
CP 231	Painting of buildings

BS 5262	External rendered finishes
BS 5385	Wall tiling
	Part 1: Internal ceramic wall tiling and mosaics in normal conditions
	Part 2: External ceramic wall tiling and mosaics
BS 5492	Internal plastering
BS 5628	Structural use of masonry
	Part 1: Unreinforced masonry

OTHER DOCUMENTS

BRE Digest 77	: Damp proof courses
BRE Digest 163	: Drying out buildings
BRE Digest 197 & 198:	Painting walls

17.4 Enforcement of specifications

In simple terms, specifications, apart from their legal aspect, are an attempt to ensure that certain important aspects are conveyed to the site. Although it could be argued that having written the specification the designer need pay them no more attention until a problem occurs, it would be wise to watch for non-compliance as work proceeds. For example, in a case where problems eventually arise with mortar, where, perhaps in the first instance it appears too soft. A long and often complicated period then follows for all parties and, in many instances, although not always fully justified, results in hardened analysis of the mortar which for arguments sake lets say indicates incorrect mix proportions. Assuming also that this was one of those jobs where the specification called for the mortar to be batched by use of gauge boxes. Eventually there will no doubt be the familiar, 'Well, of course, I've never seen a gauge box on this site anyway'. 'Oh yes you have, they make the tea on it'.

Surely if the designer considers that the specifications are important it would be far better to bring non-compliance to the attention of the contractor during and not after the event. Equally well, the contractor should accept that the designer has written the specifications for a good reason. This again returns to one of the original points made, that if the specifications are clear, simple and explicit they are more likely to be used.

Since the designer will be unable to pay attention to all specification points during the contract, the following is a short list of faults often encountered and which cause problems:

(1) unfilled perpends — particularly important in separating walls;

(2) mortar incorrectly batched;

(3) render incorrectly batched or wrong thicknesses;

(4) control joints (movement joints) incorrectly formed;

(5) units not covered or stored correctly;

(6) units used too soon after manufacture, or whilst too warm;

(7) correct bonding pattern not maintained in walls to be rendered;

(8) portions of blocks used under lintel bearings;

(9) wrong type of bed joint reinforcement or inadequate length.

17.5 References

17.1 NATIONAL BUILDING SPECIFICATION. Volumes 1—6. NBS Services, Newcastle-upon-Tyne, 1982.

17.2 BRITISH STANDARDS INSTITUTION. BS 2028, 1364: 1968 *Precast concrete blocks*. BSI, London. pp 44

17.3 BRITISH STANDARDS INSTITUTION. BS 1180: 1972 *Concrete bricks and fixing bricks*. BSI, London. pp 20

17.4 BRITISH STANDARDS INSTITUTION. BS 6073: Parts 1 and 2: 1981 *Precast concrete masonry units*. Part 1: *Specification for precast concrete masonry units* (pp 12) and Part 2: *Method for specifying precast concrete masonry units* (pp 8). BSI, London.

18

Blemishes, faults and problems

18.1 Introduction

The purpose of this Chapter is to provide general information on some of the problems which can occur in masonry construction from time to time. Detailed information on common defects in buildings and remedial measures can be found in another publication[18.1]. This Chapter deals with cracks in masonry, colour variation in walling, stains, efflorescence and lime bloom, chemical attack and rendering.

18.2 Cracks in masonry

If a building is adequately designed and there is no excessive differential foundation movement, significant cracking should not develop. There are, however, occasions when cracks do develop and this Section is intended to give guidance as to the cause of particular problems. Information on the provision of movement joints and other measures to cater for the effects of movement are presented in *Chapter 16,* which also contains some guidance on the differential movement of the various masonry materials (concrete, clay and calcium silicate) and some design and construction faults which can give rise to cracking. This Section is mainly concerned with foundation and other structural movements.

To identify the cause of cracking one of the first steps should be to try to discover the mechanism of the movement. In many instances cracks will be found to taper over the wall height. The narrowest width of the crack is taken as a fulcrum point from which the likely direction of movement can be postulated. A number of examples are given in Figure 18.1, which it is hoped can be developed to deal with the particular building under investigation.

Depending upon the relative sizes and strengths of units and mortar, the crack may appear either as a stepped crack running from bed joint to perpend alternately up the wall or it may run vertically or diagonally through the units. Before repair to any cracking can be attempted, the cause must first be determined and then a decision made as to whether or not the movement has stopped. In the case of foundation movement, remedial measures, such as underpinning, may be needed to prevent further problems. Assessment of damage in low rise buildings is given in BRE Digest 251[18.2].

Cracks due to shrinkage and thermal contraction in concrete masonry tend to be fine and are generally best left alone, particularly where the surface is rendered. Attempts at repair often make the cracks more conspicuous, unless of course the rendering is to be repainted. With rough cast type renders any cracking will normally go unnoticed. In the particular case of cracking of rendered fired-clay brickwork some consideration should be given to remedial measures since the sulphates which are present in many bricks can, as a result of moisture entering through the crack, attack the rendering. All building materials, such as bricks, blocks, timber, and so on, are continually undergoing some small movement due to changes in moisture content or temperature and complete cure of cracking is, therefore, very difficult. However, subsequent cracking will usually be far less of a problem.

Where cracks along the mortar are to be made good, the mortar should be raked back at least 25 mm, and preferably 50 mm, and slightly undercut if possible. The gap should be brushed to remove loose material and lightly wetted. A mortar of the same designation (assuming it to be correct in the first place) and materials should be pushed firmly into place and when thumb print hard should be tooled to the required profile. The repaired area should then ideally be kept moist or covered with polythene to prevent rapid drying. Another method which can be tried, particularly where further small movement is still expected, is to rake back 25—30 mm and fill with a mastic of similar colour to the existing mortar. Some of the mortar removed as a result of the cutting back can then be tooled into the mastic, and with care a good match can be achieved.

18.3 Colour variation in walling

The use of units from different manufacturing batches can lead to distinct 'banding' or 'patches' in the finished wall and is the most common cause of colour variation in masonry. The problem is, of course, most apparent with fairly smooth faced, evenly textured units, and

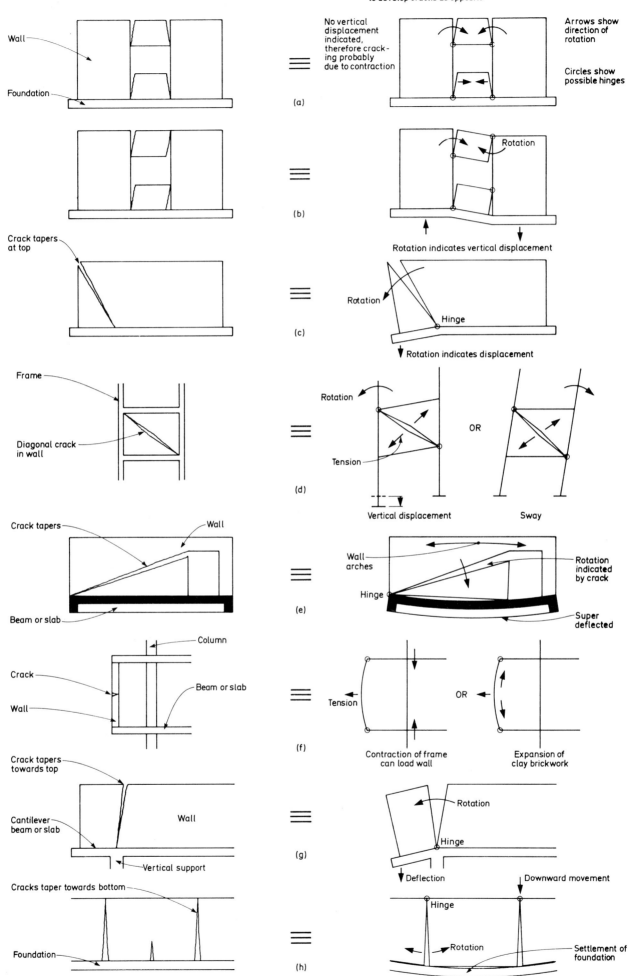

Figure 18.1 The rotation concept: (a) no displacement indicated possible contraction (b) rotation indicates displacement (c) (d) (e) floor deflection (f) (g) cantilever deflection (h) floor/foundation settlement

ideally pallets should be opened and the blocks mixed to ensure an even dispersion of colour variation. With many units natural variations occur or variations are introduced during manufacture to produce a wall with a less uniform appearance.

A second source of problems stems from the incorporation of water proofers during manufacture. If for any reason individual blocks or parts of batches have received a different dosage or no dosage of water proofer leading to more absorbent units being built into the wall, unsightly differential water retention at points where these blocks have been used will appear. The same phenomenon can also occur when blocks are made with markedly different absorption characteristics, but modern quality control procedures have made this comparatively rare.

A third source of colour variation in masonry walling occurs in the mortar joint. With some sands differences in water content of the mix can lead to very pronounced colour variations in the hardened mortar, and strict control of batching on site is needed, not allowing retempering and prolonged wet mortar life. Where coloured mortars are to be produced by means of additives the problem is even more acute and consideration should be given to the use of pre-bagged mortars to achieve greater consistency during mixing.

18.4 Stains on masonry

As a result of site activities or vandalism stains can occasionally occur on masonry and this Section has been included to give some guidance on the methods available for attempting to remove them. The removal of a stain from masonry is often a difficult process and sometimes produces disappointing results. Care has to be taken to avoid damage or spoiling of the surface of the masonry. The difficulties which may arise can be categorized by three factors:

(1) masonry surfaces are generally porous so that both stains and applied cleaning solutions tend to become absorbed in the surface texture;

(2) concrete units and mortars are chemically reactive and can dissolve in some cleaning solutions more readily than the materials causing the stain;

(3) local treatment, although removing the stain, may alter the texture or colour sufficiently to cause a different blemish.

For these reasons it is wise to remove the stain as soon as possible. The two basic methods of removing stains are chemically and mechanically.

18.4.1 Chemical cleaning

Materials which may be used for removing stains from masonry include acids, organic solvents and emulsifying agents. To combat the tendency of the masonry to absorb the cleaning liquids the materials are sometimes mixed into a paste with talc, whiting or other powder. Applied to the masonry, the mixture draws the stain out to the surface. Such pastes often need to be covered with polythene to prevent the solvents from drying out too quickly.

Corrosive and poisonous chemicals *must* be handled with extreme care. It is advisable to wear rubber gloves, goggles and so on, when applying them and indeed to seek expert advice before using the materials; particularly if large quantities are to be used. A few chemical methods for removal of the more common stains encountered are given below. It is obviously desirable to experiment on small discrete areas initially to assess the effect upon the stain and any other possible side effects. Where chemical methods are employed it is advisable to wash off residues with water after treatment.

18.4.1.1 Rust Rust is difficult to remove as it is more chemically inert than the concrete surface but light staining can sometimes be removed by lightly etching the surface with 5—10% solution of hydrochloric acid for a few minutes and then washing down with water. Alternatively, wetting the surface thoroughly with several applications of 15% sodium citrate solution and applying a layer of sodium dithionite crystals held in place by a paste of whiting and water may work.

18.4.1.2 Oil Particularly if recently spilt, oil can be removed by brushing the surface with a proprietary engine cleaning fluid and then flooding with water to flush away the emulsified oil. Alternatively, scrubbing the surface with a strong detergent solution and then washing with water can be effective. Another method which has been suggested is to make a smooth stiff paste from petrol and talc, apply to the stain and cover with polythene or similar to prevent rapid evaporation. Several applications may be needed to completely remove the stain.

18.4.1.3 Creosote Creosote can be removed by applying a paste of talc and petrol and then scouring the surface to complete the removal.

18.4.1.4 Bitumen, asphalt and coal-tar products Again these can be removed by application of a paste of talc and petrol, but as much of the material as possible should be scraped off prior to application of the paste.

18.4.1.5 Paints A certain amount of consideration is needed in the removal of paints since there are a variety of types. Oil-based paint can often be removed with a proprietary solvent or alkaline paint remover. Chlorinated rubber paints may need special strippers such as naptha. Cement paints are obviously difficult to remove without affecting the concrete surface. The information given in BRE Digest 197[18.3] may be of use in some cases. Special graffiti removing products are now also available.

Other stains can be treated with organic solvents, bleach solutions and acids to ascertain which is the best chemical to remove them. Chemical cleaning methods are basically applicable to sudden stains caused by site activity and such like. Some long term stains resulting from dirt or algal or fungal growths are often removed by mechanical methods, although algal and fungal growths can be removed chemically by applying a solution of domestic bleach and, after a few days, scrubbing off the dead material.

18.4.2 Mechanical cleaning

Mechanical methods, including high pressure water cleaning and steam cleaning, are often used to remove dirt, grime and fungal growths. Gritblasting can be used very effectively in the removal of dirt and grime, but this method also removes some of the surface, thus altering the surface texture.

18.5 Efflorescence and lime bloom

Efflorescence is the term commonly used to describe the white discolouration which forms on masonry and concrete surfaces. The formation of the discolourations vary depending upon the soluble salt or salts from which it originates. With salts such as calcium sulphate, sodium sulphate, potassium sulphate and magnesium sulphate (particularly when in combination), the salt goes into solution in water and is carried to the surface where it crystallizes as the water evaporates. Some of these salts are often present in fired-clay bricks and can be the cause of the white deposits on brickwork. This crystal formation is the medium normally responsible for the efflorescence on fired-clay brickwork.

With concrete units and mortar the predominant salt is calcium hydroxide which is formed as a product of the chemical reaction between the cement and water. Calcium hydroxide is slightly soluble in water and under certain conditions it can be carried through to the surface and there reacts with carbon dioxide from the atmosphere to produce a surface deposit of calcium carbonate. This can, and normally does, take place within the wet surface. The surface deposit is normally extremely thin which is demonstrated by the fact that when the surface is wetted, the film of water on the surface commonly renders the deposit translucent and it seemingly disappears. This deposit is thus better and more commonly referred to as 'lime bloom' or 'lime running'.

Efflorescence and indeed lime bloom or running is a function of many interrelated factors and although steps can be taken to reduce the likelihood of its occurrence, total prevention is very difficult to achieve. Where the masonry is exposed to the weather, the rainwater, which may once have helped in the formation of the deposit, being also slightly acidic, slowly dissolves the deposit which is thus reabsorbed into or washed from the wall. The continuing rainwater carrying the dissolved material will penetrate into and down the wall. The process continues until the surface deposit is removed and equilibrium conditions exist at which time any remaining salts having been washed in by the rain are insufficient to return to the surface. This condition is normally reached within a year. Occasionally,

disturbance of the equilibrium conditions can cause a recurrence of the deposits.

The cause of efflorescence or lime bloom on some new structures can often be traced to poor storage on site and construction/design faults, which permit vast quantities of water to run down and through the stored materials or constructed walls. It is impossible to prevent the normal amount of rain falling on the newly constructed walls but particular attention should be given to the possible discharge from the roof prior to the structure being waterproofed. In some designs, delays in waterproofing the roof can result in large quantities of water pouring down through the walls and causing even worse efflorescence problems. Although the deposits on the external walls may eventually be removed by rainwater, the internal walls, particularly those which are left fair faced, will have the white deposits, some of which can be brushed or washed off. Lime bloom or lime runs (calcium carbonate) can be removed by washing with 5—10% solution of hydrochloric acid.

In some instances it may be necessary to paint the surface to achieve an acceptable appearance, but it is important to determine and rectify the cause of efflorescence before painting, otherwise further development of the salts can force the paint from the surface. The most practical solution is to apply a white latex or emulsion paint, since they can be applied to damp surfaces and, more importantly, will still allow the wall to breathe. The efflorescence can then form on the surface without damaging the paint, and since most efflorescence is white, it should not be noticeable on the surface. Occasional brushing may also be beneficial.

18.6 Chemical attack

Chapter 3 which dealt with materials provided general guidance on the quality of materials recommended for normal durability situations. One item in particular which should be emphasized is that Portland cement which is used for both units and mortar is not resistant to acid attack. In such situations, for instance in a silage retaining wall, where mild acid attack may occur, the wall should be covered by two coats of chlorinated rubber or similar protective paint system.

Oil paints should not be applied to concrete surfaces without first applying an efficient alkali-resisting primer. Such paints, however, are not normally resistant to acid attack.

18.7 Rendering

If cracking occurs in the rendering but does not continue into the supporting masonry, the problem is likely to lie in the preparation and materials used for the render. This section is intended to give basic guidance on the principal items necessary for good rendering. Consideration of these items may be used for initial assessment of the problem. More comprehensive information can be found in the publication *External*

250

Rendering[18.4], published by the Cement and Concrete Association.

18.7.1 Materials

In general the materials which should be used for rendering are similar to those required for mortar except that the sand will normally need to be coarser and comply with BS 1199[18.5].

18.7.2 Preparation of background

Since there is a wide range of masonry materials, each with its own texture, size and absorption or suction characteristics, it is necessary to carefully consider each material to assess the amount and type of surface preparation required. There are so many materials that it is only possible to write in very broad terms. In general, however, the masonry can be classified into the following categories: dense strong and smooth materials; moderately strong, porous materials, and moderately weak, porous materials. Many of the materials will benefit from having the mortar joints raked out.

18.7.2.1 Dense, strong and smooth materials
Dense concrete blocks, concrete bricks, and dense clay blocks not provided with a key to take the rendering may fall into this category. Where the surface is smooth, a stipple coat may be required, particularly with larger units and where the joints are not raked. A stipple coat is a thick slurry (1 part cement to 1½ parts clean sharp sand gauged with water to which an equal quantity of 'bonding' agent has been added), vigorously brushed into the surface and immediately stippled with a bannister brush to form a close textured key.

18.7.2.2 Moderately strong, porous materials
Most lightweight aggregate blocks fall into this category, as do clay and sand lime bricks. These types of masonry material generally have fair suction and good mechanical key. Occasionally, where suction is too great or uneven suction exists, a stipple coat or spatterdash may again be required.

18.7.2.3 Moderately weak, porous materials
Autoclaved aerated concrete blocks and some lightweight aggregate blocks may fall into this category, as do some of the softer types of fired-clay brick. These materials are rather varied and a satisfactory key may be obtainable without additional preparation. Where excessive suction exists the wall may require 'damping down' (not soaking) prior to rendering, and again a stipple coat or spatterdash can be used to control suction. With some materials a water retentive admixture, such as methyl-cellulose can be used in the rendering to prevent too rapid drying out and to enable it to be worked satisfactorily.

18.7.3 Mix proportions and thickness

The type of render will primarily depend upon the background material, degree of exposure and a few other factors which may also apply. In general a type (iii) cement:lime:sand (1:1:5–6) is the type of render used on masonry walls. Richer renders than this can cause problems due to higher drying shrinkage. Obviously there are also a number of factors governing thickness of render, but the general rule is that no coat should be stronger than the coat which preceeds it. In fact, ideally, each successive coat should be made thinner than the immediately preceeding coat. The undercoat should be of maximum thickness 15 mm and should be combed to prevent undue stresses forming as the rendering hardens and shrinks and to provide a key for subsequent coats. With some dense, strong materials a maximum overall thickness (undercoat plus final coat) of 15 mm may be called for.

18.7.4 Curing

It is obviously very important to cure the rendering adequately at all its various stages. Stipple and spatterdash coats, undercoats and final coats should all be prevented from rapid drying out, particularly during hot weather. Ideally they should be kept damp for three to four days and then be allowed to dry out for a few days before application of a further coat. Protection from rain and frost may also be necessary.

18.8 References

18.1 ELDRIDGE, H J. Common defects in buildings. HMSO, London, 1976. pp 486

18.2 BUILDING RESEARCH ESTABLISHMENT. BRE Digest 251: *Assessment of damage in low rise buildings*. BRE, Garston, 1981. pp 8

18.3 BUILDING RESEARCH ESTABLISHMENT. BRE Digest 197: *Painting walls*. Part 1: *Choice of paint*. BRE, Garston,

1977. pp 8

18.4 MONKS, W. AND WARD, F. Appearance matters — 2: External rendering. Cement and Concrete Association, Slough. Publication No 47.012. pp 32

18.5 BRITISH STANDARDS INSTITUTION. BS 1198, 1199, 1200: 1976 *Building sands from natural sources*. BSI, London. pp 8

19

Statistics and quality control

19.1 Introduction

Quality control covers a very wide spectrum and takes in a large number of different theories, disciplines and tests. This Chapter concerns itself with the role statistics play in quality control, examining the statistical methods a producer might adopt to control production and the statistical tests the purchaser carries out to establish whether the product satisfies the Specification. Both the producer and the purchaser appear at opposite ends of this quality control spectrum, each assessing the quality of the product by their different methods. They are clearly different because, in the first instance, the producer has, in principle at least, the entire production at his disposal whereas within the confines of the relevant British Standard the purchaser has rather a small number of results to assess the quality. Quality then, as far as the purchaser is concerned, is often related to, and sometimes interpreted as, compliance with an associated British or other Standard. Quality is taken by the producer as the current performance relative to some pre-determined bench mark frequently selected as a minimal value required to satisfy a particular compliance clause.

In the following paragraphs statistical assessments are made of some of the compliance clauses of British Standards related to masonry, followed by statistical methods which a producer may be expected to carry out to control his production. Both are preceded by a consideration of what variability is and how it can be measured.

19.2 Variability

In any mass production it is inevitable that certain variations will exist not only within the basic materials required for production but also in the manufacturing process itself. For example, a concrete block producer may decide to adopt a target strength of 4.5 N/mm² for all his blocks. He would not expect all the blocks to be the same strength, some would be higher and some would be lower, although a large proportion should be very close to the target and a number should actually be 4.5 N/mm². These differences or errors exist for a

number of reasons. Some can be attributed to slight changes in the basic materials used, whilst others are caused by small differences in the manufacturing process itself. The errors may be random in nature, such as differences between batches of concrete for the blocks caused by weighing errors or variations in moisture content of the aggregates. Other errors may occur in a more systematic way, one example of which would be if a producer has a multi-block machine, the strength pattern within each 'drop' of blocks always appears the same, with blocks dropped in certain positions having lower strengths than others.

Variability is often measured as a standard deviation. A distinction must be drawn between a standard deviation calculated from sample data and the 'true' standard deviation of which the sample data is only an estimate. The true value is rarely known in practice, though by taking a sufficiently large sample the value can be estimated to a reasonable degree. Here we will represent the true value by the symbol σ and a standard deviation from a sample of data by the letter s.

The formulae which provides an unbiased estimate of σ is:

$$s = \sqrt{\frac{\sum_{i=1}^{n} (X_i - \overline{X}_n)^2}{n - 1}} \quad \dots\dots\dots\dots(19.1)$$

where n is the sample size, $\overline{X}_n$ is the average value of the sample and X_i is successively each result in the sample. The method of evaluation is given in the following examples.

Example 1: A concrete brick producer has the following 10 results from which a standard deviation needs to be calculated. In evaluating formula (19.1) the producer will find the calculations easier if he uses a tabular approach as shown in Table 19.1, which gives:

$$\overline{X}_n = \frac{\sum_{i=1}^{n} X_i}{n} = \frac{290.8}{10} = 29.08 \simeq 29.1 \text{ N/mm}^2$$

253

Table 19.1

Specimen number	Compressive strength (N/mm^2)	Difference from average value	Square of difference
1	36	6.9	47.61
2	36.1	− 3	9
3	30.9	1.8	3.24
4	29.1	0	0
5	35.3	6.2	38.44
6	33	3.9	15.21
7	23.7	− 5.4	29.16
8	31.4	2.3	5.29
9	26.2	− 2.9	8.41
10	19.1	−10	100
	$\sum\limits_{i=1}^{n} X_i = 290.8$		$\sum\limits_{i=1}^{n} (X_i - \bar{X}_n)^2 = 256.36$

Now, $s = \sqrt{\dfrac{\sum\limits_{i=1}^{n}(X_i - \bar{X}_n)^2}{n-1}} = \sqrt{\dfrac{256.36}{(10-1)}}$

$= \sqrt{\dfrac{256.36}{9}} \simeq 5.3$

The value of 5.3 has, therefore, been calculated from a sample of 10 specimens. Clearly if a further sample of 10 specimens were taken, the standard deviation may well be a different value to that for the first sample. It is possible to place confidence limits about a sample standard deviation in order to be confident to a certain degree that the unknown true value, σ, will be contained within the computed limits. To establish limits easily, the multipliers given in *Table A1* of *Section 19.5* may be used. For a sample of size $n = 10$ and a confidence interval of, say, 90% (i.e., we are 90% confident that σ will lie within the interval computed), the upper and lower limits are as follows:

$$1.65 \times 5.3 = 8.7$$
$$0.73 \times 5.3 = 3.9$$

Thus the brick producer may say that he is 90% confident that σ lies in the interval 3.9 to 8.7 N/mm^2. Obviously this range could be reduced either by increasing the sample size or reducing the level of confidence.

It should be noted that this method of calculating standard deviations is quickened with the use of calculating machines with pre-programmed standard deviation routines. If a calculator does not possess such a routine, the computation can still be simplified by modifying formula (19.1) to read:

$$s = \sqrt{\dfrac{\sum\limits_{i=1}^{n} X_i^2 - \dfrac{\left(\sum\limits_{i=1}^{n} X_i\right)^2}{n}}{n-1}} \quad \ldots\ldots\ldots\ldots(19.2)$$

which is computationally easier as all that is required from the data are n, $\sum\limits_{i=1}^{n} X_i^2$ and $\sum\limits_{i=1}^{n} X_i$, bypassing the problem of calculating $\bar{X}_n$ and subtracting it from each value before squaring the differences.

When the sample size is small the estimate of σ given by formula (19.1) or (19.2) will be rather poor. Generally speaking, for a good estimate a sample size of about 30 or more results will be required.

Several methods exist for approximating standard deviations. Two which are particularly useful are the mean range method and the graphical method using normal probability paper. The mean range method provides a fairly quick estimation of standard deviation from a sample:

$$s \simeq \dfrac{w}{d_n} \quad \ldots\ldots\ldots\ldots\ldots\ldots(19.3)$$

which states the approximation where w is the range within a sample of size n and d_n is a constant depending upon the sample size. Values for d_n are given in *Table A2* of *Section 19.5*.

Example 2: Estimating the standard deviation with the mean range method using the data in the previous example. The range is calculated as the highest value minus the lowest value, as given in Table 19.2, i.e., $w = 36 - 19.1 = 16.9$.

Table 19.2

Specimen number	Compressive strength (N/mm^2) X_i	
1	36	← Highest value
2	26.1	
3	30.9	
4	29.1	
5	35.3	
6	33	
7	23.7	
8	31.4	
9	26.2	
10	19.1	← Lowest value

From formula (19.3): $s \simeq \dfrac{w}{d_n}$

as the sample contains 10 items, d_n becomes d_{10} which can then be read from Table A2 (*Section 19.5*) as 3.078.

Thus:

$$s \simeq \dfrac{16.9}{3.078} \simeq 5.5$$

The value obtained using formula (19.1) was 5.3.

It will be seen from Table A2 that there are no values for d_n beyond $n = 10$. Although further values can be computed[19.6], it is found that other methods provide better estimates and so the Table has been truncated. This does not mean that it is not possible to estimate a standard deviation with n larger than 10 by the range method. The procedure is to sub-divide the sample into equal sized sub-groups arranging that the number in each sub-group is equal to or less than 10. Observe the range for each sub-group and compute the mean or average range, $\bar{w}$, of the sub-group ranges. Replacing w by $\bar{w}$ in formula (19.3), s is estimated as before; the value of d_n is selected according to how many values are in each sub-group. A certain amount of care is required to avoid bias by selecting values during sub-division of the original data. It is preferable to use a random method of assigning the data to the sub-groups otherwise any bias may falsify the results. If larger volumes of data are available, perhaps 40 results or more, then a graphical method to approximate the standard deviation may be appropriate.

Example 3: The data given are 50 test results from a concrete block manufacturer. The data are analysed for mean value and standard deviation using the graphical method and are shown in Table 19.3. In Figure 19.1 the data in Table 19.3 has been classified and plotted onto normal probability paper. From this a producer may estimate the mean strength and standard deviation of the sample as follows. By definition 50% of the results should lie above the mean value and 50% below it. Therefore $\overline{X}$ is estimated at the 50% point on the graph as indicated in Figure 19.1, in this case it is 8.1 N/mm².

Table 19.3 Block producer's data

Specimen number	Compressive strength X_i (N/mm²)	Specimen number	Compressive strength X_i (N/mm²)
1	6.82	26	8.64
2	9.55	27	8.07
3	6.23	28	9.77
4	7.27	29	9.2
5	8.07	30	9.89
6	6.71	31	8.52
7	7.61	32	9.32
8	5.23	33	6.02
9	7.16	34	11.48
10	8.64	35	7.27
11	9.32	36	8.3
12	8.63	37	7.39
13	8.41	38	8.06
14	9.32	39	9.55
15	7.5	40	6.82
16	8.64	41	7.5
17	7.39	42	9.09
18	8.18	43	5.91
19	6.82	44	6.36
20	9.77	45	7.39
21	7.16	46	6.82
22	7.5	47	8.3
23	9.09	48	7.27
24	7.39	49	9.32
25	9.09	50	8.18

The estimation of the standard deviation is just a little more involved. Table A3 *(Section 19.5)* tabulates for a normal distribution the proportion of the distribution lying outside any given multiple of the standard deviation below or above the mean value. It is evident from Table A3 that when displaced by one standard deviation below the mean value, 16% of the distribu-

tion will lie beyond. Thus when the strength below which 16% of the distribution lies is read off from the graph in Figure 19.1, this strength will be about one standard deviation below the mean value found earlier. Hence the difference between this value and the previously estimated value for $\overline{X}$ will be the estimate of *s*. From Figure 19.1 this is 1.2 N/mm². Values of 8.03 N/mm² and 1.24 N/mm² are obtainable for $\overline{X}$ and *s* when formulae are used on the data.

It should be noted that the normal probability paper shown in Figure 19.1 is valid only for normally distributed data. The paper has been constructed such that when normally distributed data are plotted, the graph should be a straight line. Most often test results will be normally distributed. Each normal distribution is defined by the two parameters: the mean value (μ) and the standard deviation (σ). The symbol μ is used here to represent the 'true' mean value in the same sense that σ represents the 'true' standard deviation. The normal distribution is symmetrical and rather bell shaped, it is the most commonly occurring frequency in nature. Figure 19.2 is a schematic representation of a normal distribution. If the data does not come from a normal distribution, the method will no longer be valid and the plotted points will appear to lie on a curved line rather than a straight line. Figure 19.3 illustrates such a situation.

Should non-normality manifest itself the conclusions from such analyses may be misleading. If this method is to be pursued with non-normal data, either the underlying distribution must be identified and the appropriate probability paper used, or a transform must be performed on the data to make them approximately normal. After transformation the normal probability paper is used as before. There are several transforms available such as taking logarithms of the data or squaring all the data, cube roots, and so on. Before attempting a transform, it would be advisable to consult a statistician. Statistical tests do exist to determine whether or not data belongs to a specified distribution[19.3].

Another way to express variability is to quote the coefficient of variation. This is simply the ratio of the standard deviation to the mean value, often expressed as a percentage. If a set of *n* data were available, the coefficient would be calculated using formula (19.4):

$$\kappa = \frac{100\,s}{\overline{X}_n} \quad ....(19.4)$$

where *s* and $\overline{X}_n$ are found as before from formula (19.1). It is possible to calculate κ directly without having to find *s* and $\overline{X}_n$ with a modified version of formula (19.4):

$$\kappa = \frac{100}{\overline{X}_n} \sqrt{\frac{\Sigma\,(X_i - \overline{X}_n)^2}{n-1}} \quad ....(19.5)$$

This is the formula given in BS 6073[19.12].

The virtues of the coefficient of variation are that it is dimensionless and that it provides a way of comparing variabilities from different strength levels; variation often rises with increasing strength level.

Example 4: Calculating the coefficient of variation using the data in *Example 1*. From *Example 1*, with formula (19.1) we have:

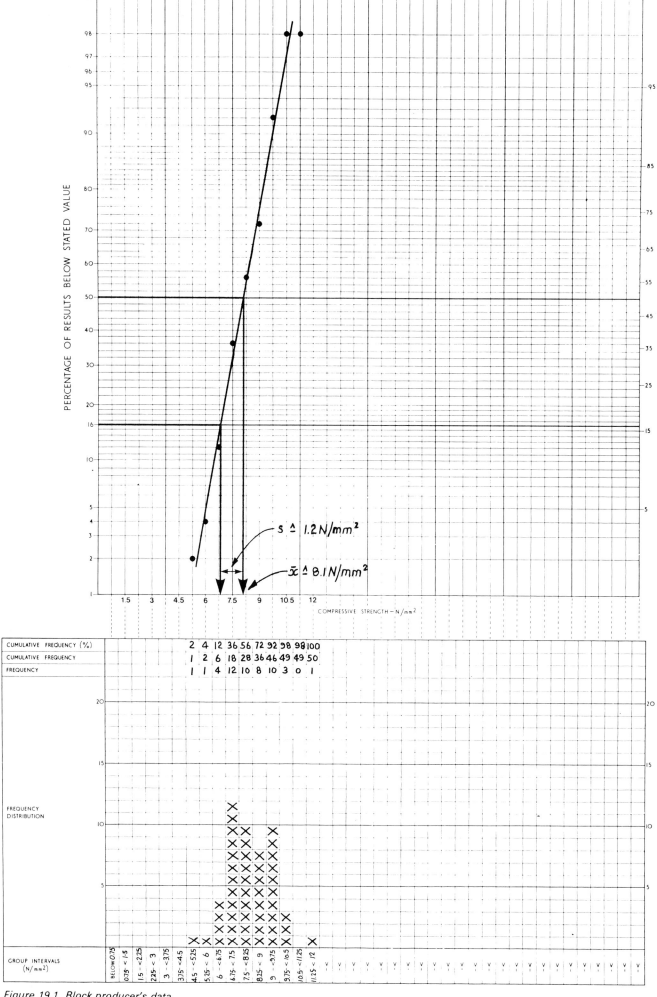

Figure 19.1 Block producer's data

256

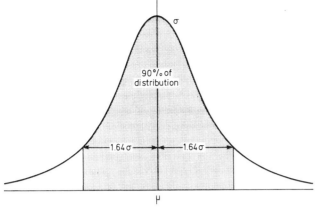

Figure 19.2 A normal distribution

$$s \simeq 5.3 \text{ N/mm}^2 \quad \overline{X} = 29.1 \text{ N/mm}^2$$

thus with formula (19.4):

$$\kappa = \frac{100 \times 5.3}{29.1} \simeq 18.2\%$$

19.3 Compliance

A producer should spend time and effort examining his data, estimating standard deviations and so on, so that he may judge where to aim his production to have a high chance of complying with any given specification. A purchaser should also understand the risks that he takes of failing to detect non-complying products with the compliance clauses available. It is not a trivial decision taken by the producer when selecting the product target strength. The first step towards reaching this decision should be to make a detailed analysis of the compliance clauses outlined within the specification and the subsequent production of an operating-characteristic (O-C) curve. An O-C curve reports the probability that a consignment of a given quality will be accepted by the compliance clauses. Generally speaking one expects that when quality is good the consignment has a very high chance of passing whereas there should be a low chance of passing when the quality is poor. Figure 19.4 provides a schematic diagram of an O-C curve. Usually, the more discriminating the compliance clauses the steeper the gradient of the O-C curve.

The method of computation of such curves can be complex and sometimes involves the use of computer simulation. Occasionally it is reasonably straightforward to calculate using ordinary probability theory. The method of calculation in detail is considered to be beyond the scope of this book and only the O-C curves of the compliance clauses where applicable are presented.

British Standards 1180[19.14] and 2028[19.4] have been superseded by a new Standard, BS 6073:1981 *Precast concrete masonry units*[19.12]. Contained therein are compliance clauses for both concrete blocks and bricks.

19.3.1 Compliance clauses for concrete blocks

The set of compliance clauses given in BS 6073 related to concrete blocks depend on whether the blocks are produced to normal or special manufacturing control. The differences between normal and special manufacturing control are explained in *Clause 27.2.1* of BS 5628:Part 1:1978[19.13] and are further defined in other sections of this handbook.

19.3.1.1 Normal manufacturing control The compliance clause for normal blocks contained in BS 6073 requires that the compressive strength is not less than the specified strength and that no individual block strength shall be less than 80% of the specified strength*. As in the case of the compliance clause relating to concrete bricks, the term compressive strength is defined as the average strength of a sample of 10 blocks and that the specified strength is supplied by the purchaser and may be taken from Table 19.4.

Table 19.4 Available strengths for specification of concrete masonry units

Blocks (N/mm²)	Bricks (N/mm²)
2.8	7
3.5	10
5	15
7	20
10	30
15	40
20	
35	

Example 5: A purchaser having specified a strength of 3.5 N/mm² has data from a sample of 10 blocks as given in Table 19.5. According to the first requirement the compressive strength required is 3.5 N/mm². The sample given provides a compressive strength of 3.8 N/mm²† and so satisfies the first requirement. The second requirement is that no individual block strength be less than 80% of the specified strength, in this example 2.8 N/mm². From Table 19.5 it can be seen that one block strength is less than 2.8 N/mm² and so the second requirement has not been met. The O-C curves of these two requirements are given in Figures 19.5 and 19.6, when the specified strength is 3.5 N/mm². Similar curves can be produced for different specified strengths.

It is quite apparent that the second requirement in this clause dominates the first and will consequently require the producer to aim at a target mean strength (TMS) higher than that which he might otherwise think necessary to provide a reasonably low producer risk. Figure 19.7 is the O-C curve of the combination of the

---

*An amendment has been agreed deleting the 80% requirement on individual blocks and replacing this by $\overline{X} \geqslant 0.9G + 0.62S$, where $\overline{X}$ = the compressive strength, G = the specified strength, S = the standard deviation.
†BS 6073 requires that for specified strengths of 7 N/mm² or less each block strength must be reported to the nearest 0.05 N/mm² and for specified strengths in excess of 7 N/mm² to the nearest 0.1 N/mm².

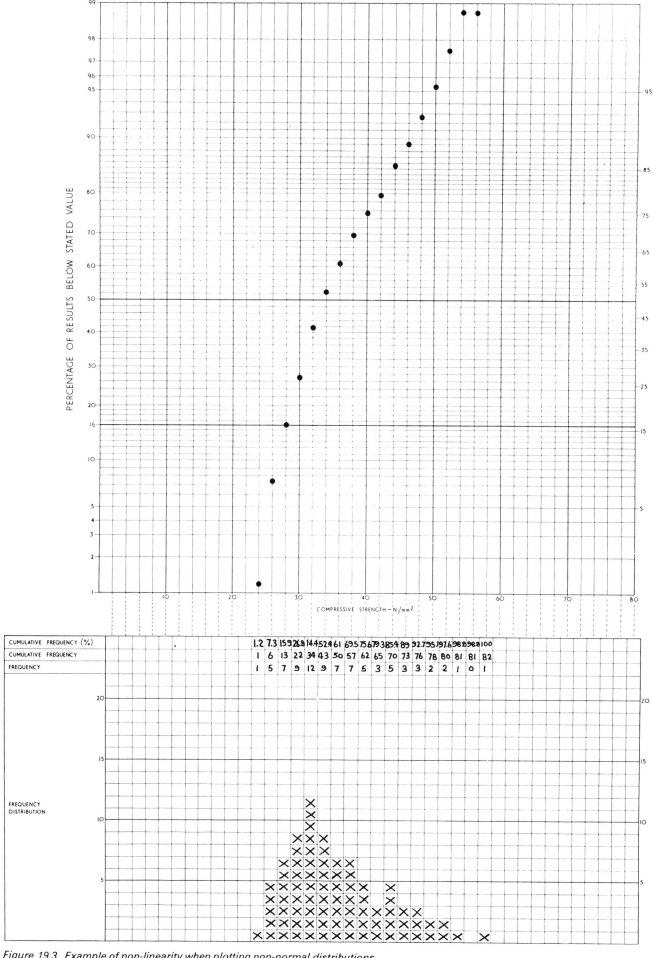

Figure 19.3 Example of non-linearity when plotting non-normal distributions

258

Figure 19.4 Schematic representation of an O –C curve

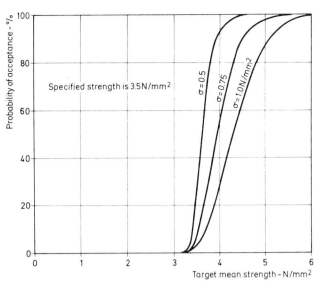

Figure 19.7 O–C curve of the whole compliance clause for blocks in BS 6073[19.12]

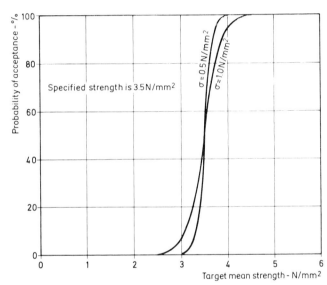

Figure 19.5 O–C curve of the compressive strength requirement for blocks in BS 6073 in BS 6073[19.12]

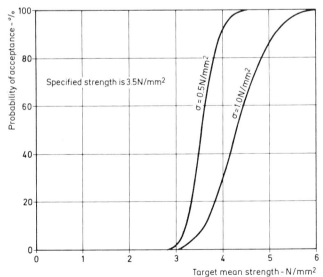

Figure 19.6 O–C curve of the 80% requirement for blocks in BS 6073[19.12]

Table 19.5

Result (i)	Strength (N/mm²)
1	3.3
2	3.65
3	4.5
4	5
5	2.85
6	4.25
7	4.55
8	2.6
9	3.65
10	3.5

two requirements of this clause and illustrates that when the specified strength is 3.5 N/mm², a producer having a standard deviation of 0.75 N/mm² should aim at 4.75 N/mm² to have a producer risk of 5%. Figure 19.7 also shows that the purchaser has virtually no risk of accepting blocks not conforming to his specified strength of 3.5 N/mm². Indeed even if a producer manufactured at 10% below the specified strength the purchaser carries virtually no risk at all of accepting, irrespective of the specified strength level or the producers standard deviation as is plain from Table 19.6.

Table 19.6 Probabilities (%) of accepting blocks 10% below specified strength

| $\frac{G}{\sigma}$ | Probability (%) of accepting blocks 10% below specified strength, G | | |
	Mean of 10 rule	80% rule	Combined
3.5	13.3	1.1	0.1
5	5.7	2.5	0.1
7	1.4	6.3	0.1
10	0.1	17.8	<0.1

G is specified strength and σ is the producer's standard deviation

19.3.1.2 Special manufacturing control The compliance clauses for special blocks are more complicated than for normal blocks in that they require a second sample to be tested should the first not provide sufficient evidence to either accept or reject the consignment. The entire procedure is illustrated in Figure 19.8 as a flow chart. Each sample comprises of 10 blocks and the compressive strength ($\overline{X}$) and the sample standard deviation (s) are calculated. The specified strength is represented by G.

Example 6: A purchaser has specified a strength of 10 N/mm² with a special category of manufacturing control. A sample of data has been obtained and the results are shown in Table 19.7.

Table 19.7

Result (i)	Strength (N/mm²)
1	12.8
2	11.9
3	13.1
4	13.7
5	10.6
6	10.7
7	12.9
8	12.4
9	12.3
10	9.4

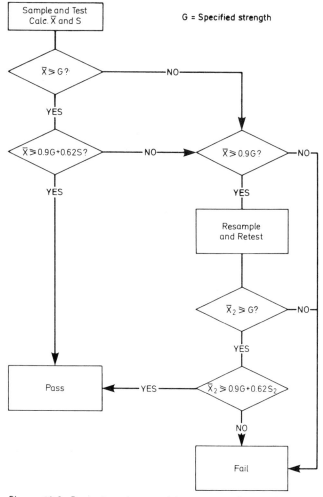

Figure 19.8 Procedure for special category of manufacturing control

From this first sample of 10 specimens the compressive strength ($\overline{X}$) and sample standard deviation (s) are calculated to be 12 N/mm²* and 1.3 N/mm² respectively. The first requirement states that the compressive strength be greater than or equal to the specified strength of 10 N/mm². As the compressive strength is 12 N/mm² the first requirement has been met. The second requirement calls for:

$$\overline{X} \geq 0.9\,G + 0.62\,s \quad\quad\quad (19.6)$$

As G is 10 N/mm² and from the sample s is 1.3 N/mm²†, the compressive strength must be equal to or greater than 9.8 N/mm². The second requirement is then satisfied and the consignment is deemed to comply.

As the procedure for judging compliance is somewhat complicated, it has been decided to present the O-C curves as those of the first requirement with those of the second requirement separately. Figure 19.9 illustrates the O-C curve of the first requirement whilst Figure 19.10 illustrates that of the second. These curves are based on the work of Sym[19.10 19.11] in developing suitable compliance clauses for special category manufacturing control. It is evident that when the standard deviation is small it is the first requirement which dominates the second and when the standard deviation is large the reverse situation is true.

19.3.2 Compliance clauses for concrete bricks *

As in the case of concrete blocks, bricks may also be produced to normal or special manufacturing control.

19.3.2.1 Normal manufacturing control BS 6073[19.12] requires that the compressive strength shall not be less than the specified strength and that the coefficient of variation for the sample shall be less than 20%.

In this compliance clause the compressive strength is taken to be the average strength of the sample of 10 bricks and the specified strength is that strength provided by the purchaser. A list of strengths available is given in BS 5628:Part 1:1978 *Code of Practice for the structural use of masonry* Part 1: *Unreinforced masonry*[19.13] and is reported in Table 19.4.

Example 7: A purchaser specifies a strength of 20 N/mm². A sample of bricks has been selected and the results are as shown in Table 19.8.

Table 19.8

Result (i)	Strength (N/mm²)
1	24
2	20
3	20
4	14.
5	25.
6	20
7	22
8	18.5
9	20
10	21.5

*BS 6073 requires that for specified strengths of 7 N/mm² or less each block strength must be reported to the nearest 0.05 N/mm² and for specified strengths in excess of 7 N/mm² to the nearest 0.1 N/mm².

†Although not reported in BS 6073 the sample standard deviation rounded to the nearest 0.05 should be accurate enough in this instance.

The compressive strength of the sample is 20.5 N/mm² and this value will satisfy the first requirement that the compressive strength is not less than the specified strength. The sample coefficient of variation may be

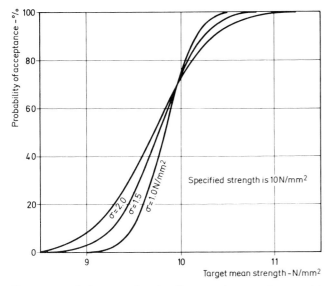

Figure 19.9 O–C curve for the first requirement for special category blocks in BS 6073[19.12]

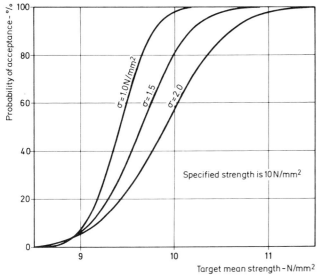

Figure 19.10 O–C curve for the second requirement for special category blocks in BS 6073[19.12]

Figure 19.11 O–C curve for the compressive strength requirement for bricks in BS 6073[19.12]

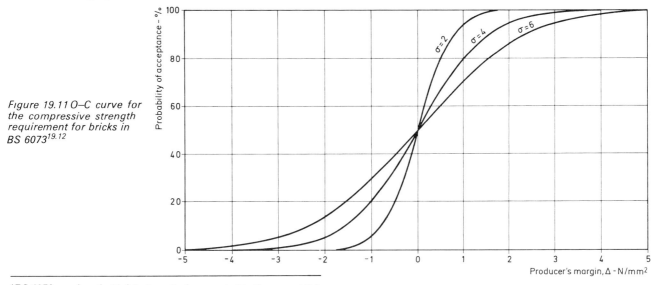

computed directly using formula (19.5), and using the above data this is found to be 15%*. As the maximum permitted value is 20%, the sample also satisfies the second requirement. The purchaser may then assume that the bricks conform to his specification.

Figure 19.11 is the O-C curve for the first requirement and illustrates the chance that a sample of 10 bricks drawn from a production having a margin of Δ N/mm² will satisfy the compressive strength requirement. The margin will be the difference between the specified strength and the target strength selected by the producer. It will be seen that a producer with a standard deviation as low as 2 N/mm² does not require as large a margin as a producer with a higher standard deviation. A producer may reasonably be expected to use a margin that will provide him with a high chance of acceptance, i.e., a lower producer risk. It is the producer's decision as to which risk he will accept; clearly the smaller the risk, the larger the margin required.

The purchaser also takes a risk of accepting bricks which are in the main of a lower strength than specified although a sample of 10 satisfy the first requirement. From Figure 19.11 it can be seen that the purchaser's risk increases with the producer's standard deviation.

When deciding upon the margin to select, the producer needs to examine the effect of the coefficient of variation requirement. The O-C curve of this second requirement is given in Figure 19.12. The producer, knowing the value of σ, may select a margin from Figure 19.11. This will fix the value of κ, i.e. $\frac{\sigma}{\mu}$. If this value, κ, is less than 15% the producer will accept a small risk of failing the second requirement. Thus, if a producer with $\sigma = 4$ N/mm² decides to accept a risk of 2% for the first requirement, the margin selected from Figure 19.11 will be 2 N/mm². If the specified strength is 20 N/mm² the producer must have a target strength of 22 N/mm². This will provide a value κ of about 18% and the producer may conclude that his margin needs to be greater as a value of 18% for κ will almost result in a 1 in 3 risk of failing the second requirement from Figure 19.12. To reduce this risk the producer should

---

*BS 6073 requires that brick strengths be reported to the nearest 0.5 N/mm² and that values for coefficient of variation be recorded as the nearest 1%.

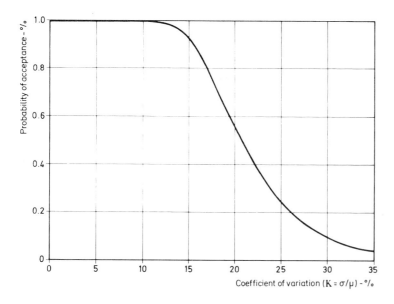

Figure 19.12 O–C curve of the coefficient of variation requirement for bricks in BS 6073[19.12]

arrange that κ be 15% or less and, as there is little chance of reducing σ the only option available is to increase μ, the target strength. In this case the target strength will need to be raised to approximately 26.5 N/mm² and in so doing the risk of failing the first requirement will be virtually nil. Clearly the inclusion of this coefficient of variation requirement can be rather costly. However, a purchaser may be comforted to know that if a producer aims the target strength at only 1 N/mm² below the specified strength, the compliance clause is almost certain to detect the low strength in only one test of the compliance rules.

19.3.2.2 Special manufacturing control The special compliance procedure for bricks is the same as given in *Section 19.3.1.2* for blocks.

19.4 Control charts

Having selected a target mean strength (TMS), a producer will decide upon a mix design and suitable manufacturing process. Once production has begun the strength level will need to be monitored as the producer cannot be sure that the chosen quantities and process will provide the selected TMS and production might begin with an achieved mean value different to the TMS. The producer will also be unsure that the achieved mean value has not differed from the selected TMS during production. In addition to all this the producer's standard deviation may fluctuate and, depending on whether it rises or falls, the producer may be holding his head or rubbing his hands!

It is important for a producer to observe these situations as an unexpected rise in strength will yield a much lower producer risk than originally chosen and would, therefore, make the production less economic. On the other hand, a fall in TMS would expose the producer to a much higher risk than he bargained for. Figures 19.5 to 19.7 and 19.9 to 19.12 all demonstrate producer risks and how they change as the target mean strength alters. As an example, a producer of bricks manufacturing to a specified strength of 20 N/mm² with a coefficient of variation of, say, 10% will need to aim at a TMS 1 N/mm² above the specified value of 20 N/mm² to provide a risk of about 5%. If this TMS slips by, say, 0.5 N/mm² the risk will increase to about 22% (see

Figures 19.11 and 19.12). A concrete block manufacturer with a standard deviation of 1 N/mm² manufacturing 3.5 N/mm² normal category blocks for a 5% producer risk would select a TMS of 5.4 N/mm², as shown in Figure 19.13. Figures 19.14 and 19.15 illustrate the effect on the producer risk if the TMS rises or falls. In the case of Figure 19.14 the producer must raise the TMS by either changing the production process or by modifying the mix design to reduce the producer risk. Figure 19.15 presents the opposite situation, the producer could reduce strength as a 1% producer risk might be regarded as excessive.

Figures 19.16 and 19.18 illustrate the effect of a changing standard deviation upon the producer risk. From Figure 19.16 it can be seen that the producer risk is at 20% whereupon the producer would wish to return to the selected 5%. It is not possible to 'control' a standard deviation directly and consequently the producer must modify the TMS to alter the producer risk. Figure 19.17 indicates the position of the TMS when σ = 1.25 N/mm² to restore the producer risk to 5% whilst Figure 19.19 shows the new TMS when σ = 0.75 N/mm². Figure 19.19 indicates that a strength of 4.7 N/mm² will be sufficient to provide a 5% producer risk. Any producer thus lowering his TMS from 5.4 N/mm² to this new level on the basis of a fall in the standard deviation from 1 N/mm² to 0.75 N/mm² is moving his TMS nearer to the specified strength of 3.5 N/mm². Should the standard deviation jump back to 1 N/mm² it would immediately expose the producer to a risk of about 25%. Caution is, therefore, recommended when reducing the TMS in line with reducing σ. Also, any producer wishing to produce special category masonry units must monitor his production, by stipulation given in BS 5628:Part 1:1978:Clause 27.2.1.2(b)[19.13]. The problem then remains of what a producer can do to monitor TMS and σ so that changes in these parameters can be seen.

19.4.1 Shewhart charts
Charts with action and warning lines drawn into them, as illustrated in Figure 19.20, are often known as Shewhart charts. The Shewhart chart is easy and straightforward to use. If a result lies outside either action line, the interpretation is that the TMS of the process has

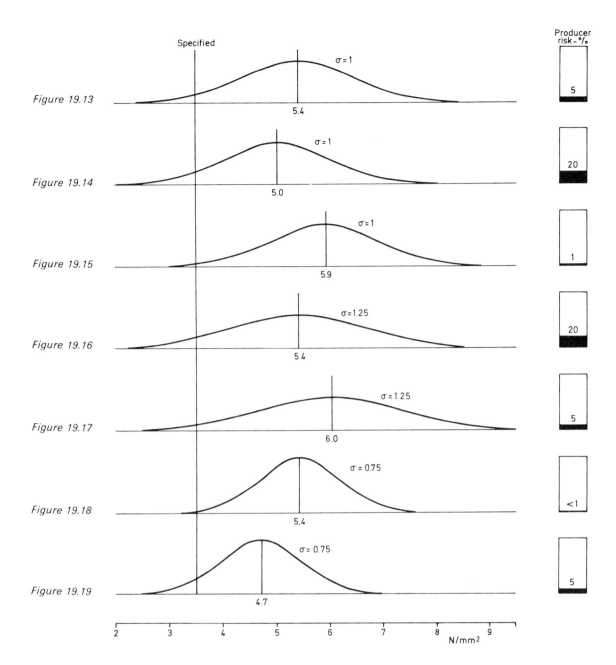

Figure 19.13

Figure 19.14

Figure 19.15

Figure 19.16

Figure 19.17

Figure 19.18

Figure 19.19

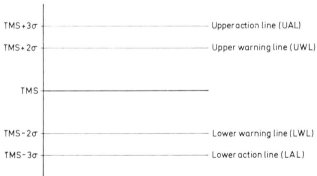

Figure 19.20 An example Shewhart chart

shifted to a different position and corrective action is required. If the result lies inside the action lines, the process is considered to be *in control* unless two consecutive results lie between the same pair of action and warning lines whereupon the interpretation is that the process TMS has moved. The positions of these lines may be chosen to suit the process under inspection and those shown in Figure 19.20 are only an example. The charts under discussion here are for normally distributed variables such as strength or density of bricks or blocks. If a non-normal variable was being monitored the design of these charts would be different.

It is most beneficial, if possible, to plot the average of four or five results onto the chart. The average of four results is a better estimate of the true process mean value than an individual result, and the variability exhibited by such averages may be calculated as the parent population standard deviation (σ) divided by the square root of the number of single results going to make up the average, i.e., $\sigma/\sqrt{n}$. This quantity is often referred to as the standard error. So, for averages of four, the standard error would be $\sigma/\sqrt{4}$ or $\sigma/2$. Thus, when plotting averages the action and warning lines will be closer to the TMS and might be positioned at TMS $\pm 3\sigma/\sqrt{n}$ and TMS $\pm 2\sigma/\sqrt{n}$ respectively. However, some people prefer to plot single results. Results are plotted sequentially across the chart as illustrated in the following example:

Example 8: A concrete block producer has a TMS at 5.3 N/mm² with a standard deviation of 0.7 N/mm². A chart with action lines set at TMS $\pm 3\sigma$ and warning lines at TMS $\pm 2\sigma$ has been selected as shown in Figure

263

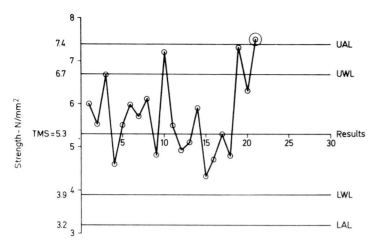

Figure 19.21 Shewart chart example (ALs:TMS $\pm$ 30σ; WLs:TMS $\pm$ 20σ)

19.21. The producer's data given in Table 19.9 may then be plotted:

Table 19.9

Result (i)	Strength (X_i) (N/mm^2)
1	6
2	5.5
3	6.7
4	4.5
5	5.5
6	6
7	5.7
8	6.1
9	4.8
10	7.2
11	5.6
12	4.9
13	5.1
14	5.9
15	4.3
16	4.7
17	5
18	4.8
19	7.3
20	6.3
21	7.5

It is evident from Figure 19.21 that result 21 exceeds the UAL. Assuming the standard deviation has not altered, the *high result* will be indicative of one of the following three situations:

(i) the TMS has risen above the chosen value of 5.3 N/mm^2;

(ii) the TMS is still at 5.3 N/mm^2 and this result is simply one of those rare but possible values;

(iii) the TMS has fallen below 5.3 N/mm^2, although this result is extremely rare.

The rule used with these charts is that if a result exceeds the UAL a rise in TMS is assumed. In the case of situation (i) above this would be the correct conclusion and the further the TMS rises above 5.3 N/mm^2 the more likely a signal above the UAL. Examining situa-

tion (ii), should this be the real situation the signal above UAL would be spurious, i.e., a false conclusion that the TMS was above 5.3 N/mm^2. The risk of such spurious signals can be calculated. For the chart in this example the action lines (ALs) are placed at TMS $\pm$ 3σ, as the data are assumed to be *normal* the probability of a result occurring above the UAL when the TMS is stationary can be estimated using a normal distribution table such as Table A3 in *Section 19.5*. Here there is a 0.15% chance that a result would naturally occur beyond 3σ above TMS, i.e., about once every 670 results. If (iii) was the true situation, the producer would be taking the opposite action to that required and therefore wrongly adjusting the TMS. However, the likelihood of this is small. The spurious signal resulting in the TMS being lowered when in reality the process mean level had fallen as suggested in (iii) is very unlikely. If the process had fallen to say 5 N/mm^2, about 0.5σ, the probability of having a signal above UAL is 0.0003, i.e., about one in 3325.

Having detected a signal on the chart the second stage is to assess how far above the 5.3 N/mm^2 the TMS has moved. It would not be enough to analyse all the data (21 results), compute the average of these and estimate the change in TMS (δ) as the difference between this average and 5.3 N/mm^2. This approach may lead to an underestimate of the real difference.

$$\delta = \overline{X} - 5.3 \text{ N/mm}^2 \ldots\ldots\ldots\ldots\ldots(19.7)$$

From the data. $\overline{X}$ = 5.7, so from formula (19.7), δ would be estimated as 0.4 N/mm^2.

It is important to inspect the data plotted on the chart. In this example the majority of the data, results 1 to 18, appear to be centred upon 5.3 N/mm^2 and only the last three results are differently centred. Thus, a better estimate of δ would be obtained by comparing the average of these last three results with 5.3 N/mm^2. In this way the estimate of δ would be 1.7 N/mm^2. In this situation the producer would be expected to be rather conservative as the strength level will be reduced. The producer might, therefore, estimate a value of the currently achieved TMS such that there is only a 10% chance that the true mean strength of the product could be lower than $\overline{X}$. Table A4 of *Section 19.5* can be used to make such estimations. As the standard deviation in the sample is given as 0.7 N/mm^2

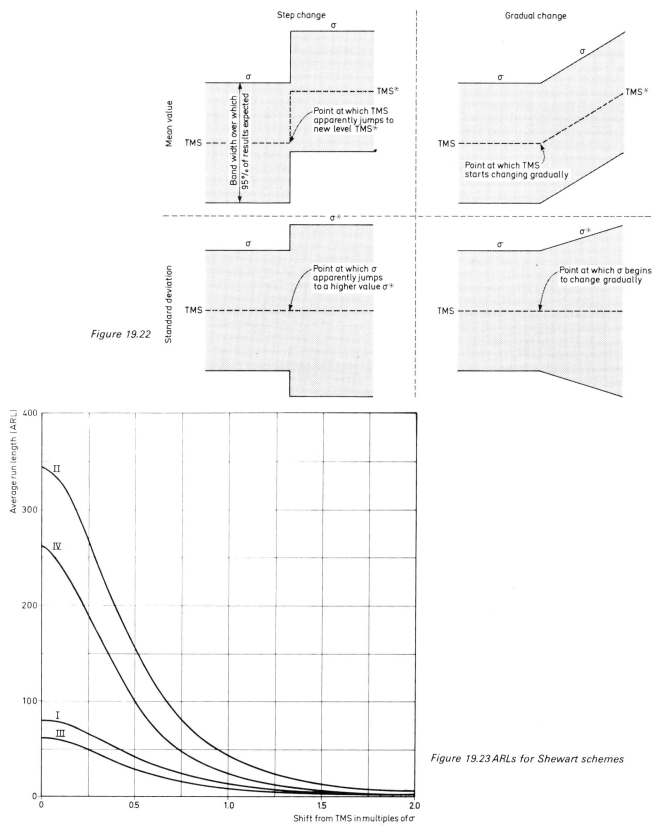

Figure 19.22

Figure 19.23 ARLs for Shewart schemes

and there are three results in the data segment under suspicion, the value of 0.52 is taken from Table A4. 0.52 is subtracted from the segment average of 7 N/mm² giving a value of 6.48 N/mm². In this way, δ should be re-estimated as 6.48 − 5.3 ≃ 1.2 N/mm². The producer now has to modify the process to remove the 1.2 N/mm² to restore the TMS to 5.3 N/mm².

The producer would be expected to investigate the reason for the process change. It may be possible to glean what might have caused the change by examining the chart for any change in the data and identifying any trends. Figure 19.22 provides a guide to the effect of changes in mean strength and standard deviation on the appearance of the data on the chart. However, there is often some interaction between the two and the subsequent patterns may become complicated and confused.

Wherever a control chart is being used it is important to know how rapidly the chart will respond to departures in TMS. An appropriate way to give the performance of the chart is to compute the average run length (ARL), i.e., the average number of results required to produce a signal when the TMS has moved by a certain amount. The ARL for four schemes are given in Table 19.10, and the ARLs of these four schemes are plotted in Figure 19.23.

Table 19.10 ARLs of four 'Shewhart' styled schemes

Shewhart scheme		Shift from TMS in multiples of σ					
		0	0.25	0.5	1	1.5	2
ALs : TMS $\pm$ 2.5 σ	I	79	65	41	15	6.2	3.2
ALs : TMS $\pm$ 3 σ	II	345	266	151	44	15	6.2
ALs : TMS $\pm$ 2.5 σ WLs : TMS $\pm$ 1.64 σ	III	61	48	29	10	4.4	2.5
ALs : TMS $\pm$ 3 σ WLs : TMS $\pm$ 2 σ	IV	263	192	99	25	8.7	4

There are two important factors in such a table or graph. Firstly, the frequency with which the producer will be taking action on spurious signals, i.e., the ARL when the TMS has not moved (the zero shift column in Table 19.10). Secondly, the ARL when the TMS has moved by an *important* amount. It is usual in setting up a scheme to obtain as small an ARL as possible for this *important* shift combined with as long an ARL as is reasonable at zero shift. Most processes do not leap from one point to another, or from one mean strength level to another, they rather drift and meander about. The *important* shift in this context would be in the region of 0.5σ. From Table 19.10 it can be seen that the charts with ALs only set at TMS $\pm$ 2.5σ are quicker at detecting these shifts than those charts with ALs set at TMS $\pm$ 3σ. The speed of detection is increased by WLs. The penalty, however, is that the ARL at zero shift is reduced. Some attention should be given to the term ARL, for in the case where the ALs and the WLs are set at $\pm$ 2.5σ and $\pm$ 1.64σ respectively, the ARL when the process is 0.5σ away from target is 29. There is a 50% chance that the run length to provide a signal will be less than 20 and a 25% chance that it will be longer than 40. When the ARL is large the distribution of run length tends to be long and flat and it is equally likely that a signal will appear in only a few plots as in a large number of plots. Charts exist to monitor standard deviation[19.3, 19.6], which are based mainly, upon the range expected between small sets of data when the true standard deviation is known, and are consequently called *range charts*. It is usual to plot the range between successive results on another chart positioned beneath the control chart for the process mean and these two interpreted together. Action lines may be drawn upon the range chart and if the plotted ranges exceed the limits, then the process variability is deemed to have changed. The factors required in setting the action lines for range chart can be found in the *Bibliography*[19.3].

If the process is reasonably stable it may only be necessary to monitor the standard deviation two or three times a year using formula (19.3). This formula is preferred here to (19.1) as over a long period it is likely that the TMS will have moved or have been moved, and perhaps several times. To use (19.1) may lead to an overestimate of σ. When using (19.3) simply sum the

differences between successive results and divide the total by $(n - 1)$ where n is the number of results. For n results there will, of course, be $(n - 1)$ differences. This average difference can then be divided by 1.128 (from Table A2 of *Section 19.5*), the outcome being the estimate of the standard deviation.

19.4.2 Cusum charts

Cusum chart methods are another form of control chart and are an alternative to Shewhart charts. The philosophical difference between them is that Shewhart charts wait for high and/or low results to signal a shift in TMS whilst cusum charts use all valid data to determine the state of the production process. The word *cusum* stands for cumulative sum. Each time a new result becomes available it is compared with the TMS. The summation of all these differences, some of which should be positive and some negative, is a cusum. The following example describes such a calculation.

Example 9: Each result in column 2 of Table 19.11 has the TMS of 11.5 N/mm^2 subtracted from it producing a series of differences in column 3, some positive and some negative. Column 4 is a running total of these differences, i.e., a cusum. When cusum values are plotted they form a cusum trace (Figure 19.24). Clearly the trend shown by the trace is an important factor in deciding whether the TMS has shifted or not. If the process is in control a horizontal trend would be expected, and should the production process begin on target and remain on target the resulting trace will have a horizontal trend centred about zero. If the achieved mean value is μ, then:

$$TMS = \mu$$

and

$$\sum_{i=1}^{n} (X_i - TMS) \simeq 0$$

If the process is out of control then depending upon whether the achieved mean is higher or lower than the TMS the cusum trace will develop an upward or downward trend:

$$TMS + \delta = \mu \text{ (achieved is higher than TMS)}$$

Table 19.11

Result (i)	Strength (N/mm^2) (X_i)	Minus TMS 11.5 N/mm^2	Cusum (C_i)
1	11.3	-0.2	-0.2
2	12	0.5	0.3
3	11.9	0.4	0.7
4	12	0.5	1.2
5	11.7	0.2	1.4
6	11.9	0.4	1.8
7	10.8	-0.7	1.1
8	11.4	-0.1	1
9	12	0.5	1.5
10	11.3	-0.2	1.3
11	10.6	-0.9	0.4
12	10.5	-1	-0.6
13	10.9	-0.6	-1.2
14	10.8	-0.7	-1.9

i.e.,
$$\sum_{i=1}^{n} (X_i - TMS) \simeq n\delta \dots\dots\dots\dots(19.8)$$

or $TMS - \delta = \mu$ (achieved is lower than TMS)

i.e.,
$$\sum_{i=1}^{n} (X_i - TMS) \simeq - n\delta \dots\dots\dots(19.9)$$

These three cases are illustrated in Figure 19.25.

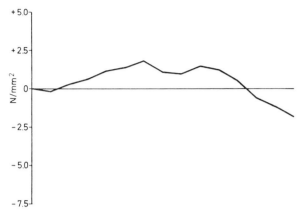

Figure 19.24 Example cusum trace

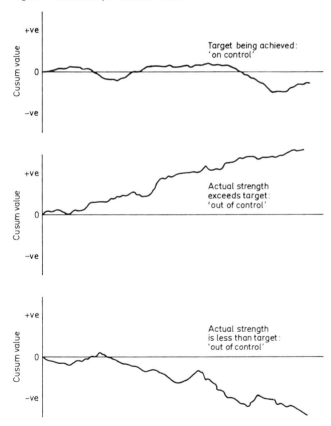

Figure 19.25 Examples of trends in cusum traces

A process may be in an off-target condition and then correct itself. This would cause a trend to develop whilst off-target but as soon as the process returns to TMS the trend will become horizontal, although no longer centred on zero. A popular misconception is that when a trace develops a positive or negative gradient, the process is missing the TMS by an increasing amount. In fact, it is a continuing statement that the process has shifted by a constant amount, δ, as suggested in formulae (19.8) and (19.9). If after n results the cusum has an absolute value of approximately $n\delta$,

then the average difference from TMS at each plotted value will be δ. If a process is moving further away from its TMS the gradient of the trace will not be constant but will be an increasing or decreasing gradient depending upon the movement in the process relative to the TMS. Not all trends will be assessed as important or significant. With a cusum system it is necessary to decide when a trace has developed a significant trend. One very successful method is to use a V-mask, which is shown in Figure 19.26. A V-mask, so called because it resembles a truncated V, has four elements: two action arms, a *lead point* and a central axis. Whenever a new cusum value is added to the cusum trace the V-mask is superimposed over the trace such that the lead point lies exactly over this latest point with the central axis of the mask kept parallel with the zero axis of the graph. Should any part of the trace extend outside either of the two action arms, it is a signal that the process is no longer at TMS. Figure 19.27 indicates a significant trend, whilst Figure 19.28 presents the data from Figure 19.24 with a V-mask superimposed on it.

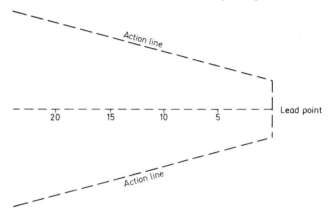

Figure 19.26 An example of a V-mask for superimposition over a cusum trace

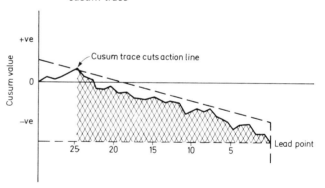

Figure 19.27 An example of a significant trend

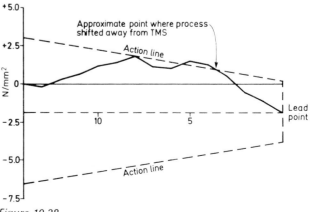

Figure 19.28

267

Unlike Shewhart charts, cusum charts provide a very clear indication from which result the process shifted. It is indicated at the most recent *cut point,* the intersection of the trace and the action arm nearest the lead point, and by counting from the lead point towards the cut point, the number of results since the shift took place are found. Then, using a formula such as (19.8) or (19.9), the shift in the process can be calculated.

The value of the cusum at the cut point may be substracted from the latest value of the cusum, i.e., the value at the lead point, and the difference divided by the number of results taken to detect the change, will yield the amount of shift:

$$\frac{(C_{lp} - C_{cp})}{n} = \delta \quad \cdots\cdots\cdots(19.10)$$

Using (19.10) and the data from Figure 19.28:

$$= \frac{(-1.9 - 0.9)}{3.5} = -0.8$$

thus, for the previous three or four results the process has not been at 11.5 N/mm² but at about 10.7 N/mm².

Having made the necessary corrections to the process, the producer must return the value of the cusum to zero, indicate the action taken on the chart, and then recommence monitoring.

Rather than have to evaluate (19.10) on each occasion, it is simpler to produce a *look-up* graph so that δ may be read off once given the number of results taken to detect the change, an example of which is provided in Figure 19.29. In some cases it may be better not to correct for the full amount δ, but a proportion of it, say, 75 or 80%. This is because the cusum can over exaggerate the real shift and, by adopting the full amount, may lead to the system *hunting* for the real shift.

The following two examples are of cusum systems[19.7]; the first designed to control the strength of concrete blocks and the second to control block densities. Figures 19.30 and 19.31 related to the first and Figures 19.32 and 19.33 to the second.

In setting up a cusum system careful thought must be given to the selection of the V-mask. Too shallow a gradient of the action arms may lead to too sensitive a

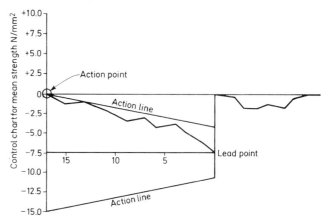

Figure 19.30 Cusum on strength (this trace on strength exhibits a significant decline – the cause was a deterioration in the steam venting system)

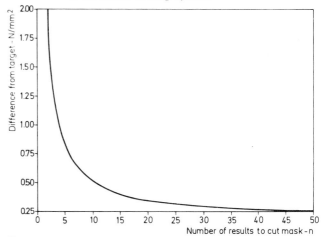

Figure 19.31 Look-up chart for mean strength

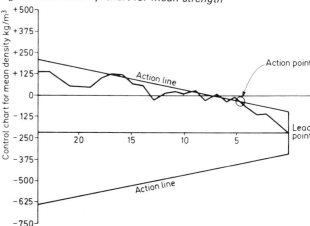

Figure 19.32 Cusum on density (the figure shows how a cusum on density had been running under control to be followed by a sudden downward trend – an investigation uncovered that a vibrator had been inadvertently switched off)

mask whilst too steep a gradient might result in the mask not being sensitive enough. The selection of the mask will depend upon several factors, one of which will be the speed, measured as ARL, at which the user wishes to detect a shift of an *important* amount. Another factor will be the ARL required for the system to detect a shift when the process is still at TMS, this is the frequency of false alarms, and the third factor is the producer's standard deviation. BS 5703[19.5] gives valuable assistance to anyone setting up a cusum system and guidance on which mask to use should be sought from a statistician. An example of a general purpose mask is given in Figure 19.34[19.2]. This mask has the following characteristics (Table 19.12):

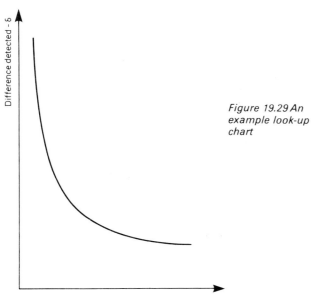

Figure 19.29 An example look-up chart

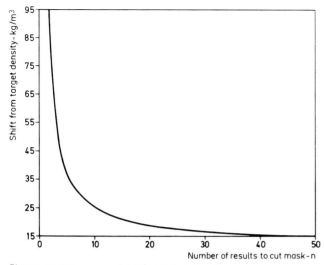

Figure 19.33 Look-up chart for mean density

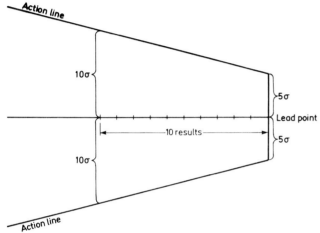

Figure 19.34 General purpose V-mask

Table 19.12 ARLs for V-mask shown in Figure 19.34

	Shift from TMS in multiples of σ					
	0	0.25	0.5	1	1.5	2
ARLs	1000	130	40	10	5.5	3.6

Having selected a mask design it is necessary to scale both the paper onto which the trace will be plotted and the mask. The choice of a suitable scale is important as the trace, as a consequence, may be too flat to show any trends or so sensitive that it resembles an Alpine mountain range. A commonly adopted scale convention is to select a convenient plotting distance on the horizontal axis and allow the same distance to represent 2σ on the cusum axis, rounding as appropriate.

An entire cusum system can be loaded into a small micro-computer costing only a few hundred pounds so relieving any arithmetic tedium. Cusums carry much more visual impact when plotted than do Shewhart charts. To illustrate this the data already given in an earlier Shewhart chart (Figure 19.21) is reproduced as a cusum trace in Figure 19.35.

Cusums are often quicker at detecting small drifts from TMS than Shewhart charts. Table 19.13 compares the ARLs of the Shewhart system with action and warning lines set at TMS $\pm 3\sigma$ and TMS $\pm 2\sigma$ respectively, and the V-mask illustrated in Figure 19.34. It can be seen that in the important drift regions of about 0.5σ, the ratio of the ARL of the Shewhart scheme to the cusum scheme is almost 2.5, that is the cusum scheme is 2.5 times quicker on average than the Shewhart scheme. With these particular schemes the cusum will produce four times less false alarms. Once the shift has reached about 1.5σ both schemes have almost the same ARLs, indeed with very large shifts the Shewhart

Table 19.13 Comparison of average run lengths

Scheme	Shift from target in multiples of σ					
	0	0.25	0.5	1	1.5	2
Shewhart	263	192	99	25	8.7	4
Cusum	1000	130	40	10	5.5	3.6
Ratio	0.26	1.48	2.48	2.5	1.58	1.11

Figure 19.35 Cusum trace of data given in Figure 19.21

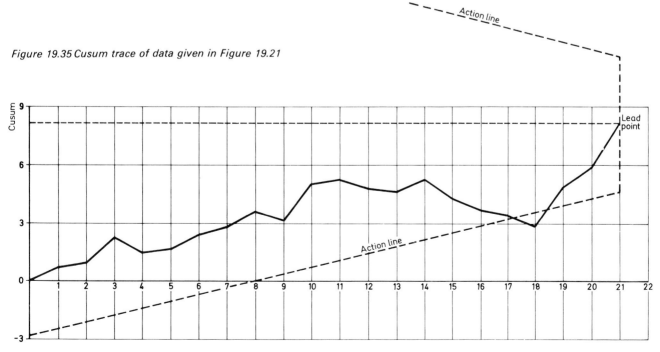

269

scheme performs slightly better than the cusum. However, with such large shifts involved a control chart is practically irrelevant as it is likely the producer will know that his process is out of control. Figure 19.36 compares the ARLs curves for these two schemes:

Because cusum analysis seeks changes in trends, unlike Shewhart charts where it can be a matter for debate, when a cusum trace cuts an action arm there is an immediate indication of where the shift began. This is of immense value in quality control systems for not only does the producer need to adjust his process in order to restore TMS, it is also necessary to investigate the reasons why the change occurred. To know the point in time of the change is likely to speed up the investigation. Because of the geometrical properties of the masks and graph paper it is a simple matter to estimate the shift in the process. With Shewhart however, it is a more difficult and sometimes misleading exercise. However, Shewhart systems are relatively cheap and easy to set up, just graph paper and a set of statistical tables[19.6] are needed, compared with cusum systems which are rather more sophisticated, sometimes requiring computer simulation which might increase the cost of setting up.

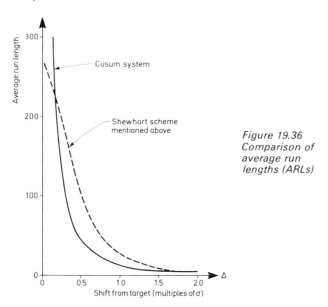

Figure 19.36 Comparison of average run lengths (ARLs)

19.5 Appendix

Table A1 Multiples for estimating confidence limits for standard deviations

Confidence level (%)	n, number in sample																		
	2	3	4	5	6	7	8	9	10	11	13	15	20	25	30	40	60	120
90	0.51	0.58	0.62	0.65	0.67	0.69	0.71	0.72	0.73	0.74	0.76	0.77	0.79	0.81	0.83	0.85	0.87	0.9
	16	4.42	2.92	2.37	2.09	1.92	1.8	1.71	1.65	1.59	1.52	1.49	1.37	1.32	1.28	1.23	1.18	1.12
95	0.45	0.52	0.57	0.6	0.62	0.64	0.66	0.68	0.69	0.7	0.72	0.73	0.76	0.78	0.8	0.82	0.85	0.89
	31.9	6.29	3.73	2.87	2.45	2.2	2.04	1.92	1.83	1.76	1.65	1.58	1.46	1.39	1.34	1.28	1.22	1.15
99	0.36	0.43	0.48	0.52	0.55	0.57	0.59	0.6	0.62	0.63	0.65	0.67	0.7	0.73	0.74	0.77	0.81	0.86
	159	14.1	6.47	4.4	3.49	2.98	2.66	2.44	2.28	2.15	1.98	1.85	1.67	1.56	1.49	1.4	1.3	1.2

Table A2 Mean range table

Number in group, n	d_n
2	1.128
3	1.693
4	2.059
5	2.326
6	2.534
7	2.704
8	2.847
9	2.97
10	3.078

Table A3 Percentage of normal distribution lying outside a given multiple of the standard deviation from the mean

Multiple of standard deviation	Total % lying outside this multiple away from mean	% in one tail only beyond multiple from mean	Multiple of standard deviation	Total % lying outside this multiple away from mean	% in one tail only beyond multiple from mean
0.1	92	46	*1.64*	*10*	*5*
0.2	84	42	1.7	9	4.5
0.3	76	38	1.8	7	3.5
0.4	69	34.5	1.9	5.8	2.9
0.5	62	31			
			1.96	*5*	*2.5*
0.6	55	27.5	2.0	4.5	2.25
0.7	48	24			
0.8	42	21	2.1	3.6	1.8
0.9	37	18.5	2.2	2.8	1.4
1.0	32	16	2.3	2.1	1.05
1.1	27	13.5	*2.33*	*2*	*1*
1.2	23	11.5	2.4	1.6	0.8
			2.5	1.2	0.6
1.28	*20*	*10*			
1.3	19	9.5	2.6	0.9	0.45
1.4	16	8	2.7	0.7	0.35
1.5	13	6.5	2.8	0.5	0.25
			2.9	0.4	0.2
1.6	11	5.5	3.0	0.3	0.15

Table A4 Additions (or subtractions), L, to $\overline{X}_n$, the segment average, to provide the upper (or lower) 90% confidence limits for the new TMS

Number of results in data segment, n	Standard deviation, σ, N/mm^2										
	0.5	0.6	0.7	0.8	0.9	1	1.1	1.2	1.3	1.4	1.5
1	0.64	0.77	0.9	1.02	1.15	1.28	1.41	1.54	1.66	1.79	1.92
2	0.45	0.54	0.64	0.72	0.81	0.91	1	1.09	1.17	1.27	1.36
3	0.37	0.44	0.52	0.59	0.66	0.74	0.81	0.89	0.96	1.03	1.11
4	0.32	0.39	0.45	0.51	0.58	0.64	0.71	0.77	0.83	0.9	0.96
5	0.29	0.34	0.4	0.46	0.51	0.57	0.63	0.69	0.74	0.8	0.86
6	0.26	0.31	0.37	0.42	0.47	0.52	0.58	0.63	0.68	0.73	0.78
7	0.24	0.29	0.34	0.39	0.43	0.48	0.53	0.58	0.63	0.68	0.73
8	0.23	0.27	0.32	0.36	0.41	0.45	0.5	0.54	0.59	0.63	0.68
9	0.21	0.26	0.3	0.34	0.38	0.43	0.47	0.51	0.55	0.6	0.64
10	0.2	0.24	0.28	0.32	0.36	0.4	0.45	0.49	0.52	0.57	0.61
11	0.19	0.23	0.27	0.31	0.35	0.39	0.43	0.46	0.5	0.54	0.58
13	0.18	0.21	0.25	0.28	0.32	0.36	0.39	0.43	0.46	0.5	0.53
15	0.17	0.2	0.23	0.26	0.3	0.33	0.36	0.4	0.43	0.46	0.5
20	0.14	0.17	0.2	0.23	0.26	0.29	0.32	0.34	0.37	0.4	0.43
25	0.13	0.15	0.18	0.2	0.23	0.26	0.28	0.31	0.33	0.36	0.38
30	0.12	0.14	0.16	0.19	0.21	0.23	0.26	0.28	0.3	0.33	0.35
40	0.1	0.12	0.14	0.16	0.18	0.2	0.22	0.24	0.26	0.28	0.3
60	0.08	0.1	0.12	0.13	0.15	0.17	0.18	0.2	0.21	0.23	0.25
120	0.06	0.07	0.08	0.09	0.1	0.12	0.13	0.14	0.15	0.16	0.18

Example: If $\overline{X}_3 = 7$ when TMS should be 5.3 and $\sigma = 0.7$ N/mm^2, then the new position for TMS $= \overline{X}_3 - 0.52$, i.e., 6.48 N/mm^2 for a 10% risk that the new TMS should really be less than 6.48 N/mm^2.

Note: (1) If $\overline{X}_n >$ TMS subtract L from $\overline{X}_n$ and if $\overline{X}_n <$ TMS add L to $\overline{X}_n$

(2) $L = \dfrac{(z_\alpha \sigma)}{\sqrt{n}}$. For 90% single sided confidence z_α from Table A3 will be 1.28

19.6 References

19.1 DOBBEN DE BRUYN, C S VAN. Cumulative sum tests — theory and practice. Charles Griffin & Co Ltd, 1968.

19.2 BISSELL, A F. An introduction to cusum charts. Institute of Statisticians, 1974.

19.3 DAVIS, O L, AND GOLDSMITH, P L (Editors). Statistical methods in research and production. 4th edition. Oliver & Boyd, 1972.

19.4 BRITISH STANDARDS INSTITUTION. BS 2028, 1364: 1968 *Precast concrete blocks*. BSI, London. pp 44

19.5 BRITISH STANDARDS INSTITUTION. BS 5703: 1980 *Guide to data analysis and quality control using cusum techniques*. BSI, London.

19.6 PEARSON, E S, AND HARTLEY, H O (Editors). Biometrica tables for statisticians. 3rd edition. Charles Griffin & Co Ltd, 1976.

19.7 HARRIS, C A R. The application of a cusum system in concrete block production. Proceedings of RILEM Symposium *Quality control of concrete structures,* Stockholm, 1979.

19.8 HARRIS, C A R. The use of a cusum system in concrete block production. *Precast Concrete, Vol 11,* No 3, March 1980.

19.9 BRITISH STANDARDS INSTITUTION. BS 5532: 1978 *Statistics — vocabulary and symbols*. BSI, London. pp 48

19.10 ORD REPORT 70 (1979). R Sym, Cement and Concrete Association.

19.11 ORD REPORT 70 (1979): Appendix A 1980. R Sym, Cement and Concrete Association.

19.12 BRITISH STANDARDS INSTITUTION. BS 6073: 1981 *Precast concrete masonry units*. BSI, London.

19.13 BRITISH STANDARDS INSTITUTION. BS 5628: Part 1: 1978 *Code of Practice for the structural use of masonry*. Part 1: *Unreinforced masonry*. BSI, London. pp 40.

19.14 BRITISH STANDARDS INSTITUTION. BS 1180: 1972 *Concrete bricks and fixing bricks*. BSI, London. pp 20